Professional DCOM Application Development

Jonathan Pinnock

Wrox Press Ltd. ®

Professional DCOM Application Development

The author and publisher have made every effort in the preparation of this book to ensure the accuracy of the information. However, the information contained in this book is sold without warranty, either express or implied. Neither the author, Wrox Press nor its dealers or distributors will be held liable for any damages caused or alleged to be caused either directly or indirectly by this book.

Published by Wrox Press Ltd. 30 Lincoln Road, Olton, Birmingham, B27 6PA
Printed in USA
ISBN 1-861001-31-2

Trademark Acknowledgements

Wrox has endeavored to provide trademark information about all the companies and products mentioned in this book by the appropriate use of capitals. However, Wrox cannot guarantee the accuracy of this information.

Credit

Author
Jonathan Pinnock

Contributing Authors
Richard Grimes
Alex Stockton

Editors
Timothy Briggs
Victoria Hudgson
Dan Maharry
Alex Stockton

Index
Nancy Humphreys
Seth Maislin

Cover
Andrew Guillaume

Technical Reviewers
Bob Beauchemin
Edward Ferron
Todd Gray
Richard Grimes
Alex Homer
Sing Li
Claus Loud
Ron Phillips
Rajesh Sankaran
Marc Simkin
Gavin Smyth
Werner Vogels
Arthur Wang
Jason Whittington

Design/Layout
Frances Olesch

Chapter divider, "Don Quixote in view of the Windmills"
Courtesy of Guenter Albrecht-Buehler,
http://pubweb.acns.nwu.edu/~gbuehler/

About the Author

Jonathan Pinnock started programming in Pal III assembler on his school's PDP 8/e, with a massive 4K of memory, back in the days before Moore's Law reached the statute books. After turning his back on computers for three years to study Mathematics at Cambridge University, he was forced back into programming in order to make a living, something that he still does from time to time. These days, he works as an independent developer and consultant, mainly in the City of London.

Jonathan lives in Hertfordshire, England, with his wife, two children and 1961 Ami Continental jukebox. He can be contacted on `jpinnock@compuserve.com`.

Dedication

This book is dedicated to my wife, Gail, who suggested it and then suffered the consequences. It's also dedicated to Mark and Rachel, our children, who just suffered the consequences.

Acknowledgements

First of all, I'd like to thank the editorial team at Wrox Press: John Franklin, who, to my amazement, agreed to let me carry out this project, and then supported and encouraged me every inch of the way, and Tim Briggs, Victoria Hudgson and Dan Maharry, who had the unenviable task of knocking my frequently confused ideas into shape. I'd also like to thank the vast army of reviewers that they assembled to cover the unusually broad spectrum of topics covered; I'd particularly like to express my appreciation to Richard Grimes and Alex Stockton for their sterling work in resolving my some of my more blatant technical faux pas.

Of the people who have helped me over the years, I'd especially like to thank Trevor Part of Kapiti, who fired me from my last permanent job, and thus saved me from a career in management. I also want to thank Carl Whitehead of M.W.Marshall and Charles Hodgson of Paribas, who gave me my first breaks as an independent. Most recently, thanks are due to David Howorth of Dow Jones Markets for giving me the opportunity to play with some really great toys, and John Moody (also of Dow Jones Markets) for a cluster of reasons.

Finally – and most important of all – I'd like to thank my family. I'll start off with my father, who tried to dissuade me from my earliest stated ambition to be an author, but – apart from that one lapse – has always supported and encouraged me in everything that I have done. I'd also like to thank my late mother, who would have been proud, if baffled. The biggest thanks go to my wife, Gail, who always persuaded me to carry on, even when her life would have become a whole lot simpler if I had packed it in, and our children, who bore my foul moods and tempers with remarkable equanimity. Last of all, I'd like to thank Albert Hall, without whose intervention, two of the foregoing would not even exist.

Oh, and special thanks to Percy the peacock, whose unexpected arrival in our garden enlivened the last few days of writing no end. A pious bird of good omen, indeed.

Table of Contents

Introduction

I wrote this book in order to benefit a group of people who, by definition, almost certainly won't read it. These people aren't interested in COM, DCOM or Visual C++. They're probably not even interested in Visual Basic. In fact, they'd rather not know anything about what goes on the other side of the computer screen at all. However, these people are the most important people in the whole software development process. Because without end-users, there would be no point in developing the stuff at all. And for a software developer, there is no bigger buzz than the one you get from seeing a real end-user – particularly a "difficult" one – actually using your stuff to improve the way they work.

The trouble is, when you start building systems that stretch over an entire enterprise, things get more complicated, and it gets more and more difficult to deliver flexible, reliable and timely solutions to your end users. For me, any tools that can simplify and standardize the process of developing enterprise-wide systems are therefore of immense significance. My view is that COM and DCOM and all the technologies that are based around them provide us with just that toolkit. I want to show you how to put them to use in building real solutions to real problems.

Raison d'être

You want transactions? Well, there's Microsoft Transaction Server (MTS). You want reliable messaging? Try Microsoft Message Queue (MSMQ). Security? Oh, we'll soon be using Kerberos. Directory services? We support Lightweight Directory Access Protocol (LDAP) now. And so on. Windows NT5 will be Microsoft's doomsday weapon. And what powers this weapon? What else but Microsoft's Component Object Model, COM, together with its distributed cousin, DCOM.

This, then, is a book about the back office. It's a book about building real, grown-up systems using Microsoft technology; systems that are distributed and have complex real-time interactions.

We won't be finding out how to build visual components. There are plenty of other books on that. We'll be learning how to build components that do real business functions. We won't be spending a lot of time on theory, either. There isn't time to spend ages looking under the hood. There are plenty of other books on that, too. We're not even going to worry too much about all that wizard-generated stuff underlying our code. If we haven't already, we're going to learn to trust Bill.

From Our Religious Affairs Correspondent...

I forgot to mention that this was a religious war. And religious wars are the most violent of them all, so it's with some trepidation that I approach this subject. But we've got to get it out in the open before we go much further. Of course DCOM is not the only game in town. There is also something called the Common Object Request Broker Architecture, or CORBA. The CORBA specification has many beautiful features, and so has DCOM, and to be honest, there really isn't that much to choose between them. How can there be? They are both solving pretty much the same problems using pretty much the same approach. The trouble is, as soon as you dare mention this self-evident truth, you suddenly find yourself accused by both sides of over-simplification and misrepresentation. Ho hum.

Personally speaking, I avoid religious wars. I make a living as an independent programmer writing software for anyone who will pay me. I'm not really interested in whether the basic architecture I use is aesthetically better or worse than its nearest rival. I'm not that interested in its origins, as long as it works and has reasonable support. What I *am* interested in is what I can use to build a solution that works in a straightforward and reliable manner so that I can hand it over, collect my fee and move on to the next one with a clear conscience. In essence, I don't really care if I use CORBA or DCOM, provided that it works.

However, this is a book about DCOM, not CORBA. That's why it says DCOM on the cover.

Is COM Difficult?

This is not a trivial question. COM is a technology that has evolved very rapidly over the few years in which it has been in existence, and the infrastructure to make it usable by anyone with an IQ less than 200 is only just emerging. There's a lovely article that you can look up on Microsoft's web site, written by Markus Horstman back in 1995, called "From CPP to COM" (at `http://www.microsoft.com/oledev/olecom/cpptocom.htm`). It's a long and technically quite complex paper (worth a read, if only for historical reasons), whose subtext is a plaintive cry, "Why oh why does COM seem so difficult?" Why indeed?

Since then, however, we've seen the introduction of the Active Template Library (ATL), and Visual Studio (which includes COM compiler support in C++ and ATL wizards, to name just two groovy gadgets in its arsenal). Maybe, just maybe, COM is beginning to get a little easier. We have gone from a time where the most appropriate quote to head this introduction would have been, "Abandon hope all ye who enter here" to a state of affairs where a little perseverance (and maybe suffering a few woes) will actually pay rich dividends. The trouble is that there is so much baggage from earlier incarnations lying around that it isn't always easy to establish how much you really need to know to get going. One of the aims of this book is to try to steer a path through all this, so that you don't get derailed by any irrelevancies.

What Does This Book Cover?

The book will cover DCOM, and all the new services on top of it that are appearing in NT5 and various pre-release forms prior to that.

- Chapter 1 takes a quick tour of COM, and sees how easy it is to create a COM object using the ATL wizard in the length of time it takes to boil an egg.
- In Chapter 2, we take a look at monikers and how to use them to overcome the difficulties of binding several clients to a central server object.
- Chapter 3 covers serializing and marshalling object data to ensure DCOM works as efficiently as possible.
- We'll look at the question of how to use a directory service to find an object in Chapter 4, and introduce the Active Directory.

- Chapters 5 through 7 are all about transactions. Chapter 5 introduces the concept of transactions and looks at how we can develop transactional programs using Microsoft Transaction Server.
- In Chapter 6, we look at the asynchronous model, where a client can make a request to a server without having to wait for an immediate response; the technology that supports this is Microsoft Message Queue. As we'll see, MTS and MSMQ together make a very powerful combination.
- In Chapter 7, we create our own resource manager and resource dispenser.
- Chapter 8 introduces Microsoft Clusters and how they bring high availability to distributed systems.
- DCOM security is covered in Chapter 9.
- We round up our tour of DCOM technologies in Chapter 10, which looks at the thorny problem of managing and monitoring this lot, and creating an MMC snap-in.

Who Is This Book For?

This book assumes that you are at least familiar with the basics of COM, using ATL. I'm not going to attempt to explain things like dual interfaces here. (In fact, pretty much all of our interfaces are going to be dual, so it's not going to be an issue). We're going to be using ATL in Visual C++. If you need a better grounding in ATL, I can recommend *Beginning ATL COM Programming*, published by Wrox Press (who else?).

This book is for experienced C++ programmers who have heard that Microsoft may be getting there at last, and want to get up to speed. It is for people in a hurry, who wish to get to grips with all the issues involved as quickly as possible. These are the kind of people who are not afraid to get their hands dirty, and will leap into the sample code before they're half way through the chapter. To be frank, they are probably the sort of people who download the sample code when it first appears on the Wrox Press site, before the book even hits the bookstores. (I know – I was that man.)

There is currently no one resource that provides this sort of information. The general approach seems to be to teach people how to use DCOM as a technology for distributing clever ActiveX controls to a wide audience. However, Microsoft's goal is somewhat broader than that, and the major thrust of NT5 is to make the OS a platform for building serious enterprise-wide applications. We are moving away from the desktop into back-office territory here.

There are two reasons for this relative lack of information: firstly, the technology is very new (indeed much of it is only available in Beta), and secondly, even if the technology is there, it is hidden away, and not emphasized in the available documentation and sample code. The paradox of Visual C++ 5 is that the new ATL Wizard is actually beginning to make COM programming something approaching a straightforward proposition; however, none of the code samples provided seem to have been generated using it.

What Do You Need to Use This Book?

Operating Systems

- NT4 Server, service pack 3
- NT4 Enterprise Edition Server (for MSCS. chapter 8)
- NT5 Server Beta 1 (for LDAP, chapter 4)

Compilers

- Visual C++ 5
- Visual Basic
- Visual Studio Service Pack 3

Other Tools

- NT Platform SDK (for MMC snap-in)
- NT 4.0 Option Pack – MTS, MSMQ, ADO 1.5
- Active Directory / ADSI SDK
- MTS SDK
- Office 97
- SQL Server 6.5

Conventions

We use a number of different styles of text and layout in the book to help differentiate between the different kinds of information. This section shows some examples of the different styles used and explains what they mean.

> **These boxes hold important, not-to-be-forgotten information which is directly relevant to the surrounding text.**

Background information, asides and references appear like this.

- **Important words** are in a bold font
- Words that appear on the screen, such as menu options or labels on buttons, are in a similar font to the one used on the screen, for example, the File menu
- Keys that you press on the keyboard are in italics, for example *Ctrl*
- File names look like this: `ConfServer.cpp`
- Functions appear like this: `CoInitialize()`

Code that is new or relevant to the current discussion is presented like this:

```
private:
   // Suitable comments here...
   CComBSTR m_bstrDescription;
   CComBSTR m_bstrShop;
```

Code that you have seen before, or that isn't directly relevant to the discussion at hand, is shown like this:

```
private:
   CComBSTR m_bstrDescription;
   CComBSTR m_bstrShop;
```

Tell Us What You Think

We have tried to make this book as accurate and enjoyable for you as possible, but what really matters is what the book actually does for you. Please let us know your views, whether positive or negative, either by returning the reply card in the back of the book or by contacting us at Wrox Press at **feedback@wrox.com**

Source Code

All the source code from the examples in this book is available for download from the Wrox Press web site:

http://www.wrox.com
ftp://ftp.wrox.com
ftp://ftp.wrox.co.uk

Errata & Updates

We've made every effort to make sure there are no errors in the text or the code. However, to err is human and as such we recognize the need to keep you, the reader, informed of any mistakes as they're spotted and corrected.

While you're visiting our web site, please make use of our *Errata* page, which is dedicated to fixing any small errors in the book, or offering new ways around a problem and its solution. Errata sheets are available for all our books – please download them, or take part in the continuous improvement of our tutorials and upload a 'fix' or pointer to the solution.

For those without access to the 'net, call us on **1-800 USE WROX** and we'll gladly send errata sheets to you. Alternatively, send a letter to:

Wrox Press Inc.,
1512 N Fremont, Ste 103
Chicago,
IL 60622-2567
USA

Wrox Press Ltd,
30, Lincoln Road,
Olton,
Birmingham,
B27 6PA
UK

1

COM Myths and Magic

"To suffer woes which hope thinks infinite,
To forgive wrongs darker than death or night,
To defy power which seems omnipotent,
Neither to change, nor falter, nor repent:
This... is to be
Good, great and joyous, beautiful and free,
This is alone life, joy, empire and victory."

"Prometheus Unbound" (Shelley)

Instant COM

In this chapter, we're going to start off by proving just how easy COM really is these days, with some ultra-rapid code generation.

From there, we're going to take a look at a couple of (moderately) advanced COM techniques that we're going to need later on in the book: **enumerators** and **connection points**.

Why are these important? Well, we'll come across enumerators all over the place as we dig into DCOM and the technologies based on it, and connection points are extremely useful for the interactive real-time systems that we'll be exploring in Chapter 2. Also, these two areas just happen to be perfect to illustrate a point about the most appropriate use of the available development technologies.

If you've done all this before, just treat it as a warm-up before we launch ourselves all the way into DCOM.

How to Time an Egg

There used to be a chap who would time his egg by how long it took him to complete The London Times crossword. History doesn't relate what his preference was, but I assume that being an Englishman, he would have preferred his eggs soft-boiled. Well, we're going to do something similar. We're going to time our egg according to how long it takes us to put together a simple COM object called `Calculator` using Visual C++. (Incidentally, I like my eggs done for about 3 minutes 45 seconds, since you ask.) I'm going to use a fairly expensive egg timer: a Pentium Pro 200-based PC with a rather light 32Mb of memory. (Well, we don't want to make things too easy, do we?)

Our COM object has only one interface, `Icalc`, which in turn has only two methods, as follows:

Method	Parameters
`Square`	`[in] double value, [out,retval] double* result`
`Root`	`[in] double value, [out,retval] double* result`

As you may have guessed, this is a small fragment of a generalized calculation object, which calculates the square or square root of a given number.

So, have you got the water boiling yet? OK, put the egg in … now!

0:00

Open Visual Studio:

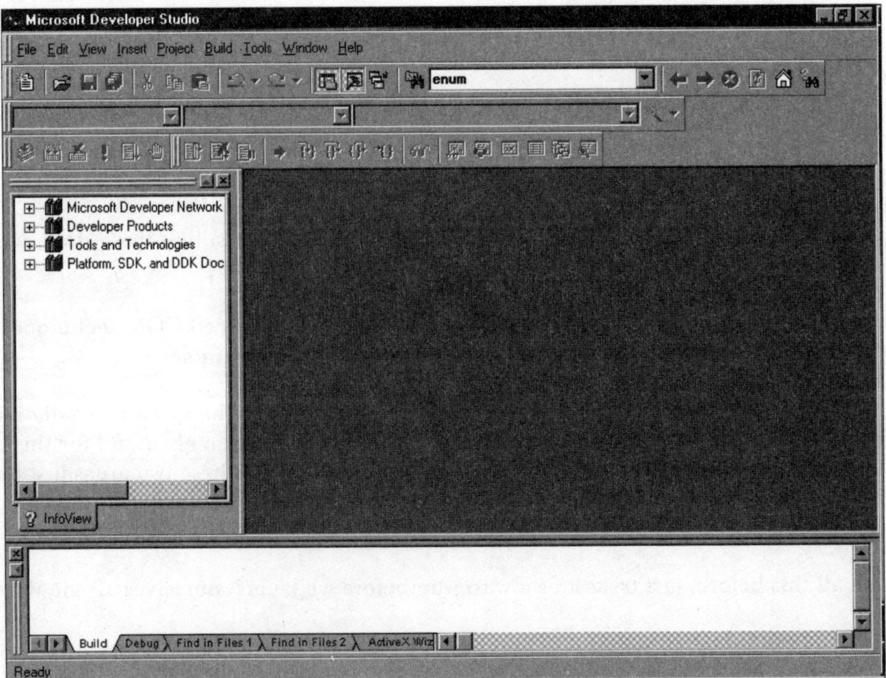

Create a new project, by using File | New. Use the ATL COM AppWizard, and call the project **`Calculator`**.

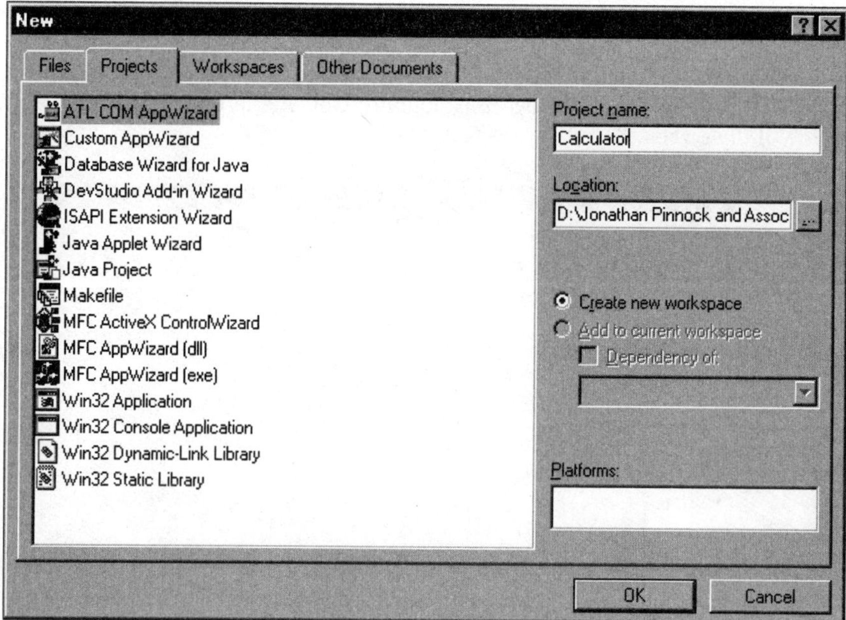

Click on OK.

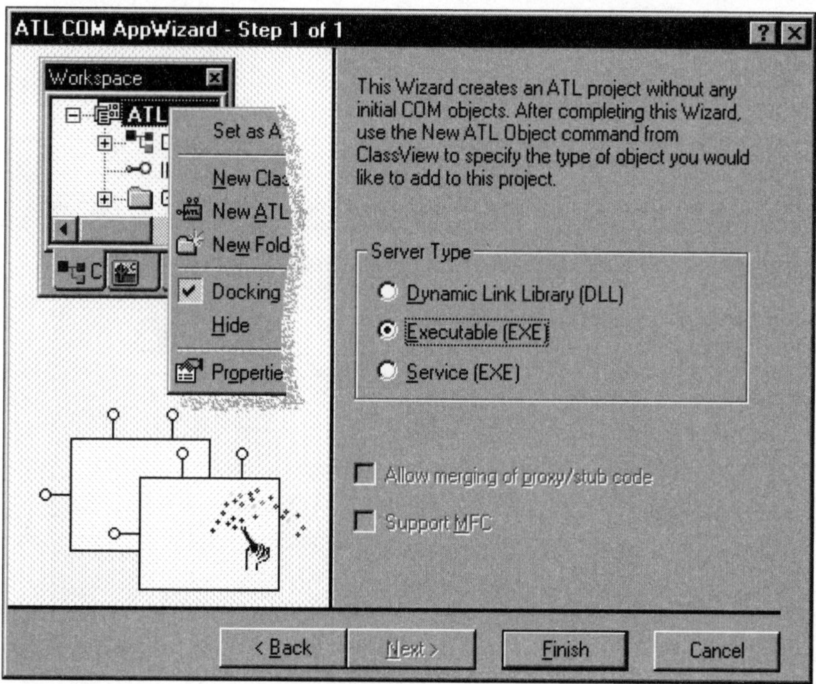

Select Executable (EXE), and then click on Finish. Confirm new project information by clicking on OK on the next screen.

0:35

Add our interface `ICalc`, by right-clicking on Calculator Classes in the Class View of the project on the left hand side of the screen. Select New ATL Object...:

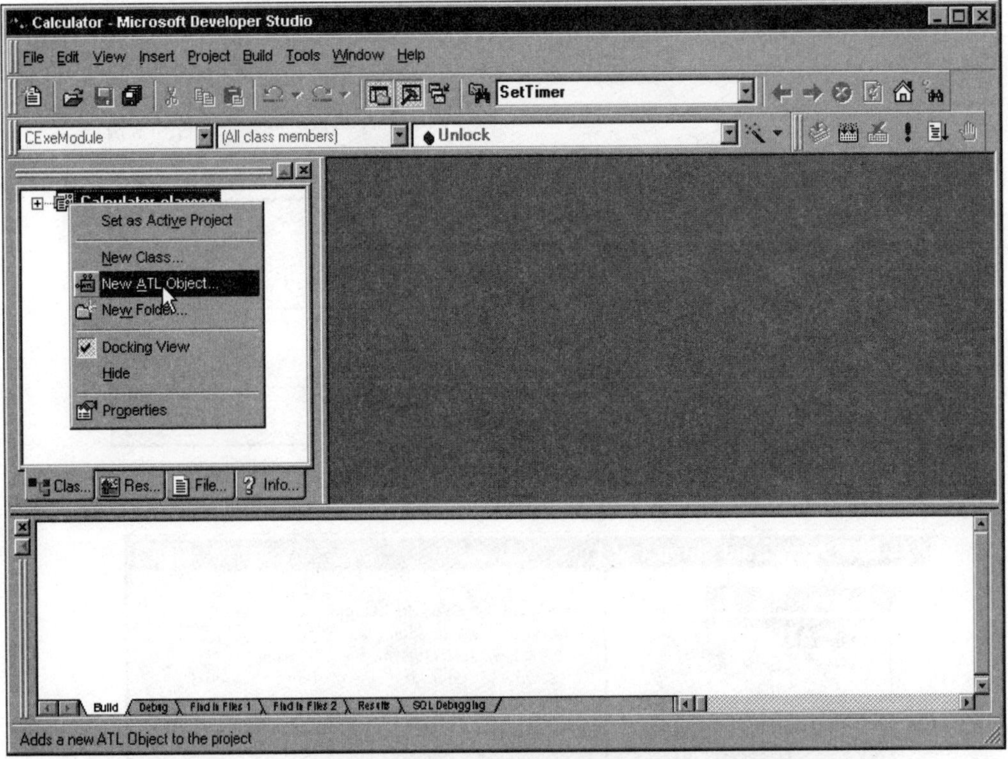

Select Simple Object, and click on Next>:

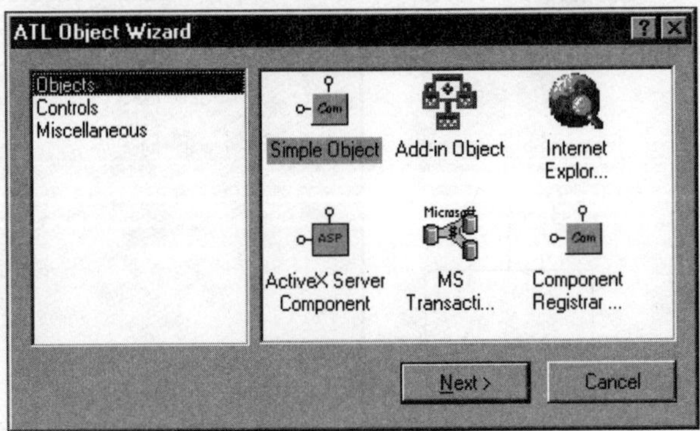

Enter the name of our object, Calc. Ignore the Attributes tab; we can assume that the defaults will be adequate for our purpose. Click on OK.

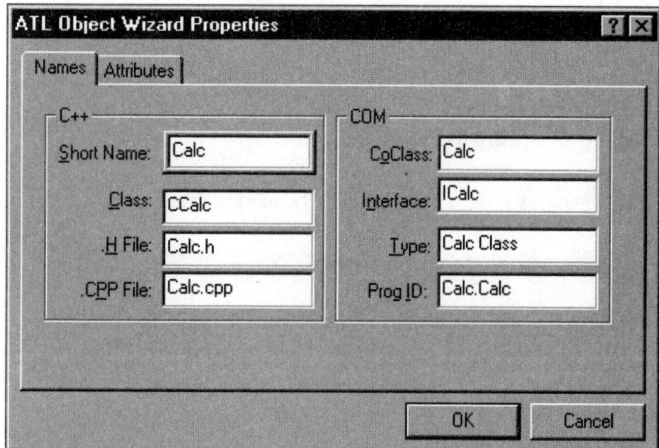

Expand the class view by clicking on the little plus sign next to Calculator classes. Add our first method **Square()**, by right-clicking over the interface ICalc in the Class View. Select Add Method...:

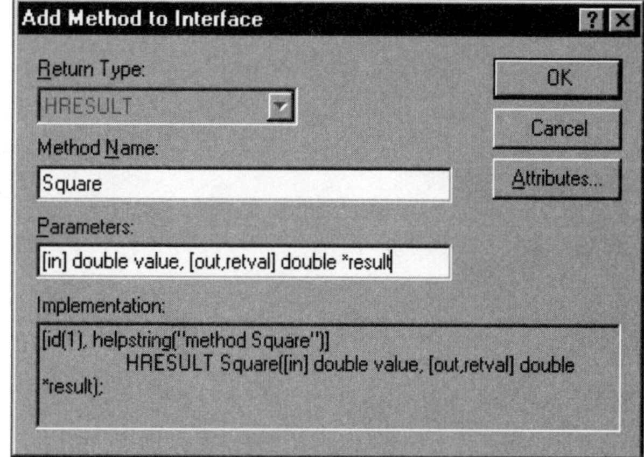

Enter the method details, and click on OK.

Add the second method, **Root()**, in the same manner:

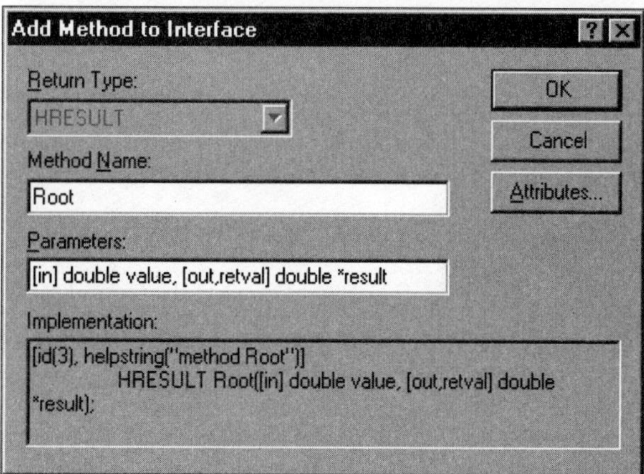

2:30

Expand the **CCalc** class in the Class View, and then the **ICalc** interface underneath it. Insert the functionality for **Square()**, by double clicking on its entry under **ICalc**, opening up **Calc.cpp** and adding the following line:

```
STDMETHODIMP CCalc::Square(double value, double * result)
{
    *result = value * value;

    return S_OK;
}
```

Insert the functionality for **Root()**, by adding the following lines to **Calc.cpp**:

```
// Calc.cpp : Implementation of CCalc
#include "stdafx.h"
#include "Calculator.h"
#include "Calc.h"

#include <math.h>

/////////////////////////////////////////////////////////////////////////////
// Ccalc

.
.
.

STDMETHODIMP CCalc::Root(double value, double * result)
{
    if (value < 0.0)
        return E_INVALIDARG;

    *result = sqrt (value);

    return S_OK;
}
```

Now build it either by pressing F7, by selecting it from the Build menu, or by pressing the build icon in the build toolbar!

3:45

We're done! Well, how was your egg? Mine was perfect. OK, I'll admit to a certain amount of creative timing. In actual fact, if I'd used the real times, my egg would have been a little soft. If I'd used a fully-spec'd machine, it would have been positively running.

There's a serious point here. Microsoft is really working very hard at making COM easier for the rest of us mortals. There's no excuse now for failing to get to grips with it.

The Client

I said that we were going to be dealing principally with the back office. However, at some point we do have to deal with clients. We programmers should get out and meet real people from time to time.

So what's the best way of developing a front-end? MFC of course! Best set of classes for handling dialogs in the world. Well, hang on a moment... It really pains me to say this, as a C/C++ programmer of far too many years' standing (indeed, as a fully paid-up member of the "Real Programmers Can Use Pointers To Go Anywhere, Even Where There Is No Data" club), but I have the feeling that Visual Basic rather has the edge these days as a front-end development environment. Blame Bill. After all, Microsoft's first ever product was a Basic compiler...

So, apologies to MFC fans out there, but I'm afraid that we're going to use Visual Basic as our front-end development environment in the main. Provided we ensure that all of our COM interfaces are described by a type library (interfaces added by the ATL Object Wizard will be) – we can use Visual Basic for testing out pretty much anything that we develop. There are so many things built into Visual Basic to make things easier for the developer to use COM objects that, in these cases, it would be crazy to waste time with MFC.

I should, perhaps, reassure you that you will still find some examples based around MFC in later chapters. For more complex front-ends, there's still a place for MFC, so we need to be able to use both technologies. Or maybe I'm just finding it hard to let go... Let's get into the spirit of things by building a quick application to test our egg-timer. We'll call it **`CalcTest.`** Here is the form:

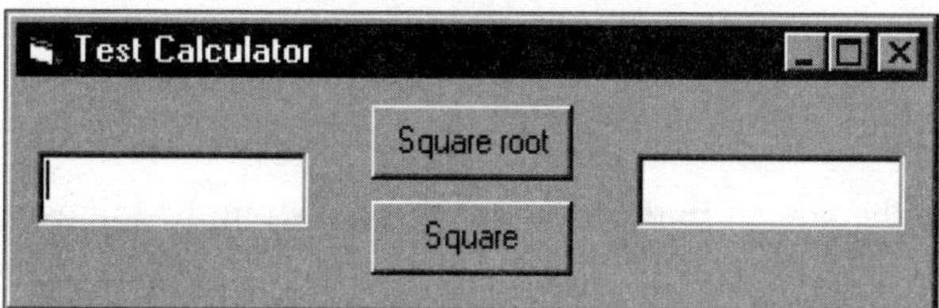

The code is very simple and looks like this:

```
Dim calculator As Calc

Private Sub Form_Load()
Set calculator = New Calc
End Sub

Private Sub Form_Terminate()
Set calculator = Nothing
End Sub

Private Sub Square_Click()
Result.Text = calculator.Square(Value.Text)
End Sub
```

```
Private Sub SquareRoot_Click()
On Error GoTo invalid

Result.Text = calculator.Root(Value.Text)
Exit Sub

invalid:
Result.Text = "Invalid"

End Sub
```

The value you want squared or square rooted goes on the left and the result appears on the right. No more explanation required.

Loading the Dice Against MFC

Whilst we're on the subject of Visual Basic versus MFC, I'd like to share a couple more examples of Microsoft really loading the dice in favor of Visual Basic. The first is presented just for fun, as part of our warming up, but the second actually has some bearing on where we are going with the rest of our project.

The first example looks at how Visual Basic provides support for **enumeration**. We're going to build a simple COM server that enables a client to enumerate a list – my shopping list, in fact.

The items to be enumerated will be `ShoppingItem`s, each of which has an interface `IShoppingItem`. All of them will be held in a collection object called `ShoppingList` which has an interface called `IShoppingList`. All collection objects have an enumerator and a `Count` property, and it is this `Count` property that allows a VB client to determine the number of items in the enumerator without iterating through all of the items.

The relationship between the objects in this example are shown in the following diagram:

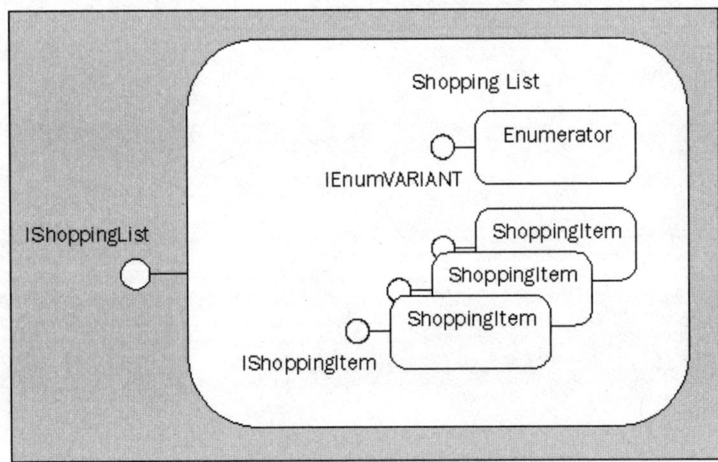

The **ShoppingList** object creates one or more **ShoppingItem** objects and gives a client access to these through the enumerator object. Clients obtain this enumerator object by accessing the **_NewEnum** property of the **IShoppingList** interface.

This example will be implemented in a **.dll** file so that access to the shopping list has the best performance. So, create a new ATL DLL project called **Shopping**, and insert a new simple object called **ShoppingItem** and add the following properties:

Property	Declaration
Description	BSTR
Shop	BSTR

Both of these properties are read/write so leave the Put Function, Get Function check boxes checked in the Add Property dialog. We'll add a couple of member variables to hold the values of these, and we'll put these in **ShoppingItem.h**:

```
// IShoppingItem
public:
	STDMETHOD(get_Shop)(/*[out, retval]*/ BSTR *pVal);
	STDMETHOD(put_Shop)(/*[in]*/ BSTR newVal);
	STDMETHOD(get_Description)(/*[out, retval]*/ BSTR *pVal);
	STDMETHOD(put_Description)(/*[in]*/ BSTR newVal);
private:
	CComBSTR m_bstrDescription;
	CComBSTR m_bstrShop;
```

These items use the ATL **CComBSTR** wrapper for **BSTR** for three reasons:

- When a **ShoppingItem** is first created these items will be initialized to the **NULL** string – you do not have to initialize them
- The **BSTR** that they wrap will be safely freed when the **ShoppingItem** is released, guarding against resource leaks
- **CComBSTR** simplifies the initialization and copying of **BSTR**s, which can only be a good thing

The property methods look like this:

```
///////////////////////////////////////////////////////////////////////////
// CShoppingItem

STDMETHODIMP CShoppingItem::get_Description(BSTR* pVal)
{
	*pVal = m_bstrDescription.Copy();

	return S_OK;
}

STDMETHODIMP CShoppingItem::put_Description(BSTR newVal)
{
```

```
        m_bstrDescription = newVal;

        return S_OK;
    }

    STDMETHODIMP CShoppingItem::get_Shop(BSTR* pVal)
    {
        *pVal = m_bstrShop.Copy();

        return S_OK;
    }

    STDMETHODIMP CShoppingItem::put_Shop(BSTR newVal)
    {
        m_bstrShop = newVal;

        return S_OK;
    }
```

Here, the **get_** methods take **[out]** parameters, hence a copy of the **BSTR** is made. The **put_** methods are used to replace the value held by the class members. **CComBSTR** helps here because the overloaded assignment operator will ensure that if the data member already has a value, it will be released before being replaced with the new value, thus preventing a resource leak.

The next task is to create the list itself. Use the ATL Object Wizard to create a simple object called **ShoppingList**. For this simple test the list will be read-only and will have hard coded items. The object will have one method and two properties:

Method	Parameters
GetItem()	**[in] long item, [out] BSTR* bstrDescription, [out] BSTR* bstrShop**

Property	Declaration
Count	**[out] long***
_NewEnum	**[out] LPUNKNOWN***

The properties are interesting. If you want Visual Basic to be able to use a collection object, you must provide these properties. The first of them returns the number of items in the list and the second returns a pointer to the **IUnknown** interface of the collection's enumerator object. Notice that these properties are read-only; you should make sure that you uncheck the Put Function check box in the Add Property dialog.

We'll come to the enumerator itself in a minute, after we've added the properties using the ATL wizard. We also need to do a little bit of manual tinkering with the **Shopping.idl** file:

```
    interface IShoppingList : IDispatch
    {
        [propget, id(1), helpstring("property Count")]
                        HRESULT Count([out, retval] long *pVal);
```

```
      [propget, restricted, id(DISPID_NEWENUM),
                       helpstring("property _NewEnum")]
                       HRESULT _NewEnum([out, retval] LPDISPATCH *pVal);
      [id(3), helpstring("method GetItem")]
                       HRESULT GetItem([in] long item,
                                            [out] BSTR *bstrDescription,
                                            [out] BSTR *bstrShop);
   };
```

VB expects to find a property with a DISPID of **DISPID_NEWENUM** (-4). However, the ClassView Property Wizard does not allow you to add a symbol or a negative value for the DISPID, so you need to change this by hand.

We'll also add a member function, **Initialize()**, to set up our shopping list, and some member variables to hold the details about the list:

```
// IShoppingList
public:
    STDMETHOD(get__NewEnum)(/*[out, retval]*/ LPUNKNOWN *pVal);
    STDMETHOD(GetItem)(/*[in]*/  long item,
                       /*[out]*/ BSTR* bstrDescription,
                       /*[out]*/ BSTR* bstrShop);
    STDMETHOD(get_Count)(/*[out, retval]*/ long *pVal);
private:
    long m_nItem;
    CComBSTR m_bstrDesc[10];
    CComBSTR m_bstrShop[10];
    void Initialize();
```

As this is a simple, illustrative example, the **BSTR** arrays are a fixed size of 10 items and have fixed values. If you wanted this example to be useful, your code should use dynamically adjustable arrays, like the STL **<vector>**, and be writeable. You could look at the example shown in Chapter 7 of Beginning ATL COM Programming. This is what the code for the shopping list looks like:

```
/////////////////////////////////////////////////////////////////////////////
// CShoppingList

STDMETHODIMP CShoppingList::get_Count(long * pVal)
{
    *pVal = m_nItem;

    return S_OK;
}

STDMETHODIMP CShoppingList::GetItem(long item, BSTR *bstrDescription,
     BSTR *bstrShop)
{
    if (item >= m_nItem || item < 0)
        return E_INVALIDARG;

    *bstrDescription = m_bstrDesc[item].Copy();
    *bstrShop = m_bstrShop[item].Copy();
```

```
    return S_OK;
}

void CShoppingList::Initialize()
{
    static LPOLESTR lpszDescr[] = {
                                   L"Lager",
                                   L"Beer",
                                   L"Pretzels",
                                   L"Tortilla chips",
                                   L"Pizza",
                                   L"Terminator 2",
                                   L"Reservoir Dogs",
                                   L"More beer",
                                   L"Batteries for remote control",
                                   L"PC World",
    };

    static LPOLESTR lpszShop[] = {
                                   L"Bottoms Up",
                                   L"Bottoms Up",
                                   L"Safeways",
                                   L"Safeways",
                                   L"Safeways",
                                   L"Blockbuster",
                                   L"Blockbuster",
                                   L"Bottoms Up",
                                   L"Dixons",
                                   L"WHSmith",
    };

    m_nItem = 10;

    for (long item = 0; item < m_nItem; item++)
    {
        m_bstrDesc[item] = SysAllocString (lpszDescr[item]);
        m_bstrShop[item] = SysAllocString (lpszShop[item]);
    }
}
```

The enumerator is fairly simple to implement. ATL 2.1 has a template class called **CComEnum<>** that allows you to implement the methods required on an enumerator object. To use the object with VB, it must be an enumerator of **VARIANT**s, and so we need to implement the **IEnumVARIANT** interface. The **CComEnum<>** class takes this interface, its IID and the type it enumerates as parameters. In addition to this, it also takes a class that provides methods to copy and initialize the items placed in the enumerator. For convenience, the following code uses a **typedef**:

```
STDMETHODIMP CShoppingList::get__NewEnum(LPUNKNOWN * pVal)
{
    typedef CComObject< CComEnum< IEnumVARIANT, &IID_IEnumVARIANT,
                                  VARIANT, _Copy<VARIANT> > > Enum;
    Enum* pEnum;
    Enum::CreateInstance(&pEnum);
    long item;
```

```
    //create the list items and put them in an array
    VARIANT* pVar = new VARIANT[m_nItem];
    for (item = 0; item < m_nItem; item++)
    {
        CComObject<CShoppingItem>* pItem;
        CComObject<CShoppingItem>::CreateInstance(&pItem);
        pItem->put_Description(m_bstrDesc[item].m_str);
        pItem->put_Shop(m_bstrShop[item].m_str);
        pVar[item].vt = VT_DISPATCH;
        pItem->QueryInterface(IID_IDispatch,
            reinterpret_cast<void**>(&(pVar[item].pdispVal)));
    }

    //put the data into the enumerator, make a copy
    pEnum->Init(&pVar[0], &pVar[m_nItem], NULL, AtlFlagCopy);

    //get rid of our copy of the list items
    for (item = 0; item < m_nItem; item++)
    {
        VariantClear(&pVar[item]);
    }

    delete [] pVar;

    return pEnum->QueryInterface(IID_IUnknown,
        reinterpret_cast<void**>(pVal));
}
```

Since **Enum** is a **CComObject<>**, it implements the **IUnknown** methods, hence the static **CreateInstance()** method can be used to create a new COM object. This enumerator must be initialized with the items that it will enumerate, which is done by calling the method **Init()**. This takes the first item together with one item after the last item of an array of **VARIANT**s, creating a temporary array and filling it with **ShoppingItem** objects initialized with the data in **m_bstrDesc** and **m_bstrShop**. The **QueryInterface()** on these **ShoppingItem** objects is important for two reasons, firstly because the **VARIANT** needs an **IDispatch** pointer, and secondly to increase the reference count to 1: the previous call to **CreateInstance()** will have initialized the reference count to zero.

Init() then makes a copy of the data, and so the items in the array must be released by calling **VariantClear()**. Finally, VB expects to get the **IUnknown** pointer of the enumerator and hence **QueryInterface()** is called on the **Enum** object. This will also ensure that the reference count of the object is 1, so that when VB releases the enumerator, it will be destroyed.

To compile this code you will need to include **ShoppingItem.h** at the top of the file.

The **IEnumVARIANT** interface has the following methods:

Method	Parameters
Next	**[in] unsigned long celt,** **[out] VARIANT FAR* rgVar,** **[out] unsigned long FAR* pCeltFetched**
Skip	**[in] unsigned long celt**
Reset	
Clone	**IEnumVARIANT FAR* FAR* ppEnum**

These methods provide everything you need to enumerate through a list.

> *The* **Clone()** *method, incidentally, simply creates a new copy of the enumerator, with the current settings.*

The parameter names are the official Microsoft ones, and, to be frank, they aren't particularly meaningful. **celt**, in particular, doesn't refer to anything Celtic, but stands for the number of elements to be fetched or skipped. The pointer **pCeltFetched** points to the number of elements found. The parameter **rgVar** refers to an array of **VARIANT**s holding the values of the enumerated elements. You've probably come across **VARIANTs** before – they're a key method of passing all types of data around OLE automation, and Visual Basic is great at interpreting them. If you want to find out more about **VARIANTs**, they're explained in much more detail in Chapter 7 of *Beginning ATL COM Programming.*

The ATL class, **CComEnum<>**, implements these methods for you so you don't have to worry about the details. This is what code re-use is all about!

Everything is in place. All we need now is a client. We'll start off with a Visual Basic client, with its display containing a single list box, called **lstShoppingList**. The code is astonishingly simple, create a Standard EXE application and use the Project|References menu item to add a reference to the Shopping 1.0 Type Library. This is the code that lies behind the form:

```
Private Sub Form_Load()
    Dim list As ShoppingList
    Dim item As ShoppingItem

    Set list = New ShoppingList

    For Each item In list
        lstShoppingList.AddItem (item.Description + " from " + item.Shop)
    Next item
End Sub
```

Yes, that really is all. Just to prove it, this is what happens when you run it:

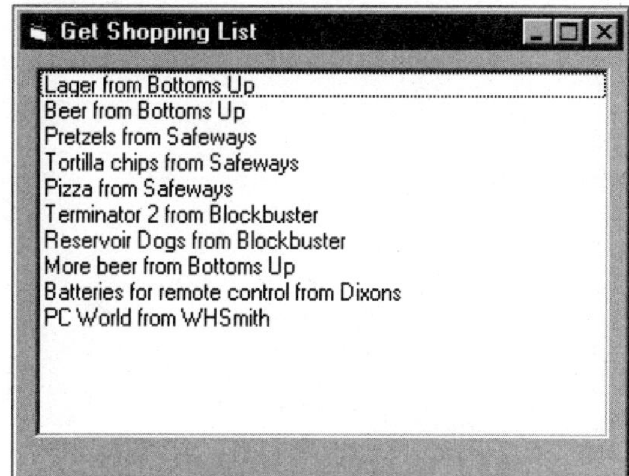

Which – to be honest – is all you really need.

Whilst we're in Visual Basic, take a look in the object browser at the definition for class **ShoppingList**. Notice anything odd? The property **_NewEnum** isn't there at all! This is because Visual Basic doesn't show any properties that start with an underscore. Of course, we don't really want to expose the internals of the enumeration process to the outside world, which is the purpose of the extra underscore in the first place. The **get__NewEnum()** method is there for the benefit of the Visual Basic container, not the client application.

MFC Has a Go

Remember what I was saying about using Visual Basic as our front-end development environment of choice? Let's see what we have to do in MFC.

Use the AppWizard to create a dialog-based app and press Finish once you've specified that. Next we need to declare an **Initialize()** method in the **CShopTestVCDlg.h** header file:

```
protected:
    HICON m_hIcon;

    // Generated message map functions
    //{{AFX_MSG(CShoppingTestVCDlg)
    virtual BOOL OnInitDialog();
    afx_msg void OnSysCommand(UINT nID, LPARAM lParam);
    afx_msg void OnPaint();
    afx_msg HCURSOR OnQueryDragIcon();
    //}}AFX_MSG
    DECLARE_MESSAGE_MAP()

private:
    Initialize();

.
.
.
```

Turning our attention to the **ShopTestVCDlg.cpp** file:

```
// ShopTestVCDlg.cpp : implementation file
//

#include "stdafx.h"
#include "ShoppingTestVC.h"
#include "ShoppingTestVCDlg.h"

#include "..\Shopping\Shopping.h"
#include "..\Shopping\Shopping_i.c"
.
.
.
BOOL CShoppingTestVCDlg::OnInitDialog()
{
    .
    .
    .
    OnInitDialog()
    SetIcon(m_hIcon, TRUE);         // Set big icon
    SetIcon(m_hIcon, FALSE);        // Set small icon

    Initialize();

    return TRUE;  // return TRUE  unless you set the focus to a control
}
.
.
.
void CShopTestVCDlg::Initialize()
{
    CoInitialize(NULL);

    IShoppingList *pList;
    CoCreateInstance(CLSID_ShoppingList, NULL, CLSCTX_SERVER,
        IID_IShoppingList, reinterpret_cast<void**>(&pList));

    long nItem;
    pList->get_Count (&nItem);

    //get the enumerator
    IUnknown *pUnk;
    pList->get__NewEnum(&pUnk);

    //don't need this pointer any more
    pList->Release();

    IEnumVARIANT *pEnum;
    pUnk->QueryInterface (IID_IEnumVARIANT,
        reinterpret_cast<void**> (&pEnum));

    //don't need this pointer either
    pUnk->Release();
    pEnum->Reset ();
```

```
    CListBox *pListBox = reinterpret_cast<CListBox *>
        (GetDlgItem (IDC_SHOPPINGLIST));

    for (long item = 0; item < nItem; item++)
    {
        VARIANT vars;
        VariantInit(&vars);
        unsigned long count;
        pEnum->Next (1, &vars, &count);

        if (!count)
            break;

        LPDISPATCH pDispItem = vars.pdispVal;

        IShoppingItem *pItem;
        pDispItem->QueryInterface(IID_IShoppingItem,
            reinterpret_cast<void **>(&pItem));

        BSTR bstrDescription;
        pItem->get_Description (&bstrDescription);
        BSTR bstrShop;
        pItem->get_Shop (&bstrShop);
        pItem->Release ();

        char szDescription[256];
        ::wcstombs (szDescription, bstrDescription, 256);
        ::SysFreeString (bstrDescription);

        char szShop[256];
        ::wcstombs (szShop, bstrShop, 256);
        ::SysFreeString (bstrShop);

        CString csListItem;
        csListItem.Format ("%s from %s", szDescription, szShop);

        pListBox->AddString (csListItem);
    }

    pEnum->Release();
}
```

Lastly you need to sort out a list box, so go into the resource editor and open the dialog resource. Add a list box and use its properties dialog to change the ID to **IDC_SHOPPINGLIST**. Now you're done! As you can see, there are quite a few more lines of code involved here. OK, it works, but, unless you've got a very good reason for using MFC, Visual Basic wins hands down.

One other point about Visual Basic before we go on. It probably won't have escaped your attention that Visual Basic is more than just a front-end development tool: you can build perfectly good COM objects with it, too. So why not use that?

My view here is that even with the continuing advances in efficiency of compiled Visual Basic code, ATL will, at least for the foreseeable future, be a better tool for developing fast, flexible objects. At the front-end, speed generally isn't so important, because after all, you're ultimately constrained by the reaction times of a slow-witted human. However, at the back-end, you're usually doing serious, labor-intensive stuff and every nanosecond counts. This is where we, the diehards of the C++ brigade, can make our last stand...

Making a Connection

In the next chapter, we're going to be looking at a multi-user interactive application that depends heavily on connection points, so I thought it would be good to spend some of our warm-up chapter preparing the ground a little. Quite coincidentally, it's also another illustration of the extraordinary power of Visual Basic against MFC; clearly, there's a masochistic streak in me somewhere.

For a part of COM which really ought to be pretty straightforward, connection points are extraordinarily complicated, and it is apparent that, over the years, Microsoft have spent a considerable amount of effort in trying to simplify them. It's actually now moderately easy to put together a COM server that sends events back to a Visual Basic client using connection points. However, what happens if the client happens to be another COM object? (Remember, we're interested in building grown-up, complex applications here.) Or what if it happens to be an MFC client?

If you've never come across connection points before, I recommend that you take a look at Chapter 6 in Beginning ATL COM Programming, *which explains the concept in more detail. Here, I'll assume that you're sufficiently familiar with them to follow this step-by-step procedure.*

This example will have an object called **`Ping`** that supports connections. This object will have a method **`Ping()`**, such that when it is called it, will generate an event called **`Pong()`**. This is illustrated in the diagram below:

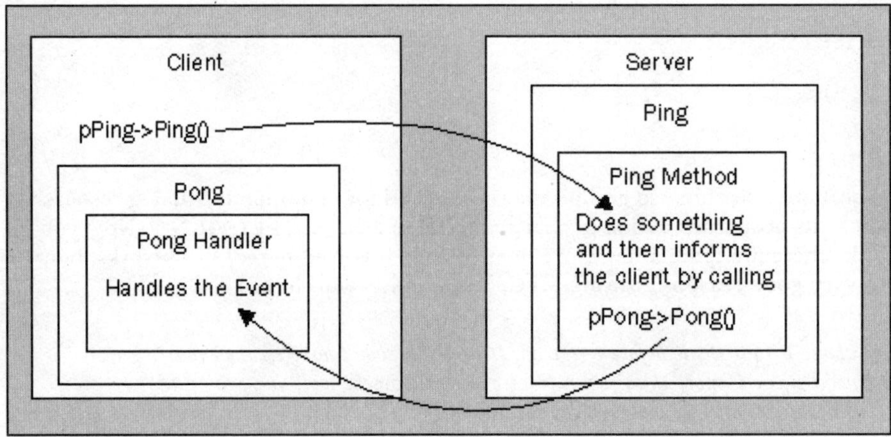

1. We'll start by creating a DLL ATL project called **PingServer** and inserting the **Ping** object. When adding the **Ping** object make, you should ensure that the Support Connection Points checkbox is checked in the ATL wizard. This will help later.

2. Add the **Ping** method to the **Ping** object

Method	Parameters
`Ping()`	`void`

3. The events are generated by calling methods on the **_PingEvents** interface, so this needs to be added as the object's **[source]** interface in the **IDL** file. To do this, go to Project | Add to Project | Components and Controls... and select Developer Studio Components and from that folder, GUID Generator, unless you've configured your Tools menu.

4. Select the 4th GUID format – registry format – and copy to the clipboard. Close **guidgen**, and paste the GUID into the following code you'll also add to the **IDL** file:

```
library PINGSERVERLib
{
    importlib("stdole32.tlb");
    importlib("stdole2.tlb");

    [
        uuid(F8BD6913-D9F6-11D1-A897-00A0C94CB8B3),
        helpstring("Event interface for Ping")
    ]
    dispinterface _PingEvents
    {
        properties:
        methods:
    };
    [
        uuid(F8BD690F-D9F6-11D1-A897-00A0C94CB8B3),
        helpstring("Ping Class")
    ]
    coclass Ping
    {
        [default] interface IPing;
        [default, source] dispinterface _PingEvents;
    };
};
```

Note that a **dispinterface** is used here because scripting clients like VBScript can only implement **dispinterfaces** (which they need to do to handle an event). VB can implement either **dispinterfaces** or custom interfaces, but *not* **dual** interfaces.

The **dispinterface** has been added as the **[default, source]** interface of the **Ping** object to indicate to VB that the **Ping** object generates events through this interface and to allow it to be used with the **WithEvents** keyword.

5. Right click on the **IDL** file and select the Compile PingServer.idl option after which **PingServer** will appear in the ClassView. Right click on it and press Add Method... to add the **void Pong** method (event).

Event	Parameters
Pong()	void

The **IDL** file will now look like this:

```
dispinterface _PingEvents
{
    properties:
    methods:
    [id(1), helpstring("method Pong")] void Pong();
}
```

6. Now you need to generate the ATL proxy code that will generate the event, but before you do this, you need compile the IDL yet again, so that the **Pong()** method is put in the type library. Then go to Project | Add to Project | Components and Controls... and select Developer Studio Components. From that folder, choose the ATL Proxy Generator and select the **PingServer.tlb** type library. Shuffle **_PingEvents** from the left box to the right, check the Connection Point is selected and say Insert.

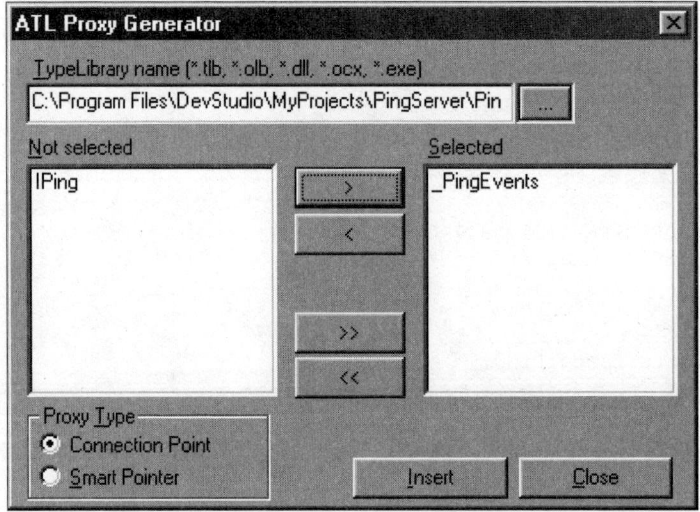

7. Save the file with the suggested name, **`CPPingServer.h`** and add the newly created header file to **`Ping.h`**:

```
// Ping.h : Declaration of the CPing

#ifndef __PING_H_
#define __PING_H_

#include "resource.h"       // main symbols
#include "CPPingServer.h"
```

8. Now, still in **`Ping.h`**, add the following lines to the code:

```
/////////////////////////////////////////////////////////////////////////////
// CPing
class ATL_NO_VTABLE CPing :
    public CComObjectRootEx<CComSingleThreadModel>,
    public CComCoClass<CPing, &CLSID_Ping>,
    public IConnectionPointContainerImpl<CPing>,
    public CProxy_PingEvents<CPing>,
    public IDispatchImpl<IPing, &IID_IPing, &LIBID_PINGSERVERLib>,
    public IProvideClassInfo2Impl<&CLSID_Ping,
                                  &DIID__PingEvents, &LIBID_PINGSERVERLib>
{
public:
    CPing()
    {
    }
```

*That's a double underscore for **`DIID__PingEvents`**, by the way.*

9. Lastly, we can add the connection point to the connection point map, made earlier by the ATL wizard:

```
BEGIN_CONNECTION_POINT_MAP(CPing)
    CONNECTION_POINT_ENTRY(DIID__PingEvents)
END_CONNECTION_POINT_MAP()
```

10. The code in the **`Ping`** class looks like this:

```
/////////////////////////////////////////////////////////////////////////////
// CPing

STDMETHODIMP CPing::Ping()
{
    Fire_Pong ();
```

```
    return S_OK;
}
```

(I told you it was simple.)

11. The **Fire_Pong()** method is in the **CPPingServer.h** file:

```
//////////////////////////////////////////////////////////////////////////////
// CProxy_PingEvents
template <class T>
class CProxy_PingEvents : public IConnectionPointImpl<T, &DIID__PingEvents,
                                                  CComDynamicUnkArray>
{
public:
//methods:
//_PingEvents : IDispatch
public:
    void Fire_Pong()
    {
        T* pT = (T*)this;
        pT->Lock();
        IUnknown** pp = m_vec.begin();
        while (pp < m_vec.end())
        {
            if (*pp != NULL)
            {
                DISPPARAMS disp = { NULL, NULL, 0, 0 };
                IDispatch* pDispatch = reinterpret_cast<IDispatch*>(*pp);
                pDispatch->Invoke(0x1, IID_NULL, LOCALE_USER_DEFAULT,
                                  DISPATCH_METHOD, &disp, NULL, NULL, NULL);
            }
            pp++;
        }
        pT->Unlock();
    }
};
```

Incidentally, if you later decide to add a second connection point to your COM object, you'll find that you have to go through the whole proxy generation process again from scratch. So be very wary of making any changes to the **CPPingServer.h** *file, as they may get lost at some point in the future – normally you should not edit this file, but the proxy generator is buggy and you may need to edit it to correct the generator's mistakes.*

Now we can build the **PingServer** and test it with a simple Visual Basic application, **PingTest**. This will be a simple form consisting of a single button:

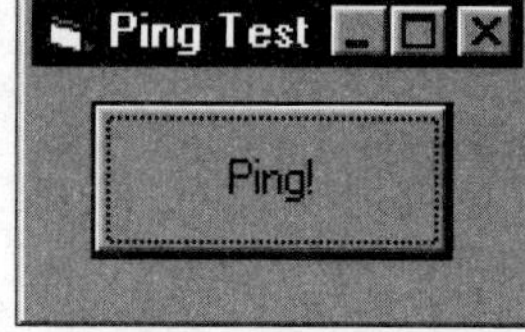

Our code looks like this:

```
Dim WithEvents pinger As Ping

Private Sub cmdPing_Click()
    pinger.Ping
End Sub

Private Sub Form_Load()
    Set pinger = New Ping
End Sub

Private Sub Form_Terminate()
    Set pinger = Nothing
End Sub

Private Sub pinger_Pong()
    MsgBox ("Pong!")
End Sub
```

Remember that you need to add a reference for the **PingServer** type library to your project. The key to receiving events back from our server is, of course, that magic word, **WithEvents**. Visual Basic very kindly recognises that, and creates a **Pinger_Pong** subroutine placeholder for you without being asked. This works fine, and our **Ping** returns a **Pong** immediately.

The Story So Far

In this chapter, we've seen that:

- COM isn't difficult at all – in fact, with ATL, it's a breeze
- Visual Basic is the tool *par excellence* for developing front-ends

And for those of us who still cling to MFC, we've realized that we're going to have to let go sooner or later, and reserve it for special occasions. Although, if you *really* insist, we've found out that we can still make use of it. Just.

In the next chapter, we'll start to look at how we can get COM objects to interact with each other in a meaningful manner. In the meantime, after that last example, I'm going to lie down for a while in a darkened room.

2

Monikers and Binding

> He did not want to compose another Quixote – which is easy – but the Quixote itself. Needless to say, he never contemplated a mechanical transcription of the original; he did not propose to copy it. His admirable intention was to produce a few pages which would coincide – word for word and line for line – with those of Miguel de Cervantes.

"Pierre Menard, Author of the Quixote *"*
(Jorge Luis Borges)

Bricks and Pieces

There are two types of people in this world: those who can do carpentry, and those who can't. I still carry the scar from the time I nearly sawed the top of my left index finger off, and the only thing I've still got that I made when I was a kid is a zither that I somehow managed to put together with considerable assistance from my school woodwork teacher. It's actually quite an unusual zither, in that I managed to assemble it with the panels the wrong way around, so that – depending on your viewpoint – it's either left-handed or upside down. It's probably the only zither in the world that plays the *Harry Lemon Theme ...*

Was my childhood marred by severe creative frustration then? Of course not, because – like anyone who has grown up in the years since World War II – I had Lego. The wonderful thing about Lego is that the hard work of making things that fit together properly has all been done for you. All you have to do is use your imagination to assemble them into what you want. And if you happen to put them together back to front, you can easily pull the bricks apart and reassemble them in the way you originally wanted.

Now it has to be said that Ole Kirk Christiansen's company hasn't been tremendously open with their interface specification – and who can blame them? In fact, the patent for the stud and tube coupling principle was filed in 1958, so you don't find hordes of two-bit Californian start-up operations (in Stud Valley, perhaps) churning out highly specialized bricks with a "Lego-compatible" logo stamped on the side. Who knows what there might be to choose from now? I mean, I remember getting freaked out when the *turntables* came along ...

Of course, things are a little different in the COM world, and this book is largely about manufacturing those specialized bricks. It's about how to make those bricks for different types of target applications. It's about developing wheels for projects that need wheels, and turntables for projects that need turntables.

So what types of project are we aiming at here? Well, in this chapter, we'll be examining a model where a number of clients can interact with each other via the same server. This will involve more than one client binding to the same central server object. It is possible to implement this using absolutely standard COM facilities, but, as we'll soon find – it's not entirely obvious at first sight. Later on in this chapter, we'll be looking at an example of this in the form of a fully functional, fully distributed teleconferencing system. We've got quite a bit of ground to cover first, though, so let's get started ...

The Binding Problem

Now you know how it is when you're just starting out in a relationship – it's very tempting to make comparisons. Right at the start of my love affair with COM, I found it very difficult not to make the observation that this sort of thing seemed to be an awful lot simpler in (whisper it quietly) CORBA. This is because, around about page 2 of any CORBA manual, it explains that whenever you access an object, you have a choice: either you can create an instance of an object (or, as we would say, `CoCreateInstance()`), or you can bind to an existing instance. This means that you can use a single object as the point of interaction between a number of calling applications, or indeed other objects. This is all pretty cool, and works very nicely, thank you.

Here's a challenge for you. Bet you anything you can't find the `bind()` command in COM. I can issue this challenge quite safely, because I know that there isn't one. The best you'll find is a thing called `BindToObject()`, which is a method of the `IMoniker` interface. Perhaps we ought to look into **monikers**, then. As it happens, after I failed to find the `bind()` function, I actually spent quite some time playing with monikers, and I also discovered the joys of the **Running Object Table**. In the event, I ended up using the Running Object Table as my way of binding to an existing object. However, it wasn't the most elegant solution by any means, and I had a feeling all along that it was really a bit of a kludge. I won't be saying anything more about the Running Object Table here, and I strongly suggest that you steer clear of it too!

However, I will be saying a *lot* more about monikers.

Introducing Monikers

Let's imagine that some time in May 1998, I create an instance of a particular COM object. I invoke a method or two, change a few properties and, provided that I'm a good boy, remember to release it. Let's also imagine that I create another instance of it two days later. If I check any of the properties that I changed last time, I'll find that they are as if nothing happened. In fact, assuming that there isn't anything peculiar going on in the constructor, I can guarantee that those two instantiations of the COM object are functionally identical to each other. The reason for this is that COM objects are **stateless**. They have no notion of **persistence** between invocations.

However, what if we want to create an instance of a COM object, and at the same time initialize it from some more persistent entity? How might we go about this – without, that is, imposing a tedious burden on our application programmers? Ladies and Gentlemen, let me introduce you to my friend **moniker**. A moniker is described in the official COM specification as a *persistent, intelligent name.* It's a name in the same way as an object's class ID is a name. It's intelligent, because not only does it carry with it details of how to create an object, but also how to initialize it. And it's persistent, because, in most cases, it has a persistent form that we can use to reconstruct it.

One of the really cool features of monikers is that, as an application programmer, you don't need to know anything about how the object that you're using was originally instantiated and initialized in order to use it. You might like to think of it as an electronic car key, as opposed to a physical one. You don't need to know the exact whereabouts of your car in the parking lot. All you need to know is that when you point your electronic key and press the button, it'll be your car that flashes its lights back at you. Actually, it's even better than that. As long as our objects support the interface that we want, we don't even need to know what their persistent representation is. The bunch of car keys in your hand may all look the same, but the cars that they open may range from a Citroen 2CV up to a Rolls Royce. However, the interface that they support (*OpenLocksAndFlashLights*) is identical.

Let's take a look at a few types of moniker:

File Monikers

The easiest to get our heads round to start with is a **file moniker**, because, after all, what is more intrinsically persistent than a file? Here's how a server COM object creates a file moniker:

```
IMoniker *pMoniker;
hResult = CreateFileMoniker (lpszPathName, &pMoniker);
```

And here's how a client application instantiates an object from it, specifying the interface **`IWhatsit`**:

```
IWhatsit *pWhatsit;
pMoniker->BindToObject (pBindCtx, NULL, IID_IWhatsit,
                        reinterpret_cast<void **>(&pWhatsit));
```

What's going on here? In the server code fragment, we're creating a moniker for some class and telling it that it's going to be initialized by loading some data from the file specified in the path name, **lpszPathName**. Now, I should add that it's not just any old file that we're talking about here, but a special type of file, called an **OLE compound document** file, which has a really interesting feature – you can associate a class ID with it.

When our client code binds to the moniker, the COM object on the server locates the required file and reads in the class ID. It uses this to instantiate the required object, with the interface that the client has specified in the bind request (in this case **IWhatsit**). I'll say a little more about how the moniker goes about initializing the object later on, but this should give you an idea of how the moniker mechanism works.

Class Monikers

Another really important class of monikers is the – er – **class moniker**. Here's some code for creating a class moniker:

```
IMoniker *pMoniker;
hResult = CreateClassMoniker (CLSID_Whatnot, &pMoniker);
```

The code for binding to it is exactly the same! Are you beginning to get some idea of the power of this? This moniker, by the way, will support binding to an instance of the object initialized to a default state.

Pointer Monikers

If our object has already been instantiated, and we've got an interface pointer to it, we can create a **pointer moniker** for it:

```
IMoniker *pMoniker;
hResult = CreatePointerMoniker (pUnknown, &pMoniker);
```

Once again, the code for binding to this is exactly the same.

Item Monikers and Composite Monikers

Things get really exciting when we start constructing composite monikers. A **composite moniker** is one that is made up of several monikers strung together. Typically, you might append an **item moniker** to a file moniker or a class moniker. This effectively parameterizes the initialization process. By composing a class moniker and an item moniker in this way, you can effectively put together a kind of super class factory. As we'll see later on, we can use this to bind to a specific existing instance of an object – something that will prove very important in our teleconferencing example.

Here's a typical fragment of code to create an item moniker:

```
IMoniker *pMoniker;
hResult = CreateItemMoniker (OLESTR("!"), L"Thingy", &pMoniker);
```

So an item moniker basically represents a string, plus something to delimit it from whatever else it's composed with.

You can make your own monikers up as well, if you want. All you need to do is create a COM object that implements the **IMoniker** interface. However, I think we've got enough in the basic set to get us through this chapter quite happily.

It's about time that we took a look at some monikers from a practical point of view, and the best place to start is with file monikers, because in many ways they're the most intuitive. File monikers depend heavily on the use of persistent storage objects, so we'll need to take a look at those first. Before that, we'll need to make a proper examination of those OLE compound document files.

Storage Solutions

I remember the first time I played with an Apple Macintosh, back in the eighties. It was one of those moments when you realize that someone has come up with a totally different way of doing things, a way that is completely different from anything else, but which at the same time is so obviously the right way. Anyway, the thing that really impressed me was the revolutionary idea that a reference to the application associated with a file could be embedded with the file itself, so that when you double-clicked on a Word file, it would launch Word, but when you double-clicked on a MacDraw file, it would launch MacDraw. To this day, I think this is the most immediate demonstration of the power of object-orientation, because,after all, what else is it but polymorphism in practice?

I've always found the Windows version of this somewhat less impressive. In Windows, applications are associated with files according to the file extension, so that – for example – **.doc** files are always associated with Word, and **.xls** files are always associated with Excel, and so on. The danger with this is that it is quite possible for the same extension to be used by two different applications, to say nothing of the fact that a user can actually change the associations and confuse the system altogether. Wouldn't it be better if a reference to the required application could somehow be embedded into the file itself? Of course, the answer is yes. And the way we do this is by using **OLE compound document files**. The most important attribute of these files is that you can associate the class ID of a COM interface with them. That sounds to me like just the kind of thing we're looking for. We'll find out more about the internals of OLE compound document files shortly, but let's just stick to opening and closing them for the time being.

Let's see this, as we build a COM object with a single interface, called **IFile**.

We'll start by creating a new workspace, called **MyFiles**. Inside this, we create a new ATL COM DLL project, called **MyFile**, and insert a simple ATL object, **File**. We'll define **IFile** to have just three methods for the time being:

Method	Parameters
`Create`	`[in] BSTR bstrFileName`
`Close`	
`Open`	`[in] BSTR bstrFileName`

Inside this object, we'll hold a pointer to an **IStorage** interface, **m_pStorage**. **IStorage** is a standard COM interface that we can use to access the data in our file.

We'll need to use a couple of API helper functions to create and open this object. The two functions are **StgCreateDocfile()** and **StgOpenStorage()**. The implementation for the three methods is shown in the code extract below, from **File.cpp**, and we'll add more code to this later.

```
//////////////////////////////////////////////////////////////////////////////
// CFile
STDMETHODIMP CFile::Create(BSTR bstrFileName)
{
    // m_pStorage must be NULL
    if (m_pStorage)
        return E_FAIL;

    if (SysStringLen(bstrFileName) == 0)
        return E_INVALIDARG;

    HRESULT hResult = StgCreateDocfile (bstrFileName,
                            STGM_SIMPLE | STGM_CREATE | STGM_READWRITE |
                            STGM_SHARE_EXCLUSIVE, 0, &m_pStorage);

    if (FAILED(hResult))
        return hResult;

    return S_OK;
}

STDMETHODIMP CFile::Close()
{
    // m_pStorage must have a value
    if (!m_pStorage)
        return E_FAIL;
    m_pStorage->Release();
    m_pStorage = NULL;

    return S_OK;
}

STDMETHODIMP CFile::Open(BSTR bstrFileName)
{
    // m_pStorage must be NULL
    if (m_pStorage)
        return E_FAIL;

    if (SysStringLen(bstrFileName) == 0)
        return E_INVALIDARG;

    HRESULT hResult = StgOpenStorage (bstrFileName, NULL,
                            STGM_READWRITE |
                            STGM_SHARE_EXCLUSIVE, NULL, 0, &m_pStorage);

    if (FAILED(hResult))
        return hResult;

    return S_OK;
}
```

The call to **StgCreateDocFile()** simply creates a file (described later) with the pathname that you pass to it, plus a COM object to access it, and returns to you a pointer to the **IStorage** interface on that object. The call to **StgOpenStorage()** opens an existing file. The code for **Create()** and **Open()** ensures that either of these must be called, but not both.

The header file, **CFile.h** needs to be amended by inserting the lines that are highlighted below. We are adding the private member variable, **m_pStorage**, which just adds a placeholder for the pointer to the storage object that we are wrapping:

```
/////////////////////////////////////////////////////////////////////////////
// CFile
class ATL_NO_VTABLE CFile :
     public CComObjectRootEx<CComSingleThreadModel>,
     public CComCoClass<CFile, &CLSID_File>,
     public IDispatchImpl<IFile, &IID_IFile, &LIBID_MYFILELib>
{
private:
     IStorage    *m_pStorage;

public:
     CFile()
     {
          m_pStorage = NULL;
     }

DECLARE_REGISTRY_RESOURCEID(IDR_FILE)

BEGIN_COM_MAP(CFile)
     COM_INTERFACE_ENTRY(IFile)
     COM_INTERFACE_ENTRY(IDispatch)
END_COM_MAP()

// IFile
public:
     STDMETHOD(Open)(/*[in]*/ BSTR bstrFileName);
     STDMETHOD(Close)();
     STDMETHOD(Create)(/*[in]*/ BSTR bstrFileName);
};
```

That's all you need to do for now, so compile the project. Let's try it out in time-honored tradition by using a VB client. Create a Standard EXE project and add a reference to the MyFile 1.0 Type Library. The form we'll use to do this is shown here:

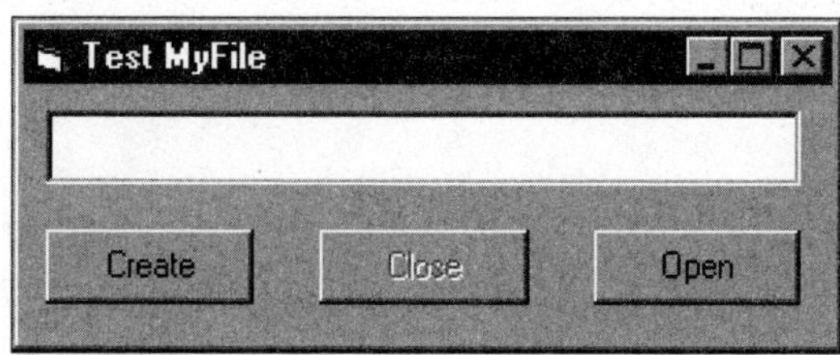

The controls on the form have been named **txtFileName**, **cmdCreate**, **cmdClose** and **cmdOpen**, and the code underlying these is really simple – I present it here with no further explanation:

```
Dim fil As File

Private Sub cmdCreate_Click()

Dim name As String

Set fil = New File

name = txtFileName.Text
fil.Create name

cmdOpen.Enabled = False
cmdCreate.Enabled = False
cmdClose.Enabled = True

End Sub

Private Sub cmdOpen_Click()

Dim name As String

Set fil = New File

name = txtFileName.Text
file.Open name

cmdOpen.Enabled = False
cmdCreate.Enabled = False
cmdClose.Enabled = True

End Sub

Private Sub cmdClose_Click()

fil.Close

cmdOpen.Enabled = True
cmdCreate.Enabled = True
cmdClose.Enabled = False

End Sub
```

If you run this client, you can create a blank file, and then open it again. So far so good, but we haven't put anything into the file yet (or indeed, associated a class ID with it – but, as you might have guessed, I'm coming to that ...)

Gently Down the Stream

A storage object can contain two types of other object: other storage objects and stream objects. In fact, you can think of a storage object as a whole file system in miniature (and there are a whole load of things that you can do with storage objects and OLE, which we haven't time to go into here). So what is a stream object? If you're thinking of the storage object as a file system, then each stream object contained in it is an individual file. Alternatively, perhaps it's more useful to think of each stream object as a variable-length field in a complex file.

Conceptually, storage objects, streams and compound files are related like this:

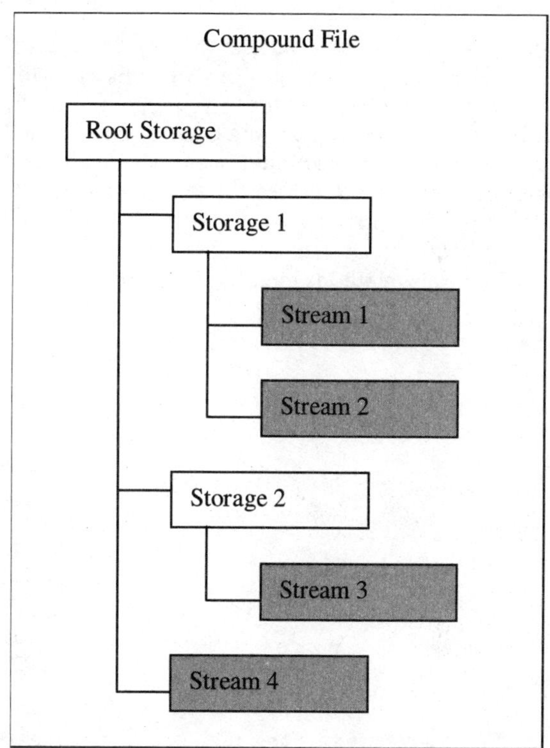

Just as directories can have files and directories, storage objects can contain other storage objects and streams. Actual data is held within streams. Storage objects and streams have names, and each compound file has a root storage object. The great advantage of using storage objects and streams is that they do not need to exist in a compound file. A storage object could be implemented in an object database or in global memory, and yet *it can be accessed by exactly the same code.*

For our example, `File`, we'll have two streams in the root storage, `Title` and `Data` and to provide the data to put in these let's add two properties to `IFile`:

Property	Type
Title	BSTR
Data	BSTR

Before we actually code this, let's have a look at the **IStream** interface, and how it relates to **IStorage**.

You can create a stream by using the **CreateStream()** method on **IStorage**. Since our example implements the root storage object in a file, this call will create the stream in the file, plus a COM object to wrap it, and it will return to you a pointer to the **IStream** interface on that object. To open an existing stream, you use the **OpenStream()** method on **IStorage**. Again, this returns you a pointer to the **IStream** interface on the associated object. Once you have your **IStream** interface, you can write to it using the **Write()** method and read from it using the **Read()** method. (Well, what did you expect?).

So what do our new methods look like?

```
STDMETHODIMP CFile::put_Title(BSTR newVal)
{
   if (!m_pStorage)
       return E_FAIL;

   if (SysStringLen(newVal) == 0)
        return E_INVALIDARG;

   IStream *pStream;

   //see if the stream already exists, and if so over write it
   HRESULT hResult = m_pStorage->OpenStream (L"Title",
      NULL, STGM_READWRITE | STGM_SHARE_EXCLUSIVE, 0, &pStream);
   if (FAILED(hResult))
   {
      // the stream does not exist so create it
      hResult= m_pStorage->CreateStream (L"Title",
         STGM_READWRITE | STGM_SHARE_EXCLUSIVE, 0, 0, &pStream);
   }

   if (FAILED(hResult))
      return hResult;

   //get the size of the title
   size_t len = wcslen(newVal);

   hResult = pStream->Write (&len, sizeof(size_t), NULL);

   if (SUCCEEDED(hResult))
      hResult = pStream->Write (newVal, len * sizeof(WCHAR), NULL);

   pStream->Release();

   return hResult;
```

```
}

STDMETHODIMP CFile::put_Data(BSTR newVal)
{
    if (!m_pStorage)
        return E_FAIL;

    if (SysStringLen(newVal) == 0)
        return E_INVALIDARG;

    IStream *pStream;

    //see if the stream already exists, and if so over write it
    HRESULT hResult = m_pStorage->OpenStream (L"Data", NULL,
        STGM_READWRITE | STGM_SHARE_EXCLUSIVE, 0, &pStream);
    if (FAILED(hResult))
    {
        // the stream does not exist so create it
        hResult = m_pStorage->CreateStream (L"Data",
            STGM_READWRITE | STGM_SHARE_EXCLUSIVE, 0, 0, &pStream);
    }

    if (FAILED(hResult))
        return hResult;

    //get the size of the data
    size_t len = wcslen(newVal);

    hResult = pStream->Write (&len, sizeof(size_t), NULL);

    if (SUCCEEDED(hResult))
        hResult = pStream->Write (newVal, len * sizeof(WCHAR), NULL);

    pStream->Release();

    return hResult;
}

STDMETHODIMP CFile::get_Title(BSTR *pVal)
{
    if (!m_pStorage)
        return E_FAIL;

    ULONG length;
    IStream *pStream;

    HRESULT hResult = m_pStorage->OpenStream (L"Title", NULL,
        STGM_READWRITE | STGM_SHARE_EXCLUSIVE, 0, &pStream);

    if (FAILED(hResult))
        return hResult;

    //read how big the title is
    size_t len;
    hResult = pStream->Read (&len, sizeof(size_t), &length);
```

```
    if (SUCCEEDED(hResult))
    {
        //create an uninitialized BSTR to hold the title
        *pVal = SysAllocStringByteLen(NULL, len * sizeof(WCHAR));
        hResult = pStream->Read (*pVal, len * sizeof(WCHAR), &length);
    }

    pStream->Release();

    return hResult;
}
STDMETHODIMP CFile::get_Data(BSTR *pVal)
{
    if (!m_pStorage)
        return E_FAIL;

    ULONG length;
    IStream *pStream;

    HRESULT hResult = m_pStorage->OpenStream (L"Data", NULL,
        STGM_READWRITE | STGM_SHARE_EXCLUSIVE, 0, &pStream);

    if (FAILED(hResult))
        return hResult;

    //read how big the data is
    size_t len;
    hResult = pStream->Read (&len, sizeof(size_t), &length);
    if (SUCCEEDED(hResult))
    {
        //create an uninitialized BSTR to hold the data
        *pVal = SysAllocStringByteLen(NULL, len * sizeof(WCHAR));
        hResult = pStream->Read (*pVal, len * sizeof(WCHAR), &length);
    }

    pStream->Release();

    return hResult;
}
```

Once again, we'll test with VB. Here is our extended form:

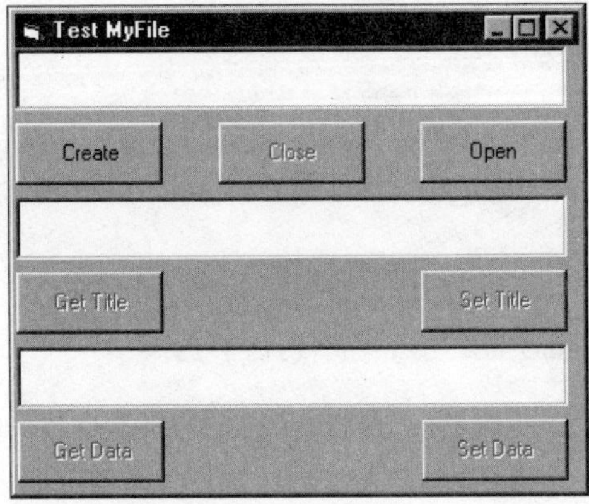

The two new text boxes have been named **txtTitle** and **txtData**, whilst the new command buttons are **cmdGetTitle**, **cmdSetTitle**, **cmdGetData** and **cmdSetData**. Add code to **cmdOpen_Click()** and **cmdCreate_Click()** to enable these new command buttons, and code to **cmdClose_Click()** to disable them. Here is the new code.

```
Private Sub cmdGetData_Click()
on error goto exitGetData
     txtData.Text = fil.Data
exitGetData:
End Sub

Private Sub cmdGetTitle_Click()
on error goto exitGetTitle
     txtTitle.Text = fil.Title
exitGetTitle:
End Sub

Private Sub cmdSetData_Click()
on error goto exitSetData
     fil.Data txtData.Text
exitSetData:
End Sub

Private Sub cmdSetTitle_Click()
on error goto exitSetTitle
     fil.Title txtTitle.Text
exitSetTitle:
End Sub
```

If you try testing the code using your new form, you should find that you can create new files, give them a title and data, and later open those same files to retrieve the data. Before we move on, I'd also like to say a quick word about a really neat tool that comes with Visual Studio package, **dfview**. You can use this program to dump out the contents of any OLE compound document file. For example, here's one I created using **MyFileTest**:

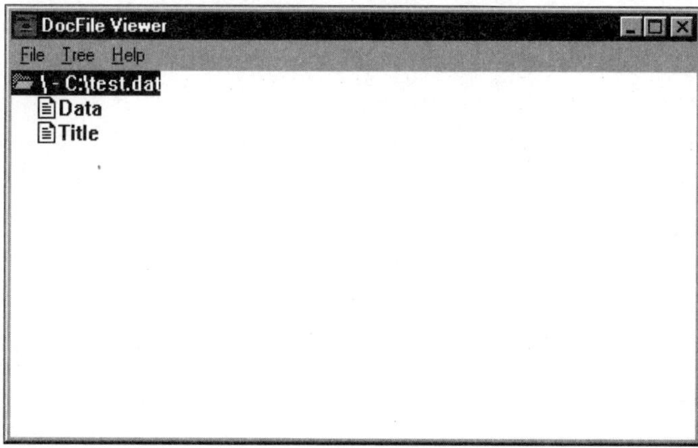

You can get the contents of any stream by simply clicking on its name. For example, here's the "Data" stream:

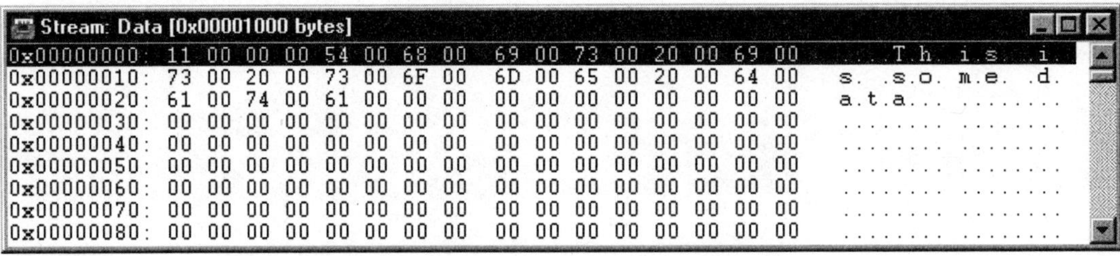

Take a look at that size, incidentally. Perhaps we should have used the **`SetSize()`** *method of* **`IStream`** *to limit the size allocated to the stream to something a little more economical!*

A Date With Moniker

OK, we've taken a brief look inside storage objects, and how streams work. Now let's see how we can make our files more intelligent. Remember that class ID that we could associate with our file? Remember that I said that a file moniker could make use of it? I think it's time to meet moniker in the flesh.

Let's step back a little before we dive into code. Can we just take a COM object that implements **`IFile`** and associates it with a moniker? Well, no. For a start, the COM object doesn't even exist at the point when we get hold of our moniker. All that is there is a file, sitting comfortably on disk and not troubling the memory manager at all. Who was that shouting at the back? Yes, you're right, This is where the storage object's class ID comes into play. But is that enough? Well, we're nearly there. The only problem is that the moniker hasn't the faintest idea how to find the file, let alone extract the class ID. So, how do we get around this one?

The answer is to extend our **`File`** object so that it implements another, standard, interface that the moniker object can use to find out how to open the file. This interface is called **`IPersistFile.`** Let's make the necessary changes to **`File.h`**:

```
/////////////////////////////////////////////////////////////////////////////
// CFile
class ATL_NO_VTABLE CFile :
      public CComObjectRootEx<CComSingleThreadModel>,
      public CComCoClass<CFile, &CLSID_File>,

      public IPersistFile,

      public IDispatchImpl<IFile, &IID_IFile, &LIBID_MYFILELib>
{
private:
      IStorage   *m_pStorage;

public:
      CFile()
      {
            m_pStorage = NULL;
      }
```

```
DECLARE_REGISTRY_RESOURCEID(IDR_MYFILE)

BEGIN_COM_MAP(CMyFile)
     COM_INTERFACE_ENTRY(IMyFile)
     COM_INTERFACE_ENTRY(IPersistFile)
     COM_INTERFACE_ENTRY(IDispatch)
END_COM_MAP()

// IFile
public:
     STDMETHOD(get_Data)(/*[out,retval]*/ BSTR *bstrData);
     STDMETHOD(get_Title)(/*[out,retval]*/ BSTR *bstrTitle);
     STDMETHOD(put_Data)(/*[in]*/ BSTR bstrData);
     STDMETHOD(put_Title)(/*[in]*/ BSTR bstrTitle);
     STDMETHOD(Open)(/*[in]*/ BSTR bstrFileName);
     STDMETHOD(Close)();
     STDMETHOD(Create)(/*[in]*/ BSTR bstrFileName);
// IPersistFile
public:
   STDMETHOD(GetClassID)(CLSID* pClassID);
   STDMETHOD(IsDirty)(void);
   STDMETHOD(Load)(LPCOLESTR pszFileName, DWORD dwMode);
   STDMETHOD(Save)(LPCOLESTR pszFileName, BOOL fRemember);
   STDMETHOD(SaveCompleted)(LPCOLESTR);
   STDMETHOD(GetCurFile)(LPOLESTR*);
};
```

We should now give some thought to what we are going to do in each of these methods. I'm actually going to cheat a little here, because for the purposes of our little experiment, we don't really need some of them, and we can get away with a minimal implementation for others. I don't want to get this discussion derailed into a detailed investigation of storage objects!

A Minimally Persistent Storage Object

I suggest that the following will be quite sufficient:

```
//   IPersistFile stuff

STDMETHODIMP CFile::GetClassID(CLSID* pClassID)
{
     *pClassID = CLSID_File;

     return S_OK;
}

STDMETHODIMP CFile::IsDirty(void)
{
     return E_NOTIMPL;
}

STDMETHODIMP CFile::Load(LPCOLESTR pszFileName, DWORD dwMode)
{
```

```
    if (pszFileName == NULL)
        return E_POINTER;
    if (wcslen(pszFileName) == 0)
        return E_INVALIDARG;
    if (m_pStorage)
        Close ();

    HRESULT hResult = StgOpenStorage (pszFileName, NULL,
        STGM_READWRITE | STGM_SHARE_EXCLUSIVE, NULL, 0, &m_pStorage);

    return hResult;
}

STDMETHODIMP CFile::Save(LPCOLESTR pszFileName, BOOL fRemember)
{
    if (pszFileName == NULL)
        return E_POINTER;
    if (wcslen(pszFileName) == 0)
        return E_INVALIDARG;

    BSTR bstrTitle = NULL;
    BSTR bstrData = NULL;
    HRESULT hResult1 = E_FAIL;
    HRESULT hResult2 = E_FAIL;

    if (m_pStorage)
    {
        hResult1 = get_Title(&bstrTitle);
        hResult2 = get_Data(&bstrData);

        Close();
    }

    HRESULT hResult = Create(CComBSTR(pszFileName));

    if (SUCCEEDED(hResult))
    {
        if (SUCCEEDED(hResult1))
            put_Title (bstrTitle);

        if (SUCCEEDED(hResult2))
            put_Data (bstrName);
    }

    SysFreeString (bstrTitle);
    SysFreeString (bstrName);

    return hResult;
}

STDMETHODIMP CFile::SaveCompleted(LPCOLESTR)
{
      // Dummy

      return S_OK;
}
```

```
STDMETHODIMP CFile::GetCurFile(LPOLESTR*)
{
      return E_NOTIMPL;
}
```

We've nearly got enough for our moniker to get to work on. There's just one thing we've forgotten. We need to add a couple of lines to the **Create()** method:

```
      HRESULT hResult = StgCreateDocfile (bstrFileName,
                                      STGM_SIMPLE | STGM_CREATE | STGM_READWRITE |
                                      STGM_SHARE_EXCLUSIVE, 0, &m_pStorage);

      if (FAILED(hResult))
            return hResult;

      hResult = m_pStorage->SetClass(CLSID_File);

      return hResult;
}
```

There we are. If we create a file moniker based on this file, it now has enough information to locate the file, open it, get hold of the class ID, create an instance of an object, and get hold of the **IFile** interface on it. Whew!

Monikers in Action

This is all very well, but I'm sure that what you really want to see is some monikers that actually do something. Our first problem is that we haven't really established where monikers actually come from. We have basically two alternatives: the client or the server. Our next example will show both of these possibilities in action.

Using A File Moniker

We'll start off by creating a small COM object that hands out monikers to anyone who asks. We'll create an EXE project call **MonServer**, and use the ATL wizard to create a COM object in it called **MonGiver**, with a single vtable-only interface **IMonGiver**:

Method	Parameters
GetMoniker()	**[in] short monNum, [out] IMoniker **pMoniker**

Don't forget to add a custom build step to the project to create and register the proxy/stub DLL – we'll need this because it's a pure vtable object.

The implementation code looks like this:

```
// MonGiver.cpp : Implementation of CMonGiver
#include "stdafx.h"
#include "MonServer.h"
#include "MonGiver.h"

////////////////////////////////////////////////////////////////////////////
// CMonGiver


STDMETHODIMP CMonGiver::GetMoniker(short monNum, IMoniker * * pMoniker)
{
    switch (monNum)
    {
        case 1:
            return CreateFileMoniker (L"C:\\MonTest.dat", pMoniker);

        default:
            return E_INVALIDARG;
    }
}
```

Here – if we pass in a value of 1, we'll get a file moniker passed back to us, which, provided that our file **C:\montest.dat** is set up correctly, will enable our client application to get hold of a **File** object that has been initialized with data from it. Don't worry about any other values for the time being, by the way, we'll add those in a little while. Let's try this out.

First of all, we'll need to create a suitable file. We'll use our **MyFileTest** VB application to do this. We'll just create the file as **C:\montest.dat**, and add a title and some data:

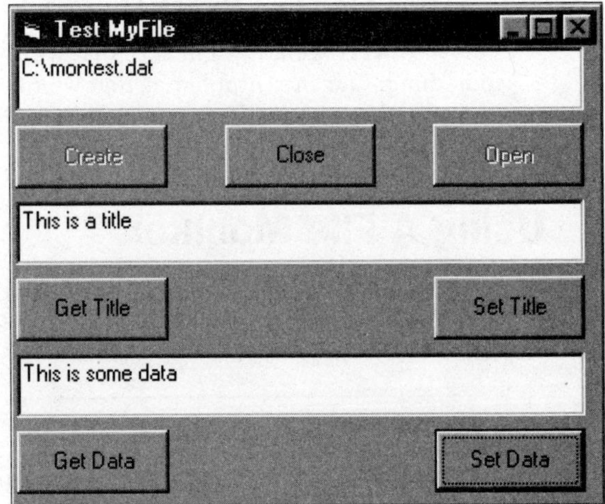

We've got a pure vtable interface here, so we'll need an MFC application. Let's create a dialog-based one called **MonUser**. Here's the dialog:

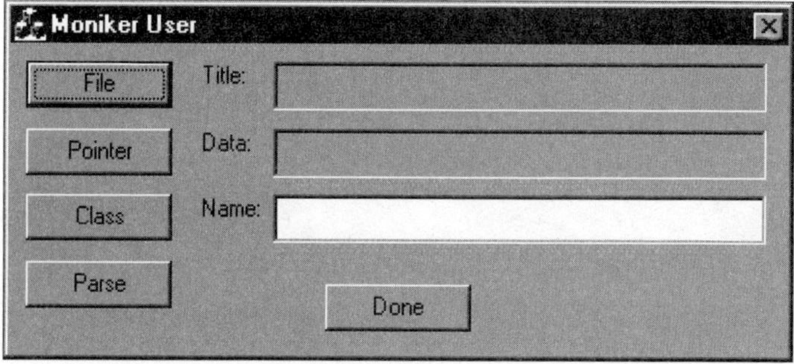

The five buttons are **IDC_FILE**, **IDC_POINTER**, **IDC_CLASS**, **IDC_PARSE** and **IDOK** respectively, all disabled except the last two (Parse and Done). The three edit fields are **IDC_TITLE**, **IDC_DATA** and **IDC_NAME**. We'll need to add this code to the end of **OnInitDialog()**:

```
   CoInitialize(NULL);

   HRESULT hResult = CoCreateInstance(CLSID_MonGiver, NULL,
                  CLSCTX_SERVER, IID_IMonGiver,
                  reinterpret_cast<void **> (&m_pGiver));

   if (FAILED(hResult))
   {
      CString csError;
      csError.Format(_T("Failed to create instance of moniker giver,
                                                            %x"),
            hResult);
      AfxMessageBox(csError);

      m_pGiver = NULL;
   }
   else
   {
      CButton *pFile = reinterpret_cast<CButton*>(GetDlgItem(IDC_FILE));
      pFile->EnableWindow(TRUE);

      CButton *pClass =
                  reinterpret_cast<CButton*>(GetDlgItem(IDC_CLASS));
      pClass->EnableWindow(TRUE);

      CButton *pPointer = reinterpret_cast<CButton*>(
                                          GetDlgItem(IDC_POINTER));
      pPointer->EnableWindow(TRUE);
   }

   return TRUE;  // return TRUE  unless you set the focus to a control
}
```

Here, we're creating our instance of **MonGiver**. We store the pointer in a member variable, and we release it when the user clicks on Done:

```
void CMonUserDlg::OnOK()
{
      if (m_pGiver)
            m_pGiver->Release();

      CDialog::OnOK();
}
```

For this code to work you need to initialize the pointer in the constructor:

```
CMonUserDlg::CMonUserDlg(CWnd* pParent)
   : CDialog(CMonUserDlg::IDD, pParent), m_pGiver(NULL)
```

And since you have initialized COM you will need to uninitialize it, the safest place to do this is in **OnClose()**, the handler for **WM_CLOSE**:

```
void CMonUserDlg::OnClose()
{
   CoUninitialize();
   CDialog::OnClose();
}
```

Here are the additions that we need to make to the header file **MonUserDlg.h**:

```
#include "..\MonServer\MonServer.h"

        .
        .
        .

// Implementation
private:
      IMonGiver *m_pGiver;
      void UseMoniker(short monNum);
      void DoMoniker(IBindCtx *pBindCtx, IMoniker *pMoniker);
```

We'll look into those member functions shortly. For now, let's go back to the dialog. First add the **MonServer** constants to the **MonUserDlg.cpp**:

```
#include "MonUserDlg.h"
#include "..\MonServer\MonServer_i.c"
```

We'll just implement the code underneath the File button for now, and it looks like this:

```
void CMonUserDlg::OnFile()
{
      UseMoniker(1);
}
```

Uh-huh. What's in **`UseMoniker()`**, then?

```
void CMonUserDlg::UseMoniker(short monNum)
{
   CString csError;

   IMoniker *pMoniker;

   HRESULT hResult = m_pGiver->GetMoniker(monNum, &pMoniker);

   if (FAILED(hResult))
   {
      csError.Format(_T("Failed to get moniker, %x"), hResult);
      AfxMessageBox (csError);
      return;
   }

   IBindCtx *pBindCtx;
   CreateBindCtx (0, &pBindCtx);

   DoMoniker(pBindCtx, pMoniker);

   pBindCtx->Release();
   pMoniker->Release();
}
```

Here, we get hold of our moniker from our **`MonGiver`** object. After this, we create a **bind context**. This is basically an object that keeps track of what's happening during a moniker binding operation. We pass this, plus our moniker, to our second private member function, **`DoMoniker()`**:

```
void CMonUserDlg::DoMoniker(IBindCtx *pBindCtx, IMoniker *pMoniker)
{
     IFile *pFile;
     HRESULT hResult = pMoniker->BindToObject(pBindCtx, NULL,
                                        IID_IFile, (void **) &pFile);

     if (FAILED(hResult))
     {
           CString csError;
           csError.Format(_T("Failed to bind to object, %x"), hResult);
           AfxMessageBox (csError);
           return;
     }

     BSTR bstrTitle;
     pFile->get_Title(&bstrTitle);

     BSTR bstrData;
     pFile->get_Data(&bstrData);

     CString csTitle = bstrTitle;
     SysFreeString (bstrTitle);
```

```
        CEdit *pTitle = reinterpret_cast<CEdit*>(GetDlgItem(IDC_TITLE));
        pTitle->SetWindowText(csTitle);
        CString csData = bstrData;
        SysFreeString (bstrData);

        CEdit *pData = reinterpret_cast<CEdit*>(GetDlgItem(IDC_DATA));
        pData->SetWindowText(csData);

        LPOLESTR olestrName;
        hResult = pMoniker->GetDisplayName(pBindCtx, NULL, &olestrName);

        CString csName;

        if (FAILED(hResult))
              csName = "No display name available";
        else
        {
              csName = olestrName;
              CoTaskMemFree(olestrName);
        }

        CEdit *pName = reinterpret_cast<CEdit*>(GetDlgItem(IDC_NAME));
        pName->SetWindowText(csName);

        pFile->Release();
    }
```

OK, this is the point at which we actually bind to our object. When we do this, we specify that we want the interface **`IFile`**. Once we've got this, we can access its properties, which, we hope, will have been magically filled in with the data from the file **`c:\montest.dat`**. Before you can compile this, you must add an **`#include`** to the **`MyFile.h`** header that describes **`IFile`**, and the **`MyFile_i.c`** that declares the constants for the interface.

Let's try it out:

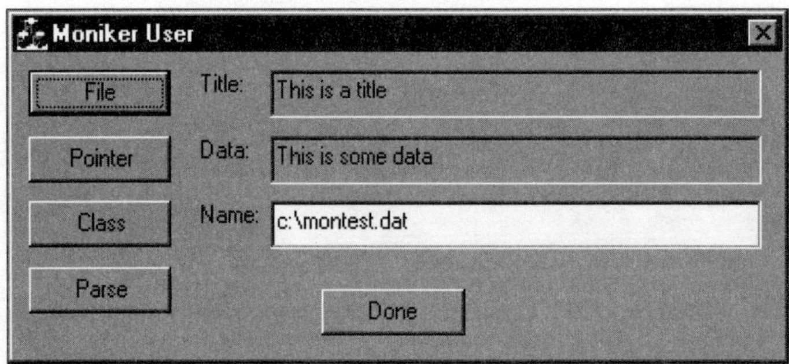

Great! By the way, did you notice that call to **`GetDisplayName()`**? That gets the persistent display name for the moniker. We'll see soon how we can use it to reconstruct the moniker without reference to our server.

Monikers as an Abstraction

OK, let's see how monikers can provide an abstraction. Let's imagine that we've got an object that's pretending to be a file, to the extent that it implements the **IFile** interface. It's not an entirely absurd notion – perhaps it's a gateway to some sort of legacy system. We'll call this object **NotFile**, and we'll implement it in the DLL project **MyNotFile**, under the **MyFiles** workspace.

The easiest way to create this is to use the ATL wizard to create an ATL object called **NotFile**. This will create an interface called **INotFile**, which we do not need, so open the IDL to remove this interface definition altogether and make the other changes highlighted here:

```
// MyNotFile.idl : IDL source for MyNotFile.dll
//

// This file will be processed by the MIDL tool to
// produce the type library (MyNotFile.tlb) and marshalling code.

import "oaidl.idl";
import "ocidl.idl";

import "MyFile.idl";

[
     uuid(4000AD50-4C90-11D1-B06A-0040951082F7),
     version(1.0),
     helpstring("MyNotFile 1.0 Type Library")
]
library MYNOTFILELib
{
     importlib("stdole32.tlb");
     importlib("stdole2.tlb");

     [
          uuid(4000AD5E-4C90-11D1-B06A-0040951082F7),
          helpstring("NotFile Class")
     ]
     coclass NotFile
     {
          [default] interface IFile;
     };
};
```

This uses the IDL and headers from the **MyFile** project, so copy over **MyFile.idl**, **MyFile.h** and **MyFile_i.c** from the **MyFile** directory to the **MyNotFile** directory. Next, we need to make a few changes to the header file **NotFile.h** so that the objects implements **IFile**:

```
// NotFile.h : Declaration of the CNotFile

#ifndef __NOTFILE_H_
#define __NOTFILE_H_
#include "resource.h"        // main symbols

#include "MyFile.h"
```

```
///////////////////////////////////////////////////////////////////////////
// CNotFile
class ATL_NO_VTABLE CNotFile :
     public CComObjectRootEx<CComSingleThreadModel>,
     public CComCoClass<CNotFile, &CLSID_NotFile>,
     public IDispatchImpl<IFile, &IID_IFile, &LIBID_MYNOTFILELib>
{
public:
     CNotFile()
     {
     }

DECLARE_REGISTRY_RESOURCEID(IDR_NOTFILE)

BEGIN_COM_MAP(CNotFile)
     COM_INTERFACE_ENTRY(IFile)
     COM_INTERFACE_ENTRY(IDispatch)
END_COM_MAP()

// IFile
public:
     STDMETHOD(get_Data)(/*[out, retval]*/ BSTR *pVal);
     STDMETHOD(put_Data)(/*[in]*/ BSTR newVal);
     STDMETHOD(get_Title)(/*[out, retval]*/ BSTR *pVal);
     STDMETHOD(put_Title)(/*[in]*/ BSTR newVal);
     STDMETHOD(Open)(/*[in]*/ BSTR bstrFileName);
     STDMETHOD(Close)();
     STDMETHOD(Create)(/*[in]*/ BSTR bstrFileName);
};

#endif //__NOTFILE_H_
```

Finally, we need to implement the **IFile** methods in **NotFile.cpp**. Well, one or two of them, anyway:

```
// NotFile.cpp : Implementation of CNotFile
#include "stdafx.h"
#include "MyNotFile.h"
#include "NotFile.h"

///////////////////////////////////////////////////////////////////////////
// CNotFile

STDMETHODIMP CNotFile::Create(BSTR bstrFileName)
{
     return E_NOTIMPL;
}

STDMETHODIMP CNotFile::Close()
```

```
{
     return E_NOTIMPL;
}

STDMETHODIMP CNotFile::Open(BSTR bstrFileName)
{
     return E_NOTIMPL;
}

STDMETHODIMP CNotFile::get_Title(BSTR *bstrTitle)
{
     *bstrTitle = SysAllocString (L"This is a dummy title");
     return S_OK;
}

STDMETHODIMP CNotFile::put_Title(BSTR bstrTitle)
{
     return E_NOTIMPL;
}

STDMETHODIMP CNotFile::get_Data(BSTR *bstrData)
{
     *bstrData = SysAllocString (L"This is dummy data");
     return S_OK;
}

STDMETHODIMP CNotFile::put_Data(BSTR bstrData)
{
     return E_NOTIMPL;
}
```

Basically, all we're doing with our **IFile** interface is setting up a dummy title and some dummy data to be returned by the **get_Title()** and **get_Data()** methods respectively. All the other methods have been left unimplemented.

We also need to add the following line to the top of **MyNotFile.cpp**:

```
#include "stdafx.h"
#include "resource.h"
#include "initguid.h"
#include "MyNotFile.h"

#include "MyNotFile_i.c"
#include "MyFile_i.c"
#include "NotFile.h"
```

Now you should build it.

In order to test it, however, we'll need to add a couple more lines to our **IMonGiver::GetMoniker()** method in the **MonServer** project. Here is what it looks like now:

```
// MonGiver.cpp : Implementation of CMonGiver
#include "stdafx.h"
#include "MonServer.h"
#include "MonGiver.h"

#include "..\MyFiles\MyNotFile\MyNotFile.h"

///////////////////////////////////////////////////////////////////////////////
// CMonGiver

STDMETHODIMP CMonGiver::GetMoniker(short monNum, IMoniker * * pMoniker)
{
     switch (monNum)
     {
          case 1:
               return CreateFileMoniker (L"c:\\montest.dat", pMoniker);

          case 2:
               IUnknown *pUnk;
               HRESULT hResult;
               hResult = CoCreateInstance(CLSID_NotFile,
                                          NULL,
                                          CLSCTX_SERVER,
                                          IID_IUnknown,
                                          reinterpret_cast<void**>(&pUnk));
               if (FAILED(hResult)) return hResult;
               hResult = CreatePointerMoniker (pUnk, pMoniker);
               pUnk->Release();
               return hResult;
          default:
               return E_INVALIDARG;
     }

     return S_OK;
}
```

Here, we're instantiating a **NotFile** object, and creating a pointer moniker based on it. So that this project has the constants for the **NotFile** object add the following to **MonServer.cpp**:

```
#include "MonServer.h"
#include "..\MyFiles\MyNotFile\MyNotFile.h"

#include "MonServer_i.c"
#include "..\MyFiles\MyNotFile\MyNotFile_i.c"
```

The project should now compile. Before going on to **MonUser**, look back at what you have just done. **IMonGiver::GetMoniker()** returns an **IMoniker** pointer, and yet this pointer can refer to one of two different objects: a **File** object or a **NotFile** object.

Now, let's go back to our **MonUser** application and try this out. We'll need to add some code under the Pointer button – use ClassView to create the **OnPointer()** handler for clicking on this button:

```
void CMonUserDlg::OnPointer()
{
    UseMoniker(2);
}
```

And we're away. If we run it up, and click on the Pointer button, here's what we see:

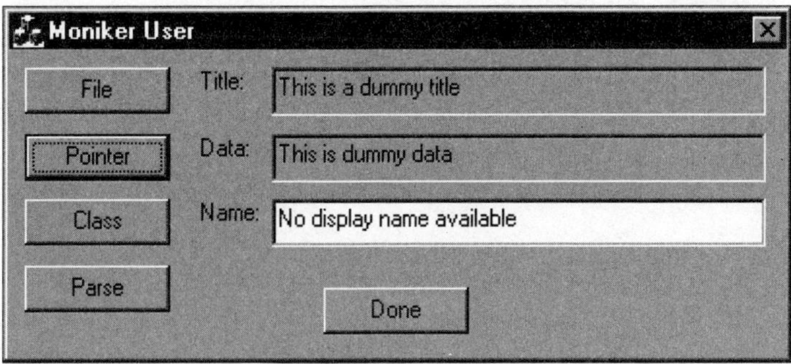

If you get an error of 0x80040002 then this means that the **IFile** *interface cannot be marshaled from* **MonServer**. *To get round this, compile and register the proxy-stub for* **IFile** *using the* **MyFileps.mk** *makefile in* **MyFile**.

Notice that there isn't a display name. That's because pointer monikers are unusual in that they don't have any persistent state. How could they? All they do is represent a pointer to one specific instance.

However, the really cool thing is that our application doesn't know whether it's dealing with something that's file oriented or not. The moniker abstracts all those considerations from us. Now let's try a class moniker.

Class Monikers

You might at first think that all we need to do for our **MonGiver** object in order to offer a class moniker is this:

```
// MonGiver.cpp : Implementation of CMonGiver
#include "stdafx.h"
#include "MonServer.h"
#include "MonGiver.h"

#include "..\MyFiles\MyFile\MyFile.h"
#include "..\MyFiles\MyNotFile\MyNotFile.h"
```

```
///////////////////////////////////////////////////////////////////////////////
// CMonGiver


STDMETHODIMP CMonGiver::GetMoniker(short monNum, IMoniker * * pMoniker)
{
      switch (monNum)
      {
            case 1:
                  return CreateFileMoniker (L"c:\\montest.dat", pMoniker);

            case 2:
                  IUnknown *pUnk;
                  CoCreateInstance(CLSID_NotFile, NULL, CLSCTX_SERVER,
                                        IID_IUnknown, (void**)&pUnk);
                  return CreatePointerMoniker (pUnk, pMoniker);

            case 3:
                  return CreateClassMoniker (CLSID_NotFile, pMoniker);

            default:
                  return E_INVALIDARG;
      }

      return S_OK;
}
```

The trouble is, it isn't quite that simple. If you bind to a class moniker, what you're actually binding to is a **class object**. Class objects are the things that create instances of a COM class and typically they implement the **IClassFactory** interface (this mechanism is described in Chapter 2 of *Professional ActiveX COM Control Programming*, by Sing Li and Panos Economopoulos, *ISBN 1-861000-37-5*). In ATL, these are buried below the surface, and most of the time you don't need to know anything about them.

If you create a moniker in this way and then try to bind to it, you'll get an **E_NOINTERFACE** error. This is because the class moniker binding mechanism gets the class object for the specified class ID, and attempts to find the **IFile** interface from it. Because the default ATL class factory object only implements **IClassFactory**, any attempt to get a different interface will fail.

So what are we to do? Basically, we have to override the standard class factory with our own. Now as it happens, all ATL objects implement **IClassFactory** as standard, so all we have to do is make sure that the class factory object used is one of our own. However, as we do this, we run the risk of making the object inaccessible by the standard routes, and our pointer moniker won't work any more. So we'll leave the **NotFile** object alone, and create a new one, **ClassFile**.

MyClassFile is the third project in the **MyFiles** workspace. You should create this in exactly the same way as we created **MyNotFile**; I won't go into it here, except to say that **get_Title()** and **get_Data()** should return a different string than **NotFile**.

Remember that you can download all the code from the examples here and in the rest of the book from the Wrox Press web site at http://www.wrox.com.

However, there is one further change that we have to make. The object must be identified as a class object and hence returned when queried by **DllGetClassObject()**. Add the following lines in **MyClassFile.cpp**:

```
STDAPI DllGetClassObject(REFCLSID rclsid, REFIID riid, LPVOID* ppv)
{
      if (rclsid == CLSID_ClassFile)
      {
            if (ppv == NULL)
                  return E_POINTER;
            CComObject<CClassFile>* pObj;
            HRESULT hResult;
            hResult = CComObject<CClassFile>::CreateInstance(&pObj);
            if (FAILED(hResult))
                  return hResult;
            hResult = pObj->QueryInterface(riid, ppv);
            if (FAILED(hResult))
            delete pObj;
            return hResult;
      }
      else
            return CLASS_E_CLASSNOTAVAILABLE;
}
```

What we're doing here is telling COM that we're going to use one of our objects as the class factory, and not the one provided by ATL. OK, let's make the last change to **MonServer**:

```
// MonGiver.cpp : Implementation of CMonGiver
#include "stdafx.h"
#include "MonServer.h"
#include "MonGiver.h"

#include "..\MyFiles\MyNotFile\MyNotFile.h"
#include "..\MyFiles\MyClassFile\MyClassFile.h"

/////////////////////////////////////////////////////////////////////////////
// CMonGiver


STDMETHODIMP CMonGiver::GetMoniker(short monNum, IMoniker * * pMoniker)
{
      switch (monNum)
      {
            case 1:
                  return CreateFileMoniker (L"c:\\montest.dat", pMoniker);

            case 2:
                  IUnknown *pUnk;
                  CoCreateInstance(CLSID_NotFile, NULL, CLSCTX_SERVER,
                                          IID_IUnknown, (void**)&pUnk);
                  return CreatePointerMoniker (pUnk, pMoniker);

            case 3:
                  return CreateClassMoniker (CLSID_ClassFile, pMoniker);
```

```
            default:
                return E_INVALIDARG;
        }

        return S_OK;
    }
```

Remember to include **MyClassFile_i.c** and **MyClassFile.h** to **MonServer.cpp**.

Oh, and we'll need to add some code under that Class button in **MonUser**:

```
void CMonUserDlg::OnClass()
{
    UseMoniker(3);
}
```

OK, let's try it out:

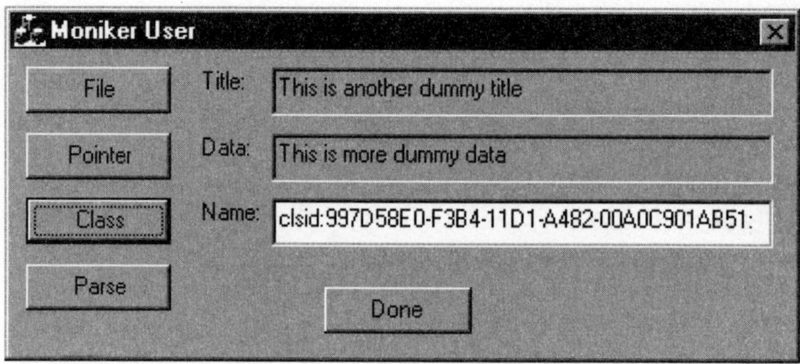

Not that your example may have a different ***CLSID****.*

Right, we're nearly done with this. But there's one more piece of magic to try out.

Making Your Own Monikers

Remember that we said that a moniker was a *persistent* intelligent name? Well, we've been looking at persistent representations of our monikers in the **IDC_NAME** field of our dialog. Could we take one of these and just turn it into a moniker? Without reference to **MonGiver** at all? Of course we can. Let's see what's hiding under the Parse button:

```
void CMonUserDlg::OnParse()
{
    USES_CONVERSION;
    CString csName;

    CEdit *pName = reinterpret_cast<CEdit*>(GetDlgItem(IDC_NAME));
    pName->GetWindowText(csName);
```

```
    IBindCtx *pBindCtx;
    CreateBindCtx (0, &pBindCtx);

    ULONG eaten;
    IMoniker *pMoniker;
    HRESULT hResult = MkParseDisplayName(pBindCtx,
                                        T2OLE(csName),
                                        &eaten, &pMoniker);

    if (FAILED(hResult))
    {
        CString csError;
        csError.Format(_T("Failed to parse display name, %x"), hResult);
        AfxMessageBox (csError);
        return;
    }

    DoMoniker(pBindCtx, pMoniker);

    pBindCtx->Release();
    pMoniker->Release();
}
```

So that you can use the conversion macros, add these to the top of the file:

```
#include <atlconv.h>
#include <atlconv.cpp>
```

The really cool thing here is that call to **`MkParseDisplayName()`**. This is an API routine that takes the persistent display name for a moniker and turns it into a moniker! So all we have to do is give our clients a string and they can use that to bind to an object.

Let's give it a go – run **`MonUser`** and then, in the Name edit box, type in: **`clsid:`** followed by your class id of **`ClassFile`**. In my case, this is:

`clsid:997D58E0-F3B4-11d1-A482-00A0C901AB51`

When you click the Parse button, you should get the same results as the last test.

It even works from VB. Here's some VB code to access the **`IFile`** interface on our **`ClassFile`** object:

```
Private Sub Bind_Click()
Dim fil As IFile
Set fil = GetObject(txtObject.Text)
txtTitle.Text = fil.Title
txtData.Text = fil.Data
End Sub
```

And this is what it looks like if we input our moniker and bind:

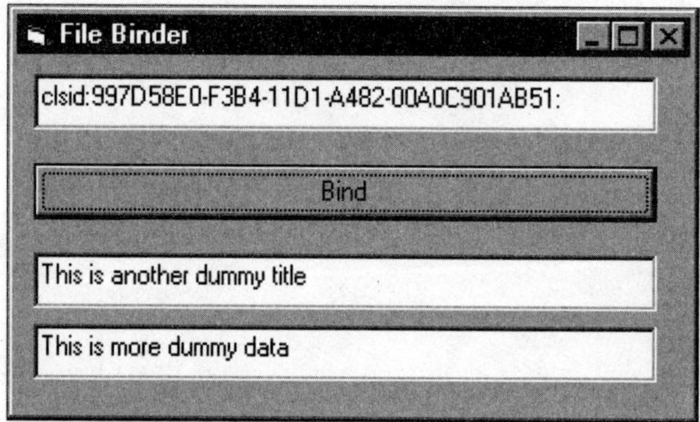

What's happening here is that the `MkParseDisplayName()` and `BindToObject()` stuff is all hidden away under that deceptively simple `GetObject()` call. Isn't VB wonderful?

OK, let's take stock of where we are:

- We've explored how to make file, pointer and class monikers
- We've looked at how to bind to them
- We've seen how we can use monikers to hide implementation details from the client
- We've seen how clients can use the persistent representation of monikers to create them without recourse to a server

Wow! But we haven't finished yet. Not by a long chalk.

A Teleconferencing System

It's time to start building our final example. We're going to develop a teleconferencing system. We'll use two objects:

- `ConfMgr` – this is going to create and control access to the conferences
- `Conference` – this is going to handle interactions within each conference

Composite Monikers

We'd like to enable our clients to access a particular conference by issuing a VB command that connects them to a specified conference. We can do this by means of a composite moniker. Here's the display representation of a composite moniker of the type that we're going to use:

```
clsid:9E0AE32E-F025-11D1-A47C-00A0C901AB51:!MyConf
```

We're going to use this to say "Connect me to a conference called *MyConf*". This looks very much like the type of thing we've seen with the `MyClassFile` example, except for `!MyConf` stuck on the end. This part represents an item moniker or, rather the `MyConf` bit does; the exclamation mark is a delimiter between the two parts of the composite.

But how on earth does the VB **`GetObject()`** function cope with this? Or, to be more accurate, how on earth does **`MkParseDisplayName()`** cope?

What the **`MkParseDisplayName()`** function does is to parse as far as it can – which, in this case, amounts to establishing that **`clsid:9E0AE32E-F025-11D1-A47C-00A0C901AB51:`** represents a class object. Having done that, it instantiates an object of that class and passes the remainder of the moniker string to the object. **`MkParseDisplayName()`** is basically saying "Hey, dude – have a look at this. Doesn't make any sense to me at all." Let's see how it does this.

In order for a class to be able to support composites, it needs to implement an interface called **`IParseDisplayName`**. This is a very simple interface, with one method, **`ParseDisplayName()`**. (How do they make these up, eh?) Let's start to build our **`ConfMgr`** object, and see what we have to do to support **`IParseDisplayName`**.

We'll create it as a stand-alone EXE project, called **`ConfServer`**, with a single ATL object **`ConfMgr`**, which implements a single *custom* interface **`IConfMgr`**. This interface won't actually have any methods of its own, so you can remove all references to it in the header (delete the reference in the interface map and make sure that the class does not derive from it). We'll need to make a couple of other changes to the generated header file:

```
// ConfMgr.h : Declaration of the CConfMgr

#ifndef __CONFMGR_H_
#define __CONFMGR_H_

#include "resource.h"        // main symbols

/////////////////////////////////////////////////////////////////////////////
// CConfMgr
class ATL_NO_VTABLE CConfMgr :
      public CComObjectRootEx<CComSingleThreadModel>,
      public CComCoClass<CConfMgr, &CLSID_ConfMgr>,
      public IParseDisplayName
{
public:
      CConfMgr()
      {
      }

DECLARE_REGISTRY_RESOURCEID(IDR_CONFMGR)

BEGIN_COM_MAP(CConfMgr)
      COM_INTERFACE_ENTRY(IParseDisplayName)
END_COM_MAP()

// IParseDisplayName
public:
      STDMETHOD(ParseDisplayName)(IBindCtx *pbc,
                  LPOLESTR pszDisplayName, ULONG *pchEaten,
                  IMoniker **ppmkOut);
};

#endif //__CONFMGR_H_
```

You will also have to remove **IConfMgr** from the IDL, so that the **coclass** entry will compile you must specify a **[default]** interface, so replace **IConfMgr** with **IParseDisplayName**:

```
coclass ConfMgr
{
    [default] interface IParseDisplayName;
};
```

Here's the implementation of **IParseDisplayName**:

```
// ConfMgr.cpp : Implementation of CConfMgr
#include "stdafx.h"
#include "ConfServer.h"
#include "ConfMgr.h"

/////////////////////////////////////////////////////////////////////////////
// CConfMgr

STDMETHODIMP CConfMgr::ParseDisplayName (struct IBindCtx *pbc,
                                         LPOLESTR pszDisplayName,
                                         ULONG *pchEaten,
                                         struct IMoniker **ppmkOut)
{
     *pchEaten = wcslen (pszDisplayName);

     return CreateItemMoniker (L"!", pszDisplayName + 1, ppmkOut);
}
```

What happens here is that **MkParseDisplayName()** passes the part of the composite moniker that it can't understand... to us in the string **pszDisplayName**. In the case that we looked at earlier, we'd get the string **"MyConf"** passed to us. The approach taken here is that whatever we get, we'll assume that it represents an item. We set the amount of characters processed ("eaten"!) to the full length of the incoming string. We strip off the leading exclamation mark, and create an item moniker out of the rest. We pass the item moniker back to **MkParseDisplayName()**.

So, to recap — **MkParseDisplayName()** is trying to construct a moniker. It manages to extract a class moniker from the composite display name, but it can't understand the rest. So, it instantiates an object and interrogates it for **IParseDisplayName**. Once it finds this, it asks the object to convert the part of the composite that it can't understand into a moniker. The object obliges by returning an item moniker.

What happens next is that **MkParseDisplayName()** composes the two monikers together into one composite moniker. Our client now tries to bind to this (either explicitly in C++ by using **BindToObject()**, or as part of the underlying logic beneath **GetObject()** in VB). In order to make any sense of the item moniker, however, the binding process needs to interrogate another standard interface, **IOleItemContainer**. Hence we need to extend our **ConfMgr** object to implement this as well:

```
// ConfMgr.h : Declaration of the CConfMgr

#ifndef __CONFMGR_H_
#define __CONFMGR_H_

#include "resource.h"        // main symbols

/////////////////////////////////////////////////////////////////////////////
// CConfMgr
class ATL_NO_VTABLE CConfMgr :
     public CComObjectRootEx<CComSingleThreadModel>,
     public CComCoClass<CConfMgr, &CLSID_ConfMgr>,
     public IOleItemContainer
{
public:
     CConfMgr()
     {
     }

DECLARE_REGISTRY_RESOURCEID(IDR_CONFMGR)

BEGIN_COM_MAP(CConfMgr)
     COM_INTERFACE_ENTRY(IParseDisplayName)
     COM_INTERFACE_ENTRY(IOleItemContainer)
END_COM_MAP()

// IParseDisplayName
public:
     STDMETHOD(ParseDisplayName)(struct IBindCtx *pbc,
               LPOLESTR pszDisplayName, ULONG *pchEaten,
               struct IMoniker **ppmkOut);
// IOleContainer
     STDMETHOD(EnumObjects)(DWORD grfFlags, IEnumUnknown **ppenum);
     STDMETHOD(LockContainer)(BOOL fLock);
// IOleItemContainer
     STDMETHOD(GetObject)(LPOLESTR pszItem, DWORD dwSpeedNeeded,
               IBindCtx *pbc, REFIID riid, void **ppvObject);
     STDMETHOD(GetObjectStorage)(LPOLESTR pszItem, IBindCtx *pbc,
               REFIID riid, void **ppvStorage);
     STDMETHOD(IsRunning)(LPOLESTR pszItem);
};

#endif //__CONFMGR_H_
```

As it happens, **IOleItemContainer** derives from **IOleContainer** which, in turn, derives from **IParseDisplayName**, so we don't need to reference **IParseDisplayName** explicitly, except in the COM map, where it's essential in order for **MkParseDisplayName()** to be able to access it. Thus, the ATL class derives from **IOleItemContainer** and not **IParseDisplayName**.

The heart of the **IOleItemContainer** interface is the **GetObject()** method, which is where we return a pointer to the required interface on the object that the caller really wants.

The Conference Object

Before we take a look at our implementation of **IOleItemContainer**, however, we're going to have to look at our **Conference** object. This object has a single **dual** interface, **IConference**, with one method:

Method	Parameters	Description
Broadcast()	[in] BSTR message	Broadcast message to all users connected to conference

It also has a couple of properties:

Parameter	Type	Description
Count	short	Count of number of connected users
_Name	BSTR	Name of conference

Count is read-only, but **_Name** is read/write.

It has also got a single event:

Event	Parameters	Description
Transmit	[in] BSTR message	Transmit message

Let's start off by creating the object using the ATL wizard in the usual manner. We'll add it to the **ConfServer** project, as there's no real reason why a conference should be geographically separated from the conference manager. The object is created with a dual interface, but remember to add support for connection points. We add the method and the properties in the usual manner using ClassView.

We handle the event by means of a connection point, so we've now got to go through the mildly tedious process of setting up the proxy. This is very similar to the process that I described for the Ping example in Chapter 1, so I won't go through it all again. Suffice to say that your IDL file should end up looking like this:

```
// ConfServer.idl : IDL source for ConfServer.dll
//

// This file will be processed by the MIDL tool to
// produce the type library (ConfServer.tlb) and marshalling code.

import "oaidl.idl";
import "ocidl.idl";
      [
            object,
            uuid(9E0AE330-F025-11D1-A47C-00A0C901AB51),
            dual,
```

```
            helpstring("IConference Interface"),
            pointer_default(unique)
        ]
        interface IConference : IDispatch
        {
            [id(1), helpstring("method Broadcast")]
                                  HRESULT Broadcast([in] BSTR message);
            [propget, id(2), helpstring("property Count")]
                                  HRESULT Count([out, retval] short *pVal);
            [propget, id(3), helpstring("property _Name")]
                                  HRESULT _Name([out, retval] BSTR *pVal);
            [propput, id(3), helpstring("property _Name")]
                                  HRESULT _Name([in] BSTR newVal);
        };
    [
        uuid(9E0AE320-F025-11D1-A47C-00A0C901AB51),
        version(1.0),
        helpstring("ConfServer 1.0 Type Library")
    ]
    library CONFSERVERLib
    {
        importlib("stdole32.tlb");
        importlib("stdole2.tlb");

        [
            uuid(06360550-F34E-11d1-A481-00A0C901AB51),
            helpstring("Event for Conference")
        ]
        dispinterface _ConferenceEvents
        {
            properties:
            methods:
            [id(1)] void Transmit(BSTR message);
        };

        [
            uuid(9E0AE32E-F025-11D1-A47C-00A0C901AB51),
            helpstring("ConfMgr Class")
        ]
        coclass ConfMgr
        {
            [default] interface IParseDisplayName;
        };
        [
            uuid(9E0AE331-F025-11D1-A47C-00A0C901AB51),
            helpstring("Conference Class")
        ]
        coclass Conference
        {
            [default] interface IConference;
            [default,source] dispinterface _ConferenceEvents;
        };
    };
```

We'll also add a single member variable to **CConference**, a **CComBSTR** object called **m_name** for the **_Name** property. This will be used to hold the name of the conference. This is what the **Conference.h** header file should look like:

```
// Conference.h : Declaration of the CConference

#ifndef __CONFERENCE_H_
#define __CONFERENCE_H_

#include "resource.h"       // main symbols
#include "CPConfServer.h"

/////////////////////////////////////////////////////////////////////////////
// CConference
class ATL_NO_VTABLE CConference :
     public CComObjectRootEx<CComSingleThreadModel>,
     public CComCoClass<CConference, &CLSID_Conference>,
     public IConnectionPointContainerImpl<CConference>,
     public CProxy_ConferenceEvents<CConference>,
     public IDispatchImpl<IConference, &IID_IConference,
                                                        &LIBID_CONFSERVERLib>,
     public IProvideClassInfo2Impl<&CLSID_Conference,
                        &DIID__ConferenceEvents, &LIBID_CONFSERVERLib>
{
private:
     CComBSTR m_name;

public:
     CConference() : m_name("")
     {}

DECLARE_REGISTRY_RESOURCEID(IDR_CONFERENCE)

BEGIN_COM_MAP(CConference)
     COM_INTERFACE_ENTRY(IConference)
     COM_INTERFACE_ENTRY(IDispatch)
     COM_INTERFACE_ENTRY_IMPL(IConnectionPointContainer)
END_COM_MAP()

BEGIN_CONNECTION_POINT_MAP(CConference)
     CONNECTION_POINT_ENTRY(DIID__ConferenceEvents)
END_CONNECTION_POINT_MAP()
// IConference
public:
     STDMETHOD(get__Name)(/*[out, retval]*/ BSTR *pVal);
     STDMETHOD(put__Name)(/*[in]*/ BSTR newVal);
     STDMETHOD(get_Count)(/*[out, retval]*/ short *pVal);
     STDMETHOD(Broadcast)(/*[in]*/ BSTR message);
};

#endif //__CONFERENCE_H_
```

The file **CPConfServer.h** is automatically generated by the ATL proxy generator as usual. Now let's take a look at the code for the **Conference** object. The **Broadcast()** method is very simple:

```
STDMETHODIMP CConference::Broadcast(BSTR message)
{
      Fire_Transmit (message);
      return S_OK;
}
```

Remember that **Transmit()** is the only event offered, and that **Fire_Transmit()** is implemented by the proxy (check **CPConfServer.h** if you're unsure). Whenever a broadcast is received by the object, it gets sent out to all attached connection points. All? Just check out the code in the proxy – you'll see that *all* the connection points get triggered! Which is pretty useful for our application, as we'll find out.

The code to read and write the name property is very simple:

```
STDMETHODIMP CConference::get__Name(BSTR * pVal)
{
      *pVal = m_name.Copy();
      return S_OK;
}

STDMETHODIMP CConference::put__Name(BSTR newVal)
{
      m_name = newVal;
      return S_OK;
}
```

Incidentally, why is the property called **_Name** rather than **Name**? The reason is that we don't want our VB clients arbitrarily changing the name of the conference in mid-stream, because the name is what we're going to use to determine which conference we're going to access. If we add an underscore at the front, it won't be visible to VB.

Now for the interesting bit. I wanted to have a property that would tell us how many clients were attached. I didn't particularly want to re-implement **IUnknown**, so I thought the best way would be to borrow a bit of code from the connection point proxy:

```
STDMETHODIMP CConference::get_Count(short * pVal)
{
      short count = 0;

      IUnknown** pp = m_vec.begin();
      while (pp < m_vec.end())
      {
            if (*pp != NULL)
                  count++;
            pp++;
      }
```

```
        *pVal = count;

        return S_OK;
    }
```

Neat, huh? The **m_vec** array keeps a list of all the connection points, so we can be sure that, provided that our clients are releasing their references – the count ought to be accurate.

OK, that's about it for the **Conference** object. Let's go back and see how we go about finding the right conference object for our clients.

Binding to a Composite

Remember where we were before we dived off into the **Conference** object? We were looking at the problem of binding to a composite class/item moniker. I said that in order for this to work, the class that was being bound to would have to implement **IOleContainer**. I also said that the real meat of the implementation was in the **GetObject()** method of this interface. As we'll see soon, this method is all about finding the right conference object from an array of available ones.

However, before we look at that, there's one important addition that we've got to make to the **ConfMgr** class. We need to add a private member, **m_conference[10]**:

```
// ConfMgr.h : Declaration of the CConfMgr

#ifndef __CONFMGR_H_
#define __CONFMGR_H_

#include "resource.h"        // main symbols

#include "Conference.h"

/////////////////////////////////////////////////////////////////////////////
// CConfMgr
class ATL_NO_VTABLE CConfMgr :
    public CComObjectRootEx<CComSingleThreadModel>,
    public CComCoClass<CConfMgr, &CLSID_ConfMgr>,
    public IOleItemContainer
{
private:
    CComObjectGlobal<CConference> m_conference[10];

public:
    CConfMgr()
    {
    }

DECLARE_REGISTRY_RESOURCEID(IDR_CONFMGR)

BEGIN_COM_MAP(CConfMgr)
    COM_INTERFACE_ENTRY(IParseDisplayName)
    COM_INTERFACE_ENTRY(IOleItemContainer)
END_COM_MAP()
```

```
// IParseDisplayName
public:
     STDMETHOD(ParseDisplayName)(struct IBindCtx *pbc,
               LPOLESTR pszDisplayName, ULONG *pchEaten,
               struct IMoniker **ppmkOut);
// IOleContainer
public:
     STDMETHOD(EnumObjects)(DWORD grfFlags, IEnumUnknown **ppenum);
     STDMETHOD(LockContainer)(BOOL fLock);
// IOleItemContainer
public:
     STDMETHOD(GetObject)(LPOLESTR pszItem, DWORD dwSpeedNeeded,
               IBindCtx *pbc, REFIID riid, void **ppvObject);
     STDMETHOD(GetObjectStorage)(LPOLESTR pszItem, IBindCtx *pbc,
               REFIID riid, void **ppvStorage);
     STDMETHOD(IsRunning)(LPOLESTR pszItem);
};

#endif //__CONFMGR_H_
```

Believe it or not, **m_conference[10]** is an array of our conference objects. We declare them as **CComObjectGlobal<>** so that they can be single instances, shared by a number of clients. I'm using a static array of 10 of them to avoid cluttering the rest of the code up with loads of dynamic allocation and re-allocation. I would think that 10 conferences will do for starters.

We want to ensure that the **Conference** objects are only created by the **ConfMgr** object, rather than being externally creatable, so you should remove the object entry for **CConference** from the object map in **ConfServer.cpp**. Your object map should then look like this:

```
BEGIN_OBJECT_MAP(ObjectMap)
   OBJECT_ENTRY(CLSID_ConfMgr, CConfMgr)
END_OBJECT_MAP()
```

Also, you should remove **CComCoClass<>** base class from the **CConference** definition in the header file.
So how do we get use of this? Well, here's the implementation of **IOleItemContainer**:

```
STDMETHODIMP CConfMgr::EnumObjects(DWORD grfFlags, IEnumUnknown **ppenum)
{
     return E_NOTIMPL;
}

STDMETHODIMP CConfMgr::LockContainer(BOOL fLock)
{
     return E_NOTIMPL;
}


STDMETHODIMP CConfMgr::GetObjectStorage(LPOLESTR pszItem,
                         IBindCtx *pbc, REFIID riid, void **ppvStorage)
{
     return E_NOTIMPL;
}
```

```
STDMETHODIMP CConfMgr::IsRunning(LPOLESTR pszItem)
{
      return E_NOTIMPL;
}

STDMETHODIMP CConfMgr::GetObject(LPOLESTR pszItem, DWORD dwSpeedNeeded,
    IBindCtx *pbc, REFIID riid, void **ppvObject)
{
      HRESULT hResult;

      // see if the requested conference exists
      for (int conf = 0; conf < 10; conf++)
      {
             BSTR bstrName;
             hResult = m_conference[conf].get__Name(&bstrName);

             if (FAILED(hResult))
                   return hresult;

             if (wcscmp(pszItem, bstrName) == 0)
             {
                   ::SysFreeString(bstrName);
                   return m_conference[conf].QueryInterface(riid, ppvObject);
             }

             ::SysFreeString(bstrName);
      }

      // find an empty conference
      for (conf = 0; conf <10; conf++0
      {
             short count;
             hResult = m_conference[conf].get_Count(&count);
             if (FAILED(hResult))
                   return hResult;
             if (count == 0)
                   break;
      }

      // no empty conferences
      if (conf == 10)
             return MK_E_NOOBJECT;

      // assign the conference to this name
      m_conference[conf].put__Name(CComBSTR(pszName));
      return m_conference[conf].QueryInterface(riid, ppvObject);;
}
```

As you can see, most of the methods return **E_NOTIMPL**; frankly, they're superfluous to this application. The real fun is in the **GetObject()** method. As we can see, this goes through the static list of objects, searching for one with a name that matches the incoming item (that's the same item that was stuck on the end of the class ID in the display name). If it finds one, it **QI**'s for the requested interface and returns the pointer to the caller. If it doesn't find a match, it searches through the list again for the first slot with no connected users – that's one of the reasons I wanted that **Count** property! If it finds a free slot, it writes the name of the conference into that slot, and **QI**'s the object for the requested interface.

And, believe it or not, that's pretty much it for our teleconferencing server. Apart from one thing, that is. The eagle-eyed among you may be standing on your chairs and shouting "Class Factory!" at me. Yes, because we're using a class moniker to get access to the **ConfMgr** object. In the previous example the object was implemented in a DLL, so the change was in **DllGetClassObject()**. This example has the object implemented in an EXE, in which case classes are registered by a call in **WinMain()**. Make the following change to **ConfServer.cpp**:

```
.
.
.

if (bRun)
{
    DWORD dwReg;
    CComObjectNoLock<CConfMgr>* mgrClassObject
        = new CComObjectNoLock<CConfMgr>;
    hRes = CoRegisterClassObject(CLSID_ConfMgr,
        reinterpret_cast<IOleItemContainer*>(mgrClassObject),
        CLSCTX_LOCAL_SERVER, REGCLS_MULTIPLEUSE, &dwReg);
    _ASSERTE(SUCCEEDED(hRes));

    MSG msg;
    while (GetMessage(&msg, 0, 0, 0))
          DispatchMessage(&msg);

    CoRevokeClassObject(dwReg);
}

.
.
.
```

The **ConfMgr** object will be used to give access to the **Conference** objects. It is created using **CComObjectNoLock<>** to ensure that creating this object will not affect the module's lock count. If **CComObject<>** had been used instead, it would add a lock to the module and this will never be released, hence the EXE would never be unloaded.

This code uses **new** rather than **CreateInstance()**, this is quite safe because **FinalConstruct()** and **FinalRelease()** are not used, so **CreateInstance()** is essentially a call to **new**. If you do use the **FinalConstruct()** or **FinalRelease()** methods, then you *must* call **CreateInstance()**. Also, notice the use of the cast to **IOleItemContainer***, this is to get access to the **IUnknown** interface of the object: a cast direct to **IUnknown*** will fail due to ambiguities.

OK, all we need now is a client.

The Teleconferencing Client

Our VB client is simplicity itself. Here's the form:

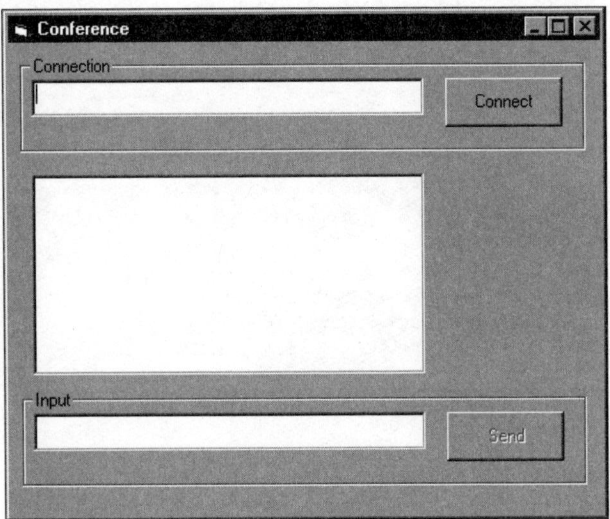

Basically, all we do is specify a conference to join, and then everything we type in the box at the bottom gets sent to everyone else who's attached to that conference. The controls at the top are a text box called **txtConf** and a button called **cmdConnect**. In the center is a list box called **lstMessages** and a label called **lblCount** to its right, and at the bottom is a text box called **txtMessage** and a button called **cmdSend**. Once you have created this form add a reference to ConfServer 1.0 Type Library.

The code, shown below, is really quite simple:

```
Dim WithEvents conf As Conference

Private Sub conf_Transmit(ByVal mess As String)
lstMessages.AddItem mess
lblCount = Str$(conf.Count) + " connected"
End Sub

Private Sub cmdConnect_Click()
Dim obj As String
obj = "clsid:9E0AE32E-F025-11D1-A47C-00A0C901AB51:!" + txtConf

On Error GoTo failure
Set conf = GetObject(obj)
lblCount = Str$(conf.Count) + " connected"

cmdConnect.Enabled = False
cmdSend.Enabled = True
txtMessage.SetFocus
```

```
Exit Sub

failure:
MsgBox "Failed to connect to " + txtConf

End Sub

Private Sub cmdSend_Click()

conf.Broadcast txtMessage
txtMessage = ""
txtMessage.SetFocus

End Sub
```

The key point is the **`GetObject()`** statement in the **`cmdConnect_Click`** function. That's the point at which the display name for the composite class/item moniker is constructed and used to attach to the right conference object. Once that connection is made, we're home and dry. Note that I've used the **`Count`** property to give the user an idea of how many others are connected to the conference.

You can try this out by running, say, three copies on the same machine. Start up the client three times and use the same connection each time. You should be able to see stuff like this:

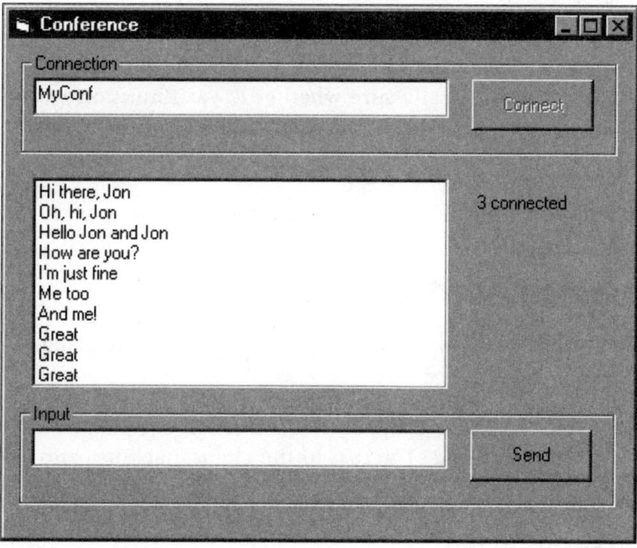

Well, there's only so much you can say to yourself ...

Just to re-iterate what I said earlier, nowhere did I specify that the connection point logic should call back to all the clients. It just happened because that's the way the connection point proxy works by default.

Here's the key section of code in **CPConfServer.h**:

```
.
.
.

while (pp < m_vec.end())
{
      if (*pp != NULL)
      {
            pvars[0].vt = VT_BSTR;
            pvars[0].bstrVal= message;
            DISPPARAMS disp = { pvars, NULL, 1, 0 };
            IDispatch* pDispatch = reinterpret_cast<IDispatch*>(*pp);
            pDispatch->Invoke(0x1, IID_NULL, LOCALE_USER_DEFAULT,
                              DISPATCH_METHOD, &disp, NULL, NULL, NULL);
      }
      pp++;
}

.
.
.
```

(This is the bit that I borrowed for the **get_Count** method, by the way.) The **m_vec** array holds details of all the connection points that are to be serviced, and the proxy code simply goes through each one in turn. When I first tried this, I thought that I was going to have to play around with all the **EnumConnectionPoints** functionality that the Visual Studio help files describe at great length. (And, to be honest, I wasn't really sure whether it was **EnumConnections** or **EnumConnectionPoints** even ...) I was really pleasantly surprised to find out that I didn't have to!

We've nearly finished our example. There's one more crucial issue to be resolved ...

Distributing the Application

Ah! DCOM at last! Well, we might as well make this a proper teleconferencing application, and it's actually very simple to do.

First of all, let's register the **ConfServer** proxy stub DLL on our client workstations. We do this by simply copying **ConfServerps.dll** across to the client machines and typing the following command:

```
regsvr32 ConfServerps.dll
```

This allows the clients to access the **IConference** interface on the remote object. Next, you need to indicate to COM on a client machine that a remote machine should be used. This is where the task gets a bit grungy. The problem is that VB is not DCOM aware (don't let anyone convince you otherwise – VB only knows about COM objects on a single machine). DCOM helps however; there is a 'legacy' setting called **RemoteServerName** that can be used to indicate that, if COM cannot find a server on the local machine, it should ask COM on another machine for the object.

RemoteServerName is a value under a class specific key in **HKEY_CLASSES_ROOT\AppID**. This 'class specific key' can be any GUID you like as long as it is unique and is mentioned as a value under the class's **CLSID** key. When you create an EXE server with the ATL AppWizard, it will create an AppID, and I have copied this into the following REGEDIT script:

```
REGEDIT4

[HKEY_CLASSES_ROOT\AppID\{29906F15-F940-11D1-A5C7-0080C8879C82}]
@="ConfServer"
"RemoteServerName"="Athena"

[HKEY_CLASSES_ROOT\AppID\ConfServer.EXE]
"AppID"="{29906F15-F940-11D1-A5C7-0080C8879C82}"

[HKEY_CLASSES_ROOT\CLSID\{29906F22-F940-11D1-A5C7-0080C8879C82}]
@="ConfMgr Class"
"AppID"="{29906F15-F940-11D1-A5C7-0080C8879C82}"

[HKEY_CLASSES_ROOT\TypeLib\{29906F14-F940-11D1-A5C7-0080C8879C82}]

[HKEY_CLASSES_ROOT\TypeLib\{29906F14-F940-11D1-A5C7-0080C8879C82}\1.0]
@="ConfServer 1.0 Type Library"

[HKEY_CLASSES_ROOT\TypeLib\{29906F14-F940-11D1-A5C7-0080C8879C82}\1.0\0]

[HKEY_CLASSES_ROOT\TypeLib\{29906F14-F940-11D1-A5C7-0080C8879C82}\1.0\0\win32]
@="ConfServer.tlb"

[HKEY_CLASSES_ROOT\TypeLib\{29906F14-F940-11D1-A5C7-0080C8879C82}\1.0\FLAGS]
@="0"

[HKEY_CLASSES_ROOT\Interface\{29906F25-F940-11D1-A5C7-0080C8879C82}]
@="_ConferenceEvents"

[HKEY_CLASSES_ROOT\Interface\{29906F25-F940-11D1-A5C7-
0080C8879C82}\ProxyStubClsid32]
@="{00020420-0000-0000-C000-000000000046}"

[HKEY_CLASSES_ROOT\Interface\{29906F25-F940-11D1-A5C7-0080C8879C82}\TypeLib]
@="{29906F14-F940-11D1-A5C7-0080C8879C82}"
"Version"="1.0"
```

I have highlighted two important lines. The first lists the **RemoteServerName** as **Athena**, obviously you should change this to the name of the machine that has the **ConfServer** executable. The second line has the path to the type library of the **ConfServer** *on the local machine*. You should add the complete path here and copy **ConfServer.tlb** from the server machine to this directory on the client. The type library is required because it is used to marshal calls to the **_ConferenceEvents dispinterface** when events are generated.

Finally, in order to get our teleconferencing application to work, we need to think about security. It's about connection points. Our server hasn't a clue what user it's talking back to with these things, and it has no idea what the security arrangements are. We need to change the settings on the server so that it makes the connection back to the client under a specific user name that the client knows about. If you're running NT, you should run up `DCOMcnfg`, on the server, select `ConfMgr Class` and then go for the `Identity` tab. Select `This user`, and specify the name of user known to all the clients that will attach to the server:

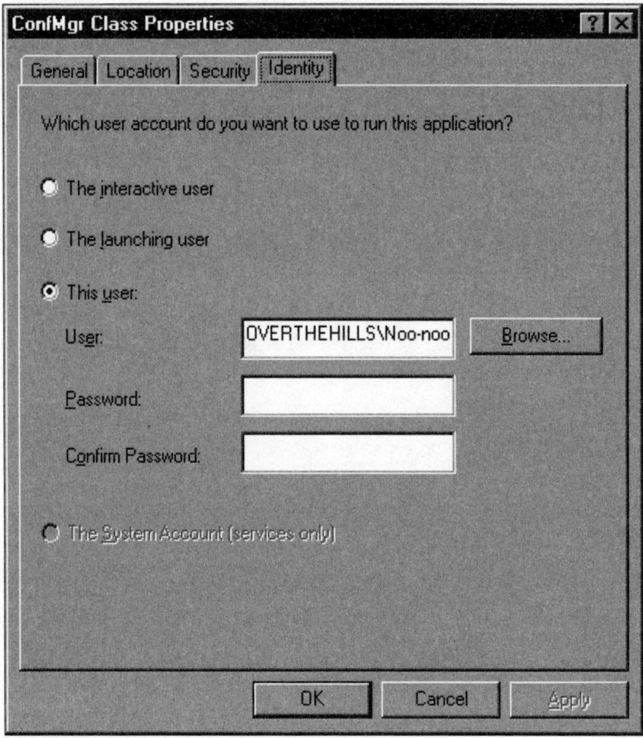

Now we should be able to start up the client on one or more machines and start teleconferencing. We've done it!

COM With a Longer Wire?

So that was DCOM, eh? Just a question of tinkering with `DCOMcnfg` to tell the client where to find the server executable, bit of messing about with the security settings, and that's it. Hmmm.

DCOM has been described as being "Location Transparent" – in other words, a client can't tell whether the COM objects that it is using are running locally or remotely. This leads to the description of DCOM simply being "COM with a longer wire".

How true is this?

I'll tell you a little story about location transparency. All the negotiations prior to writing this book were conducted via e-mail. I sent my proposals to the editor at his address at `wrox.com`, and he replied to me at my address at `compuserve.com`. I assumed that because Wrox Press had an American office, I was dealing with someone in the USA (because of the `.com` domain). Equally, the people at Wrox Press assumed that I was in the States, for precisely the same reason. It was only when they asked me for my home address so that they could send me a contract that we realized that we were both located in the United Kingdom. That strikes me as good an illustration of location transparency as you'll find.

But here's the pay-off. Now that I realized we were both in the UK, I was in a position to ask to be paid in sterling, rather than US dollars, thus eliminating my exposure to foreign exchange risk. There is a limit to location transparency. In my case, the limit was the fact that we haven't yet reached a common currency in Europe yet, let alone the whole world. In the case of DCOM, the limit is the fact that we don't yet have infinite bandwidth.

In some cases, then, pure DCOM simply isn't efficient enough. (Incidentally, if you want to get some idea of what gets sent between client and server during a COM method call, take a look at Chapter 6 of Richard Grimes' book "Professional DCOM Programming" – it's pretty scary.) There are some occasions when what you really need to do is create your object locally, invoke some local method calls, and then send it over to the server. In order to do this, we need to get to grips with serialization and marshaling, which are the subjects of the next chapter.

3

Streaming, Marshaling and Other DCOM Stuff

> "So the future designers of transporters will have a choice. Either they must find an energy source that will temporarily produce a power that exceeds the total power consumed on the entire Earth today by a factor of about 10,000...or...discover a way to heat up a human being instantaneously to roughly a million times the temperature at the center of the Sun."

The Physics of Star Trek,
Lawrence M. Krauss

How Long is a Piece of Wire?

As every schoolkid knows, DCOM is merely COM with a longer wire. Of course, this is an absolutely true statement in theory, and it would be absolutely true in practice as well ... if we had infinite bandwidth. Unfortunately, most of us aren't blessed with infinite bandwidth, so this chapter explores some of the issues that we need to consider when designing and implementing distributed components in the real world. The goal is still to hide as much as possible of the distributed nature of the system from the application developer – it's not in their remit to worry about all that – but we may have to make a few changes to the way in which we implement the underlying components.

It's a Wide World

Let's start by constructing a slightly absurd example.

Imagine that we've got an application that requires some kind of order form to be filled in. When the order is complete, we'll insert it into a database. In real life, this form might have as many as twenty fields, but for simplicity's sake, we'll keep it down to a round five. Each of these fields has to be validated, and – because we really hate those forms that let you fill in the whole lot before it tells you that you got the first field wrong – we're going to insist on field-by-field validation.

So, what do we do? Well, because we're fans of object orientation, we define an order object. And because we're fans of COM, we'll make it a COM object. This is particularly useful, because we know that our host computer is in Tierra del Fuego (mainly for tax reasons) and most of our users are in Ulaanbaatar. Since we've used COM to develop our objects, we should be able to distribute our components without any software changes. At least, that's how DCOM is billed.

Before we go any further, let's put a little flesh on this, and imagine that our punters in Mongolia are going to submit orders for secondhand LPs featuring late sixties psychedelia (for which I happen to know there is enormous demand out there; trust me on this).

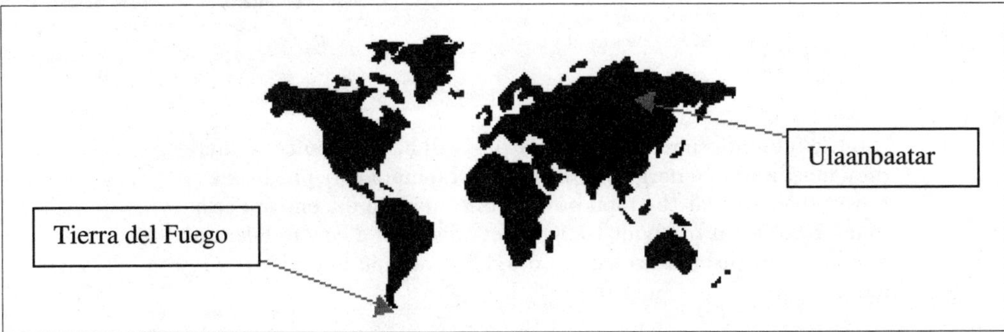

Our fields are as follows:

Field	Validation
Customer ID	Must be present, and be alphabetic
Artist	Must be present, and be alphabetic
Title	Must be present, and be alphanumeric
Label	May be blank; if present, must be alphabetic
Price	Must be valid dollar price

Let's create an EXE project called **SimpleOrder**. We'll use the ATL Object Wizard to create our object (a Simple Object called **Order**, with a single dual interface, **IOrder**). We can construct our component from five write-only **BSTR** properties (one for each field) and one parameter-less method, **Submit()**. We can add these properties and methods using ClassView.

We'll also need some validation routines – things like **MandatoryAlphanumeric()**, which checks that a given field:

- Is present
- Only contains alphanumeric characters.

We need to add these functions and some member variables to the **Order.h** header file:

```
// Order.h : Declaration of the COrder

#ifndef __ORDER_H_
#define __ORDER_H_

#include "resource.h"        // main symbols

/////////////////////////////////////////////////////////////////////////////
// COrder
class ATL_NO_VTABLE COrder :
   public CComObjectRootEx<CComSingleThreadModel>,
   public CComCoClass<COrder, &CLSID_Order>,
   public IDispatchImpl<IOrder, &IID_IOrder, &LIBID_SIMPLEORDERLib>
{
private:
   HRESULT MandatoryAlphabetic(/*[in]*/ BSTR bstrValue);
   HRESULT OptionalAlphabetic(/*[in]*/ BSTR bstrValue);
   HRESULT MandatoryAlphanumeric(/*[in]*/ BSTR bstrValue);
   HRESULT OptionalAlphanumeric(/*[in]*/ BSTR bstrValue);
   HRESULT MandatoryPrice(/*[in]*/ BSTR bstrValue);
   void Write(/*[in]*/ IStorage* pStorage, /*[in]*/ LPOLESTR lpszField,
              /*[in]*/ CComBSTR& bstr);

   CComBSTR m_bstrCustomerID;
   CComBSTR m_bstrArtist;
   CComBSTR m_bstrTitle;
   CComBSTR m_bstrLabel;
   CComBSTR m_bstrPrice;
public:
   COrder()
   {
   }

DECLARE_REGISTRY_RESOURCEID(IDR_ORDER)

BEGIN_COM_MAP(COrder)
   COM_INTERFACE_ENTRY(IOrder)
   COM_INTERFACE_ENTRY(IDispatch)
END_COM_MAP()
```

```
// IOrder
public:
    STDMETHOD(put_CustomerID)(/*[in]*/ BSTR newVal);
    STDMETHOD(put_Artist)(/*[in]*/ BSTR newVal);
    STDMETHOD(put_Title)(/*[in]*/ BSTR newVal);
    STDMETHOD(put_Label)(/*[in]*/ BSTR newVal);
    STDMETHOD(put_Price)(/*[in]*/ BSTR newVal);
    STDMETHOD(Submit)();
};

#endif //__ORDER_H_
```

Here's the code for implementing the methods of **IOrder**:

```
// Order.cpp : Implementation of COrder
#include "stdafx.h"
#include "SimpleOrder.h"
#include "Order.h"

///////////////////////////////////////////////////////////////////////////////
// COrder

STDMETHODIMP COrder::put_CustomerID(BSTR newVal)
{
    HRESULT hResult = MandatoryAlphabetic(newVal);
    if (FAILED(hResult))
        return hResult;

    m_bstrCustomerID = newVal;

    return S_OK;
}

STDMETHODIMP COrder::put_Artist(BSTR newVal)
{
    HRESULT hResult = MandatoryAlphabetic(newVal);
    if (FAILED(hResult))
        return hResult;

    m_bstrArtist = newVal;

    return S_OK;
}

STDMETHODIMP COrder::put_Title(BSTR newVal)
{
    HRESULT hResult = MandatoryAlphanumeric(newVal);
    if (FAILED(hResult))
        return hResult;

    m_bstrTitle = newVal;

    return S_OK;
}
```

```
STDMETHODIMP COrder::put_Label(BSTR newVal)
{
   HRESULT hResult = OptionalAlphabetic(newVal);
   if (FAILED(hResult))
      return hResult;

   m_bstrLabel = newVal;
   return S_OK;
}

STDMETHODIMP COrder::put_Price(BSTR newVal)
{
   HRESULT hResult = MandatoryPrice(newVal);
   if (FAILED(hResult))
      return hResult;

   m_bstrPrice = newVal;
   return S_OK;
}

STDMETHODIMP COrder::Submit()
{
   CComPtr<IStorage> pStorage;
   HRESULT hResult = StgCreateDocfile(L"C:\\Order.dat",
                     STGM_SIMPLE | STGM_CREATE | STGM_READWRITE |
                     STGM_SHARE_EXCLUSIVE, 0, &pStorage);
   if (FAILED(hResult))
      return hResult;

   Write(pStorage, L"CustomerID", m_bstrCustomerID);
   Write(pStorage, L"Artist", m_bstrArtist);
   Write(pStorage, L"Title", m_bstrTitle);
   Write(pStorage, L"Label", m_bstrLabel);
   Write(pStorage, L"Price", m_bstrPrice);

   return S_OK;
}
```

As you can see, the property **put_** methods devolve the real work to the validation functions. The **Submit()** method is something of a dummy as far as this implementation is concerned. In real life, the order would be put into some database or other; here, we're just writing it to an OLE compound document file. At least this way we can check that it's OK by using the **dfview** utility that I mentioned in the last chapter. Each field is written to a separate stream, using this member function:

```
void COrder::Write(IStorage* pStorage, LPOLESTR lpszField, CComBSTR& bstr)
{
   CComPtr<IStream> pStream;
   pStorage->CreateStream(lpszField, STGM_READWRITE |
                         STGM_SHARE_EXCLUSIVE, 0, 0, &pStream);

   bstr.WriteToStream(pStream);
}
```

Finally, the validation is performed in these member functions:

```
HRESULT COrder::MandatoryAlphabetic(BSTR bstrValue)
{
   int length = SysStringLen(bstrValue);
   if (length == 0)
      return E_INVALIDARG;

   return OptionalAlphabetic(bstrValue);
}

HRESULT COrder::OptionalAlphabetic(BSTR bstrValue)
{
   int length = SysStringLen(bstrValue);

   for (int iChar = 0; iChar < length; iChar++)
   {
      if (!iswspace(bstrValue[iChar]) &&
           !iswalpha(bstrValue[iChar]))
         return E_INVALIDARG;
   }

   return S_OK;
}

HRESULT COrder::MandatoryAlphanumeric(BSTR bstrValue)
{
   int length = SysStringLen(bstrValue);
   if (length == 0)
      return E_INVALIDARG;

   return OptionalAlphanumeric(bstrValue);
}

HRESULT COrder::OptionalAlphanumeric(BSTR bstrValue)
{
   int length = SysStringLen(bstrValue);

   for (int iChar = 0; iChar < length; iChar++)
   {
      if (!iswspace(bstrValue[iChar]) &&
           !iswalnum(bstrValue[iChar]))
         return E_INVALIDARG;
   }

   return S_OK;
}

HRESULT COrder::MandatoryPrice(BSTR bstrValue)
{
   // Get the locale ID for the US with default sorting
   LCID lcid = MAKELCID(MAKELANGID(LANG_ENGLISH, SUBLANG_ENGLISH_US),
                        SORT_DEFAULT);
```

```
    // Define a variable to hold the returned currency
    CURRENCY cy = {0};
    // Convert the string to a currency value
    HRESULT hr = VarCyFromStr(bstrValue, lcid, 0, &cy);

    // If the function failed, bstrValue is not a valid US currency
    if (FAILED(hr))
       return E_INVALIDARG;

    // Finally, check that the currency value is positive
    if (cy.int64 < 0)
       return E_INVALIDARG;

    return S_OK;
}
```

This time, we'll use a VBA form as our front end. Here's the code (written using Word 97 and the Microsoft Forms controls). Don't forget we're insisting on field-by-field validation:

The code uses the controls' **`Tag`** *property to store whether the field is valid. Mandatory fields start with this value being false, optional fields start with it being true. The tag is updated as the controls get visited.*

```
Option Explicit

Dim m_order As SIMPLEORDERLib.Order

Private Sub HandleError(ctrl As Control)
   If (Err.Number = 5) Then
      lblError.Caption = "Invalid input - please re-enter"
   ElseIf (Err.Number = &H80004005) Then
      lblError.Caption = "This field is mandatory"
   Else
      lblError.Caption = Err.Description
   End If
   ctrl.Tag = False
End Sub

Private Sub HandleSuccess(ctrl As Control)
   lblError.Caption = ""
   ctrl.Tag = True
End Sub

Private Sub UserForm_Initialize()
   Set m_order = New SIMPLEORDERLib.Order
End Sub

Private Sub txtCustomerID_Exit(ByVal Cancel As MSForms.ReturnBoolean)
On Error GoTo TryAgain
   m_order.CustomerID = txtCustomerID.Text
   HandleSuccess txtCustomerID
   Exit Sub
```

```
    TryAgain:
    HandleError txtCustomerID
    Cancel = True
End Sub
Private Sub txtTitle_Exit(ByVal Cancel As MSForms.ReturnBoolean)
On Error GoTo TryAgain
    m_order.Title = txtTitle.Text
    HandleSuccess txtTitle
    Exit Sub

TryAgain:
    HandleError txtTitle
    Cancel = True
End Sub

Private Sub txtArtist_Exit(ByVal Cancel As MSForms.ReturnBoolean)
On Error GoTo TryAgain
    m_order.Artist = txtArtist.Text
    HandleSuccess txtArtist
    Exit Sub

TryAgain:
    HandleError txtArtist
    Cancel = True
End Sub

Private Sub txtLabel_Exit(ByVal Cancel As MSForms.ReturnBoolean)
On Error GoTo TryAgain
    m_order.Label = txtLabel.Text
    HandleSuccess txtLabel
    Exit Sub

TryAgain:
    HandleError txtLabel
    Cancel = True
End Sub

Private Sub txtPrice_Exit(ByVal Cancel As MSForms.ReturnBoolean)
On Error GoTo TryAgain
    m_order.Price = txtPrice.Text
    HandleSuccess txtPrice
    Exit Sub

TryAgain:
    HandleError txtPrice
    Cancel = True
End Sub

Private Sub cmdConfirm_Click()
    ' Make sure that all mandatory controls have been filled
    Dim ctrl As Control
    For Each ctrl In Me.Controls
       If InStr(1, ctrl.Name, "txt", vbBinaryCompare) = 1 Then
```

```
            If ctrl.Tag <> "True" Then
                lblError = "This field is mandatory"
                ctrl.SetFocus
                Exit Sub
            End If
        End If
    Next ctrl
      m_order.Submit
    Unload Me
End Sub
```

And here's what the form looks like in operation:

Order Entry

Customer ID: JMP

Title: Mass in F Minor

Artist: Electric Prunes

Label: Reprise

Price ($US): $0.99

Confirm

Well, I never promised you an *elegant* form. I'm only really interested in the underlying components. (But isn't that what COM's all about? Leave the user interface design to the experts, and leave the business logic to us!)

Now, what happens when our Strawberry Alarm Clock fans in Ulaanbaatar start entering their orders? Well, the first thing that happens is that a blank order object is instantiated in Tierra del Fuego. Our man in Mongolia drums his fingers for a few seconds, and then he enters his name in the first field. As he tabs on to the next field, there is an ominous pause whilst the client process invokes the **`put_CustomerID()`** method at the bottom end of Argentina. The good news is that Argentina is happy with the name, and the client process in Ulaanbaatar can respond to the tab by moving on to the next item.

And so on. Each field involves a separate interaction with the server. Imagine a form that required twenty fields! The Mongolians are a patient and hardy people, but I don't think our system would last more than an afternoon there. OK, maybe I've stretched things a little, but I hope that you appreciate my point – DCOM can only be COM with a longer wire when the wires get fast enough. In the meantime, we can't ignore geography.

Beam Me Up, Scotty

If we are to make our system more usable, we have two basic alternatives.

Firstly, we could simply do all our validation in one go. We could let our user fill in the entire form, and invoke a single order entry method. This method could have one argument for each element of data (or maybe a variant array would be a little more elegant). Invoking this method from Ulaanbaatar would effectively send the whole order down the wire to Tierra del Fuego. Tierra del Fuego would in turn check it for validity and either return a successful status or an array of flags indicating which fields were invalid. It wouldn't be particularly slick, but it would work. This is the sort of solution frequently used in Web applications backed up by Active Server Pages or CGI.

Alternatively, we could instantiate our object *locally* in Ulaanbaatar. We could then carry out our validation (as far as possible) on-site, before re-instantiating the validated object in Patagonia. This is a bit like beaming our object down from Mongolia down to Argentina using the transporter. Although it's a little more straightforward, of course, since we are dealing with bits rather than atoms...

Note the proviso "as far as possible" in the paragraph above. For many real-world applications, some validation must be carried out on the server – in our example, we could validate that the customer ID is in the right form using client-side rules, but we can't tell at the client end whether the customer ID actually exists or not.

So, how do we go about transporting an object? What we basically want to do is take the object's current state and pack that up into a flat form that we can represent as a pure string of bytes. Having done that, we create another instance of the object in the target location. Then we restore the object's state from the byte string.

If we were in MFC land, we'd refer to this process as **serialization**. Every MFC object is intrinsically serializable, because it derives from `CObject`, which has the `Serialize()` method built into it. If we want to make our object serializable, all we have to do is override the default `Serialize()` method with our own code to either save our object's state to an archive or restore the state from an archive. The whole process is triggered by the calling application invoking either `ReadObject()` or `WriteObject()` on an archive, specifying our object as the argument. What we need is the nearest COM equivalent.

Streaming

If we're looking for a COM object to hold a flat array of bytes, we could do worse than look at a **stream**. We've already seen in Chapter 2 how streams can be used to build up a structured storage object. We'll see in this chapter how streams are used in several other places where we need to move flat strings of bytes around. From now on, then, instead of serialization, we're going to refer to **streaming**.

Streams are useful because they provide a standard and well-supported way of saving data. COM provides implementations of stream objects (objects that implement the `IStream` interface) for writing to and reading from memory and compound files. You saw the compound file implementation in use in the last chapter; you'll see how to create a stream based on global memory shortly.

Almost all control containers and many other COM clients expect to be able to save a control to a stream, so COM defines a standard stream persistence interface, **`IPersistStream`**. Since a stream is little more than an interface to a stream of bytes, other persistence interfaces such as **`IPersistStorage`** and **`IPersistFile`** are often implemented in terms of **`IPersistStream`**. Later in the chapter, we'll define and implement our own persistence interface, **`IPersistVariant`**, that also relies on an implementation of **`IPersistStream`** for its functionality.

`IPersistStream` inherits from **`IPersist`** and has the following methods (in vtable order and ignoring the usual methods inherited from **`IUnknown`**, of course):

Method	Parameters	Description
`GetClassID`	`[out] CLSID* pClassID`	Returns class identifier. Inherited from **`IPersist`**.
`IsDirty`		Checks to see if the object has changed since it was last saved (returns **`S_OK`** or **`S_FALSE`**)
`Load`	`[in] IStream* pStream`	Loads the object from the specified stream
`Save`	`[in] IStream* pStream,` `[in] BOOL fClearDirty`	Saves the object to the specified stream
`GetSizeMax`	`[out] ULARGE_INTEGER* pcbSize`	Returns size of stream needed to save object

COM also defines a similar interface, **`IPersistStreamInit`**, with an extra **`InitNew()`** method at the end of the vtable. Apart from this extra method, the signatures and semantics of the remaining methods are the same in both interfaces.

Method	Parameters	Description
`InitNew`		Initializes the object to a default state. This method is called instead of **`Load()`** for new objects. The presence of the **`InitNew()`** method allows objects to avoid performing needless and potentially lengthy initializations just before being loaded with data.

Although, **`IPersistStreamInit`** is vtable-compatible with **`IPersistStream`**, the two interfaces are not related by inheritance. Although both interfaces derive from **`IPersist`**, **`IPersistStreamInit`** does not derive from **`IPersistStream`**. COM objects should support only one of these interfaces at a time.

Either of these interfaces provides just the mechanism we need to save our object to a stream and to restore it from one. If we wanted, we could implement one of these interfaces to enable client applications to stream our object simply by invoking the **`Save()`** and **`Load()`** methods.

However, if we were to implement **`IPersistStream`** or **`IPersistStreamInit`** ourselves, I'd feel like we were doing all the hard work, and COM was getting all the credit. Fortunately, ATL provides us with a default implementation for these interfaces – all we need to do is tell it about the properties we want to stream, and it does all the rest. Excellent! Now *ATL* can do all the hard work, and *we'll* get all the credit.

First of all, let's have a look at ATL's implementation class, which is called **`IPersistStreamInitImpl<>`**. Unsurprisingly, this class provides default implementations for **`IPersistStreamInit`**'s methods. In this implementation, the **`InitNew()`** method does nothing more than return **`S_OK`** and isn't an integral part of the implementation, so this class is equally good for implementing **`IPersistStream`**. The class takes your derived class as a template parameter.

In theory, implementing **`IPersistStream`** should be as easy as deriving from this class template, and providing a property map containing the items to be persisted. In reality (in the current version of ATL), we have to do a little more work. Currently, **`IPersistStreamInitImpl<>`** is tied into ATL's control framework via the **`CComControl<>`** class (where stream-based persistence is most commonly used), so these are the steps that you need to make use of ATL's implementation today:

1. Derive your class from **`IPersistStreamInitImpl<CYourClass>`**
2. Add the entry for the interface to your class' COM map.
   If you want to expose **`IPersistStream`**, use:
   `COM_INTERFACE_ENTRY_IMPL_IID(IID_IPersistStream, IPersistStreamInit)`
   If you want to expose **`IPersistStreamInit`** use:
   `COM_INTERFACE_ENTRY_IMPL(IPersistStreamInit)`
3. Ensure all the persistable properties appear in a property map within your class
4. Derive your class from **`CComControl<CYourClass>`**
5. Provide an implementation of **`ProcessWindowMessage()`** by adding an empty message map to your class
6. Add the required ATL header and source files to your project

Expect the need for Steps 4 and 5 to disappear in some future version of ATL.

Implementing IPersistStream

Let's try this out with our order object. We'll make a clone of the **`SimpleOrder`** project, and rename the project folder to **`SerialOrder`** (so that you can find the relevant code on the web site) then we'll apply the changes to the **`SerialOrder`** project.

We'll start off with the class definition in the **`Order.h`** header file, where we'll add the two new base classes, **`IPersistStreamInitImpl<>`** and **`CComControl<>`**:

```
class ATL_NO_VTABLE COrder :
   public CComObjectRootEx<CComSingleThreadModel>,
   public CComCoClass<COrder, &CLSID_Order>,
   public IDispatchImpl<IOrder, &IID_IOrder, &LIBID_SIMPLEORDERLib>,
   public IPersistStreamInitImpl<COrder>,
   public CComControl<COrder>
```

We also need to add the interface to our COM map, to ensure that it's visible to the outside world. In this case, we'll use **IPersistStreamInitImpl<>** to implement the **IPersistStream** interface in our component, so we use the **COM_INTERFACE_ENTRY_IMPL_IID()** macro as shown:

```
BEGIN_COM_MAP(COrder)
   COM_INTERFACE_ENTRY(IOrder)
   COM_INTERFACE_ENTRY(IDispatch)
   COM_INTERFACE_ENTRY_IMPL_IID(IID_IPersistStream, IPersistStreamInit)
END_COM_MAP()
```

Next, we need to make a couple of changes to **StdAfx.h**:

```
extern CExeModule _Module;
#include <atlcom.h>
#include <atlctl.h>
```

And we need to make similar changes to **StdAfx.cpp**:

```
#include <atlimpl.cpp>
#include <atlwin.cpp>
#include <atlctl.cpp>
```

If we try to compile the code as it stands at the moment, we'll see that the **CComObject<>** base class can't be instantiated because the **ProcessWindowMessage()** member function is missing. This member function is usually provided by the class' message map, so let's give it one:

```
public:
   COrder()
   {
   }

BEGIN_MSG_MAP(COrder)
END_MSG_MAP()
```

Don't worry about this message map – it won't be used! It's just there to get the code to compile cleanly by defining the **ProcessWindowMessage()** function.

OK, now how is **IPersistStreamInitImpl<>** going to find out what properties it's going to read from and write to the stream? The answer lies in the **property map** – another one of those nifty little macro blocks that tend to appear in ATL header files.

If you've ever created full controls with ATL, you'll be familiar with the property map. The property map is just a macro-wrapped structure that collects 'descriptions' of properties so that they can be used by ATL's implementation classes. ATL uses the property map to provide the data that drives its implementations of ***IPerPropertyBrowsing****,* ***IPersistPropertyBag****,* ***ISpecifyPropertyPages*** *and, of course,* ***IPersistStreamInit****.*

In our case, we need to insert a property map that looks like this just after the COM map:

```
BEGIN_PROPERTY_MAP(COrder)
   PROP_ENTRY("CustomerID", 1, CLSID_NULL)
   PROP_ENTRY("Artist", 2, CLSID_NULL)
   PROP_ENTRY("Title", 3, CLSID_NULL)
   PROP_ENTRY("Label", 4, CLSID_NULL)
   PROP_ENTRY("Price", 5, CLSID_NULL)
END_PROPERTY_MAP()
```

Each entry in this map consists of a **PROP_ENTRY()** macro with three arguments:

- The first argument is a text descriptor
- The second is the DISPID that we'll find in the IDL file for the property in question
- The last argument is the class ID for the class that provides the property page

Since we don't have property pages for our properties, we can pass **CLSID_NULL** in every case.

But wait one moment. We've specified which properties that we're going to want **IPersistStreamInitImpl<>** to stream. So all it has to do is call their **get_** methods when it saves them, and their **put_** methods when it loads them, right? But didn't we define our properties as **put_**-only? Oops.

Let's go back to our IDL file, and do some cutting and pasting to add the **get_** properties to the interface definition:

```
interface IOrder : IDispatch
{
   [propput, id(1), helpstring("property CustomerID")]
         HRESULT CustomerID([in] BSTR newVal);
   [propget, id(1), helpstring("property CustomerID")]
         HRESULT CustomerID([out, retval] BSTR* pVal);
   [propput, id(2), helpstring("property Artist")]
         HRESULT Artist([in] BSTR newVal);
   [propget, id(2), helpstring("property Artist")]
         HRESULT Artist([out, retval] BSTR* pVal);
   [propput, id(3), helpstring("property Title")]
         HRESULT Title([in] BSTR newVal);
```

```
    [propget, id(3), helpstring("property Title")]
         HRESULT Title([out, retval] BSTR* pVal);
    [propput, id(4), helpstring("property Label")]
         HRESULT Label([in] BSTR newVal);
    [propget, id(4), helpstring("property Label")]
         HRESULT Label([out, retval] BSTR* pVal);
    [propput, id(5), helpstring("property Price")]
         HRESULT Price([in] BSTR newVal);
    [propget, id(5), helpstring("property Price")]
         HRESULT Price([out, retval] BSTR* pVal);
    [id(6), helpstring("method Submit")] HRESULT Submit();
};
```

Next, we add them to **Order.h**:

```
// IOrder
public:
   STDMETHOD(put_CustomerID)(/*[in]*/ BSTR newVal);
   STDMETHOD(get_CustomerID)(/*[out, retval]*/ BSTR* pVal);
   STDMETHOD(put_Artist)(/*[in]*/ BSTR newVal);
   STDMETHOD(get_Artist)(/*[out, retval]*/ BSTR* pVal);
   STDMETHOD(put_Title)(/*[in]*/ BSTR newVal);
   STDMETHOD(get_Title)(/*[out, retval]*/ BSTR* pVal);
   STDMETHOD(put_Label)(/*[in]*/ BSTR newVal);
   STDMETHOD(get_Label)(/*[out, retval]*/ BSTR* pVal);
   STDMETHOD(put_Price)(/*[in]*/ BSTR newVal);
   STDMETHOD(get_Price)(/*[out, retval]*/ BSTR* pVal);
   STDMETHOD(Submit)();
```

And finally, we provide their implementations in **Order.cpp**:

```
STDMETHODIMP COrder::get_CustomerID(BSTR* pVal)
{
   *pVal = m_bstrCustomerID.Copy();
   return S_OK;
}

STDMETHODIMP COrder::get_Artist(BSTR* pVal)
{
   *pVal = m_bstrArtist.Copy();
   return S_OK;
}

STDMETHODIMP COrder::get_Title(BSTR* pVal)
{
   *pVal = m_bstrTitle.Copy();
```

```
    return S_OK;
}

STDMETHODIMP COrder::get_Label(BSTR* pVal)
{
    *pVal = m_bstrLabel.Copy();
    return S_OK;
}
STDMETHODIMP COrder::get_Price(BSTR* pVal)
{
    *pVal = m_bstrPrice.Copy();
    return S_OK;
}
```

OK, we're ready to start streaming our object.

Trip Away

Let's think about what we've achieved here. We now have an **Order** object with a set of properties that we can read from and write to, a **Submit()** method that enters the order in a 'database', and the ability to persist this object to a stream.

We'd like to be able to instantiate our **Order** object on our client machine in Ulaanbaatar, so that the local object can carry out local validation up to the point that the order needs to be submitted. At that point, we'd like to magically transport all the data from the object in Ulaanbaatar over to a new object in Tierra del Fuego and have that submit the order. If we can succeed in this, we have minimized the number of remote calls.

So far our implementation of **IPersistStream** seems to be the answer to these problems; we could follow these steps:

1. Get our client in Ulaanbaatar to create an **Order** object in Ulaanbaatar
2. Populate the **Order**'s properties and use it to provide validation
3. Create a stream object using **CreateStreamOnHGlobal()**
4. Save the **Order** object's state to the stream
5. Create a new **Order** object in Tierra del Fuego using **CoCreateInstanceEx()**
6. Load the new **Order** object's state from the stream
7. Call **Submit()** on the **Order** object in Tierra del Fuego

Sounds good doesn't it? According to this outline, it looks like we have just three remote calls – the last three steps shown above – and we could even reduce these to just two remote calls by combining the last two steps in a new interface method.

Unfortunately, there are a couple of problems. The most important problem is that Step 6 actually hides a large number of remote calls. If we pass a stream object created in Ulaanbaatar to an order object created in Tierra del Fuego via **IPersistStream::Load()**, there will be a long distance call across the wire for every property in the **Order** object. The ATL implementation of **IPersistStream::Load()** calls **IStream::Read()** once for each property in the property map. This is a disaster!

The other problem is that we want our object to be usable from Visual Basic clients. Visual Basic doesn't much like the **IStream** interface[1], and the client programmers won't be too interested in all the grunge work necessary to create stream objects, so we need to provide a simpler mechanism for the data to be passed.

The solution is to define a new persistence interface – this interface must be similar to existing persistence interfaces, it must be fully Visual Basic compatible and it must ensure that all the data is passed in one go. The proposed solution is **IPersistVariant** defined with the IDL below:

IPersistVariant

```
// IPersistVariant.idl : IDL source for IPersistVariant.tlb

import "oaidl.idl";
import "ocidl.idl";
    [
        object,
        uuid(79215722-F8CC-11D1-99A7-444553540000),
        dual,
        helpstring("IPersistVariant Interface"),
        pointer_default(unique)
    ]
    interface IPersistVariant : IDispatch
    {
        [id(1), helpstring("method GetClassID")]
        HRESULT GetClassID([out, retval] BSTR* pbstrCLSID);
        [id(2), helpstring("method IsDirty")]
        HRESULT IsDirty([out, retval] VARIANT_BOOL* pbDirty);
        [id(3), helpstring("method Save")]
        HRESULT Save([in] VARIANT_BOOL bClearDirty,
                     [out, retval] VARIANT* pvar);
        [id(4), helpstring("method Load")]
        HRESULT Load([in] VARIANT var);
    };

[
    uuid(79215725-F8CC-11D1-99A7-444553540000),
    version(1.0),
    helpstring("IPersistVariant 1.0 Type Library")
]
library IPersistVariantLib
```

[1] This problem is caused by the standard definition of **IStream** using types for which Visual Basic has no equivalents. However, there are a couple of devious ways around this problem. Check out the book *Hardcore Visual Basic* (Microsoft Press, ISBN 1-57231-422-2) and the following URL for hints to solving this problem:

http://microsoft.ease.lsoft.com/scripts/wa.exe?A2=ind9710A&L=DCOM&D=0&m=9090&P=21833

```
{
    importlib("stdole32.tlb");
    importlib("stdole2.tlb");

    interface IPersistVariant;
};
```

Here you can see that we have defined a dual interface with all the best methods of the standard persistency interfaces – **`GetClassID()`**, **`IsDirty()`**, **`Load()`** and **`Save()`**. All these methods use **`VARIANT`**-compatible (and, therefore, Visual Basic-compatible) data types, and use **`[out, retval]`** parameters as much as possible for the convenience of our Visual Basic clients. The data itself will be passed as a safe array of bytes (in a **`VARIANT`** of type **`VT_UI1 | VT_ARRAY`**) to and from the **`Load()`** and **`Save()`** methods.

Note that this IDL file provides a type library section. This is important since the type library serves a number of roles:

- It provides information about this interface to Visual Basic (and other) clients
- It provides marshaling information for this interface (when the type library is registered)
- It allows the information about this interface to be **`importlib()`**'d into other type libraries.

File Generation and Housekeeping

Once you have defined an interface like this, you'll usually want to generate the header, IID and type library files from the IDL, and register the type library. The easiest way to do this is define a batch file called **`BuildIDL.bat`** with the contents shown.

```
midl /Oicf /h "%1.h" /iid "%1_i.c" "%1.idl"
regtlb32 %1.tlb
```

If you put this in a directory in your path, you can call **`BuildIDL`** to compile any IDL file and register the generated type library like this:

`BuildIDL` ***`idlname`***

In this case ***`idlname`*** is **`IPersistVariant`** since our IDL file is called **`IPersistVariant.idl`**.

> `Regtlb32` **is a command line tool that allows you to register type libraries. You can download it from** `http://www.worldofatl.com/`

To make this interface (or any other interface that you define) generally available in any of your projects, the IDL file and the generated files should be stored in a folder that is registered with Developer Studio as containing Include files. To allow the type library to be **`importlib()`**'d, the folder also needs to be registered in the list of directories containing Executable files. You can achieve both of these ends by using Developer Studio's Tools | Options... menu item to display the Options dialog and adjusting the settings on the Directories page.

IPersistVariantImpl<>

Now that we've defined an interface that will solve our problems, it's up to us to implement it. This class will follow ATL style throughout, so the class will be a template called **IPersistVariantImpl<>**.

The single template parameter, **T**, will be used to pass the derived class to the **IPersistVariantImpl<>** base class so that we can do safe downcasting of the **this** pointer:

```
// T is a class derived from IPersistVariantImpl<T>
// 'this' is an IPersistVariantImpl<T>*
// The following code shows how to get a T* from 'this':
T* pT = static_cast<T*>(this);
```

Our implementation of **IPersistVariant** will leverage ATL's **IPersistStreamInitImpl<>** class for its functionality.

Here's the complete header file for the class. We'll discuss each section as we reach it:

Prologue

```
// IPersistVariantImpl.h

#if !defined(_IPERSISTVARIANTIMPL_H____INCLUDED_)
#define _IPERSISTVARIANTIMPL_H____INCLUDED_

#if _MSC_VER >= 1000
#pragma once
#endif // _MSC_VER >= 1000

#include "IPersistVariant.h"

      /////////////////////////////////////////////////////
      // Don't forget to register IPersistVariant.tlb! //
      /////////////////////////////////////////////////////

// T must supply the following members (or compatible alternatives)
//    const CLSID& GetObjectCLSID();
//             usually from CComCoClass<>
//    BOOL m_bRequiresSave;
//             possibly from CComControlBase via CComControl<>
//    HRESULT IPersistStreamInit_Load(LPSTREAM pStm,
//                                    ATL_PROPMAP_ENTRY* pMap);
//             usually from IPersistStreamInitImpl<>
//    HRESULT IPersistStreamInit_Save(LPSTREAM pStm, BOOL bClearDirty,
//                                    ATL_PROPMAP_ENTRY* pMap);
//             usually from IPersistStreamInitImpl<>
//    static ATL_PROPMAP_ENTRY* GetPropertyMap();
//             usually from BEGIN_PROPERTY_MAP() macro
```

The first section of the header file consists of little more than guards, documentation, and a **#include** for **IPersistVariant.h**. The comments are quite explicit about the members the class expects the template parameter **T** to supply, and where these members can be found in existing ATL classes.

As you'll see, our implementation assumes that the derived class will also derive from **CComCoClass<>** and **IPersistStreamInitImpl<>**, but the beauty of templates is that this expectation is not forced upon the class **T** as long it can provide the desired members to satisfy the compiler.

IDispatchImpl<> Base Class

```
template <class T>
class IPersistVariantImpl :
     public IDispatchImpl<IPersistVariant,
                          &IID_IPersistVariant, &LIBID_IPersistVariantLib>
{
public:
```

Our implementation class derives from ATL's **IDispatchImpl<>** class, which provides the implementation of the dispatch portion of the interface, based on information in a type library. Here, we have passed the underlying interface, **IPersistVariant**, as the first template argument, the IID of that interface as the second, and the LIBID of the **IPersistVariant** type library as the third.

GetClassID()

```
STDMETHOD(GetClassID)(BSTR* pbstrCLSID)
   {
      T* pT = static_cast<T*>(this);
      LPOLESTR pstr = NULL;
      HRESULT hr = StringFromCLSID(pT->GetObjectCLSID(), &pstr);
      if (FAILED(hr))
         return hr;

      *pbstrCLSID = SysAllocString(pstr);
      if (!*pbstrCLSID)
         return E_OUTOFMEMORY;

      CoTaskMemFree(pstr);
      return S_OK;
   }
```

GetClassID() simply returns the object's class ID to the caller in the form of a **BSTR**. We can get an ATL object's CLSID by calling **GetObjectCLSID()**, a function supplied by **CComCoClass<>**. We then convert the **CLSID** into an OLE string and from there into a **BSTR**.

IsDirty()

```
STDMETHOD(IsDirty)(VARIANT_BOOL* pbDirty)
{
   T* pT = static_cast<T*>(this);
   *pbDirty = pT->m_bRequiresSave ? VARIANT_TRUE : VARIANT_FALSE;
   return S_OK;
}
```

`IsDirty()` simply returns a **`VARIANT_BOOL`** representation of the dirty state of an object. **`m_bRequiresSave`** may be a **`BOOL`** member (and will be if it's obtained from **`CComControl<>`**), so we're careful to make a valid translation between the two boolean types because **`VARIANT_TRUE`** is **`-1`**, whereas **`TRUE`** is **`1`**.

Load()

```
STDMETHOD(Load)(VARIANT var)
{
   if (V_VT(&var) != (VT_UI1 | VT_ARRAY))
      return E_INVALIDARG;

   T* pT = static_cast<T*>(this);
   HRESULT hr = S_OK;
   SAFEARRAY* pArray = V_ARRAY(&var);

   long lBound;
   hr = SafeArrayGetLBound(pArray, 1, &lBound);
   if (FAILED(hr))
      return hr;

   long uBound;
   hr = SafeArrayGetUBound(pArray, 1, &uBound);
   if (FAILED(hr))
      return hr;

   ULONG size = uBound - lBound + 1;

   ULARGE_INTEGER cbSize = {0};
   cbSize.LowPart = size;
   cbSize.HighPart = 0;

   CComPtr<IStream> pStream;
   hr = CreateStreamOnHGlobal(NULL, TRUE, &pStream);
   if (FAILED(hr))
      return hr;

   hr = pStream->SetSize(cbSize);
   if (FAILED(hr))
      return hr;

   HGLOBAL hgData;
   hr = GetHGlobalFromStream(pStream, &hgData);
   if (FAILED(hr))
      return hr;

   BYTE* pStreamData = static_cast<BYTE*>(GlobalLock(hgData));

   BYTE* pData = NULL;
   hr = SafeArrayAccessData(pArray, reinterpret_cast<void**>(&pData));
   if (FAILED(hr))
      return hr;

   memcpy(pStreamData, pData, size);

   SafeArrayUnaccessData(pArray);
   GlobalUnlock(hgData);
```

```
      hr = pT->IPersistStreamInit_Load(pStream, T::GetPropertyMap());
      return hr;
   }
```

Although there's a lot of code in the **Load()** method, the concepts are quite simple. The byte array passed in to the method contains the data that needs to be loaded. We just create a stream object using **CreateStreamOnHGlobal()**, copy the data from the array into the area of memory used by the stream object, then pass the stream object to ATL's implementation of **IPersistStreamInit::Load()**. Easy!

Note that ATL's **IPersistStreamInit::Load()** implementation is actually handled by the **IPersistStreamInit_Load()** member which takes an **IStream*** and a pointer to the property map of the class.

Save()

```
   STDMETHOD(Save)(VARIANT_BOOL bClearDirty, VARIANT* pvar)
   {
      T* pT = static_cast<T*>(this);

      CComPtr<IStream> pStream;
      HRESULT hr = CreateStreamOnHGlobal(NULL, TRUE, &pStream);
      if (FAILED(hr))
         return hr;

      hr = pT->IPersistStreamInit_Save(pStream,
                  bClearDirty == VARIANT_TRUE ? TRUE : FALSE,
                  T::GetPropertyMap());
      if (FAILED(hr))
         return hr;

      STATSTG stat = {0};
      pStream->Stat(&stat, STATFLAG_NONAME);
      ULONG cbSize = stat.cbSize.LowPart;
      if (!cbSize)
         return E_FAIL;

      HGLOBAL hgData = NULL;
      hr = GetHGlobalFromStream(pStream, &hgData);
      if (FAILED(hr))
         return hr;

      BYTE* pStreamData = static_cast<BYTE*>(GlobalLock(hgData));

      SAFEARRAY* pArray = SafeArrayCreateVector(VT_UI1, 0, cbSize);
      if (!pArray)
         return E_OUTOFMEMORY;

      BYTE* pData = NULL;
      hr = SafeArrayAccessData(pArray, reinterpret_cast<void**>(&pData));
      if (FAILED(hr))
         return hr;

      memcpy(pData, pStreamData, cbSize);
```

```
        SafeArrayUnaccessData(pArray);
        GlobalUnlock(hgData);

        V_VT(pvar) = VT_UI1 | VT_ARRAY;
        V_ARRAY(pvar) = pArray;

        return S_OK;
    }
```

Like **Load()**, the **Save()** method requires a lot of dirty code to handle the safe arrays, but once again the concepts are pretty simple: create a stream, save the object to the stream using ATL's **IPersistStreamInitImpl<>** class, convert the underlying stream memory to a safe array and return. Nothing to it...

As before, the **IPersistStreamInit::Save()** implementation is actually handled by the **IPersistStreamInit_Save()** member provided by **IPersistStreamInitImpl<>**.

Epilogue

```
};

#endif // !defined(_IPERSISTVARIANTIMPL_H____INCLUDED_)
```

Don't forget to close the class, and end the preprocessor guard.

IPersistVariantImpl.cpp

Finally, we need an implementation file to match the header. The implementation file won't contain any code, it will just contain the definition for the GUIDs used by the class. When someone wants to use **IPersistVariantImpl<>**, they can just include the header file at relevant points in their project and include this source file in **StdAfx.cpp**.

```
// IPersistVariantImpl.cpp
// Implementation file for IPersistVariantImpl<>
// This file just ensures that the IPersistVariant.h header
// is included before IPersistVariant_i.c
// (Need to do this for the extern uuids to avoid link errors)
#include "IPersistVariant.h"
#include "IPersistVariant_i.c"
```

We could just leave it up to the user to realize that they need to include **IPersistVariant_i.c** somewhere in their project (and that it must appear after **IPersistVariant.h**), but providing this implementation file reduces the likelihood of problems.

Using IPersistVariantImpl<>

Now using this class to implement **IPersistVariant** in our **Order** object is as simple as can be. First we'll copy the existing **SerialOrder** folder and name the copy **PersistOrder** (once again, so that you can find the corresponding code on the web site).

Now add the following code to **StdAfx.h**:

```
#include <atlctl.h>
#include "IPersistVariantImpl.h"
```

#include the implementation file in **StdAfx.cpp**:

```
#include <atlctl.cpp>
#include "IPersistVariantImpl.cpp"
```

Add **IPersistVariantImpl<>** to the list of base classes in **Order.h**:

```
class ATL_NO_VTABLE COrder :
   public CComObjectRootEx<CComSingleThreadModel>,
   public CComCoClass<COrder, &CLSID_Order>,
   public IDispatchImpl<IOrder, &IID_IOrder, &LIBID_SIMPLEORDERLib>,
   public IPersistStreamInitImpl<COrder>,
   public CComControl<COrder>,
   public IPersistVariantImpl<COrder>
```

Change the COM map to expose the **IPersistVariant** interface and disambiguate (!) **IDispatch** as shown:

```
BEGIN_COM_MAP(COrder)
   COM_INTERFACE_ENTRY(IOrder)
   COM_INTERFACE_ENTRY(IPersistVariant)
   COM_INTERFACE_ENTRY2(IDispatch, IOrder)
   COM_INTERFACE_ENTRY_IMPL_IID(IID_IPersistStream, IPersistStreamInit)
END_COM_MAP()
```

These are all the source code changes we need. In the project's IDL file, add **IPersistVariant.idl** to the list of **import**ed files

```
import "oaidl.idl";
import "ocidl.idl";
import "IPersistVariant.idl";
```

Finally, add **IPersistVariant.tlb** to the list of **importlib()**'d libraries in the **library** section, and add the **IPersistVariant** interface to the list of interfaces supported by the **Order** coclass:

```
library SIMPLEORDERLib
{
   importlib("stdole32.tlb");
   importlib("stdole2.tlb");
   importlib("IPersistVariant.tlb");

   [
      uuid(DBDFAF30-F88A-11D1-99A7-A7FE6B055E09),
      helpstring("Order Class")
```

```
    ]
    coclass Order
    {
       [default] interface IOrder;
       interface IPersistVariant;
    };
};
```

Now you can rebuild the example to update the code and type information.

Client

We can change the VBA client we saw earlier with the addition of a new function and a small change in the existing code. The function we'll define is a simple, generic VBA function to clone any object that implements **IPersistVariant**:

```
Public Function Clone(Source As IPersistVariant, _
                      Optional ByVal ServerName As String, _
                      Optional ByVal Context As Long = CLSCTX_SERVER) _
                                                        As IPersistVariant

   ' Create the clone (potentially on another machine)
   Set Clone = CreateObjectEx(Source.GetClassID(), ServerName, Context)

   ' Save the source data to a variant
   Dim Data As Variant
   Data = Source.Save(True)

   ' Load the target with the variant data
   Clone.Load Data
End Function
```

The **Clone()** function presented here takes an **IPersistVariant** reference, plus an optional server name and a **CLSCTX** to determine the machine on which to create the clone. The function creates the clone object then just calls **Save()** on the source object and **Load()** on the clone.

This function uses **CreateObjectEx()**, a VBA wrapper to **CoCreateInstanceEx()**. The wrapper takes a string (which may be a ProgID or a CLSID) identifying the object to create, an optional machine name identifying the server on which to create the object, and an optional context. If successful, **CreateObjectEx()** returns an **IUnknown** reference to the newly created object. You can find the full code for this function in Appendix B (and, of course, you can also find the complete code for this example on the Wrox Press web site).

With the **Clone()** function defined, the only change that needs to be made to the previous client implementation is in **cmdConfirm_Click()**. Previously, the order was submitted with this code:

```
m_order.Submit
```

We can change this to allow the order to be cloned and submitted from another machine using this code:

```
Dim itfOrder As Order
Set itfOrder = Clone(m_order, "\\DIPSY")
itfOrder.Submit
```

Alternatively, you can change the code to allow the server to be specified administratively by omitting the server name and specifying **CLSCTX_REMOTE_SERVER** as the context:

```
Set itfOrder = Clone(m_order, , CLSCTX_REMOTE_SERVER)
```

If you do this, you'll need to set up **DCOMCnfg** so that the **Order** component can be run both locally (for the initial object) and remotely (for the clone):

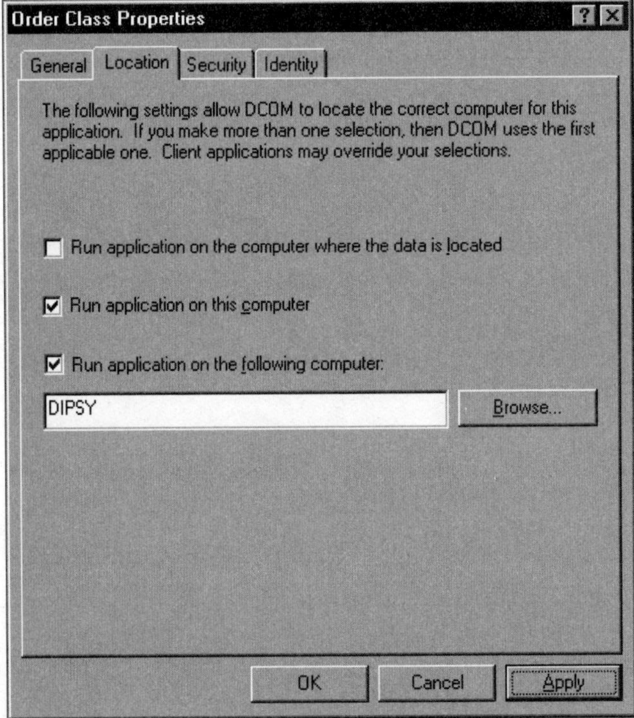

The VB client will create the first **Order** object locally using **New**, but by specifying **CLSCTX_REMOTE_SERVER** to the **Clone()** function, the clone object will be created on the specified remote host, and that's where the order eventually gets written to file.

Of course to run this example, the **Object** server and the **IPersistVariant** type library need to be registered on both client and server machines.

You could increase the efficiency of the code further by rewriting the `Clone()` function in C++ and making it less general by returning the `IOrder` interface on the clone object. You could use `CoCreateInstanceEx()` to query for the `IPersistVariant` and `IOrder` interfaces at the same time to avoid an extra trip across the network.

You could also design `Clone()` as a COM interface method on the `Order` object, doing away with the need for the first parameter, and allowing direct access to the CLSID without having to translate back and forth between string and `CLSID` form.
These improvements are left as an exercise.

MBV Motivation

OK, we've got a generic interface, `IPersistVariant`, that can be used from Visual Basic to save and load objects in a byte array, an easy-to-use ATL implementation class for this interface, and a `Clone()` function that allows us to transport any object that implements `IPersistVariant` to any machine on the network. By using these tools in the `Order` class, our clients are in a great position to write reasonably efficient code.

The major problem is that it requires our clients to do more work than they need. Every time a client needs to read the values of an `Order` object that's on a different machine, it has to explicitly clone the object to its own machine in order to get efficient access to the object's properties. If the client doesn't do this, each attempt to read one of the object's properties will result in a call over the network – something we're keen to avoid.

What we need is some kind of caching system, whereby the initial access to the `Order` object automatically loads the whole thing up locally, so that the client can play around with the order to its heart's content without troubling the network. Passing an `IOrder` interface to an object on another machine should be all it needs to trigger this mechanism, removing an extra burden from the client programmers.

This kind of problem screams out for a technique known as **marshal-by-value**, or **MBV**. You'll find that it has a *lot* in common with the kind of thing we've been playing with up until now. In order to use MBV, we must first understand **custom marshaling**.

Marshal Arts

I feel that it is part of my mission with this book to try and remove some of the general veneer of voodoo and mysticism that surrounds COM and DCOM. More than any other technology I've come across, COM is often, at first sight, so counter-intuitive that you often feel like an outsider who has been trying to penetrate some kind of secret society, where real enlightenment is only given after you've been through some painful initiation ceremony. But the wonderful thing is that every time you run up against something that seems so completely opaque that you feel like giving up, eventually the penny drops and it makes absolute, perfect, beautiful sense, and you wonder why you ever had problems with it in the first place.

And nowhere have I felt this more so than in the area of *custom marshaling.* Maybe I'm just slow, but I read everything I could on the subject, and it still failed to make any sense whatsoever. Finally, I just got stuck in and tried programming it, step by step, plastering the whole thing with debug statements, and then at last it all began to fall into place.

Let's take a look at it, then.

I like to think of the way DCOM works as a bit like one of those remote pairs of hands that workers in nuclear installations use to handle unfriendly materials. You know the sort of thing – on *this* side of the glass you stick your hands in a pair of magic gloves, twiddle them about, and then somehow on the *other* side of the glass, a pair of robotic hands echo your movements.

Let's try and add some tentative details to this analogy. Your hands are of course the **client**. The Plutonium sample is the COM object that you're invoking methods on. The magic gloves are the **proxy** for the object within the local client, and the robotic hands on the other side of the protective glass are the **stub**. The magic gloves – assuming a realistic tactile feel (maybe we're really talking VR here!) – are the sample's representative on this side of the glass, and the robotic hands are our representative on the sample's side of the glass. Similarly, in DCOM, the *proxy* is basically the representative of the object to the client, whilst the *stub* is the representative of the client to the object.

In our nuclear installation, the key to the efficacy of the Plutonium-handling system is the mechanics linking the magic glove and the robotic arm. Similarly, the key to the success of DCOM is the implementation of *marshaling* that takes place within the standard DCOM proxy/stub code. In most circumstances, the standard implementation will be perfectly adequate, but if we wish to change it (to handle local caching, for example), we'll have to do our own marshaling. It's a bit like changing the mechanism linking the magic gloves to the robotic hands.

The IMarshal Interface

If we want to do our own custom marshaling, we're going to have to provide an implementation of the `IMarshal` interface. There is tremendous scope for confusion here, because `IMarshal` is really two interfaces combined into one – some of the methods are invoked solely on the server object itself, and some on the proxy. Here is its definition, with the methods listed in the order in which they are usually invoked:

Method	Parameters	Invoked on	Description

`GetUnmarshalClass`	`[in] REFIID riid,`
	`[in] void* pv,`
	`[in] DWORD dwDestContext,`
	`[in] void* pvDestContext,`
	`[in] DWORD mshlflags,`
	`[out] CLSID* pCid`
		Server Object	Get the identifier of the class that we are going to use to create our proxy

Method	Parameters	Invoked on	Description

`GetMarshalSizeMax`	`[in] REFIID riid,`
	`[in] void* pv,`
	`[in] DWORD dwDestContext,`
	`[in] void* pvDestContext,`
	`[in] DWORD mshlflags,`
	`[out] ULONG* pSize`
		Object	Get the maximum size of the stream used to hold information that will initialize the proxy

`MarshalInterface`	`[in] IStream* pStm,`
	`[in] REFIID riid,`
	`[in] void* pv,`
	`[in] DWORD dwDestContext,`
	`[in] void* pvDestContext,`
	`[in] DWORD mshlflags`
		Object	Load the stream with the information needed to initialize the proxy

`UnmarshalInterface`	`[in] IStream* pStm,`
	`[in] REFIID riid,`
	`[out] void** ppv`
		Proxy	Get initialization information from the incoming stream, and return pointer to specified interface

`ReleaseMarshalData`	`[in] IStream* pStm`	Object	Dispose of unwanted data from stream after failure to invoke proxy
`DisconnectObject`	`[in] DWORD dwReserved`	Object	Handle unexpected disconnection

So, what happens?

First of all, the client attempts to instantiate a server object, requesting interface **IWhatever**. The COM environment queries the server object for the **IMarshal** interface. If the object doesn't implement it, COM carries on and uses standard marshaling. If the object *does* implement **IMarshal**, the COM environment invokes **GetUnmarshalClass()** on the server object to determine which class of object is going to act as our proxy. If it's not stretching the analogy too far, you can think of this as a question of determining which type of magic gloves to use, depending on the type of operation that you're going to be carrying out on your radioactive substance.

Next, COM invokes **GetMarshalSizeMax()** on the server object to find out the maximum size of the proxy initialization stream. This is the stream of data that we use to put our object into its initial state. We'll see what we might insert in this stream in a little while. Then, having set up the stream to receive the proxy initialization data, COM invokes **MarshalInterface()** on the server object.

COM has now got everything it needs from the object, so it can create the proxy, getting hold of its **IMarshal** interface. Having done that, it invokes **UnmarshalInterface()** on the proxy. This tells the proxy to initialize itself (using the data from the stream, which you can bet is a memory-based stream – remember **CreateStreamOnHGlobal()** a while back?).

At this point, the proxy can make its connection to its stub partner. The choice of technology for connecting proxy to stub is entirely up to you as the developer. In some cases, as you'll see, we may do all the work inside the proxy, and not make a connection to a stub at all! Having done this, the proxy returns a pointer to an implementation of **IWhatever** that it knows about; in fact, the proxy will usually implement **IWhatever** itself.

From here on, all method calls on the marshaled interface are received by the proxy, and it's up to the proxy to process them in whatever way is appropriate to the implementation. This might be to stream the arguments for the call over to a stub for processing there (which, after all, is what RPC does for us in standard marshaling). Perhaps we might use a TCP/IP socket as our transport mechanism, or – and here's an interesting possibility – perhaps we could use Microsoft Message Queue.

OK, that's enough talk. Let's see how it happens in practice. Remember what our goal was? We've got a remote object that we want to cache locally for easy manipulation without imposing any undue strain on our network. It's time to take a look at how we can achieve this using custom marshaling to implement marshal-by-value.

Marshaling By Value

Now that you've seen how custom marshaling works, it should start to become clearer how we can implement our local **Order** cache. We know that a remote client will have a proxy to an **Order** object. If we create a custom proxy, we just need to initialize it with the complete state of the remote **Order** object (as represented by the **IOrder** interface), implement the **IOrder** interface and serve the client's requests with the locally cached information.

This is the central idea of MBV – the proxy *is* the implementation. In fact, in most cases, the proxy object and the server object are identical, and have the same class ID, although this isn't a requirement.

IMarshalByValueImpl<>

To help implement marshal-by-value, we can use a generic template class to provide the implementation for **IMarshal** in both proxy and server. The template class, **IMarshalByValueImpl<>**, is extremely simple. The template assumes that the server object implements **IPersistStream** (or provides compatible methods) so it can save the state of the server object in **MarshalInterface()** using **IPersistStream::Save()**. It also assumes that the proxy object implements **IPersistStream** (or provides compatible methods) so that it can load the proxy with the previously saved state with a call to using **IPersistStream::Save()**.

The complete header file for **IMarshalByValueImpl<>** is shown below:

```
// IMarshalByValueImpl.h
// Implementation of IMarshal for marshal by value objects
// Original code by Jonathan Borden posted to the DCOM mailing list:
// Based on MBV code by Don Box
// Minor changes made by Alex Stockton

#if !defined(_IMARSHALBYVALUEIMPL_H____INCLUDED_)
#define _IMARSHALBYVALUEIMPL_H____INCLUDED_

#if _MSC_VER >= 1000
#pragma once
#endif // _MSC_VER >= 1000

// Remember that proxies must be implemented in DLLs with
// the 'Both' threading model

// Note that ATL 2 returns E_NOTIMPL from IPersistStreamInit::GetSizeMax()
// Either implement this method yourself, or override GetMarshalSizeMax()
// in your class

// Expose the IMarshal interface in your object's COM map like this:
// COM_INTERFACE_ENTRY_IMPL_IID(IID_IMarshal, IMarshalByValue)

// T must supply the following members (or compatible alternatives)
//       const CLSID& GetObjectCLSID();
//             usually from CComCoClass<>
//       HRESULT GetSizeMax(ULARGE_INTEGER* pcbSize);
//             usually from IPersistStreamInitImpl<>
//       HRESULT Load(IStream* pStm);
//             usually from IPersistStreamInitImpl<>
//       HRESULT Save(IStream* pStm, BOOL bClearDirty);
//             usually from IPersistStreamInitImpl<>
//       IUnknown* GetUnknown();
//             usually from BEGIN_COM_MAP() macro

template <class T>
class ATL_NO_VTABLE IMarshalByValueImpl : public IMarshal
{
public:
// IMarshal
   STDMETHODIMP GetUnmarshalClass(REFIID riid, void* pv,
      DWORD dwDestContext, void* pvDestContext, DWORD mshlflags,
      CLSID* pCid)
```

```
{
   ATLTRACE(_T("GetUnmarshalClass\n"));
   T* pT = static_cast<T*>(this);

   *pCid = pT->GetObjectCLSID();
   return S_OK;
}

STDMETHODIMP GetMarshalSizeMax(REFIID riid, void* pv,
   DWORD dwDestContext, void* pvDestContext, DWORD mshlflags,
   DWORD* pSize)
{
   ATLTRACE(_T("GetMarshalSizeMax\n"));
   T* pT = static_cast<T*>(this);

   // Use IPersistStreamInit::GetSizeMax() (or compatible alternative)
   ULARGE_INTEGER uli = {0};
   HRESULT hr = pT->GetSizeMax(&uli);
   if (SUCCEEDED(hr))
      *pSize = uli.LowPart;
   return hr;
}

STDMETHODIMP MarshalInterface(IStream* pStm, REFIID riid,
   void* pv, DWORD dwDestContext, void* pvDestCtx,
   DWORD mshlflags)
{
   ATLTRACE(_T("MarshalInterface\n"));
   T* pT = static_cast<T*>(this);

   // Use IPersistStreamInit::Save() (or compatible alternative)
   HRESULT hr = pT->Save(pStm, FALSE);
   return hr;
}

STDMETHODIMP UnmarshalInterface(IStream* pStm, REFIID riid,
   void** ppv)
{
   // This method is invoked on the proxy
   ATLTRACE(_T("UnmarshalInterface\n"));
   T* pT = static_cast<T*>(this);

   // Use IPersistStreamInit::Load() (or compatible alternative)
   HRESULT hr = pT->Load(pStm);
   if (FAILED(hr))
      return hr;

   IUnknown* pUnk = pT->GetUnknown();
   if (!pUnk)
      return E_FAIL;

   return pUnk->QueryInterface(riid, ppv);
}

STDMETHODIMP ReleaseMarshalData(IStream* pStm)
{
   ATLTRACE(_T("ReleaseMarshalData\n"));
```

```
        // Nothing to release
        return S_OK;
    }

    STDMETHODIMP DisconnectObject(DWORD dwReserved)
    {
        ATLTRACE(_T("DisconnectObject\n"));
        // Nothing to do
        return S_OK;
    }
};

#endif // !defined(_IMARSHALBYVALUEIMPL_H____INCLUDED_)
```

Let's take a quick look at these methods. The first method, **`GetUnmarshalClass()`**, is called on the server object and returns the class ID of the proxy that we're going to use. For this implementation, the CLSID of the proxy is the CLSID of the server. We get this CLSID by calling **`GetObjectCLSID()`**, which is usually provided by **`CComCoClass<>`**.

The second method, **`GetMarshalSizeMax()`**, sets up the size of the initialization stream, so that it will be big enough to hold our object's state when it's been streamed. It does that by calling **`GetSizeMax()`**, one of the **`IPersistStream`** methods implemented by **`IPersistStreamInitImpl<>`**. At least, it *should* be implemented by **`IPersistStreamInitImpl<>`** – the ATL implementation actually returns **`E_NOTIMPL`**. This is acceptable to many clients and containers (which provide resizable streams) but not when marshaling. You must provide a full implementation of **`GetSizeMax()`** in your server object to use the **`IMarshalByValueImpl<>`** class. We'll see how to implement **`GetSizeMax()`** for the **`Order`** example shortly.

Now take a look at the next method, **`MarshalInterface()`**. All that this one does is use the **`Save()`** method – again from **`IPersistStreamInitImpl<>`** – to actually stream the server's current state.

As you can see, all the server side of the marshaling code does is:

- Determine who's going to act as the proxy
- Stream the object's state

The remaining piece of the jigsaw is the call to **`UnmarshalInterface()`** on the proxy. It's no real surprise that the bulk of the work is once again carried out by a method provided by **`IPersistStreamInitImpl<>`** – this time the **`Load()`** method. The proxy's **`UnmarshalInterface()`** implementation just loads itself up with data from the incoming stream, and passes the requested interface on itself back to the caller. Hey presto! One object ready and waiting to be interrogated.

The remaining **`IMarshal`** methods don't require any code at all.

Code

Let's see this in action by implementing MBV in our **Order** object. We'll start by creating yet another version of our **Order** server by copying the **SerialOrder** folder and renaming the new copy **MarshalOrder**. You'll remember that the **SerialOrder** version of the project had **get_** and **put_** methods for all the properties in the **IOrder** interface, as well as an implementation of **IPersistStream**. This is just the base needed by the **IMarshalByValueImpl<>** class.

The changes that you need to make to the header file **Order.h** are shown below. First, include the header file for **IMarshalByValueImpl<>** at the top of **Order.h**:

```
#include "resource.h"        // main symbols
#include "IMarshalByValueImpl.h"
```

Add **IMarshalByValueImpl<>** to the list of base classes:

```
class ATL_NO_VTABLE COrder :
   public CComObjectRootEx<CComSingleThreadModel>,
   public CComCoClass<COrder, &CLSID_Order>,
   public IDispatchImpl<IOrder, &IID_IOrder, &LIBID_SIMPLEORDERLib>,
   public IPersistStreamInitImpl<COrder>,
   public CComControl<COrder>,
   public IMarshalByValueImpl<COrder>
```

And add an interface entry to the COM map:

```
BEGIN_COM_MAP(COrder)
   COM_INTERFACE_ENTRY(IOrder)
   COM_INTERFACE_ENTRY(IDispatch)
   COM_INTERFACE_ENTRY_IMPL_IID(IID_IPersistStream, IPersistStreamInit)
   COM_INTERFACE_ENTRY_IMPL_IID(IID_IMarshal, IMarshalByValue)
END_COM_MAP()
```

The only thing left to do in the server code is implement **GetSizeMax()** to return a useful value. We'll add a quick implementation to the **COrder** class like this:

```
// IPersistStream
   STDMETHOD(GetSizeMax)(ULARGE_INTEGER* pcbSize)
   {
      // Return size of data to be written to stream in bytes

      // ATL Version
      pcbSize->QuadPart = sizeof(DWORD);

      // User Data
      pcbSize->QuadPart +=
         SizeOfBSTR(m_bstrCustomerID) +
         SizeOfBSTR(m_bstrArtist) +
         SizeOfBSTR(m_bstrTitle) +
```

```
            SizeOfBSTR(m_bstrLabel) +
            SizeOfBSTR(m_bstrPrice);
        return S_OK;
    }
```

Here we have worked out the size to return by looking at the implementation of **IPersistStreamInitImpl<>::Save()** to see precisely what is written to the stream. The answer turns out to be a **DWORD** (representing the version of ATL doing the saving) plus the five **CComBSTR** members. Our implementation of **GetSizeMax()** just adds together the number of bytes for this data to get the maximum size of the stream.

SizeOfBSTR() is a simple inline function that we define to return the number of bytes used by ATL to write a **CComBSTR** to a stream.

```
inline ULONG SizeOfBSTR(/*[in]*/ BSTR bstr)
{
    return (bstr ? SysStringByteLen(bstr) + sizeof(OLECHAR) : 0)
           + sizeof(ULONG);
}
```

Our MBV server is now complete, but there's just one more thing that we need to do – make sure that the registration of our EXE server will not remove all existing registry entries for that CLSID when the server registers or unregisters itself. This is because we are about to create an in-process version of the server that we can use as the proxy with the same CLSID. Proxies must be in-process and Both-threaded to ensure that they are always accessed directly (imagine having to marshal to get to a proxy – my head's beginning to spin!). There'll be no end of confusion if we allow the EXE server to remove the registration entries for the DLL or vice versa. To avoid this, open the **Order.rgs** file and change **ForceRemove** to **NoRemove** on the line shown.

```
NoRemove CLSID
{
    NoRemove {DBDFAF30-F88A-11D1-99A7-A7FE6B055E09} = s 'Order Class'
```

The Proxy Side

To create the proxy object, create a new ATL DLL project called **OrderProxy** (in a subdirectory of **MarshalOrder** for convenience). Use the ATL Object Wizard to create a new Simple Object called **Order** and ensure that you select Both as the Threading Model on the Attributes page of the wizard. The wizard should inform you that a CLSID already exists in the registry for this class, and ask whether you'd like to use the existing CLSID. You should select Yes.

Once the object is generated, you should see that the CLSID in the **Order.rgs** file for the new project is the same as the one used in the **MarshalOrder** project. If the CLSIDs are different, you should edit the CLSIDs in the new **.rgs** file to match the original. While you have the new **Order.rgs** file open, you should also change **ForceRemove** to **NoRemove** just as we did for the executable.

```
    NoRemove CLSID
    {
        NoRemove {DBDFAF30-F88A-11D1-99A7-A7FE6B055E09} = s 'Order Class'
```

Next we need to edit the IDL file, so that it uses exactly the same information as the **MarshalOrder** project. Open the IDL file and remove the existing **interface** and **coclass** definitions then add the **import** and **importlib()** statements shown:

```
import "oaidl.idl";
import "ocidl.idl";
import "../SimpleOrder.idl";

[
   uuid(16B8BD42-FBA0-11D1-A1DD-0060087B1844),
   version(1.0),
   helpstring("OrderProxy 1.0 Type Library")
]
library ORDERPROXYLib
{
   importlib("stdole32.tlb");
   importlib("stdole2.tlb");
   importlib("../SimpleOrder.tlb");
};
```

Now copy the **Order.h** and **Order.cpp** files from the **MarshalOrder** directory into the **OrderProxy** directory, replacing the existing files. You'll need to edit **Order.cpp** to refer to the **OrderProxy.h** file:

```
#include "stdafx.h"
#include "OrderProxy.h"
#include "Order.h"
```

And you'll need to change the threading model class used by **COrder** from **CComSingleThreadModel** back to **CComMultiThreadModel** in **Order.h**.

```
class ATL_NO_VTABLE COrder :
   public CComObjectRootEx<CComMultiThreadModel>,
```

You should add the **AtlCtl.h** header file to **StdAfx.h** so that the **IPersistStreamInitImpl<>** base class will compile.

```
#include <atlcom.h>
#include <atlctl.h>
```

And you'll need to add the following **#includes StdAfx.cpp**:

```
#include <atlimpl.cpp>
#include <atlwin.cpp>
#include <atlctl.cpp>
#include "SimpleOrder.h"
#include "SimpleOrder_i.c"
```

Finally, add the **OrderProxy**'s parent directory (**..**) as an additional include directory in the project settings for all configurations.

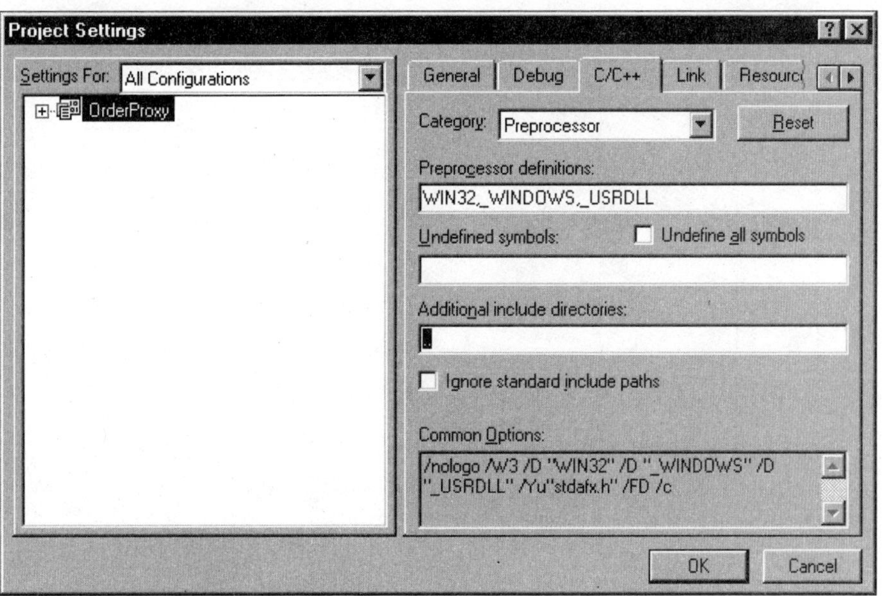

At this stage you can build the **OrderProxy** DLL.

We now have an in-process version of the **MarshalOrder** project, which also uses MBV. COM will automatically use the **Order** class within the **OrderProxy** project to act as the proxy for any **Order** objects within the **MarshalOrder** executable. But, more than that, **OrderProxy** can act as a server in its own right with exactly the same functionality as the executable.

In fact, the EXE version of the project becomes redundant unless we change it so that it populates itself with data as it starts up. To see why this is, consider the fact that all clients must access the executable through the proxy, and the proxy will never communicate back to the original server.

To see how we can extend the EXE to make it useful again, suppose we have a client in Chicago that needs to read an order from the database in Tierra del Fuego. If we changed the EXE so that it automatically read the order from a database when it started up (in **FinalConstruct()**),we could use the proxy to automatically transfer all the data across in one go. This would allow the client to retrieve the data efficiently in the form of an **Order** object without any effort.

Here's the sequence of events in this case:

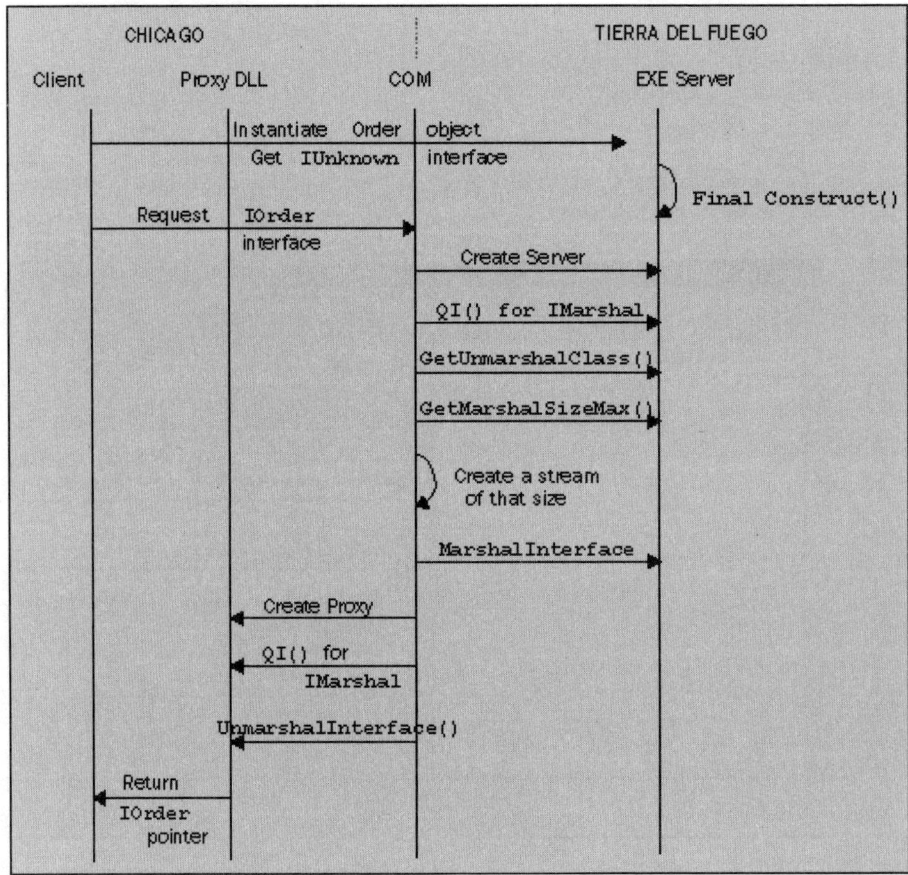

1. Client in Chicago instantiates an **`Order`** object in Tierra del Fuego.
2. Remote object is populated in the **`FinalConstruct()`** method.
3. Client requests the **`IOrder`** interface.
4. The COM environment queries the object for the **`IMarshal`** interface, and discovers that it is implemented.
5. The remote object's **`GetUnmarshalClass()`** is invoked; the object gives the class ID of the proxy (which happens to be its own CLSID).
6. COM wants to find out how to initialize the proxy object, so it invokes **`GetMarshalSizeMax()`** on the server object to find out how big the initialization stream should be.
7. COM creates the stream and invokes the **`MarshalInterface()`** method to request it to marshal its data into it; our object saves its data into the stream that it's been given.
8. We've finished with the remote object. Now COM can instantiate the proxy in Chicago.

9. COM queries the proxy for the **IMarshal** interface, and discovers that it is implemented.

10. COM invokes the **UnmarshalInterface()** method on the proxy, passing in a stream of initialization data; the proxy uses the data from the stream to populate itself, and it is now an exact clone of the original remote object.

Let's try this out. First of all, you'll need to add the following declarations to the **COrder** class in the **MarshalOrder** (EXE) project:

```
public:
   HRESULT FinalConstruct();
private:
   void Read(IStorage* pStorage, LPOLESTR lpszField, CComBSTR& bstr);
```

The implementations can go in **Order.cpp**:

```
HRESULT COrder::FinalConstruct()
{
   CComPtr<IStorage> pStorage;
   HRESULT hr = StgOpenStorage (L"C:\\Order.dat", NULL,
         STGM_READ | STGM_SHARE_EXCLUSIVE, NULL, 0, &pStorage);
   if (FAILED(hr))
      return hr;

   Read(pStorage, L"CustomerID", m_bstrCustomerID);
   Read(pStorage, L"Artist", m_bstrArtist);
   Read(pStorage, L"Title", m_bstrTitle);
   Read(pStorage, L"Label", m_bstrLabel);
   Read(pStorage, L"Price", m_bstrPrice);
   return S_OK;
}

void COrder::Read(IStorage* pStorage, LPOLESTR lpszField, CComBSTR& bstr)
{
   CComPtr<IStream> pStream;
   HRESULT hr = pStorage->OpenStream(lpszField, NULL,
                STGM_READ | STGM_SHARE_EXCLUSIVE, 0, &pStream);
   if (FAILED(hr))
      return;

   bstr.ReadFromStream(pStream);
}
```

This code just loads up the order from the same **Order.dat** file used by the **Submit()** method to save the data.

Now we'll create a new Visual Basic (or VBA) client consisting of a single form. The form just needs some text boxes to display the values of the **Order** object and a button to create the object. Here's the code:

```
Option Explicit
Private Const CLSID_Order = "{DBDFAF30-F88A-11D1-99A7-A7FE6B055E09}"
Dim m_order As Order

Private Sub cmdCheck_Click()
   Set m_order = CreateObjectEx(CLSID_Order, "dipsy", CLSCTX_REMOTE_SERVER)

   With m_order
      txtCustomerID = .CustomerID
      txtTitle = .Title
      txtArtist = .Artist
      txtLabel = .Label
      txtPrice = .Price
   End With
End Sub
```

Note that we've used **CreateObjectEx()** to specify the machine on which to create the **Order** object. We can't use **New** in this case since the proxy has the same CLSID as the EXE server, is in-process (and therefore has a higher precedence than the remote server), and must be able to be run on the client machine.

I've defined the **m_order** object as a member of the form class so that we can hang on to its reference long enough to check the task window on the remote machine to see if the object is still running there. If you check while the form is running, you'll see that the EXE server is not in the list. Only the local proxy is responsible for serving the client with data.

This is what we see when we run the program:

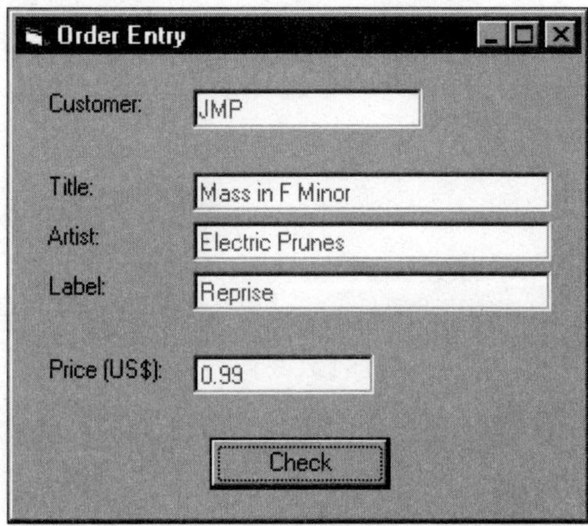

Object Transportation Using MBV

Now let's go back to our order-entry example, and see if we can apply MBV to this, too. In the last order entry example we saw, an **Order** object was created locally by the client, then explicitly cloned to a remote machine and the **Submit()** method was called on the clone.

With our MBV example, we can create the **Order** object in the same process as the client. At the point of submitting an order, we'll create another object (of a new, totally different type – let's call it **SubmitOrder**) on the server, passing it the **IOrder*** of our local **Order** object. The

SubmitOrder object then retrieves the fields from the **Order** object using the standard **get_** methods and takes responsibility for entering the information in the database (or writing it to file in our case). The great thing is that by the time the **SubmitOrder** object gets hold of the **Order**, COM has streamed everything over into the proxy on the remote machine through the magic of custom marshaling – all of the **get_** method calls are in-process.

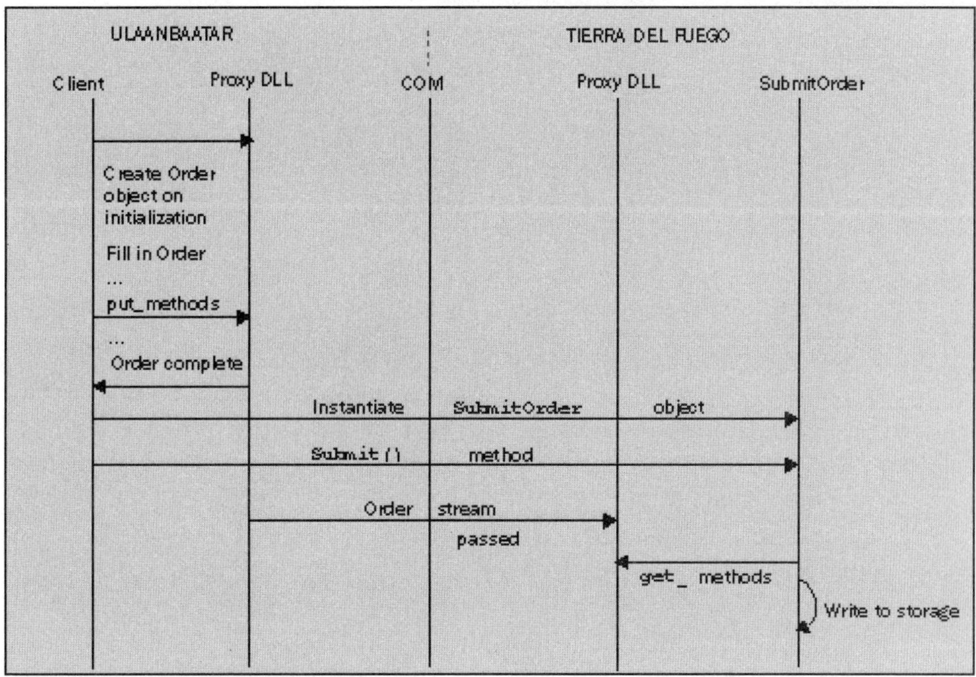

We already have the code for the in-process proxy (which we can also use as a server in its own right), so the only thing that we need to do is create a new ATL EXE project called **SubmitOrderProj** with a single simple object called **SubmitOrder**. This object needs one interface, **ISubmitOrder**, with the just the following method:

Method	Parameters	Description
`Submit`	`[in] IOrder* pOrder`	Write order to file

As usual, we **import** the **Order** project's IDL file, **importlib()** its type library into **SubmitOrderProj.idl**, and **#include** its **.h** and **_i.c** files in **SubmitOrderProj.cpp**.

The implementation of this class is simply based on the implementation of the **Submit()** method in the **Order** class:

```
STDMETHODIMP CSubmitOrder::Submit(IOrder* pOrder)
{
```

```
    CComPtr<IStorage> pStorage;
    HRESULT hr = StgCreateDocfile(L"C:\\Order.dat",
                      STGM_SIMPLE| STGM_CREATE | STGM_READWRITE |
                      STGM_SHARE_EXCLUSIVE, 0, &pStorage);
    if (FAILED(hr))
       return hr;

    CComBSTR bstr;

    hr = pOrder->get_CustomerID(&bstr);
    if (FAILED(hr)) return hr;
    Write(pStorage, L"CustomerID", bstr);

    hr = pOrder->get_Artist(&bstr);
    if (FAILED(hr)) return hr;
    Write(pStorage, L"Artist", bstr);

    hr = pOrder->get_Title(&bstr);
    if (FAILED(hr)) return hr;
    Write(pStorage, L"Title", bstr);

    hr = pOrder->get_Label(&bstr);
    if (FAILED(hr)) return hr;
    Write(pStorage, L"Label", bstr);

    hr = pOrder->get_Price(&bstr);
    if (FAILED(hr)) return hr;
    Write(pStorage, L"Price", bstr);

    return S_OK;
}

void CSubmitOrder::Write(IStorage* pStorage, LPOLESTR lpszField,
                         CComBSTR& bstr)
{
    CComPtr<IStream> pStream;
    pStorage->CreateStream(lpszField, STGM_READWRITE |
                     STGM_SHARE_EXCLUSIVE, 0, 0, &pStream);

    bstr.WriteToStream(pStream);
}
```

Visual Basic Client

The Visual Basic client code doesn't have to change much at all. Where we previously called **m_order.Submit** in the original client, now we have the code shown highlighted below:

```
Private Sub cmdConfirm_Click()
    ...

    Dim subber As SubmitOrder
    Set subber = CreateObjectEx(CLSID_SubmitOrder, "dipsy", _
                                CLSCTX_REMOTE_SERVER)
    subber.Submit m_order
```

```
    Unload Me
End Sub
```

It's as easy as that.

Practical DCOM

In this chapter, we've explored how we can make the best use of DCOM under real world limitations. We've looked at some ways in which the impact of low bandwidth on location transparency can be minimized, so that at least we can achieve some kind of location translucence. Which has to be better than location opacity.

Custom marshaling is a very powerful tool. When we come on to Microsoft Message Queue in Chapter 6, I'll show you another implementation that you can use in order to achieve a kind of "one-way" functionality. This might be appropriate for occasions when you're not too fussy about getting an immediate confirmation that a remote operation has completed.

What other uses might there be for custom marshaling? Why restrict ourselves to just one destination host? What if we were to implement, say, a *multi-cast* protocol within the proxy? Then you'd no longer be restricted by having to service multiple point-to-point connections. Imagine the possibilities: your client invokes a method, apparently on a local object – meanwhile, that method is actually invoked on a thousand other servers! Imagine, further, that each of those servers then raises an event to a thousand clients ... Truly, the possibilities are limitless.

The next area that I want to look into is the question of actually finding our objects. What we need is a proper directory service, and it just so happens that Windows NT is in the process of acquiring one...

Directories and Finding Things

"When Laura was here I had the records arranged alphabetically; before that I had them filed in chronological order, beginning with Robert Johnson, and ending with Wham!, or somebody African, or whatever else I was listening to when Laura and I met. Tonight, though, I fancy something different, so I try to remember the order I bought them in ..."

Nick Hornby,
High Fidelity

Catalogs

Anyone with a reasonably large collection of records (or books, or indeed anything) will be familiar with the problem of finding the item that you want in as short a time as possible. Do you file them in purely alphabetical order (in which case you end up with Bob Marley next to Bohuslav Martinu), do you store them by category (in which case is Philip Glass' *Low Symphony* "classical" or "rock"?) or do you keep all the ones with the same label together? It's a real dilemma, but at least the items in question are self-cataloging.

It gets considerably more complex if you indulge in home taping. I used to do an awful lot of this (even to the extent of having an amateur recording license in the days when you could get one). The problem was that you couldn't guarantee that the two things that you had recorded on either side of the cassette would be sufficiently similar to each other to enable you to treat the cassette as a single entity from the point of view of classification. (We're entering the *seriously* sad zone here, but let's stick with it – it's a useful analogy.) In the end, the only viable way to store them was to number them in the order in which you recorded them, and keep a separate card index, cross-referencing artists and records with the appropriate cassettes.

Libraries, of course, have a similar problem, only far, far worse. Let's imagine that I go to my local library in search of a copy of, say, Bill Gates' *The Road Ahead*; as I'm feeling in need of a little self-improvement. If I can't find the book on the shelves, I might search the library's CD-ROM to find out its Dewey decimal classification, so I can check to see if I was looking in the right place. If the book definitely isn't there, I'll go and ask the librarian.

The first thing that they will do is search their own database to establish whether or not they have a copy at all, and, if so, whether or not it is currently out on loan. Suppose they don't have a copy – the next step is to search the other libraries in the county. Fortunately, they find out that the central library in the next town has two, although both are currently out on loan. Reluctantly, I pay my fee to request the book, and wait to achieve enlightenment.

Here we have a reasonably typical example of a distributed directory search. You don't even really need computers for it. In the old days, your friendly librarian would have simply got on the phone and called up the other libraries to ask them. The problem, however, is basically the same: How do you find something that you need as quickly as possible, even if it's stored in a totally different geographical location?

Incidentally, once you have located the object in question, getting hold of it is a different matter – but that's outside the jurisdiction of the directory service.

Directories and Windows

What is the single biggest thing that has so far held Windows back from becoming *the* operating system of choice for large-scale distributed systems? There's no question in my mind that the answer is the lack of a decent directory service. Anyone who has been anywhere with DCOM has found out that in order to use remote components, you had to copy the executable on to your local machine, and then run `DCOMcnfg` to turn the entry in your registry into a remote reference. The end result is that every single remote component is independently registered in every single client registry, so that you have a completely unmanageable mesh. Or mess, even.

What you really need is a mechanism whereby you can make a simple call to some directory service to say, "Can you find me the nearest copy of an object with UUID *x*?" Maybe it would even instantiate the object and return to you a pointer to the interface you asked for. This would be something pretty close to nirvana. The good news is that it's on its way. But before we talk about that, let's step back a bit and take a look at directory services in general, because it's not just components that we're interested in finding. This is, after all, a book about distributed systems, and we might want to get hold of all sorts of things...

What is the difference between a directory service and a conventional database? To answer this question, I can do no better than to quote from the University of Michigan's Administrator's Guide to SLAPD and SLURPD[1], which are two of the standard processes that control LDAP (Lightweight Directory Access Protocol) implementations under Unix:

---

[1] Two gorgeous process names that seem to have been lost from the Windows LDAP implementation, more's the pity.

> *A directory is like a database, but tends to contain more descriptive, attribute-based information. The information in a directory is generally read much more often than it is written. As a consequence, directories don't usually implement the complicated transaction or rollback schemes regular databases use for doing high-volume complex updates. Directory updates are typically simple all-or-nothing changes, if they are allowed at all. Directories are tuned to give quick-response to high-volume lookup or search operations. They may have the ability to replicate information widely in order to increase availability and reliability, while reducing response time. When directory information is replicated, temporary inconsistencies between the replicas may be OK, as long as they get in sync eventually.*

Sounds cool? Let's have a look at Active Directory, then.

One word of warning before we dive in, though. This is a *very* big subject, and we can't hope to cover it all in one chapter. In the very near future, I predict that there will be whole books devoted to the subject, and a substantial number of people charging very high fees for setting up and managing directories on Windows installations. It's also one of those technologies (like the Internet) that Microsoft have chosen to realign considerable parts of Windows around – indeed, recent versions of NT (from 5.0 beta 1 on) fire up with the banner "Windows NT *with Active Directory*" (my italics).

We're going to start off the chapter by taking a look at the Active Directory Services Interfaces (ADSI), which we'll use to develop a little program to trawl through a directory and see what we find. As we go along, we'll discuss what we find out about the structure of Active Directory. Later in the chapter, we'll take a look at LDAP (Lightweight Directory Access Protocol) and develop a program to search for objects through Active Directory.

The examples shown in the first part of the chapter can be tried under either NT4 or NT5, but if you want to try out the examples in the LDAP sections in the latter part of this chapter, you'll need to get hold of a copy of NT5. The examples here were tested under NT5 beta 1. In order to build the sample applications, you'll also need to have the Windows Platform SDK installed. You can download this from `http://www.microsoft.com`, or alternatively if you're in the MSDN program, it's on one of the CDs.

Active Directory isn't part of the standard Windows NT4 release. However, you can download an NT4-compatible implementation of version 1.0 of it from `http://www.microsoft.com`. This includes all the binaries for accessing it, plus the WinNT provider. It also claims to have an LDAP provider, but, at the time of writing – this is just a dummy.

Active Directory Services Interface

The **Active Directory Services Interface** (**ADSI**) is one of Microsoft's initiatives to impose a consistent component object layer on top of a number of disparate underlying services. We'll meet another one, Active Data Objects (ADO), when we look into Microsoft Transaction Server (MTS) later on. The name of the game is to extract whatever is common, whilst isolating the differences, so as to enable application writers to develop software that, with minimal tweaking, can be made to work on all the different varieties of underlying service.

The problem is that there are a number of conflicting alternatives to use for a directory service. More importantly, from the client's point of view, there are conflicting alternatives to use for a directory namespace structure and the associated access protocol. There is a standard client access protocol emerging called LDAP (which we will look at in greater detail later), but there are plenty of legacies to cope with in the meantime. Without Active Directory, any programs that used a directory would have to be implemented differently for each type of namespace structure, and changed every time a new namespace was added. Some of those implementations, moreover, would involve some pretty hideous network-specific API calls.

Let's take a look at how Active Directory reconciles the differences between all these alternatives, and offers the client a consistent, well-defined programming interface.

There are two sides to ADSI: **clients** and **providers**. Each directory service that is to be supported must have its own provider, which essentially acts as a gateway between the directory service's view of the world and that of Active Directory. If you want to develop a provider, there is an API (structured as a set of COM interfaces) to assist you in doing so. An ADSI client is a COM client like any other. ADSI includes a set of dual interface COM objects that allow you to use automation to access Active Directory. If performance is an issue, some providers also support a pure, vtable-based set of COM objects for directory searching.

The Active Directory structure looks something like this:

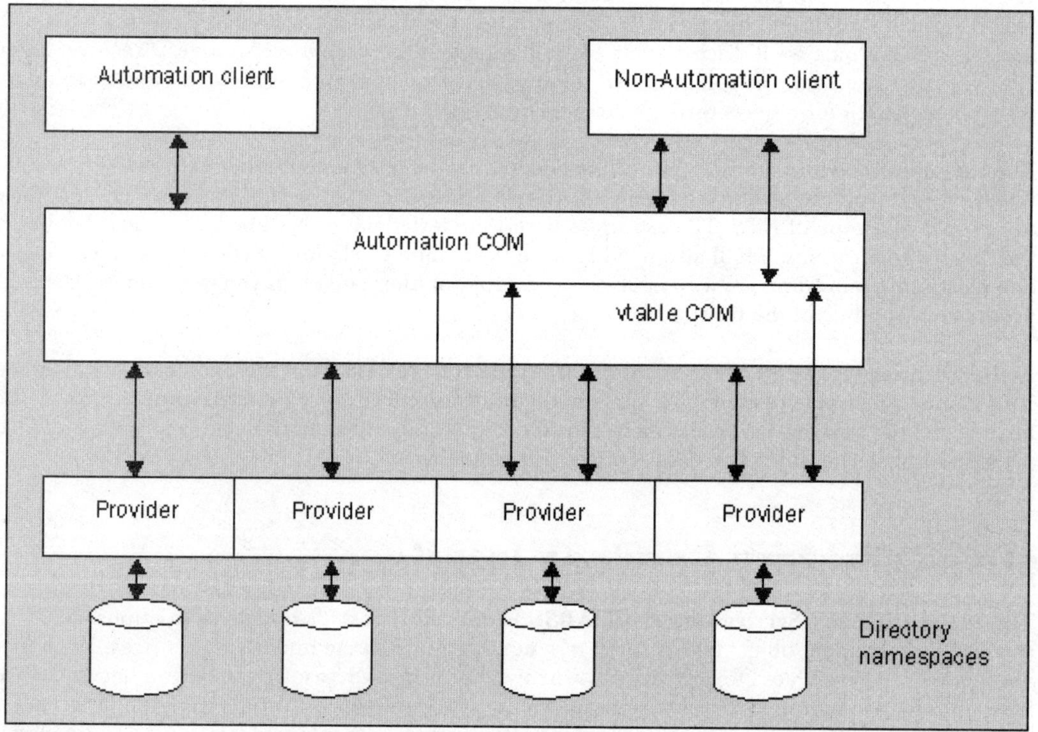

Let's start off by looking at the automation-compatible version of ADSI.

The ADSI Automation Interfaces

This is the point at which I have to issue a terminology ambiguity alert. The things that Active Directory holds information about are called **objects**. Unfortunately, we're not talking about COM objects or indeed, any other sort of object in the restricted sense that we OO freaks use. When we talk about an Active Directory object, we mean just about anything that can have information about it stored. Examples of such include:

- A computer
- A user
- A print queue

The ambiguity gets worse, alas, because Active Directory also has the concept of a **class**. Unsurprisingly, these classes have nothing to do with OOP classes. They are simply collections of characteristics that a number of objects have in common with each other.

Let's take a look at some of the attributes that each object in Active Directory must possess. First of all, it must have a **name**. It may also have a UUID. It must have a class. The class is very important, as this determines the characteristics of the object. One of the neat features of Active Directory, incidentally, is that class definitions are stored as objects (of class "Class"), just like any other.

What sort of characteristics can a class have, then? First of all, a class can either be a **container** or a **leaf**. The easiest analogy here is with folders and files. You can embed folders inside folders inside folders, until eventually you come to a file or files at the end. Similarly, containers can contain containers, which can contain containers, and so on, until you get to the leaves inside the final container. If an object belongs to a container class, it is a container; if it does not, it isn't. Where containers differ from folders is that being a container is simply an attribute of the class – so there can be several different types of container.

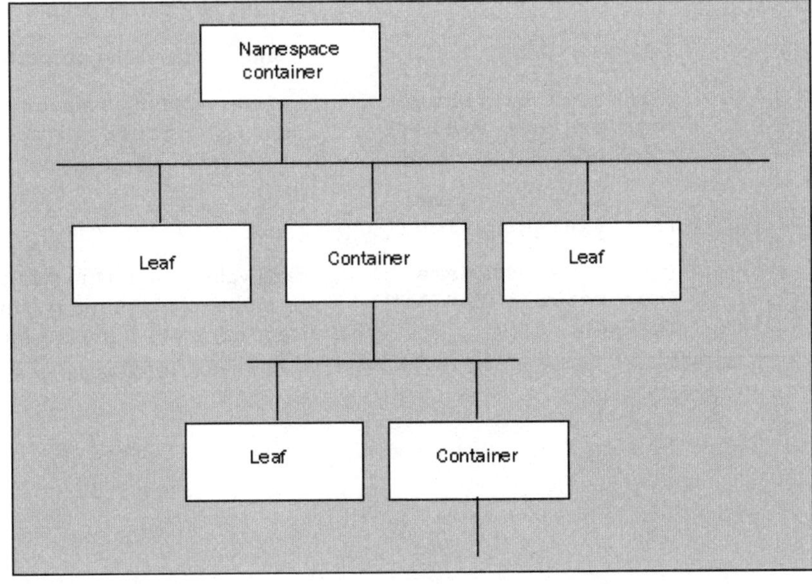

Classes also have a number of **properties**, which are attributes that every object belonging to that class can have. Some properties are **mandatory** and some are **optional**. All properties are, inevitably, Active Directory objects themselves. The most important characteristic of a property is its **syntax**. Again, syntax definitions are Active Directory objects as well. The class, property and syntax objects are all leaves in a special container, called the **schema**.

How does this map onto the ADSI object structure?

The IADs Interface

Every object in the Active Directory hierarchy must support the interface `IADs`. (You'll get used to that *Shift-AD-No shift-s* combination by the time you've finished with this chapter, believe me.) This interface has the following properties:

Property	Type	Description
`Name`	`BSTR`	Name of object
`AdsPath`	`BSTR`	Full directory path to object
`Class`	`BSTR`	Class of object
`GUID`	`BSTR`	GUID of object
`Parent`	`BSTR`	Directory path to parent container
`Schema`	`BSTR`	Directory path to schema object; we'll look at the schema a little later on

It also has the following methods:

Method	Parameters	Description
`GetInfo()`		Reload object with property values
`SetInfo()`		Commit changes to property values
`Get()`	`[in] BSTR bstrName, [out,retval] VARIANT *pvProp`	Get the value of a named property, invoking `GetInfo()` if none is found
`Put()`	`[in] BSTR bstrName, [in] VARIANT vProp`	Set the value of a property
`GetEx()`	`[in] BSTR bstrName, [out,retval] VARIANT *pvProp`	Gets values for a named single-valued or multi-valued property, invoking `GetInfoEx()` if none is found

Table Continued on Following Page

Method	Parameters	Description

`PutEx()`	`[in] LONG lnControlCode,`
	`[in] BSTR bstrName,`
	`[in] VARIANT vProp`
		Sets values for a named single- or multi-valued property; also, by setting `lnControlCode` to `ADS_PROPERTY_CLEAR`, you can remove a property altogether

`GetInfoEx()`	`[in] VARIANT vProps,` `[in] LONG lReserved`	This does the same as `GetInfo()`, except that it attempts to cut down on network traffic by specifying which properties are to be loaded, as an array of `BSTR`s.

The IADsContainer Interface

As well as supporting the **IADs** interface, containers must also support the **IADsContainer** interface. This has the following properties:

Property	Type	Description
`Count`	`long`	Count of the number of objects in the container
`_NewEnum`	`LPUNKNOWN`	Enumerator for objects in the container
`Filter`	`VARIANT`	This is an array of `BSTR`s, each of which is a filter specification, which either consists of a class name or a provider-specific specification
`Hints`	`VARIANT`	This is an array of properties that works in the same manner as the property array in `IADs::GetInfoEx()`.

It also has the following methods:

Method	Parameters	Description

`GetObject()`	`[in] BSTR bstrClass,`
	`[in] BSTR bstrRelativeName,`
	`[out, retval] LPDISPATCH *pNewObject`
		Get a dispatch pointer to the specified object within this container

`Create()`	`[in] BSTR bstrClass,`
	`[in] BSTR bstrRelativeName,`
	`[out, retval] LPDISPATCH *pNewObject`
		Create a new object with the specified class within this container (although it isn't written away until `IADs::SetInfo()` is called on the object)

Table Continued on Following Page

Method	Parameters	Description
`Delete()`	`[in] BSTR bstrClass, [in] BSTR bstrRelativeName`	Delete the specified object from this container
`CopyHere()`	`[in] BSTR bstrSource, [in] BSTR bstrNewName, [out, retval] LPDISPATCH* pNewObject`	Make a copy of the object specified by the source path in this container (but not across directory systems)
`MoveHere()`	`[in] BSTR bstrSource, [in] BSTR bstrNewName, [out, retval] LPDISPATCH* pNewObject`	Move the object specified by the source path to this container (but not across directory systems)

We'll see these interfaces in action when we use them in a practical example. So, let's take a breather from all these definitions and write some code. We've got a couple more interfaces to tackle yet, but we've got enough to get going.

Putting ADSI to Work

Let's create a new dialog-based MFC application using the MFC AppWizard. We'll start off by simply dumping out a list of all the objects in a container.

I've called the project **`DirManager`**. The main dialog is called **`IDD_DIRMANAGER_DIALOG`**, and its user interface is pretty simple. There are four buttons:

- **`IDC_ENUMERATE`** (the default)
- **`IDC_NEW`**
- **`IDC_CLASS`**
- **`IDOK`**

We'll see what these buttons do as we work our way through the application. There's a single-line edit field, **`IDC_PATH`**, which is used for inputting an Active Directory path, and a listbox, **`IDC_OBJECTS`**, which is used to display all the objects found starting from that path.

The dialog is shown below:

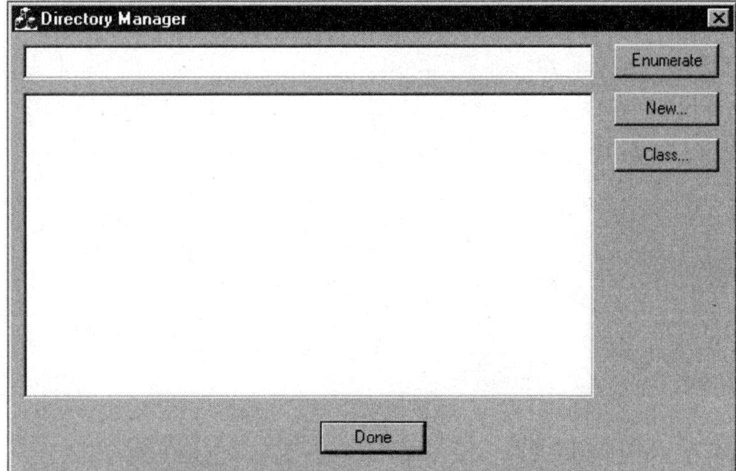

Don't worry about any of the buttons apart from Enumerate for the time being. We'll start with this one. The user should type the starting container in the edit field at the top, and when the Enumerate button is pressed, we'll enumerate all the objects in the specified container and output the names to the list box below. As well as their names, we're also going to display their Active Directory pathnames; this is a slightly sneaky way of making sure that our application has ready access to the pathnames, so we don't have to hold boring arrays of object interface pointers.

Since we'll be using Visual C++'s COM smart pointers, you'll need to include **comdef.h** in **StdAfx.h**, along with our simplified **typedef** macro:

```
#include <comdef.h>
#define SMARTPTR_TYPEDEF(x)    \
   typedef _com_ptr_t<_com_IIID<x, &IID_##x> > x##Ptr;
```

You'll need to reference one of the header files from the Platform SDK at the top of **CDirManagerDlg.cpp**, and also define **typedef**s for the interfaces that we'll be using:

```
#include "activeds.h"
SMARTPTR_TYPEDEF(IADsContainer);
SMARTPTR_TYPEDEF(IADs);
SMARTPTR_TYPEDEF(IADsProperty);
SMARTPTR_TYPEDEF(IADsSyntax);
```

Here is the first part of the code that gets executed when the user hits Enumerate:

```
void CDirManagerDlg::OnEnumerate()
{
```

```
CListBox* pObjects = static_cast<CListBox*>(GetDlgItem(IDC_OBJECTS));
pObjects->ResetContent();

// Get path from user, and get corresponding container object

CString csPath;
GetDlgItemText(IDC_PATH, csPath);

IADsContainerPtr pContainer;
HRESULT hr = ADsGetObject(_bstr_t(csPath), IID_IADsContainer,
   reinterpret_cast<void**>(&pContainer));

if (FAILED(hr))
{
   DisplayComError(_T("Failed to get object"), hr);
   return;
}
```

`ADsGetObject()` is a neat little helper function that gets hold of an ADSI interface on an object given its path. You might be interested to know that it does this by means of a **moniker**. (Remember the fun we had with those in Chapter 2?) **`ADsGetObject()`** actually uses our old friend **`MkParseDisplayName()`** to get hold of a moniker for the object based on its path, and then it calls **`BindToObject()`** to get hold of the ADSI interface. In this case, it's the ADSI provider itself that is implementing **`IParseDisplayName`**.

There are several other helper functions provided with ADSI. In fact, here are a couple more:

- **`ADsBuildEnumerator()`**
- **`ADsEnumerateNext()`**

We'll use these to enumerate all the objects in our container. (Note that we could use **`get__NewEnum()`** to get a new enumerator object, and then use the **`IEnumVARIANT`** interface of the object directly, but then why bother if ADSI is going to do the hard work for us?)

*In the call to **`ADsEnumerateNext()`**, the value of **`1`** for the second argument indicates that we want to fetch just one object at a time, and the **`NULL`** for the fourth argument indicates that we aren't interested in finding out how many were actually found (we're using the **`HRESULT`** for that).*

```
// Construct enumerator

IEnumVARIANTPtr pEnum;
hr = ADsBuildEnumerator(pContainer, &pEnum);

if (FAILED(hr))
{
   DisplayComError(_T("Failed to build enumerator"), hr);
   return;
}
```

```
// Go through list of children

while (true)
{
   _variant_t vChild;
   hr = ADsEnumerateNext(pEnum, 1, &vChild, NULL);
   if (hr != S_OK)
      break;

   // Get main ADS interface for child

   IADsPtr pChild;
   hr = vChild.pdispVal->QueryInterface(IID_IADs,
                               reinterpret_cast<void**>(&pChild));

   if (FAILED(hr))
   {
      DisplayComError(_T("Failed to QI for child"), hr);
      continue;
   }
```

At this point, we've got our **IADs** interface, so we can interrogate it for its name and path:

```
// Get name ...

BSTR bstrName;
pChild->get_Name(&bstrName);
CString csName = bstrName;
SysFreeString(bstrName);

// ... and path

BSTR bstrChildPath;
pChild->get_ADsPath(&bstrChildPath);
CString csChildPath = bstrChildPath;
SysFreeString(bstrChildPath);

// Construct entry for list and add to listbox

CString csItem;
csItem.Format("%s (%s)", static_cast<LPCSTR>(csName),
                             static_cast<LPCSTR>(csChildPath));

pObjects->AddString(csItem);
}
}
```

Path Names

This is all very well, but alert readers may have notice that we have skipped over the $64000 question, namely, what does an Active Directory path look like? And where do we start?

There are actually two forms of pathname supported. One of these is only provided for compatibility with the original **COM format** for display names. (We saw those in our discussion of monikers in Chapter 2.) For the record, a COM format pathname is basically like this:

```
@<Namespace>!<Provider-specific stuff>
```

However, we won't be using this format in our discussions here. The more usual format used in Active Directory is **URL format**. URL format pathnames look like this:

```
<Namespace>:
```

Or:

```
<Namespace>://<Provider-specific stuff>
```

Frankly, this gives the system plenty of scope. As you've probably realized by now, my preferred method of gaining insight into what the theory actually means in practice is to throw some code together, and see what it does. So let's run up our directory manager application, and see which paths it takes us down. We do need one major clue as to where to start –that the master namespace of all is called... oh, go on, guess. Yes, it's called "ADS". And that means that the mother of all pathnames is `ADS:`. Let's see what happens when we enumerate all the objects in the container starting at `ADS:` ...

The answer will depend on what sort of directories you have set up on your system, but I'm willing to bet that you have one called `WinNT:` and one called `LDAP:`, amongst others. For example, this screenshot is from an NT4 Enterprise Edition system:

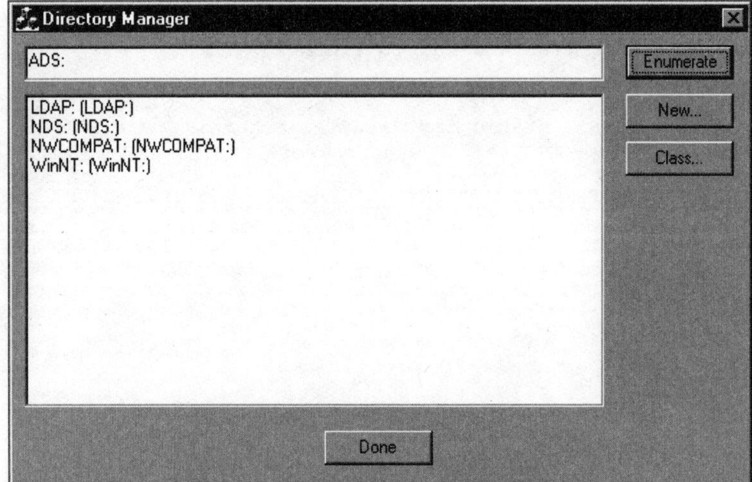

The result under the NT5 Beta 1 system looks very similar.

We'll steer clear of **LDAP:** for the time being, although we'll find out much more about it later. For now, we'll take a look at **WinNT:**. Let's make a small change to the application. Wouldn't it be good if you could double click on one of the items in the list box, and if it happens to represent a container, it re-starts the enumeration from there.
Here we go ...

```
void CDirManagerDlg::OnDblclkObjects()
{
   // Get currently selected item

   CListBox* pObjects = static_cast<CListBox*>(GetDlgItem(IDC_OBJECTS));
   int index = pObjects->GetCurSel();

   CString csObject;
   pObjects->GetText(index, csObject);

   // Extract pathname from object

   int start = csObject.Find('(');
   int end = csObject.Find(')');

   CString csPath = csObject.Mid(start + 1, end - start - 1);

   // Get hold of object interface

   IADsPtr pObject;
   HRESULT hr = ADsGetObject(_bstr_t(csPath), IID_IADs,
                             reinterpret_cast<void**>(&pObject));

   if (FAILED(hr))
   {
      DisplayComError(_T("Failed to get object"), hr);
      return;
   }
```

This time around, we don't know if we've got a container interface, so we'd better kick off with the straight object, and **QI** for the container ...

```
   // Find out if it's a container

   IADsContainerPtr pContainer;
   hr = pObject->QueryInterface(IID_IADsContainer,
                                reinterpret_cast<void**>(&pContainer));

   if (hr == S_OK)
   {
   // If it is, move this entry to main field and enumerate again

      SetDlgItemText(IDC_PATH, csPath);
      OnEnumerate();
      return;
   }

   ...
}
```

If the end result is a leaf object, rather than a container, we'll do something a bit different. But let's leave that for a while. Instead, let's try out the new code to see what happens as we delve into **`WinNT:`**.

If you double click on **`WinNT:`** to make that our enumeration start point, you should see a list of workspace or domain pathnames appear. For example, here's the NT4 enterprise edition one that I showed earlier:

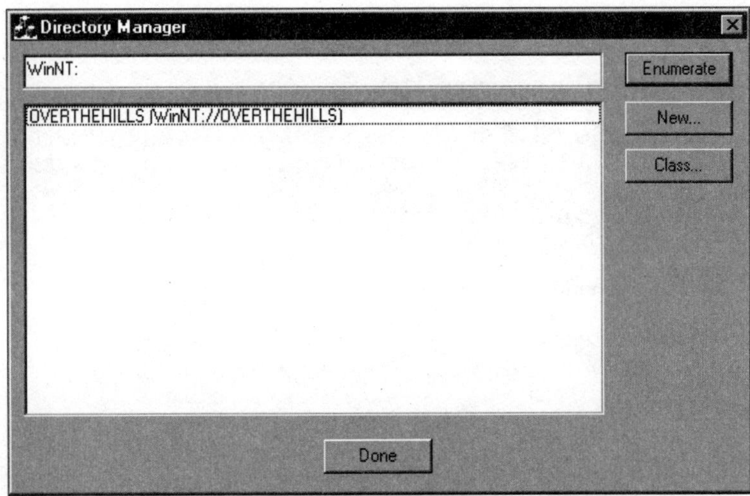

Double-click on this one, and we get a list of whole list of domain-specific objects:

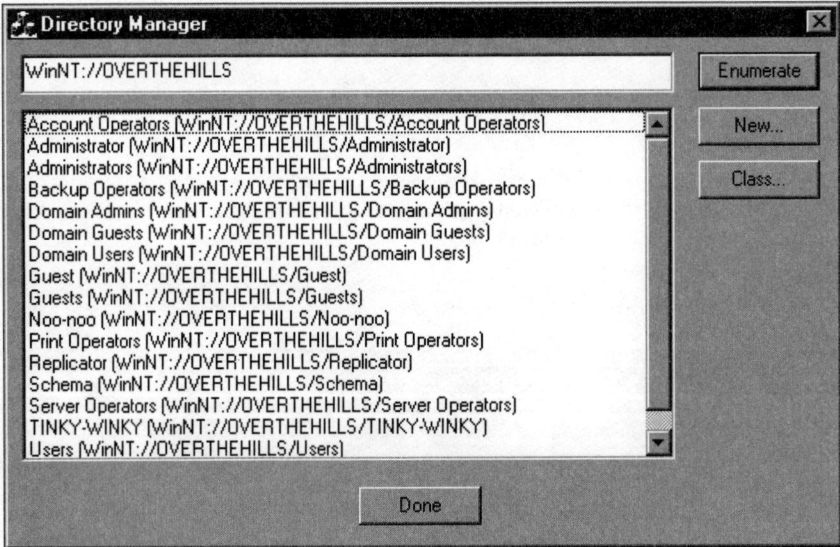

Take a look at some of these, such as **`Administrator`** (pathname **`WinNT://OVERTHEHILLS/Administrator`**). This sounds suspiciously like a user object, but how can we find out for sure? Wouldn't it be nice to be able to find out which class it's in? Even better, wouldn't it be fun to find out more about that class? Well, this is where that Class... button in our dialog box comes in, but more of that later. First, we're going to have to complete our tour of the main ADSI interfaces.

ADSI Classes

Remember that all objects in a directory have to support the **`IADs`** interface? Remember also that class definitions are stored as objects as well? No surprises, then, to find out that class definitions have to support an interface called **`IADsClass`**.

The IADsClass Interface

This is by far the most complex interface in ADSI, and it contains the following properties:

Property	Type	Description
`PrimaryInterface`	**`BSTR`**	UUID of optional provider-specific interface that can be used for direct access to this class's properties.
`CLSID`	**`BSTR`**	Class identifier of optional provider-specific associated COM object
`OID`	**`BSTR`**	Provider-specific Object Identifier defining the class
`Abstract`	**`VARIANT_BOOL`**	Abstract class flag; if set, this class cannot be instantiated, although other classes can be derived from it
`Auxiliary`	**`VARIANT_BOOL`**	Auxiliary class flag; if set, this class cannot be instantiated, although other classes can use it as a source of additional properties (see **`AuxDerivedFrom`** below)
`MandatoryProperties`	**`VARIANT`**	Array of names of mandatory properties
`OptionalProperties`	**`VARIANT`**	Array of names of optional properties

Table Continued on Following Page

Property	Type	Description
`NamingProperties`	`VARIANT`	Array of names of properties that go to make up the **Relative Distinguished Name** (**RDN**) for this class of object; the RDN is a set of properties that uniquely identifies the object
`DerivedFrom`	`VARIANT`	Array of pathnames of classes that this class is derived from
`AuxDerivedFrom`	`VARIANT`	Array of pathnames of auxiliary classes that this class is derived from
`PossibleSuperiors`	`VARIANT`	Array of pathnames of classes that can contain instances of this class
`Containment`	`VARIANT`	Array of pathnames of classes that can be contained within this class
`Container`	`VARIANT_BOOL`	Flag indicating whether or not objects of this class are containers
`HelpFileName`	`BSTR`	Name of help file (may not be implemented)
`HelpFileContext`	`long`	Help context identifier (may not be implemented)

It also has a single method, which may optionally be implemented:

Method	Parameters	Description
`Qualifiers()`	`[out, retval] IADsCollection **ppQualifiers`	Returns collection of objects describing additional qualifiers

We needn't concern ourselves too much with some of the more obscure features of this interface for the time being. Instead, let's just pick out a couple for special attention:

- `PrimaryInterface`
- `OID`

Firstly, take a look at that `PrimaryInterface` property. For a lot of object classes, there is a further interface available to allow easy access to the properties contained therein. For example, all objects of class `User` implement a further ADSI interface called `IADsUser`, which has about three pages of properties like `FullName` and `FirstName` and so on. If you want to use these, I recommend that you take a look at the Microsoft documentation for the interface in question.

The next interesting property is **OID**, the Object Identifier. We won't be seeing any value in this slot for the **WinNT:** namespace, but it will acquire greater significance later on, when we look at LDAP. This is a universally unique identifier for the class. Unfortunately, it's not a UUID as we have come to know and love them, but rather a sequence of numbers allocated by a central standards authority. I'll come back to this a little later on.

By far the most important *properties* in the interface are, of course, the ... er ... properties themselves, mandatory and optional. We're in severe danger of terminology overlap here, and there is a shift in the more recently developed interfaces towards the use of the term **attribute** rather than property. However, provided we keep our wits about us, we shouldn't get too confused. These two lists of properties (or attributes) effectively define every object that is a member of this class. Going back to our **User** class example, we have things like **FullName**, **Description**, **LastLogin** and so on.

The IADsProperty Interface

The next question we should ask ourselves is how are properties defined? I mentioned earlier that they were held as Active Directory objects, and you won't be in the least bit surprised when I present to you the **IADsProperty** interface, which provides access to these objects. This interface has these properties (that word again):

Property	Type	Description
OID	BSTR	Unique Object Identifier
Syntax	BSTR	Syntax pathname
MaxRange	long	Maximum number of values (multi-valued properties only)
MinRange	long	Minimum number of values (multi-valued properties only)
MultiValued	VARIANT_BOOL	Multi-valued property flag

Like the **IADsClass** interface, it also has a single method, which may optionally be implemented:

Method	Parameters	Description
Qualifiers()	[out, retval] IADsCollection **ppQualifiers	Returns collection of objects describing additional qualifiers

This is pretty self-explanatory, apart from that **Syntax** property. And that brings us to the last interface in the sequence, **IADsSyntax**.

The IADsSyntaxInterface

This interface must be implemented by all Active directory syntax objects. This is very simple, as it contains only one property:

Property	Type	Description
`OleAutoDataType`	`long`	This is the OLE automation data type representing this syntax (for example, **VT_BSTR**, **VT_I4** and so on). Syntaxes that can't be mapped to OLE types are mapped to **VT_U1 | VT_ARRAY**.

Using ADSI Classes

I think we should get back to our code, and dig a little deeper into the **IADsClass** interface. We'll attach some code to our Class... button so that it will give the class details of the currently selected object. For this to work, we need to have an object selected, so we should have the button disabled initially and only enable it when the user selects an object:

```
void CDirManagerDlg::OnSelchangeObjects()
{
   // Object selected - enable "Class" button
   GetDlgItem(IDC_CLASS)->EnableWindow(TRUE);
}
```

We'll also disable the button at the end of **OnEnumerate()**:

```
         pObjects->AddString(csItem);
   }

   // Disable "Class" button, as no item selected
   GetDlgItem(IDC_CLASS)->EnableWindow(FALSE);
}
```

This is what actually happens when we click on the Class... button:

```
void CDirManagerDlg::OnClass()
{
   // Get currently selected item

   CListBox* pObjects = static_cast<CListBox*>(GetDlgItem(IDC_OBJECTS));
   int index = pObjects->GetCurSel();

   CString csObject;
   pObjects->GetText(index, csObject);

   // Extract pathname

   int start = csObject.Find('(');
   int end = csObject.Find(')');
```

```
    CString csPath = csObject.Mid(start + 1, end - start - 1);

    // Get object details

    IADsPtr pObject;
    HRESULT hr = ADsGetObject(_bstr_t(csPath), IID_IADs,
                                    reinterpret_cast<void**>(&pObject));

    if (FAILED(hr))
    {
       DisplayComError(_T("Failed to get object"), hr);
       return;
    }

    // Get class path

    BSTR bstrClassPath;
    hr = pObject->get_Schema(&bstrClassPath);

    if (FAILED(hr))
       AfxMessageBox(_T("No class path defined"));

    else
    {
    // Pass class path in to class dialog

       CString csClassPath = bstrClassPath;
       SysFreeString(bstrClassPath);

       CClassDlg dlg(csPath, csClassPath);
       dlg.DoModal();
    }
}
```

The critical line is that call to **get_Schema()**, which gets hold of the pathname to our class object. In certain cases, there won't be a class object; for example, the **Schema** itself doesn't have a class, and neither do any of the **Properties** defined in it.

We pass the class pathname, along with the pathname of our selected object, into a second dialog, **CClassDlg**. The dialog looks like this:

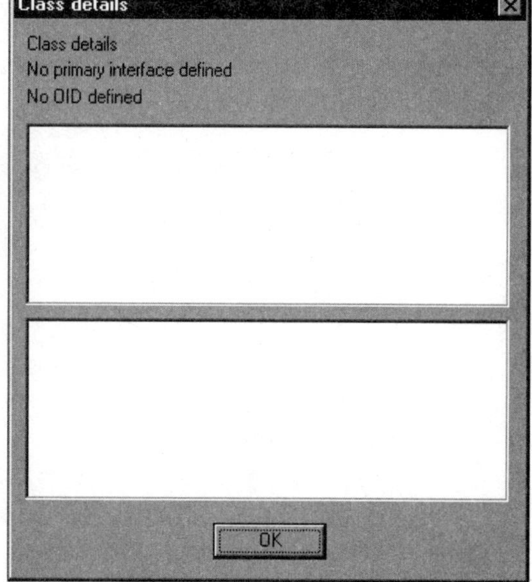

We have two list boxes:

- **IDC_MANDATORY** for mandatory properties
- **IDC_OPTIONAL** for optional properties

There are three static text fields at the top of the dialog:

- **IDC_CLASS**
- **IDC_PRIMARY**()
- **IDC_OID**

Make these three as wide as will fit on the dialog (we've got a UUID to fit in one of them!). Inside the class dialog, we extract the class information, like this:

```
BOOL CClassDlg::OnInitDialog()
{
   CDialog::OnInitDialog();

   // Get hold of object from path passed in

   IADsPtr pObject;

   if (m_csObjectPath != _T(""))
   {
      HRESULT hr = ADsGetObject(_bstr_t(m_csObjectPath), IID_IADs,
         reinterpret_cast<void**>(&pObject));

      if (FAILED(hr))
      {
         DisplayComError(_T("Failed to get object"), hr);
         EndDialog(IDOK);
         return TRUE;
      }
   }
```

This dialog can also be used to get the class details if we double-click on a class item in the main list, so we might not have an object path set up.

```
   // Get hold of class from path passed in
   IADsClassPtr pClass;
   HRESULT hr = ADsGetObject(_bstr_t(m_csClassPath), IID_IADsClass,
      reinterpret_cast<void**>(&pClass));

   if (FAILED(hr))
   {
      DisplayComError(_T("Failed to get class object"), hr);
      EndDialog(IDOK);
      return TRUE;
   }
```

Once we have got a pointer to the class interface, we can extract a few of its properties:

```
// Get hold of class name and determine whether or not it's a container

BSTR bstrName;
pClass->get_Name(&bstrName);

CString csName = bstrName;
SysFreeString(bstrName);

VARIANT_BOOL bContainer;
pClass->get_Container(&bContainer);

// Format header and output to form

CString csHeader;

if (bContainer == VARIANT_TRUE)
  csHeader.Format("Class <%s> (container)",
                                        static_cast<LPCSTR>(csName));
else
  csHeader.Format("Class <%s> (not a container)",
                  static_cast<LPCSTR>(csName));

SetDlgItemText(IDC_CLASS, csHeader);

// Find out primary interface name and output to form

BSTR bstrPrimary;
hr = pClass->get_PrimaryInterface(&bstrPrimary);

if (hr == S_OK)
{
   CString csPrimary = bstrPrimary;
   SysFreeString(bstrPrimary);

   csHeader.Format("Primary i/f: %s", static_cast<LPCSTR>(csPrimary));

   SetDlgItemText(IDC_PRIMARY, csHeader);
}

// Find out OID and output to form

BSTR bstrOID;
hr = pClass->get_OID(&bstrOID);

if (hr == S_OK)
{
   CString csOID = bstrOID;
   SysFreeString(bstrOID);

   csHeader.Format("OID: %s", static_cast<LPCSTR>(csOID));

   SetDlgItemText(IDC_OID, csHeader);
}
```

And now we can look at the object's mandatory and optional property settings. They get returned to us as an array of **VARIANTs** ...

```
    // Get list of mandatory properties

    _variant_t vProps;
    hr = pClass->get_MandatoryProperties(&vProps);

    if (FAILED(hr))
    {
       DisplayComError(_T("Failed to get mandatory properties"), hr);
       EndDialog(IDOK);
       return TRUE;
    }

    // Output to screen

    OutputArray(vProps, pObject, IDC_MANDATORY);

    // Get list of mandatory properties

    hr = pClass->get_OptionalProperties(&vProps);

    if (FAILED(hr))
    {
       DisplayComError(_T("Failed to get optional properties"), hr);
       EndDialog(IDOK);
       return TRUE;
    }

    // Output to screen

    OutputArray(vProps, pObject, IDC_OPTIONAL);

    return TRUE;  // return TRUE unless you set the focus to a control
                  // EXCEPTION: OCX Property Pages should return FALSE
}
```

Here we go through the slightly tedious process of extracting our property values from the incoming **VARIANT** array:

```
void CClassDlg::OutputArray(const VARIANT& vData, IADs* pObject, int nID)
{
    // Extract safe array from incoming variant

    COleSafeArray array(vData);

    long lBound;
    array.GetLBound(1, &lBound);

    long uBound;
    array.GetUBound(1, &uBound);

    int nItem = uBound - lBound;
```

```
VARIANT HUGEP* pVData;
array.AccessData(reinterpret_cast<void**>(&pVData));

// Cycle through array, outputting property names and values to screen
for (int item = 0; item < nItem; item++)
{
   CString csProp;
   csProp = pVData[item].bstrVal;
```

Now we've got the property name, we can see if it's got a value for the current object:

```
      CString csItem;

      if (pObject)
      {
         _variant_t vValue;
         HRESULT hr = pObject->Get(pVData[item].bstrVal, &vValue);

         if (hr == S_OK)
         {
            CString csValue;

            switch (vValue.vt)
            {
               case VT_BSTR:
                  csValue = vValue.bstrVal;
                  break;

               case VT_I4:
                  csValue.Format("%ld", vValue.lVal);
                  break;

               case VT_DATE:
                  csValue = COleDateTime(vValue).Format();
                  break;

               default:
                  csValue.Format("type %d data", vValue.vt);
                  break;
            }

            csItem.Format("%s = %s", static_cast<LPCSTR>(csProp),
                        static_cast<LPCSTR>(csValue));
         }

         else
            csItem.Format("%s (unset)", static_cast<LPCSTR>(csProp));
      }

      else
         csItem = csProp;

      static_cast<CListBox*>(GetDlgItem(nID))->AddString(csItem);
   }

   array.UnaccessData();
}
```

Finally, we need two alternative constructors, one where we're just getting information on a class, and one where we have an object path defined:

```
CClassDlg::CClassDlg(const CString& csPath, CWnd* pParent /*=NULL*/)
   : CDialog(CClassDlg::IDD, pParent)
{
   //{{AFX_DATA_INIT(CClassDlg)
      // NOTE: the ClassWizard will add member initialization here
   //}}AFX_DATA_INIT

   m_csObjectPath = _T("");
   m_csClassPath = csPath;
}

CClassDlg::CClassDlg(const CString& csObjectPath,
                     const CString& csClassPath, CWnd* pParent /*=NULL*/)
   : CDialog(CClassDlg::IDD, pParent)
{

   m_csObjectPath = csObjectPath;
   m_csClassPath = csClassPath;
}
```

We'll also need to add a couple of private members to the **CClassDlg** class:

```
   CString m_csObjectPath;
   CString m_csClassPath;
```

If we now build and run the application, and get to the list that we had before, let's see what happens if we select a typical object (say the one that we saw before, with pathname **WinNT://OVERTHEHILLS/Administrator**), and click on the Class... button, we see something like this:

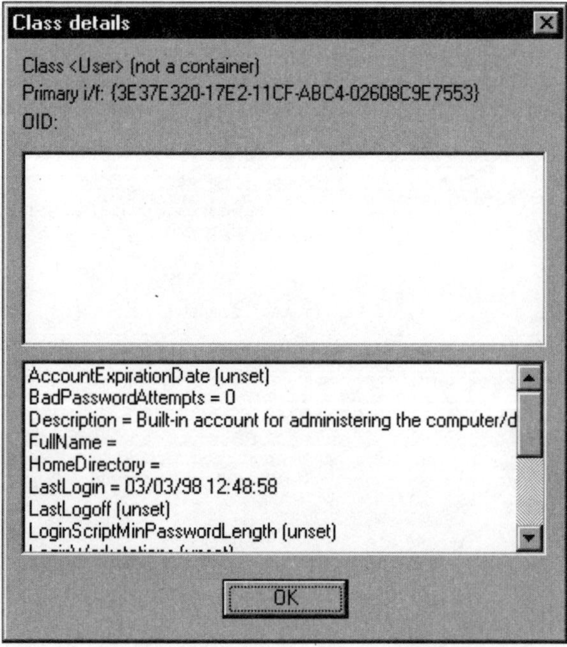

Here we see one or two recognizable features in the optional properties list, such as the description that we see in the standard user administration tool, and the details of last log-in time and so on. Notice that UUID for the primary interface; if you look at the type library for **IADs**, you'll find that it is indeed the IID for the **IADsUser** interface.

OK, so we can extract the class details for an Active Directory object. But where are these class definitions kept, and, furthermore, can we add some of our own?

Let's put the second question to one side for a moment and concentrate on the first. In the **WinNT:** namespace, the class definitions are kept in the **Schema** container. Run up the **DirManager** application again, and take a look at the list that we found our **Administrator** object in. If you look here, you should find another object called **Schema**. (If you try to get the class for this, by the way, you'll find that – as I mentioned earlier – the class pathname isn't defined.) Double-click on this item to open up the container, and you should see a whole list of objects, like this:

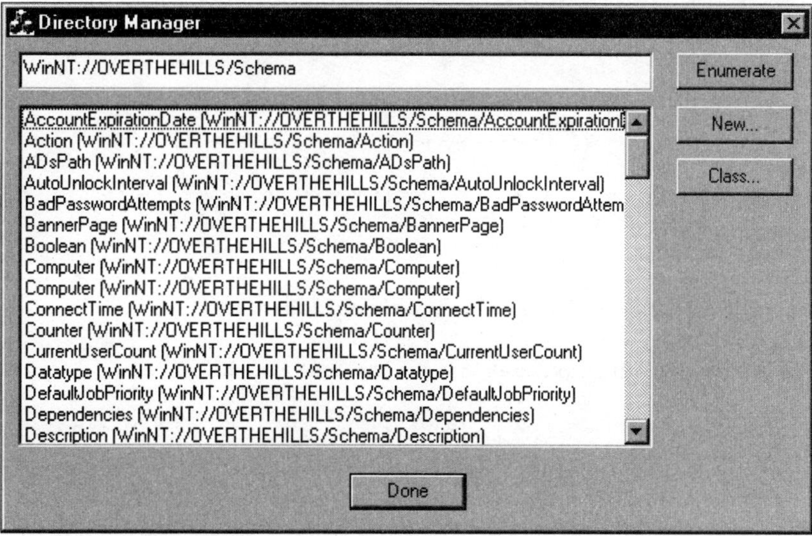

All of these objects are classes, properties or syntaxes. At this point, we can finish off the code executed on the double-click of an item in the box. Let's do something different when we choose a leaf rather than a container; if the object is a class, we'll output the class definition using the same dialog as for displaying the class details:

```
// Get class type for item

BSTR bstrClass;
pObject->get_Class(&bstrClass);
CString csClass = bstrClass;
SysFreeString(bstrClass);

// If it's a class, set up class path and invoke class details dialog

if (csClass == _T("Class"))
{
   CClassDlg dlg(csPath);
   dlg.DoModal();
}
```

If it's a property, we can show the syntax instead:

```
      else
      {
         CString csDetails;

         // Otherwise, if it's a property, get syntax and output to user

         if (csClass == _T("Property"))
         {
            IADsPropertyPtr pProperty;
            hr = pObject->QueryInterface(IID_IADsProperty,
                                          reinterpret_cast<void**>(&pProperty));
            if (FAILED(hr))
            {
               DisplayComError(_T("Failed to QI for property interface"), hr);
               return;
            }

            BSTR bstrSyntax;
            pProperty->get_Syntax(&bstrSyntax);
            CString csSyntax = bstrSyntax;
            SysFreeString(bstrSyntax);

            csDetails.Format("Property with syntax %s",
                             static_cast<LPCSTR>(csSyntax));
         }
```

And if it's a syntax, on the other hand, let's show the OLE data type:

```
         // If it's a syntax, get data type and output to user

         else if (csClass == _T("Syntax"))
         {
            IADsSyntaxPtr pSyntax;
            hr = pObject->QueryInterface(IID_IADsSyntax,
                                            reinterpret_cast<void**>(&pSyntax));

            if (FAILED(hr))
            {
               DisplayComError(_T("Failed to QI for syntax interface"), hr);
               return;
            }

            long lType;
            pSyntax->get_OleAutoDataType(&lType);

            csDetails.Format("Syntax of type %ld", lType);
         }
```

Finally, if it's a plain old object, let's just show the class type:

```
        // Otherwise, it's just an object - output its class

        else
           csDetails.Format("Object with class %s",
                        static_cast<LPCSTR>(csClass));

        AfxMessageBox(csDetails);
    }

}
```

Let's try this code out with some of the objects in the **Schema** folder. We can see, to take just a few examples, that **Computer** is a class object, **OperatingSystem** is a property of syntax **String** and **String** is a syntax of type **8** (which turns out to be **VT_BSTR** – so no surprises there). Notice, incidentally, that there isn't a class object in the list called **Class** – I was quite disappointed to find out that it's hard-wired, but I suppose you'd get into a hideous self-referential loop if it wasn't.

Before we leave the **WinNT:** namespace and dive into LDAP, we've one more important topic to cover. It's time we did something with that New... button.

Adding Objects

Actually, adding objects is simplicity itself. The code that sits underneath the New... button in our application simply passes the current pathname to a new dialog:

```
void CDirManagerDlg::OnNew()
{
   // Get current container path

   CString csPath;
   GetDlgItemText(IDC_PATH, csPath);

   // Pass in to new object dialog

   CNewObjectDlg dlg(csPath);
   dlg.DoModal();

   // Re-enumerate in case something has been added

   OnEnumerate();
}
```

The dialog, which will appear when the New... button is clicked, looks like this:

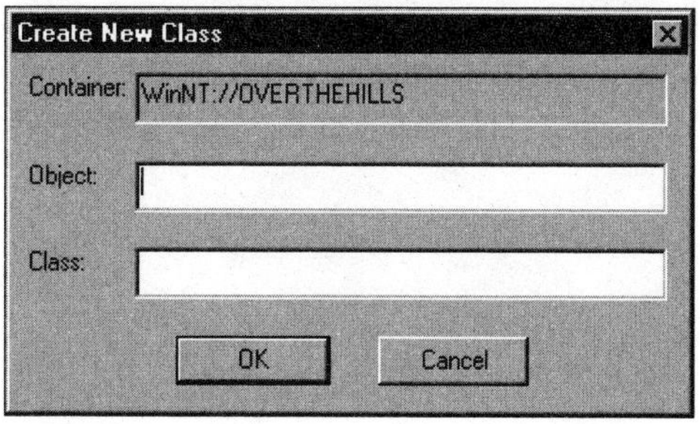

Create New Class

Container: WinNT://OVERTHEHILLS

Object:

Class:

OK Cancel

The edit boxes have been called **IDC_CONTAINER**, **IDC_OBJECT** and **IDC_CLASS** respectively. The code for the **OnInitDialog()** method is shown below:

```
BOOL CNewObjectDlg::OnInitDialog()
{
   CDialog::OnInitDialog();

   // Outputting incoming container name

   SetDlgItemText(IDC_CONTAINER, m_csContainer);

   // Get container object

   HRESULT hr = ADsGetObject (_bstr_t(m_csContainer), IID_IADsContainer,
      reinterpret_cast<void**>(&m_pContainer));

   if (FAILED (hr))
   {
      DisplayComError(_T("Failed to get container"), hr);
      EndDialog (IDCANCEL);
      return TRUE;
   }

   return TRUE;  // return TRUE unless you set the focus to a control
                 // EXCEPTION: OCX Property Pages should return FALSE
}
```

Here's the constructor:

```
CNewObjectDlg::CNewObjectDlg(const CString& csContainer,
                                    CWnd* pParent /*=NULL*/)
   : CDialog(CNewObjectDlg::IDD, pParent)
{
   //{{AFX_DATA_INIT(CNewObjectDlg)
      // NOTE: the ClassWizard will add member initialization here
   //}}AFX_DATA_INIT

   m_csContainer = csContainer;
}
```

This simply initializes the two private members in **CNewObjectDlg**:

```
CString m_csContainer;
IADsContainerPtr m_pContainer;
```

And this is the business end of the code:

```
void CNewObjectDlg::OnOK()
{
   // Get name and class of new object
   CString csObject;
   GetDlgItemText(IDC_OBJECT, csObject);

   CString csClass;
   GetDlgItemText(IDC_CLASS, csClass);

   // Create new object with specified class in this container
   IDispatchPtr pDispatch;
   HRESULT hr = m_pContainer->Create(_bstr_t(csClass), _bstr_t(csObject),
                                     &pDispatch);
   if (FAILED(hr))
   {
      DisplayComError(_T("Failed to create new object"), hr);
      return;
   }

   // Get main ADS interface for new object
   IADsPtr pNewObject;
   hr = pDispatch->QueryInterface(IID_IADs,
                                  reinterpret_cast<void**>(&pNewObject));
   if (FAILED(hr))
   {
      DisplayComError(_T("Failed to QI for IADs"), hr);
      return;
   }

   // Confirm settings
   pNewObject->SetInfo();

   CDialog::OnOK();
}
```

The critical points here are the use of the **`Create()`** method on the **`IADsContainer`** interface to create our new object with the required class, and the use of the **`SetInfo()`** method on the **`IADs`** interface of the new object in order to commit the change to the directory. In fact, we haven't set up any of the properties of the object in this implementation, but if we choose our object carefully, it won't matter. Try, for example, creating an object of class **`User`** with name, say, **`Wallace`**. Lo and behold, it appears in the list when we complete the dialog. Moreover, it's still there when we look in the user administration facility. I should perhaps add that this will only work if the current user has sufficient privilege to add users – which is at least reassuring from the security point of view!

Now for the big question: can you create new classes? In other words, can you extend the schema? Well, in theory, all you have to do is create an object of type "Class", or indeed "Property" or "Syntax". The trouble is that if you try this, you run up against an error in the **`WinNT:`** namespace. In LDAP, it's a different matter altogether, as we'll see shortly.

Moving to LDAP

Trawling through the **WinNT:** namespace as we have been, it may have occurred to you that it's a bit, well, *flat.* There's very little use made of containers, for example, the schema is limited, and it's unlikely to scale very well when we move towards large distributed systems – we're talking about systems requiring directories of millions of objects here. Microsoft has realized this, and is now making a major push towards the **Lightweight Directory Access Protocol**, or **LDAP**. Now, who said that Microsoft ignores existing non-proprietary standards and persists with its own? Actually, I can think of just two proprietary standards that Microsoft has stuck to in the face of pressure from the rest of the software industry: *Windows* and *COM.* Everywhere else the move has been towards implementing standards such as LDAP. Mind you, the proprietary standards that they have kept to aren't at all bad. Say what you like about Windows, but COM is a thing of pure beauty ... but then we all knew that, didn't we?

LDAP was developed at the University of Michigan as a front-end to the more complex X500 directory protocol, and was formalised in 1995 in RFC 1777. If you want to do some more extensive reading, the best place to start is the University of Michigan's LDAP page, located at URL `http://www.umich.edu/~dirsvcs/ldap/`. This has got links to just about every resource to do with LDAP.

There are five distinct aspects to the LDAP definition:

- The Data Model,
- The Organizational Model
- The Security Model
- The Functional Model
- The Topological Model

The **Data Model** defines the syntax of the data in the directory. The model is centered around **entries**, which are composed of **attributes**; each attribute has a **type** and one or more **values**. Remember what I said about ADSI properties being increasingly referred to as attributes these days? Guess why.

The **Organizational Model** defines how the data is organized in the directory. Entries are organized in a **Directory Information Tree** and divided among servers in a geographical and organizational distribution. Each entry has a **Distinguished Name (DN)**, each component of which is called a **Relative Distinguished Name (RDN)**. We'll see some of these very soon.

The **Security Model** defines how the information in the directory is accessed in a secure manner. This is based on the **Kerberos** authentication model, which we'll be looking at briefly in Chapter 9.

The **Functional Model** defines the operations for querying and modifying the directory. This defines how to carry out such operations as adding entries, deleting entries, modifying entries and making queries. There is in fact an entire LDAP 'C' API specified and supported by Microsoft, which you can use in place of ADSI if you're feeling perverse. (ADSI's a whole lot more straightforward!)

The **Topological Model** defines how the directory service integrates with other directory services to form a global internet-based directory service. One or more LDAP servers together make up the directory tree. If an LDAP client makes a request of an LDAP server, and that server can't satisfy the request, it passes the request on to another that can. All this is completely transparent to the client – in marked contrast to the WinNT style of directory. Note also that the remote server doesn't have to be running Windows, provided that it supports LDAP.

One word of terminology here – an LDAP *server* is a piece of software that implements the LDAP protocol. An LDAP *provider*, on the other hand, implements the OLE DB-based ADSI provider protocol on one side, and LDAP on the other; it's a gateway between ADSI and LDAP.

> *Note that in order to run the rest of the examples in this chapter, you'll need to be running the NT5 beta.*

If you run our **DirManager** application again, and explore the **LDAP:** namespace, you'll notice some significant differences. First of all, the pathnames have a different format. For example, the first container that you'll come to under **LDAP:** has a pathname like this:
LDAP://DC=OverTheHills,O=Internet

(Depending on which version of Active Directory you're using, you may or may not see the **O=Internet** part – this is being phased out).

The part to the right of the **LDAP:** namespace identifier is referred to as the distinguished name (or DN), and it identifies the domain that holds the object, as well as the complete path to reach the object through the hierarchy of containers. You read the DN from right to left. Typical components in a DN are organizations (identified by **O=**), domain components (identified by **DC=**) and common names (identified by **CN=**). If your domain looks like, say, **microsoft.com**, you'll have two segments in your DNs: **CN=microsoft,CN=COM**.

Domains can be linked together into domain trees and forests by trust relationships. Here's a typical transitive domain trust relationship:

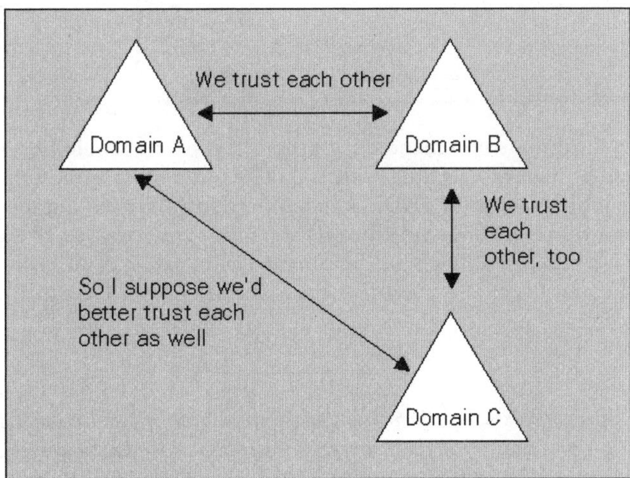

Let's dig a little further into our **`LDAP:`** namespace by double-clicking on the entry for the domain component. Here we come across our second major difference: the namespace is fully containerized! There are containers here for entities like **`Users`**, **`Computers`** and so on. One curious thing, though: the schema isn't part of the standard tree; in the **`LDAP:`** implementation, the schema is hidden – we'll see where in a little while.

If we open up the **`Users`** container, we get to an administrator object, similar to the one we found earlier in the **`WinNT:`** namespace. This time, however, it's got a pathname of: **`LDAP://CN=Administrator,CN=Users,DC=OverTheHills,O=Internet`**.

What else is different about it?

If you click on the Class... button to display its properties, the most striking thing is the sheer number of properties that have been specified for this class (of type **`user`**). Here is a screen shot of my ADS object for user **`Administrator`**:

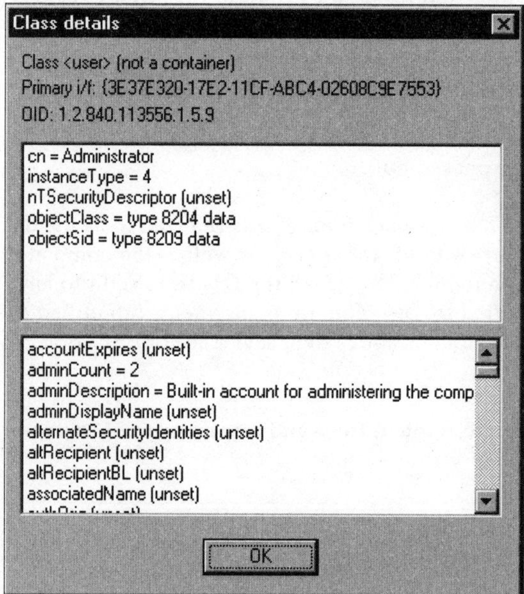

As you can see, we've now got some mandatory properties, plus a whole host of optional properties (I've only shown some of the ones starting with 'a'!). The other interesting thing is that our user class now has an Object Identifier (or OID). Remember that OIDs are unique identifiers, which are issued by international standards organizations in much the same way as IP addresses. If you explore further, you'll probably notice that the **`container`** class has an OID of 1.2.840.113556.1.3.23, and that the **`computer`** class has an OID of 1.2.840.113556.1.3.30, which suggests that Microsoft have probably been allocated the space 1.2.840.113556 in the universal ISO-ITU OID tree.

> *The fact that we have got this far without changing a single line of code in our* **`DirManager`** *application (which was – quite frankly – a pretty rudimentary demonstration of ADSI) is, I think, pretty impressive. It is a testament to the way in which ADSI has successfully hidden from us the provider-specific aspects of the two namespaces that we have been exploring.*

Let's consider the implications of these OIDs. The OID structure in LDAP is about nothing more than setting up an environment in which any type of object in the entire world can be uniquely parameterised. You could, in theory, put together all the LDAP directory systems in the world, using one single schema, and they would all work together without any class ambiguity! It's an astonishingly powerful concept, and ever so slightly scary. (For some reason, the *SkyNet* system in the *Terminator* films comes to my mind whenever I think of this ...)

However, a significant corollary of this is that you really should think twice before extending the schema. The chances are, unless your object class is really obscure and unusual, there's something already out there that will do. If you really must, then OK, go ahead and contact your friendly neighborhood ISO, get your OID space and set up your own internal standards organization to manage it within your corporation. Once you've set up the logistics of managing the allocation of OIDs, creating them is child's play using ADSI. It's just a question of creating new objects in the schema container using the ADSI methods that we've already encountered.

Ah! The schema container. In the **LDAP:** namespace, this is hidden away in the highly non-standard path of **LDAP://schema**. If you take a look at it using our sample application, you'll find all the usual suspects, plus a host of others. All the properties are there, too. In **LDAP:**, however, the syntax objects are built in – you can't change these or add to them. Here's a screen shot of the start of the schema:

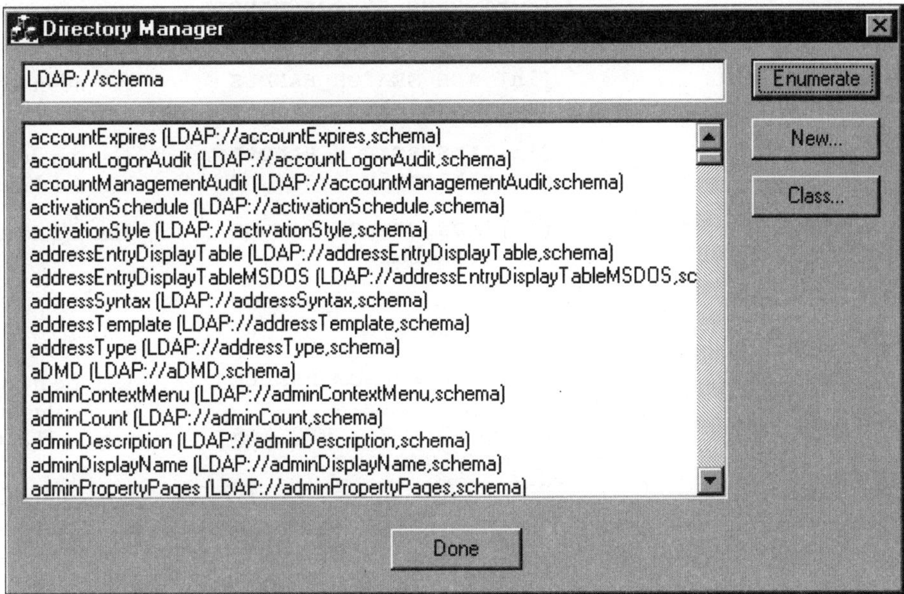

Rapid Searching

One of the advertised features of LDAP, as opposed to the standard Windows directory, is the ability to make highly efficient searches. The way to use this facility in ADSI is via one of the pure COM interfaces available, called `IDirectorySearch`. This interface has the following methods:

Method	Parameters	Description
`SetSearchPreference()`	`[in] PADS_SEARCHPREF_INFO pSearchPrefs, [in] DWORD dwNumPrefs`	Set up search preferences; this enables you to define time limits for the search, size limits, and so on
`ExecuteSearch()`	`[in] LPWSTR pszSearchFilter, [in] LPWSTR __RPC_FAR *pAttributeNames, [in] DWORD dwNumberAttributes, [out] PADS_SEARCH_HANDLE phSearchResult`	Start search; the filter specifies which properties are to be searched for, in LDAP format-
`AbandonSearch()`	`[in] ADS_SEARCH_HANDLE hSearchResult`	Abandon a search
`GetFirstRow()`	`[in] ADS_SEARCH_HANDLE hSearchResult`	Get the first row of retrieved data
`GetNextRow()`	`[in] ADS_SEARCH_HANDLE hSearchResult`	Get the next row
`GetPreviousRow()`	`[in] ADS_SEARCH_HANDLE hSearchResult`	Get the previous row
`GetNextColumnName()`	`[in] ADS_SEARCH_HANDLE hSearchHandle, [out] LPWSTR __RPC_FAR *ppszColumnName`	Get the name of the next column of retrieved data

Table Continued on Following Page

Method	Parameters	Description
`GetColumn()`	`[in] ADS_SEARCH_HANDLE hSearchResult, [in] LPWSTR szColumnName, [out] PADS_SEARCH_COLUMN pSearchColumn`	Get the details of the property settings for the specified column into a column descriptor
`FreeColumn()`	`[in] PADS_SEARCH_COLUMN pSearchColumn`	Free a column descriptor
`CloseSearchHandle()`	`ADS_SEARCH_HANDLE hSearchResult`	Release search resources

Much of this style of searching has strayed in from OLE DB. This is hardly surprising, as ADSI providers are OLE DB providers. This incidentally means that there is an OLE DB interface to the Active Directory database as well, but that's outside the scope of this book.

The idea is that you specify a search by saying what you are looking for (rows), and optimize it by saying what properties you're actually interested in (columns). The search then returns you a grid full of data, which you can then navigate your way around using the methods provided.

This sounds fine, but how do we get **`IDirectorySearch`** in the first place? Easy! It's just another interface implemented by **`ADs`** objects. Let's take it for a spin, and write ourselves a little search application.

Once again, we'll use MFC (and COM smart pointers). We need to get the user to specify the start path for the search, the search filter, and the list of properties to fetch. The dialog looks like this:

We have two edit fields at the top of the dialog:

- **IDC_PATH** – the user will use this box to specify the start path for the search
- **IDC_FILTER** – this is where the user enters the search filter

The two list boxes are:

- **IDC_PROPERTIES** – we'll display all the properties from the schema container in this list box, and the user can select the ones that they are interested in retrieving from this box
- **IDC_VALUES** – this is the list box where the results of the search will be displayed

The buttons are **IDC_SEARCH** and **IDOK**.

In order to help the user select the properties from a list, we'll provide them with a full list of the available ones. We'll populate this list in the **OnInitDialog()** method by enumerating the schema:

```
BOOL CDirSearchDlg::OnInitDialog()
{
   ...

   // Get hold of LDAP schema container

   IADsContainerPtr pContainer;
   HRESULT hr = ADsGetObject(L"LDAP://schema", IID_IADsContainer,
                              reinterpret_cast<void**>(&pContainer));
   if (FAILED(hr))
   {
      DisplayComError(_T("Failed to get schema container"), hr);

   }

   // Construct enumerator

   IEnumVARIANTPtr pEnum;
   hr = ADsBuildEnumerator(pContainer, &pEnum);

   if (FAILED(hr))
   {
      DisplayComError(_T("Failed to build enumerator"), hr);
      return TRUE;
   }

   CListBox* pProperties =
                     static_cast<CListBox*>(GetDlgItem(IDC_PROPERTIES));

   // Cycle through items in schema

   while (true)
   {
```

```
      // Get next child (i.e. property, because we're in the schema)

      _variant_t vChild;
      hr = ADsEnumerateNext(pEnum, 1, &vChild, NULL);

      if (hr != S_OK)
         break;

      // Get property interface

      IADsPropertyPtr pChild;
      hr = vChild.pdispVal->QueryInterface(IID_IADsProperty,
                              reinterpret_cast<void**>(&pChild));

      if (hr != S_OK)
         continue;

      // Extract name and add to displayed list

      BSTR bstrName;
      pChild->get_Name(&bstrName);
      CString csName = bstrName;
      SysFreeString(bstrName);

      pProperties->AddString(csName);
   }

   return TRUE;  // return TRUE  unless you set the focus to a control
}
```

Notice that we eliminate all the non-property objects by the simple expedient of **`QI`**'ing for the **`IADsProperty`** interface. This is derived from **`IADs`**, so we get access to **`get_Name()`** without any further **`QI`**'s. This is what our user sees:

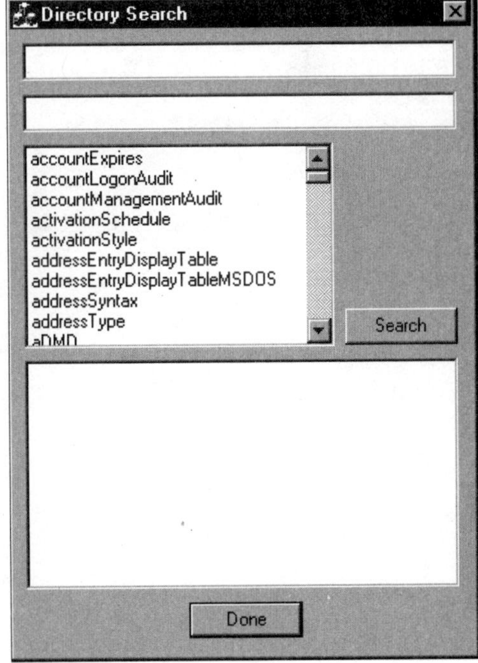

Our user can now select whichever properties are to be fetched, a start point and a search path. Here is the code that handles the search:

```
void CDirSearchDlg::OnSearch()
{
   // Get path from user input

   CString csPath;
   GetDlgItemText(IDC_PATH, csPath);

   // Construct search object based on current path

   IDirectorySearchPtr pSearch;
   HRESULT hr = ADsGetObject(_bstr_t(csPath), IID_IDirectorySearch,
      reinterpret_cast<void**>(&pSearch));

   if (FAILED(hr))
   {
      DisplayComError(_T("Failed to get search object"), hr);
      return;
   }
```

Remember that the directory search was simply another interface on the ADS object?

```
   // Get filter from user input

   CString csFilter;
   GetDlgItemText(IDC_FILTER, csFilter);

   // Build list of selected properties

   CListBox* pProperties =
                        static_cast<CListBox*>(GetDlgItem(IDC_PROPERTIES));
   int nProp = pProperties->GetSelCount();

   LPWSTR* pwstrProps = NULL;

   if (nProp)
   {
      pwstrProps = new LPWSTR[nProp];

      int prop = 0;
      CString csProp;

      int nItem = pProperties->GetCount();

      for (int item = 0; item < nItem; item++)
      {
         if (pProperties->GetSel(item))
         {
            pProperties->GetText(item, csProp);
            pwstrProps[prop++] = csProp.AllocSysString();
         }
      }
   }
```

```
// Execute search based on filter and required properties

ADS_SEARCH_HANDLE hSearch;
hr = pSearch->ExecuteSearch(_bstr_t(csFilter), pwstrProps, nProp,
                            &hSearch);

for (int prop = 0; prop < nProp; prop++)
   SysFreeString(pwstrProps[prop]);

delete[] pwstrProps;

if (FAILED(hr))
{
   DisplayComError(_T("Failed to execute search"), hr);
   return;
}

CListBox* pValues = static_cast<CListBox*>(GetDlgItem(IDC_VALUES));
pValues->ResetContent();
```

The critical line is that call to **`ExecuteSearch()`**. We pass this the filter string and the list of properties that we want to fetch (from **`IDC_FILTER`** and **`IDC_PROPERTIES`** respectively), and it returns us a handle, **`hSearch`**. We'll use this in the next code segment to traverse through the data. There's one row for each object found:

```
// Go through returned data, row by row

while (true)
{
   hr = pSearch->GetNextRow(hSearch);

   if (hr != S_OK)
      break;

   CString csValues;
```

There's also one column for every property that we specified:

```
// Go through row, column by column

while (true)
{
   LPWSTR wstrColumn = NULL;
   hr = pSearch->GetNextColumnName(hSearch, &wstrColumn);

   if (hr != S_OK)
      break;

// Get hold of column details

   ADS_SEARCH_COLUMN column;
    hr = pSearch->GetColumn(hSearch, wstrColumn, &column);
```

```
            CoTaskMemFree(wstrColumn);

            if (FAILED(hr))
            {
               DisplayComError(_T("Failed to get column"), hr);
               pSearch->CloseSearchHandle(hSearch);
               return;
            }

         // Extract column name ...

            CString csAttr = column.pszAttrName;
            CString csValue;

         // ... and value

            switch (column.pADsValues->dwType)
            {
               case ADSTYPE_CASE_EXACT_STRING:
               case ADSTYPE_CASE_IGNORE_STRING:
               case ADSTYPE_PRINTABLE_STRING:
                  csValue = column.pADsValues->PrintableString;
                  break;

               default:
                  csValue.Format("(unsupported type %d)",
                                 column.pADsValues->dwType);
                  break;
            }

         // Construct entry segment for displayed list

            CString csItem;
            csItem.Format("%s = %s", static_cast<LPCSTR>(csAttr),
                          static_cast<LPCSTR>(csValue));

         // Append segment to current entry

            if (!csValues.IsEmpty())
               csValues += "\t";

            csValues += csItem;

            pSearch->FreeColumn(&column);
         }

      // Add entry to list

         if (!csValues.IsEmpty())
            pValues->AddString(csValues);
      }

      pSearch->CloseSearchHandle(hSearch);
   }
```

So how do we actually use this? Well, let's just try specifying our domain pathname (**`LDAP://DC=OverTheHills,O=Internet`** in my case) for the start path, and, say, a search filter of **`adminDescription=Built-in account for administering the computer/domain`**. Why? Well, I happen to know that this will find the **`Administrator`** user object. (OK, I admit it. I only know this because I looked at the properties for the **`Administrator`** user object using the first code sample in this chapter ...):

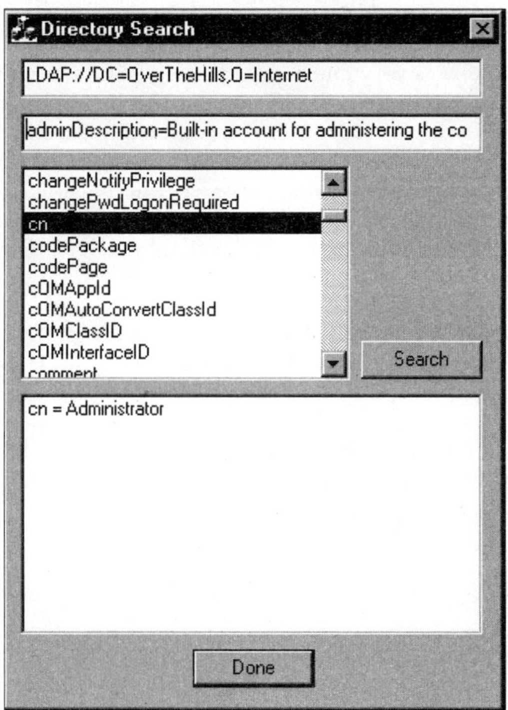

Neat. More seriously, you can use this mechanism to find all users with a given attribute, or all computers in a particular geographical location, or frankly, wherever your imagination leads you.

The Class Store

Now for what we've all been waiting for. Hands up who thinks DCOMcnfg is a really cool tool. Uh-uh. And hands up if at some point during this chapter you thought, "Hey! Wouldn't this Active Directory thing be a great place to store details of how to find objects?" Everyone? Well, the good news is that Microsoft is doing the hard work for you.

At the time of writing, the Class Store is very much an emerging feature, which may or may not appear with NT5.0. However, what we can be sure of is that it will be implemented as an Active Directory container. By the use of new class definitions to completely describe COM objects (including key attributes, such as location of executables), this class store will permit systems administrators to install COM components once, but run everywhere. No longer will we have to configure every single interested registry. If required, on-demand installation can be specified instead, so that the COM component is downloaded to the client machine if required and installed correctly there.

To me, this is what Active Directory is really all about. Once the Class Store is in place, we can start to develop truly distributed COM systems, without having to worry about the hassle of deploying them to our end-users. Nirvana, indeed.

We're going to change direction a little in the next few chapters, and take a look at the Microsoft Transaction Server, which is revolutionizing the way in which we structure COM clients, and which forms the central plank of Microsoft's thrust into the Back Office.

5

Transactions (and a Bit About Data)

"Do not despise the snake because he has no horns,
For who is to say he will not become a dragon?"

Ancient Chinese Saying

Enter the Dragon

One of the most exciting developments in COM is the emergence of Microsoft Transaction Server (MTS). Up until pretty recently, transactions were one of those areas in systems development which were surrounded by an aura of voodoo, black magic and, above all, exorbitant consulting fees. All this is about to change. Transaction-based development is going mainstream, and one of the prime movers here is Microsoft. Precisely *how* mainstream is indicated by the fact that, some time back, Microsoft actually merged their Transaction Server and COM teams together. Microsoft Transaction Server is absolutely central to the future strategy of Windows – so much so that, from Version 5 of NT onwards, MTS is actually going to be part of the operating system itself.

Why is this?

Very simply, it's because transactions are central to all human activity.

But what exactly is a transaction?

We'll get onto a more precise definition in a little while, but for the time being, we can take a transaction as meaning simply a number of events that must either all take place or none at all. The standard example is taken from the world of commerce and usually involves transferring money from account A to account B. The money must either end up in account B (and nowhere else), or, if something goes wrong, stay in account A (and go nowhere else). But, just to show how universal the concept of a transaction is, here are a few more examples:

- Software change control. Each new version of a software package potentially involves changes to several of the underlying source files. The new version is only defined when every single one of the changes has been made. Just try supporting a product with loads of intermediate versions.
- Arranging a tennis match. A time must be agreed when all four players can be there. If only three can turn up, it won't be much of a game. The actual transaction may fail many times before a mutually convenient time is agreed.
- Almost any military maneuver involving more than one unit.
- Taking off in an airplane. This involves an enormous of elements. For example, all the fuel must be on board, all the doors must be closed, air traffic control must have granted clearance, all the baggage must be on, etc. etc..

Inevitably, *most* transactions in life are to do with commerce, and basically involve ensuring electronically that money transfers, foreign exchange deals and so on do happen in a controlled manner with the minimum risk of something going wrong. Once you get into this, you start looking for transactions everywhere ... every time you use your credit card, for instance. It's fascinating stuff.

This is why Microsoft has invested so much time and money into developing the product that they code-named Viper. The next three chapters will all look at various aspects of MTS:

- This chapter examines what we can do with our DCOM applications to take advantage of Microsoft Transaction Server (including a look at how we can use ActiveX Data Objects to access database resources)
- The next chapter looks at how it fits in with Microsoft Message Queue Server.
- The third chapter in the sequence opens up the hood a little and looks at how we can develop resource managers to work with MTS. You won't often need to do this, but, believe me, MTS will make a whole load more sense after we've done it.

In this chapter, we'll look specifically at:

- Transaction theory
- Setting up SQL server
- How to use ActiveX Data Objects
- Object-oriented programming, components and tiered application development
- How MTS runs the show
- Transaction context
- Resource dispensers
- The shared property manager

ACID Culture

OK, I think we're ready for a little theory. Generally speaking, my view on computer science theory is that it's all very well, but you can get a much better idea of what is going on in a system by kicking it in various places and finding out which bit squeaks. However, despite this, and the fact that this is very much intended to be a practical treatise, we need a small dose of the cerebral stuff before we go ahead with transactions. In the interests of reducing the general levels of stress in the world, though, I'll keep it short...

Transaction theory was invented in California in the late sixties, which is the reason why any explanation of it usually starts with ACID. According to the ACID theory, all transactions should have the following properties:

- **Atomicity**: A transaction is *atomic.* However many different components the transaction involves, and however many different method calls there are on those components, the system treats it as *one single operation* which either entirely succeeds or entirely fails. If it fails, the system is left in the same state as if the transaction had never happened.
- **Consistency**: All changes are done in a consistent manner. The system goes from one valid state to another.
- **Isolation**: Transactions that are going on at the same time are isolated from each other. If transaction A changes the system from state S1 to state S2, transaction B will see the system in *either* state S1 *or* S2, but *not* some half-baked state in between the two. However the transactions are actually executed in practice, this requirement ensures that the developer can treat a set of transactions as executing serially.
- **Durability**: If a transaction has been committed, the effect will be permanent, even if the system fails.

At this point, it's worth considering what implications all this is likely to have on the underlying components. How on earth can you ensure that all the changes in the system can be unwound if the transaction is aborted at some point? Think about it: maybe you've changed a couple of items in shared memory, you've updated countless database files, you're sending messages off to some other system and you're just about to make the last change *when something goes wrong.*

Fortunately, help is at hand, in the shape of **resource managers**. A resource manager is the software that manages (remembers) the changes made to some resource – different types of resource need different resource managers. Physically committing, or rolling back, the changes to a resource is the resource managers' job.

Any changes that you make to the system through resource managers automatically come under the control of MTS. This means that we can we leave MTS to deal with the tedious task of ensuring that our transaction passes the ACID test, while we get on with the more interesting job of putting together an application that actually serves a useful business purpose. Such is the beauty of MTS.

And that's about all the theory we need for now. You may notice that I have left out explanations of key transaction theory phrases that you might have come across, such as *two-phase commit,* but I think we can do without that for the time being. As it happens, MTS takes away all worries about that sort of thing from us; we'll have to face up to it when we write our own resource manager in Chapter 7, but we can ignore it for now. Personally speaking, I'm itching to do some coding.

First of all, then, we need to decide on an application to try out MTS. Personally speaking, I'm bored with examples that involve banks, and I'd like something a little more frivolous. So, without further ado (although we'll come across ADO soon enough), I offer you (ta-da!)...

The Kidnap Game

The rules of this game are pretty simple. Player 1 "kidnaps" someone, sets a ransom for them but doesn't tell Player 2 what the ransom amount is. Player 1 also sets the amount of money that Player 2 has available to pay the ransom, but doesn't tell Player 2 this either. The object of the game is for Player 2 to free the hostage by paying the minimum amount that he or she can get away with, in as few goes as possible.

In this game, the transaction involves an exchange of money for a hostage. Either the deal goes through, in which case the hostage is freed and Player 2 is worse off, or the deal fails, in which case the hostage remains in captivity but Player 2 still has the same amount of money that he or she started with. There are two reasons why the deal may fail:

- Player 2 may try to offer more money than he or she has available
- Player 2 may not offer enough money.

We'll start the design process by considering what resources we are playing with. We have two types of resource: hostages and money.

A hostage resource has the following attributes:

- Name
- State (free/in captivity)
- Ransom

A money resource (strictly speaking, a bank account resource) has the following attributes:

- Account name
- Balance

How can we represent these electronically? Well, these resources look like a database to me, so we'd better start looking for databases that support transactions, and, somewhat inevitably, we end up at *SQL Server*. Incidentally, don't worry too much about using SQL Server if you haven't had much experience of it; we'll be hiding most of the SQL behind Microsoft's ActiveX Data Objects (ADO), and we won't be doing anything very complicated. This isn't a database book, after all!

The trouble is that MTS doesn't show its true colors unless we use a resource manager, and there aren't too many of them about – unless we want to tie ourselves in to a particular third party database management system (DBMS), such as Oracle. The list of supported resources is growing, but, at the time of writing, the only other alternative is to use Microsoft Message Queue (which we'll look at in the next chapter) or write our own resource manager (which we'll be doing in the one after that).

Also, if you're just interested in trying this out, you don't necessarily need to rush out and buy SQL Server. A developer's version comes with Visual Studio, and, if you happen to have NT4 Server Enterprise Edition available, when you install Microsoft Message Queue on Enterprise Edition, you'll actually get a stripped down copy of SQL Server thrown in for free. The Message Queue system uses this to hold all its static data, and we can borrow a small section of it for ourselves.

In SQL Server, then, we define two databases, called **`kidnap1`** and **`kidnap2`**. **`kidnap1`** has one table, **`hostages`** and **`kidnap2`** also has one table, **`accounts`**. (I've put them in separate databases just to make sure that they are as independent of each other as possible. It doesn't actually matter from the point of view of the application – I just wanted to make sure that the various data sources were seen to be as distinct from each other as possible.)

The **`hostages`** table has the following columns:

Key	Name	Datatype	Size	Default
✓	`name`	`char`	255	
	`free`	`bit`	1	0
	`ransom`	`int`	4	

and the **`accounts`** table has the following columns:

Key	Name	Datatype	Size	Default
✓	`name`	`char`	255	
	`balance`	`int`	4	

Let's see how we go about setting all this up.

Setting Up the Database

In a little while, we're going to look at how we use ADO to make a simple database connection. In order to do this, however, we need to define an ODBC connection to SQL Server, and then configure our databases. If you're a SQL Server guru, please feel free to skip this section. However, database expertise isn't one of the prerequisites for this book's readership, so I'll go through the process in case you're unfamiliar with it.

Defining an ODBC Connection

We'll start off by creating an ODBC connection. We need to go into the Control Panel and double click on the ODBC button.

Select the File DSN (data source name) tab and click on the Add... button. This dialog appears:

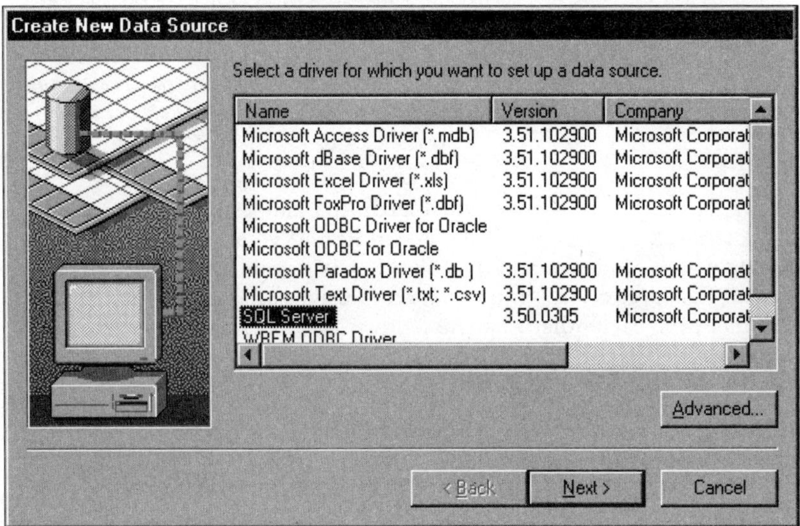

Select SQL Server, as shown and click on the Next > button. Now we tell ODBC what our data source name is going to be:

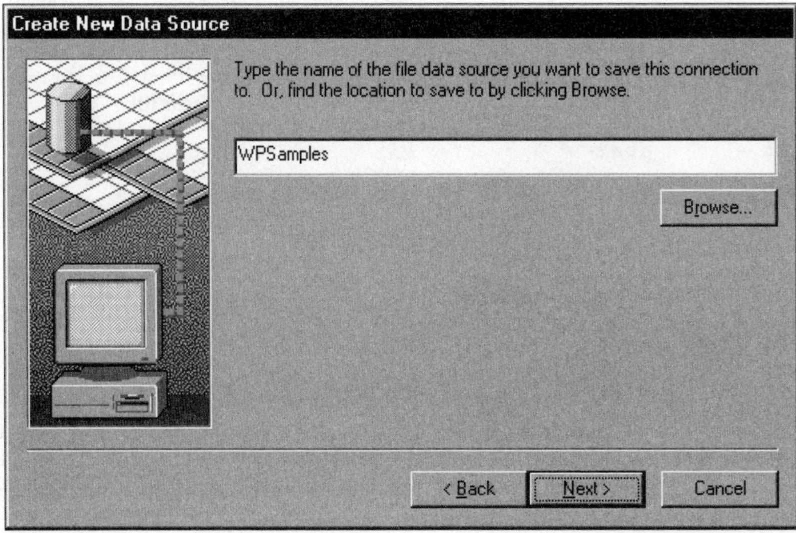

Clicking Next > again shows a confirmation dialog. If we click on Finish, we go into the SQL Server-specific part of the set-up:

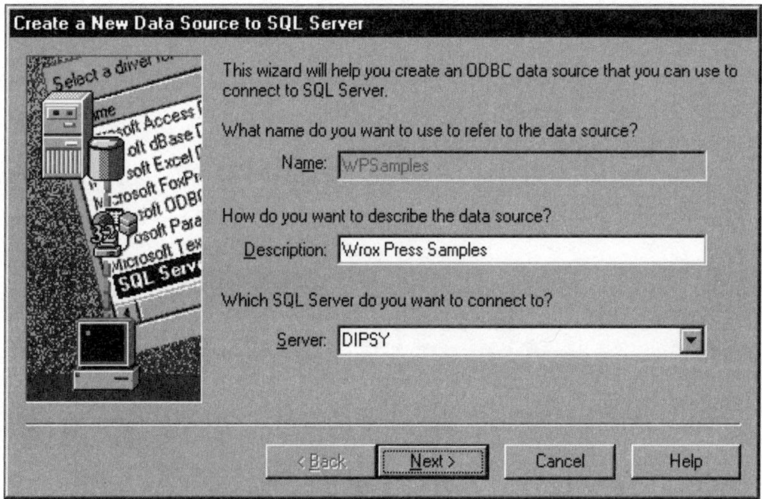

Here we enter the name of the server to which we're connecting, and a textual description of the connection. If we click on Next >, we move on, to decide how we are going to log onto the server. Accept the default, and keep going, and do the same in the next three dialogs.

Hurrah! We're finished. We now get a confirmation screen, and we're asked if we want to test the connection:

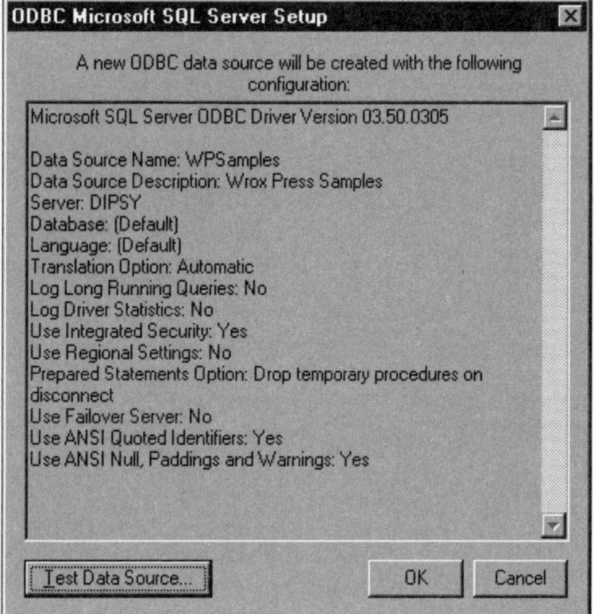

Oh, yes please! (I *love* pressing buttons...) Now we need to set up our databases.

Defining the Database

Let's start up the SQL Enterprise Manager. This is what we see (I'm using SQL Server version 6.5 here, by the way):

You may need to register your server machine, if you haven't done so already. Just select Server | Register Server... *to do just that.*

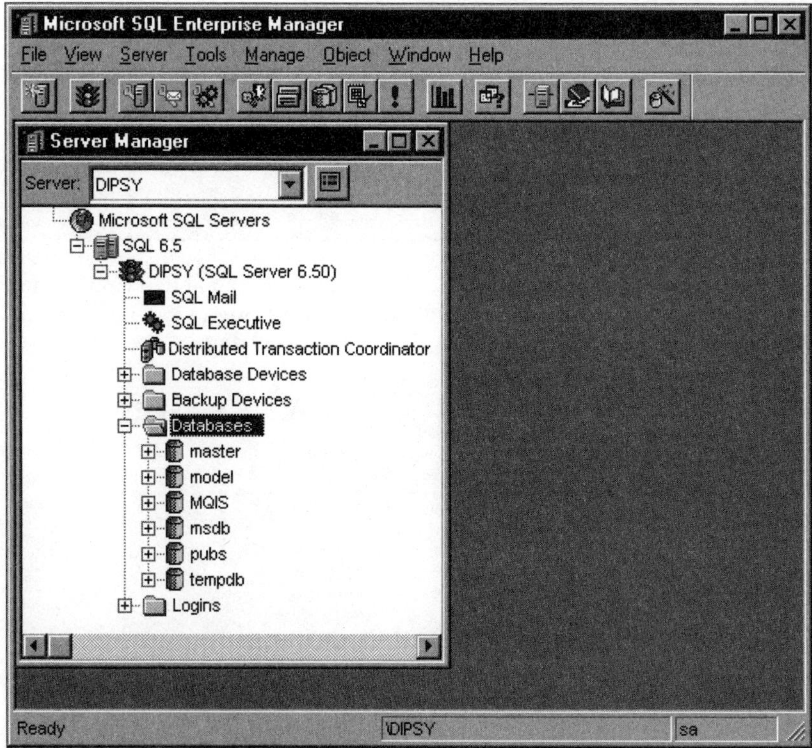

If we right-click on the Databases folder and select New Database from the drop-down menu, we see the following dialog:

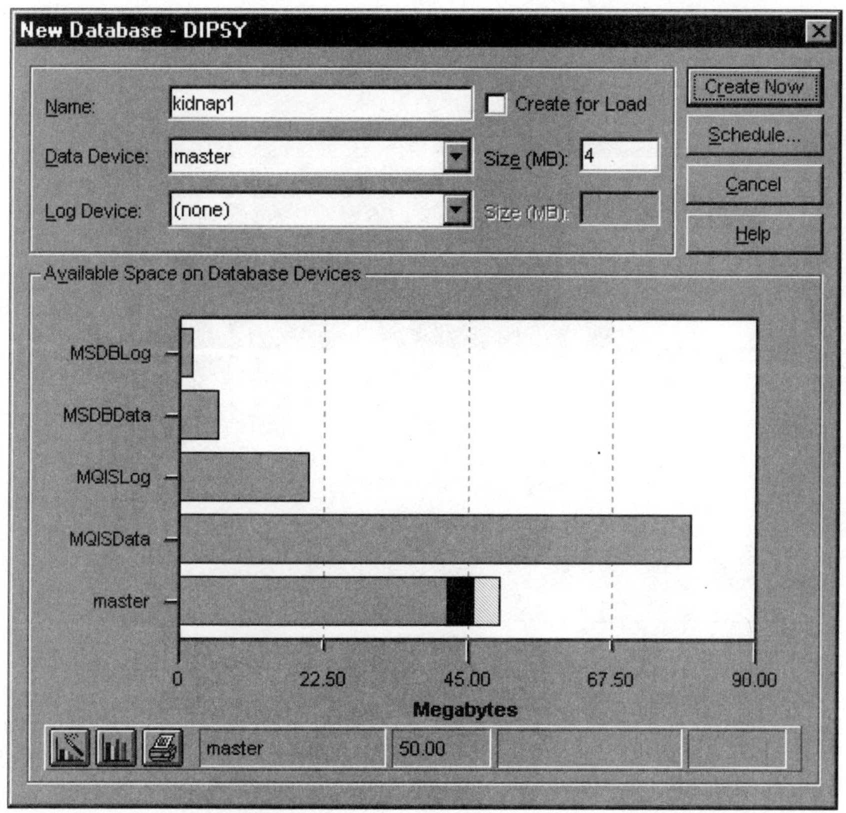

As you can see, my Message Queue installation has very generously left me with 8Mb of space to play with. Well, that's plenty enough for the kidnap game. Let's allocate half of it to **`kidnap1`**, and click on the Create Now button.

Our first database set-up is now complete, and we need to move on to setting up the **`hostages`** table within it. Back in the Server Manager window, we need to expand the **`kidnap1`** database, then the Objects folder, and right-click on the Tables folder underneath the **`kidnap1`** database. In the next dialog, we define all the fields in our **`hostages`** table:

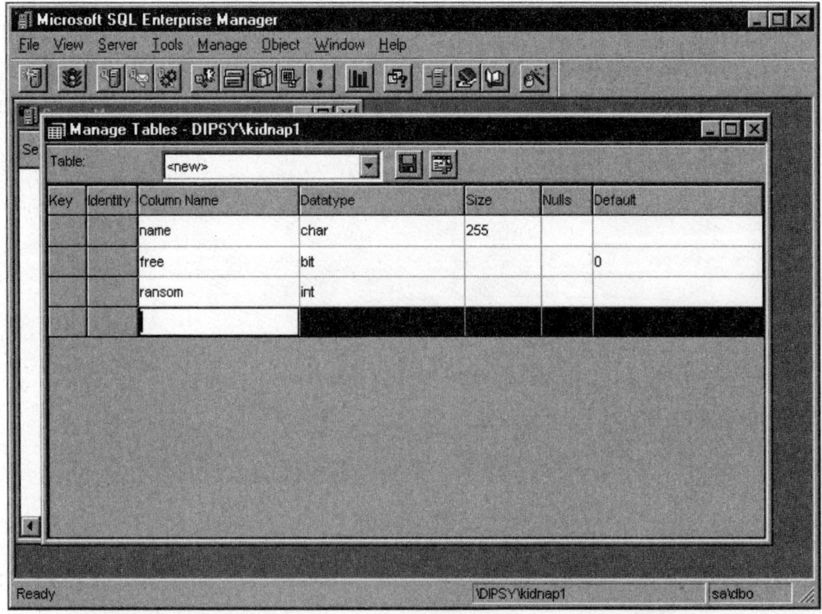

We now have to decide which of these fields is going to be the key, so click on the button with the plus sign to get to the advanced features. By the way, you *have* to specify the key at this stage. You can't come back later on and set it, because you won't be allowed access to that field. It's obvious when you think about it – key settings are pretty fundamental to database structure, and you can't just go changing them willy-nilly.

In the advanced settings part of the dialog, we set the **`name`** to be the key:

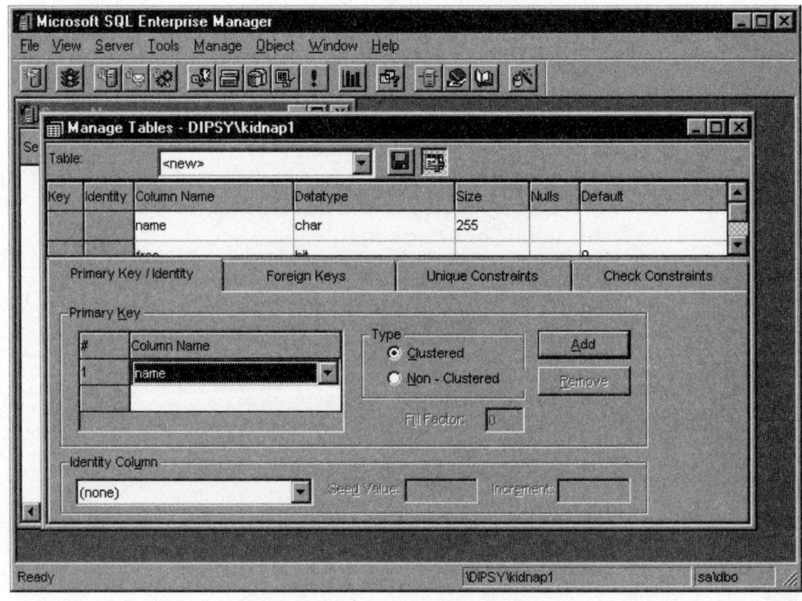

That's all we need to do here. Click on the disk icon to save our table, and specify **`hostages`** as the table name in the little dialog. Here's our table now in all its glory:

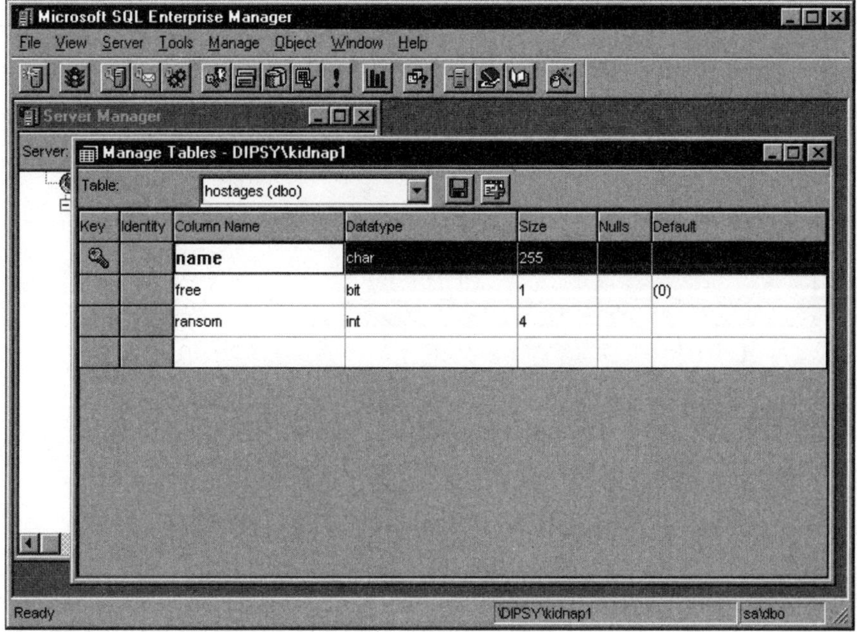

One database set up and ready for action. All we have to do is repeat the process for the **`kidnap2`** database (including the **`accounts`** table).

Next, we have to look at how we're going to program our database access. I know you're itching to get programming MTS – so am I – but we've got to sort out some resources first. The easiest way to get access to our resources is by using **ActiveX data objects**, or **ADO**.

Much ADO About Something — or Other

Well, every single article I've come across about ADO starts with the words "Much ADO", so why make an exception? I'm pretty certain, by the way, that the reason for this is simply to establish that the author of the article knows the name of at least one *Shakespearean play. Besides, "Timon of Athens" wouldn't really make much sense. Yeah, I know the names of* two *Shakespeare plays.*

One of the key goals of programming is to make everything look the same as everything else. After all, only a programmer would try to convince people that a 3½" floppy disk was really the same thing as a 32Gbyte hard disk. In every physical respect (apart from the fact that they both use magnetism to store information) they're completely different. But they look the same to you and me, don't they, because their drivers hide the differences from us.

The same holds at higher levels, too. In the last chapter, we saw how the isolation layer in the ADSI components enabled us to write an application that talked in the same way to both a conventional Windows NT directory and an LDAP-oriented one. We're going to look at something now that does the same trick for databases.

ADO is the latest in a long series of Microsoft Data access technologies, and it effectively supersedes the old Data Access Objects (DAO) and Remote Data Objects (RDO) objects. This is where it sits in the Microsoft **Universal Data Access** hierarchy:

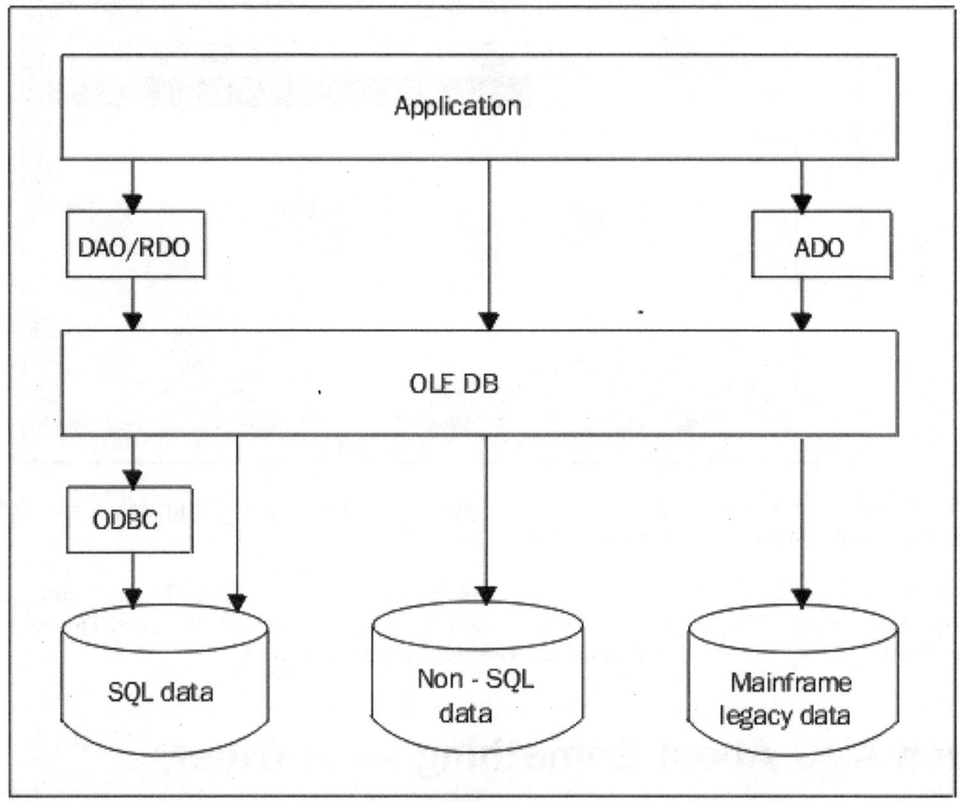

So, from the top down, we have our application that either talks directly to **OLE DB** or via ADO. ADO talks to OLE DB. Databases either present themselves as **OLE DB providers** or via **ODBC drivers**, which in turn presents itself as an OLE DB provider.

We could easily spend an entire chapter looking at ADO, but it's really outside the scope of this book. Instead, we'll proceed on a kind of "need to know" basis, and pick up enough to put together a simple application. To be honest, once you've got started on ADO, it's pretty intuitive. You'll probably find that you can easily explore further yourself, without any interfering authors breathing down your neck.

As our vehicle for exploring ADO, we're going to develop `DBManager`, the database management program that will be used by Player 1 in the Kidnap Game. In some ways, VB would be the perfect vehicle for developing this, as ADO objects are fully automation compliant and fit very well with VB. However, we're going to be accessing the database from one of our ATL components later on, so we'd better get used to using Visual C++. So our application is going to be written using MFC.

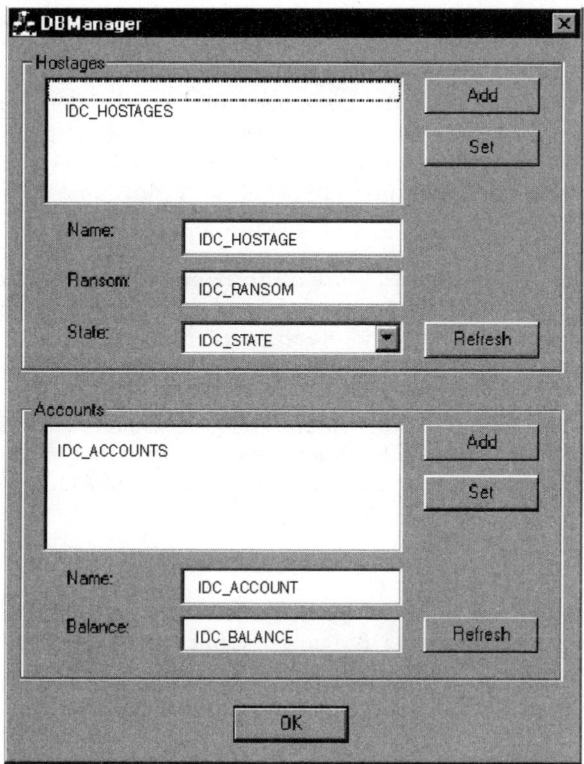

In order to develop against ADO, we'll need to include a couple of header files in both **`DBManager.cpp`** and **`DBManagerDlg.cpp`** – **`adoid.h`** and **`adoint.h`**. We'll also need to add the library **`adoid.lib`** to the list of libraries with which we link.

> **As I've noted in the code, I've used ADO 1.5, that comes with MTS 2.0. This is the same as the one included in the OLEDB SDK from Microsoft. The version that comes with Visual C++ has a different number of parameters (three not four) for the `ADOConnection::Open()` method. I've therefore put the MTS include and library files first in the listings on the Tools | Options Directory tab.**

There are seven objects in the ADO object model. I'd like to concentrate first of all on the **`Connection`**, **`Recordset`** and **`Field`** objects.

A **`Connection`** object, not surprisingly, represents a connection to a database. For our purposes, the key methods are **`Open()`**, which opens up a **`Recordset`**, **`Close()`**, which closes one, and **`Execute()`**, which executes a command.

So what's a **Recordset**? A **Recordset** is a collection of records. This collection may be the result of a database query (perhaps implemented by a command passed to the **Execute()** method of a **Connection** object), or it may simply represent the entire contents of a table.

A **Recordset** is the most important object in ADO, because this is the object on which you carry out all the manipulations. For example, you can add a new record to it using the **AddNew()** method, you can delete one or more records using the **Delete()** method, and you can navigate through it using the various **Move()** methods. Not surprisingly, fields in records from a **Recordset** are represented by **Field** objects.

You can do a lot with just these three objects. More complex provider-specific commands can be implemented using a **Command** object, perhaps in tandem with a **Parameter** object. Provider-specific properties of a **Connection**, **Command**, **Recordset** or **Field** object can be manipulated using a **Property** object. Finally, errors can be determined via an **Error** object.

The only unfortunate aspect of ADO is that it's optimized for OLE automation, so it's chock full of **VARIANT**s, which are a real pain as far as C++ is concerned. Anyway, we're halfway through the chapter already and we haven't done any coding, so let's take a look at ADO as we dig into our DBManager application.

ADO in Action

The first thing that happens on running our DBManager application is that this fragment of code gets executed at the end of **DBManagerDlg**'s **OnInitDialog()**:

```
   .
   .
   .

   HRESULT hResult = CoInitialize (NULL);

   if (FAILED (hResult))
   {
      Log (hResult, "Initialize COM");
      return TRUE;
   }

   ListHostages ();
   ListAccounts ();

   return TRUE;  // return TRUE  unless you set the focus to a control
}
```

Looking at **DBManagerDlg.h**, we need the following private methods for our code:

```
// DBManagerDlg.h : header file

...
```

```
#include <comdef.h>
#define ADO_SMARTPTR_TYPEDEF(x)    \
   typedef _com_ptr_t<_com_IIID<x, &IID_I##x> > x##Ptr;

ADO_SMARTPTR_TYPEDEF(ADOConnection);
ADO_SMARTPTR_TYPEDEF(ADORecordset);
ADO_SMARTPTR_TYPEDEF(ADOFields);
ADO_SMARTPTR_TYPEDEF(ADOField);
ADO_SMARTPTR_TYPEDEF(ADOErrors);
ADO_SMARTPTR_TYPEDEF(ADOError);

/////////////////////////////////////////////////////////////////////////////
// CDBManagerDlg dialog

...

// Implementation
private:
   ADOConnectionPtr OpenDatabase (CString csDatabase);
   ADORecordsetPtr OpenRecordset (ADOConnection *pConnection,
                                  CString csTable);
   ADORecordsetPtr FindRecordset (ADOConnection *pConnection,
                       CString csTable, CString csField, CString csValue);
   void ListHostages ();
   void ListAccounts ();
   void Log (HRESULT hResult, CString csLocation);
   void Log (HRESULT hResult, CString csLocation,
                              ADOConnection *pConnection);
```

Let's start by taking a look at the member function, **ListHostages()**. It uses the **OpenDatabase()** and **OpenRecordset()** functions, to which we'll come shortly.

```
void CDBManagerDlg::ListHostages ()
{
   CListBox *pList = static_cast<CListBox *> (GetDlgItem (IDC_HOSTAGES));
   pList->ResetContent ();

   ADOConnectionPtr pConnection;
   pConnection = OpenDatabase ("kidnap1");

   if (pConnection == NULL)
      return;

   ADORecordsetPtr pRecordset;
   pRecordset = OpenRecordset (pConnection, "hostages");

   if (pRecordset == NULL)
         return;

   // Check for end of file

   VARIANT_BOOL bEOF;
   HRESULT hResult = pRecordset->get_EOF (&bEOF);
```

```
// Scroll through all records in recordset
   while ((SUCCEEDED (hResult)) && (bEOF == VARIANT_FALSE))
   {
      ADOFieldsPtr pFields;
          hResult = pRecordset->get_Fields (&pFields);

      long count;
      hResult = pFields->get_Count (&count);

      CString csHostage = "";
      CString csRansom = "";
      CString csState = "";

      // Search through fields for the data we need

      for (long field = 0; field < count; field++)
      {
         ADOFieldPtr pField;
         hResult = pFields->get_Item (COleVariant (field), &pField);

         BSTR bstrName;
         hResult = pField->get_Name (&bstrName);
         CString csName = bstrName;
         SysFreeString (bstrName);

         _variant_t vValue;
         hResult = pField->get_Value (&vValue);

         CString csValue = "";
         long lValue;

         switch (vValue.vt)
         {
            case VT_BSTR:
               csValue = V_BSTR (&vValue);
               break;

            case VT_I4:
               lValue = V_I4 (&vValue);
               break;

            case VT_BOOL:
               if (vValue.boolVal == VARIANT_TRUE)
                  csValue = "free";
               else
                  csValue = "held";
         }

         if (csName == "name")
            csHostage = csValue.Left (20);
         else if (csName == "ransom")
            csRansom.Format ("%ld", lValue);
         else if (csName == "free")
            csState = csValue;
      }
```

```
CString csData;
      csData.Format ("%s %s (%s)", static_cast<LPCSTR> (csHostage),
            static_cast<LPCSTR> (csRansom),
            static_cast<LPCSTR> (csState));

      pList->AddString (csData);

      // Move on to the next record
      pRecordset->MoveNext ();
      pRecordset->get_EOF (&bEOF);
   }
}
```

This opens up a connection to our **kidnap1** database (using the **OpenDatabase()** method, which we'll see shortly), opens the **hostages** recordset, and simply scrolls through all the records that it finds there, formatting a display string containing the data from the fields in the record. Notice that, once we've got a connection to the database, one call to **OpenRecordset()** (which we'll also see soon) is all we need to get hold of a recordset containing all the records in the table that we want.

Opening a Connection

Here's the code to open a connection to a database passed in as a parameter:

```
ADOConnectionPtr CDBManagerDlg::OpenDatabase(CString csDatabase)
{
   // Create connection object
   ADOConnectionPtr pConnection;
   HRESULT hResult = CoCreateInstance (CLSID_CADOConnection, NULL,
      CLSCTX_INPROC_SERVER,
      IID_IADOConnection,
      reinterpret_cast<void**>(&pConnection));

   if (FAILED (hResult))
   {
         Log (hResult, "Create connection");
        return NULL;
   }

   // Format the connection string
   CString csConnection;
     csConnection.Format("FILEDSN=WPSamples;Database=%s;UID=sa;PWD=;",
                                   static_cast<LPCSTR> (csDatabase));
     _bstr_t bstrConnection = csConnection.AllocSysString ();

   // Open the database
   // Note that MTS 2.0 and OLEDB SDK include files, adoid.h and
   // adoint.h, and their corresponding library, are a more modern
   // version of ADO than that in Visual C++ 5.
   // We've used the MTS version of ADOConnection's Open() method, with
   // four parameters

     hResult = pConnection->Open(bstrConnection, NULL, NULL, NULL);

   if (FAILED (hResult))
```

```
    {
        Log (hResult, "Open connection", pConnection);
        return NULL;
    }

    return pConnection;
}
```

In the string that gets passed to the **`Open()`** method, we've specified that our FileDSN is **`WPSamples`** (remember setting that up in the ODBC configuration earlier on in the chapter?). The database is set to whatever we passed in (**`kidnap1`** or **`kidnap2`**), and the UID for SQL Server is set to **`sa`**, which is set up by default as the SQL Server administrator UID (so we know it'll work – I'm not too bothered about SQL Server security here).

Opening a Recordset

Here's how we open up our recordset:

```
ADORecordsetPtr CDBManagerDlg::OpenRecordset(ADOConnection *pConnection,
CString csTable)
{
    // Create a recordset object
    ADORecordsetPtr pRecordset;
    HRESULT hResult = CoCreateInstance(CLSID_CADORecordset, NULL,
        CLSCTX_INPROC_SERVER,
        IID_IADORecordset,
        reinterpret_cast<void**>(&pRecordset));

    if (FAILED(hResult))
    {
        Log(hResult, "Create recordset");
        return NULL;
    }

    _variant_t vTable(csTable);
    _variant_t vConnection(pConnection);

    hResult = pRecordset->Open(vTable, vConnection, adOpenKeyset,
                                        adLockPessimistic, adCmdTable);

    if (FAILED (hResult))
    {
        Log (hResult, "Open recordset", pConnection);
        return NULL;
    }

    return pRecordset;
}
```

Notice here that we're not actually issuing a command to the database to populate our recordset. Instead, we instantiate a recordset independently of the connection, and then invoke its **`Open()`** method to attach it to the connection, specifying the required table (that's what the **`adCmdTable`** parameter is saying – later on we'll see another way of opening a recordset, by issuing a command).

We can now use the recordset that we've just defined to manipulate the records in the table. We've already seen how we can scroll through them to list them, in the **`ListHostages()`** function; but we can also update the table, for example, by adding a new record. Let's take a look at how that happens.

Adding a Record

Here's the code that gets triggered when the user hits the Add button in the hostage section of the dialog:

```
void CDBManagerDlg::OnAddHostage()
{
   // Get data from dialog fields

   CString csHostage;
   CEdit *pHostage = static_cast<CEdit *> (GetDlgItem (IDC_HOSTAGE));
   pHostage->GetWindowText (csHostage);

   CString csRansom;
   CEdit *pRansom = static_cast<CEdit *> (GetDlgItem (IDC_RANSOM));
   pRansom->GetWindowText (csRansom);
   long lRansom = atol (static_cast<LPCSTR> (csRansom));

   CString csState;
   CComboBox *pState = static_cast<CComboBox *> (GetDlgItem (IDC_STATE));
   pState->GetWindowText (csState);

   VARIANT_BOOL bFree = VARIANT_FALSE;

   if (csState == "free")
      bFree = VARIANT_TRUE;

   // Open up recordset

   ADOConnectionPtr pConnection;
   pConnection = OpenDatabase ("kidnap1");

   if (pConnection == NULL)
      return;

   ADORecordsetPtr pRecordset;
   pRecordset = OpenRecordset (pConnection, "hostages");

   if (pRecordset == NULL)
      return;
```

```
    // Set up variant array containing details of new hostage

    COleSafeArray arrField;
    arrField.CreateOneDim(VT_VARIANT, 3);

    COleVariant varField;
    long rgIndices[1];

    varField = L"name"
    rgIndices[0] = 0;
    arrField.PutElement(rgIndices, reinterpret_cast<void*>(&varField));

    varField = L"ransom"
    rgIndices[0] = 1;
    arrField.PutElement(rgIndices, reinterpret_cast<void*>(&varField));

    varField = L"free"
    rgIndices[0] = 2;
    arrField.PutElement(rgIndices, reinterpret_cast<void*>(&varField));

    COleSafeArray arrValue;
    arrValue.CreateOneDim(VT_VARIANT, 3);

    COleVariant varValue;

    varValue = csHostage.AllocSysString();
    rgIndices[0] = 0;
    arrField.PutElement(rgIndices, reinterpret_cast<void*>(&varValue));

    varValue = lRansom;
    rgIndices[0] = 1;
    arrField.PutElement(rgIndices, reinterpret_cast<void*>(&varValue));

    varValue = bFree;
    rgIndices[0] = 2;
    arrField.PutElement(rgIndices, reinterpret_cast<void*>(&varValue));

    // Add new record to recordset

    HRESULT hResult = pRecordset->AddNew (arrField, arrValue);

    if (FAILED (hResult))
        Log (hResult, "Add new record", pConnection);
}
```

The key call in this code segment is the invocation of the **AddNew()** method on the recordset object. Notice, incidentally, that nowhere have we incorporated anything in the code that is specific to SQL Server; such is the power of ADO. Actually, there's just one line of code in this application that is specific to SQL Server, and that's coming up in a minute.

Finding and Updating a Record

Here's what happens when the user clicks on the Set button in the hostage section of the dialog:

```
void CDBManagerDlg::OnSetHostage()
{
   // Get data from dialog fields

   CString csHostage;
   CEdit *pHostage = static_cast<CEdit *> (GetDlgItem (IDC_HOSTAGE));
   pHostage->GetWindowText (csHostage);

   CString csRansom;
   CEdit *pRansom = static_cast<CEdit *> (GetDlgItem (IDC_RANSOM));
   pRansom->GetWindowText (csRansom);
   long lRansom = atol (static_cast<LPCSTR> (csRansom));

   CString csState;
   CComboBox *pState = static_cast<CComboBox *> (GetDlgItem (IDC_STATE));
   pState->GetWindowText (csState);

   VARIANT_BOOL bFree = VARIANT_FALSE;

   if (csState == "free")
      bFree = VARIANT_TRUE;

   // Find recordset for this hostage

   ADOConnectionPtr pConnection;
   pConnection = OpenDatabase ("kidnap1");

   if (pConnection == NULL)
      return;

   ADORecordsetPtr pRecordset;
   pRecordset = FindRecordset (pConnection, "hostages", "name", csHostage);

   if (pRecordset == NULL)
      return;

   // Set up variant array containing details of change to hostage

   COleSafeArray arrField;
   arrField.CreateOneDim(VT_VARIANT, 2);

   COleVariant varField;
   long rgIndices[2];

   varField = L"ransom";
   rgIndices[0] = 0;
   arrField.PutElement(rgIndices, reinterpret_cast<void*>(&varField));

   varField = L"free";
   rgIndices[0] = 1;
   arrField.PutElement(rgIndices, reinterpret_cast<void*>(&varField));
```

```
    COleSafeArray arrValue;
    arrField.CreateOneDim(VT_VARIANT, 2);

    COleVariant varValue;

    varField = lRansom;
    rgIndices[0] = 0;
    arrField.PutElement(rgIndices, reinterpret_cast<void*>(&varField));

    varField = bFree;
    rgIndices[0] = 1;
    arrField.PutElement(rgIndices, reinterpret_cast<void*>(&varField));

    // Update record

    HRESULT hResult = pRecordset->Update (vFields, vValues);

    if (FAILED (hResult))
       Log (hResult, "Update record", pConnection);
}
```

This time, we're finding a recordset that relates to a specific individual record, so we call a different member function, **`FindRecordSet()`** (which we'll see next). Once we've got the record, we update it using the **`Update()`** method on the recordset object. Here's our **`FindRecordSet()`** function:

```
ADORecordsetPtr CDBManagerDlg::FindRecordset(ADOConnection *pConnection,
                         CString csTable, CString csField, CString csValue)
{
    ADORecordsetPtr pRecordset;
    HRESULT hResult = CoCreateInstance (CLSID_CADORecordset, NULL,
       CLSCTX_INPROC_SERVER,
       IID_IADORecordset,
       reinterpret_cast<void**>(&pRecordset));

    if (FAILED (hResult))
    {
          Log (hResult, "Create recordset");
       return NULL;
    }

    CString csCommand;
    csCommand.Format ("SELECT * FROM %s WHERE %s = '%s'",
       static_cast<LPCSTR> (csTable),
       static_cast<LPCSTR> (csField),
       static_cast<LPCSTR> (csValue));

    _variant_t vCommand(csCommand);
    _variant_t vConnection(pConnection);

    hResult = pRecordset->Open (vCommand, vConnection, adOpenKeyset,
                                adLockPessimistic, adCmdText);

    if (FAILED (hResult))
    {
```

```
            Log (hResult, "Open recordset", pConnection);
        return NULL;
    }

    return pRecordset;
}
```

Whoa there! SQL alert! This is the one provider-specific line that I mentioned earlier. Actually, this is a very simple piece of SQL, which fetches all the records for which the specified field has the specified value. Because the field we've specified ("name") is a unique key, we're guaranteed to get a maximum of one record. Notice that this time, we're specifying open by *command* rather than open by table – that's what the **`adCmdText`** parameter is doing.

I won't bore you rigid by showing you the code for the rest of DBManager; we've covered as much ADO as we're going to need for now, and it's time to move on.

Having defined our resources, we now need to ask what our application logic is going to look like. This is where it gets interesting, and the answer is going to strike at the heart of our preconceptions about object-oriented programming. Let's step back a bit, and think back to what we were taught when we first starting using objects.

Unlearning Object-Oriented Theory

Back in the programming nursery, life seemed simple. An object was introduced to us as a data structure that you could give instructions to, using things called *methods.* We were taught all about inheritance, encapsulation and polymorphism, and a great future beckoned. All we had to do was use objects all the time and our software would be better structured, more maintainable and, joy of joys, *reusable*! So, every time we saw something that looked like a data structure, we dutifully wrapped it up inside an object, and waited to reap the rich rewards that would in time accrue to us.

Since then, one or two curious things have happened.

- First of all, reusable software is still largely a fiction that exists only in the minds of managers who are eager to cut costs. I recently met an object-oriented design guru, who, of all people, would surely have been eager to promote the concept. However, according to him, the standard greeting when one object-orientation guru meets another at a conference is "Seen any re-use yet?" to which the standard reply is "Nah."
- Secondly, Visual C++ and Visual Basic have emerged to dominate the market for object-oriented software on the Windows platform. Setting aside any question of whether Visual Basic is object-oriented or not, the net result is that object-oriented programming is often seen simply as a neat way of wrapping up the idiosyncrasies of Windows messaging, and making the manipulation of visual controls simpler.
- Thirdly, object-oriented databases have (so far) failed to deliver, and the relational model remains firmly entrenched. There seems to be little value in maintaining persistent data in an object-oriented format.

Does this mean, then, that we should pack non-visual objects in altogether? Obviously not, because, for one thing, that would undermine most of the rationale for this book. Besides, objects (and COM objects in particular) turn out to be excellent vehicles for representing business *processes*, and, in particular, *transactions*. However, if we are to develop really useful business objects, we're going to have to separate the business logic from the underlying data.

I think it's time to introduce the **three-tier model**. (I'm still itching to do some MTS coding, by the way. It's just that there's a lot of stuff we need to get out of the way before we get going...)

Three Tiers for Microsoft

When you start to get involved with Microsoft Transaction Server, you start to hear an awful lot about "three-tier applications". So what precisely is a three-tiered application?

We're all familiar with the idea of breaking down functionality into layers. In this sort of software model, each layer performs a specific role on behalf of the layer above. Each layer can then be developed using the most appropriate tools, by programmers with the most appropriate skills and experience. Provided that the interfaces between the layers are correctly defined, development can proceed in parallel, and we can even substitute alternatives for one layer without affecting the others.

In the three-tier model, the *bottom* tier handles all the nitty-gritty database stuff – what we've done so far. As far as we are concerned with MTS, this is where the resource managers sit. The *top* tier handles the user interface (i.e. all the web page or Visual Basic stuff) – MTS calls it the **base client**. The *middle* tier is the most interesting one, because that's the one that forms the bridge between the two. This is the tier that defines the business logic of the application, and is the absolute heart of the application. Leave the bottom layer to the database experts and the top layer to the user-interface whizzes – the middle tier is to be *our* territory.

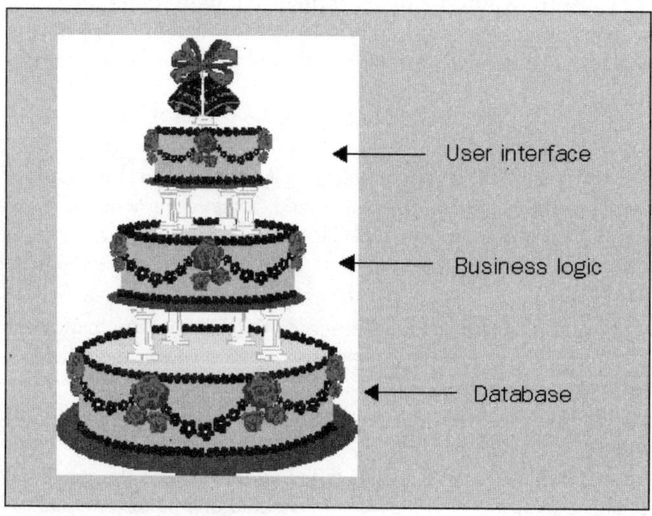

Let's get a little more concrete, and consider what the middle tier might look like in our kidnap game example. Remember, we're looking for *processes* here. One good way to identify processes is to look for the type of people who might be involved, for instance, a *negotiator*. A negotiation *process* will certainly be in progress during the kidnap game, involving the offering of a sum of money for the release of a hostage. Can we represent this as a COM object?

Of course we can. We'll give it an interface called `INegotiator` and this definition:

Method	Parameters	Description
`DealWithKidnappers`	`[in] int amount,` `[out,retval] VARIANT_BOOL *pbFree`	Offer amount for hostage, and find out if this is sufficient to free them

Property	Type	Description
`Hostage`	`BSTR`	Hostage name
`Account`	`BSTR`	Account to take ransom from

This is actually a pretty good example of a COM business object, in that it gets instantiated for a short period of time, it does its job and then goes away again. Business objects are a bit like specialized consultants: you hire them for a short-term contract, they do the job that they were hired to do and then you let them go. In our kidnap case, we hire a specially trained hostage negotiator.

Where does MTS fit in with all this? Well, as I'm sure you won't be surprised to find out, MTS is excellent at making use of COM business objects. In fact, you can make a business object transactional simply by registering it with MTS, provided it meets some simple criteria. And, in the most basic case, you can set it up so that a transaction is automatically started whenever the object is instantiated, and completed when the object is destroyed. Everything that goes on in the meantime is treated as part of a transaction.

> *Needless to say MTS offers you more control and flexibility than that, through the use of a* ***context object****, but it doesn't get any more difficult than that.*

Can you see why we have moved away from the traditional data-focused view of objects? If we used objects that represented data, we wouldn't be able to use their instantiation and destruction to signal the start and end of a transaction. And if data hung around in objects in between transactions, the MTS environment (full as it is of phrases like "recycled object instances" and "multi-user") might very well have invalidated it the next time you used it. Thus the only valid data is in the underlying database.

A Word of Warning

Let me confess to a glorious misconception early on in my career with MTS, to which I will own up, so that you don't make the same mistake. The project on which I was working was a prototype implementation of a distributed object system. We decided to do the whole thing by the book, so we used an object-oriented design tool as the first step. We identified our data items, decided on some of the operations that we would carry out on them, fed them into the tool and turned the handle to generate the code stubs. The net result was a whole rat's nest of object references inside object references, which we then went on to turn into COM objects. (To confuse matters further, we also isolated the COM layer from the underlying objects, so that we could put a CORBA wrapper round the objects as well – yep, it was one of those projects)

Of course, we knew that you could register any object with MTS and make it transactional, so we tried to do this with ours. You can guess what happened: we failed, miserably. Because our objects were so closely tied to their underlying data, they were all far too "stateful" for MTS to make any sense of them whatsoever. We had totally failed to understand the three-tier model. We had concentrated on the *data*, and we had completely ignored the *processes.*

What do I mean by **stateful**? A stateful object is one that maintains its state over a prolonged period of time. There's a spectrum of "statefulness" really. It stretches from objects that are just a collection of atomic methods that do a job and then return a result to the base client, and are then ready for the next call, to objects whose collective state is needed by the base client for some time (that is, over some method calls). If you want an example of a seriously stateful object, think back to our teleconferencing example in Chapter 2 – the conference objects can actually exist for quite a long period of time.

This is a good time to point out that, if you use stateful objects in MTS, you'll have to take some steps to ensure that the particular instances of the objects are retained for that base client. MTS doesn't guarantee that the business object instance it uses for a particular client won't change between two method calls. MTS is desperate to commit transactions wherever possible and get everything out of the way.

To put this in an example – imagine your MTS objects acquire their state from a persistent store when they are instantiated. Doing whatever validation it is that grown-up business objects do, they yield the relevant information to the base client that called them into existence. The base client information is updated (at typing and thinking speed) and then a different method of the client (behind the Submit button) calls the business objects with just those properties it's updated. Those objects then persist their state entire. But, by default, there's no reason that those business objects will be the same – cue potential embarrassment.

> *At the risk of running ahead of myself a little, let me tell you how you ensure MTS assumes nothing. You just call the* `DisableCommit()` *method of the context object, to set the objects' progress in the transaction to an indeterminate state while you make your various calls. The* `EnableCommit()` *method re-enables the default.*

And to cap it all, the more state an object has, though, the greater the performance hit in MTS.

A better scenario under MTS is to use business objects that acquire data, analyze it, pass it on to the base client per their request, and then finish their job with a smile. When the base client wants to upload the modified data, the business objects are reinstantiated and do their updating stuff to the database.

I think we're about ready to have a go at some MTS coding. Let's have a look at the source of our **Negotiator** object.

A Non-MTS-aware Negotiator Object

We're going to start off with a simple, non-MTS-aware project, called **SimpleNegotiator**, and import it into MTS and see what happens. We'll build it as an in-process DLL, despite the fact that we'll want to be able to access it remotely. This is because all MTS objects run inside transaction server proxies. This means that everything that the object does is wrapped up inside MTS control logic. We use the ATL object wizard to create our single object, called **Negotiator** (with the one interface, **INegotiator**) and we add the method and two properties that I've specified above.

*As with **DBManager**, we need to include the ADO headers from the MTS installation in our source, and add the library to the link section of the project settings.*

Starting off with our two properties, the code for these is very simple; all we're really doing here is parameterizing the object:

```
STDMETHODIMP CNegotiator::put_Hostage(BSTR newVal)
{
   m_bstrHostage = newVal;

   return S_OK;
}

STDMETHODIMP CNegotiator::put_Account(BSTR newVal)
{
   m_bstrAccount = newVal;

   return S_OK;
}
```

We need to declare the two private CComBSTR variables, **m_bstrHostage** and **m_bstrAccount**, in **Negotiator.h**:

```
private:
   ...
   CComBSTR m_bstrHostage;
   CComBSTR m_bstrAccount;
```

This is what the code for our **DealWithKidnappers()** method looks like:

```
STDMETHODIMP CNegotiator::DealWithKidnappers
                  (int amount, VARIANT_BOOL* pbFree)
{
   HRESULT hResult = TakeCashFromAccount(amount, pbFree);

   if (FAILED(hResult))
      return hResult;

   if (*pbFree == VARIANT_TRUE)
      return ReleaseHostage(amount, pbFree);

   return S_OK;
}
```

Again, this is very simple; the real action is in the two local method calls **TakeCashFromAccount()** and **ReleaseHostage()**. However, it's worth noting at this stage how the two halves of the transaction, represented by these local methods, have been separated out from each other; we'll see later on how they get tied back together.

Inside **TakeCashFromAccount()**, we hit ADO for the first time:

```
HRESULT CNegotiator::TakeCashFromAccount(int amount, VARIANT_BOOL* pbFree)
{
   // Find recordset for this account

   CComPtr<ADOConnection> pConnection = OpenDatabase(L"kidnap2");

   if (pConnection == NULL)
      return E_FAIL;

   CComPtr<ADORecordset> pRecordset = FindRecordset(pConnection, L"accounts",
                                            L"name", m_bstrAccount);

   if (pRecordset == NULL)
      return E_FAIL;

   // Extract current data from fields

   CComPtr<ADOFields> pFields;
   pRecordset->get_Fields(&pFields);

   long count;
   pFields->get_Count(&count);

   long lBalance = 0;

   for (long field = 0; field < count; field++)
   {
      CComVariant vField(field);

      CComPtr<ADOField> pField;
      pFields->get_Item(vField, &pField);
```

```
        CComBSTR bstrName;
        pField->get_Name(&bstrName);

        CComVariant vValue;
        pField->get_Value(&vValue);

        if (!wcscmp(bstrName, L"balance"))
        {
           lBalance = V_I4(&vValue);
           break;
        }
     }

     *pbFree = VARIANT_FALSE;
     HRESULT hResult = S_OK;

     if (amount <= lBalance)
     {
        // Set up variant containing change to database

        CComVariant vFields(L"balance");
        CComVariant vValues(lBalance - amount);

        // Update record

        hResult = pRecordset->Update(vFields, vValues);

        if (FAILED (hResult))
           Log(hResult, "Update record", pConnection);
        else
           *pbFree = VARIANT_TRUE;
     }

     pRecordset->Close();

     return hResult;
  }
```

That shouldn't look that much different from the logic that we had in the **DBManager** application. The code for the **OpenDatabase()** and **FindRecordset()** member functions is identical, bar the use of **CComPtr**s, to that used in **DBManager**, so I won't repeat it here. They too are declared as private member variables of **CNegotiator**.

All we are actually doing is opening up a connection to the SQL Server **kidnap2** database, getting hold of the record in the **accounts** table for the specified account, and decrementing the **amount** column by the specified amount – if there are sufficient funds to enable us to do so.

If the **TakeCashFromAccount()** method is successful, we invoke the **ReleaseHostage()** method:

```
HRESULT CNegotiator::ReleaseHostage(int amount, VARIANT_BOOL* pbFree)
{
   // Find recordset for this hostage

   CComPtr<ADOConnection> pConnection = OpenDatabase(L"kidnap1");

   if (pConnection == NULL)
      return E_FAIL;

   CComPtr<ADORecordset> pRecordset = FindRecordset(pConnection, L"hostages",
                                                   L"name", m_bstrHostage);

   if (pRecordset == NULL)
      return E_FAIL;

   // Extract current data from fields

   CComPtr<ADOFields> pFields;
   pRecordset->get_Fields(&pFields);

   long count;
   pFields->get_Count(&count);

   long lRansom = 0;

   for (long field = 0; field < count; field++)
   {
      CComVariant vField(field);

      CComPtr<ADOField> pField;
      pFields->get_Item(vField, &pField);

      CComBSTR bstrName;
      pField->get_Name(&bstrName);

      CComVariant vValue;
      pField->get_Value(&vValue);

      // If hostage is already free, don't do anything else
      if (!wcscmp (bstrName, L"free"))
         if ((vValue.vt == VT_BOOL) && (vValue.boolVal == VARIANT_TRUE))
         {
            pRecordset->Close();
            return E_INVALIDARG;
         }

         // Extract ransom
      if (!wcscmp (bstrName, L"ransom"))
      {
         lRansom = V_I4(&vValue);
         break;
      }
   }
```

```
    // Set up variant array containing changes to database

    *pbFree = VARIANT_FALSE;
    HRESULT hResult = S_OK;

    if ((amount >= lRansom)) && (lRansom != 0))
    {
       CComVariant vFields(L"free");
       CComVariant vValues(true);

       hResult = pRecordset->Update(vFields, vValues);

       if (FAILED (hResult))
          Log(hResult, "Update record", pConnection);
       else
          *pbFree = VARIANT_TRUE;
    }

    pRecordset->Close();

    return hResult;
}
```

This method opens up a connection to the **`kidnap1`** database, extracts the record for the specified hostage from the **`hostages`** table, and checks to see if the incoming funds are greater than the required ransom amount. If they are, the **`free`** column in the record is set to 1, to indicate that the hostage has been successfully freed.

Before we test it, we need a simple Visual Basic application. We'll call this **`NegotiatorClient`**, and here's the form:

In this application, we simply set up the account name, the hostage name and the attempted ransom amount, and try to deal. Here's the complete source:

```
Private Sub cmdDeal_Click()

    Dim neg As Negotiator
    Dim result As Boolean

    Set neg = New Negotiator

    neg.Hostage = txtHostage.Text
    neg.Account = txtAccount.Text

On Error GoTo failed
    result = neg.DealWithKidnappers(txtAmount.Text)

    If result = True Then
       MsgBox ("Freed!")
    Else
       MsgBox ("Still captive")
    End If

    Exit Sub

failed:
    If (Err.Number = 5) Then
       MsgBox ("Already free")
    Else
       MsgBox (Err.Description)
    End If

End Sub
```

Try setting up a few accounts and hostages using **`DBManager`**. Then run the client, try to make a deal and see what happens. You should see that whatever the result of the attempt to release the hostage, any changes made to the account still stand. This is because outside of MTS, no attempt is made to enforce the transaction logic. In other words, the kidnappers always get to keep the ransom, even if you didn't stump up enough. This isn't wholly satisfactory from the point of view of the negotiator. Furthermore, if something horrendous goes wrong during the negotiation process (for example, a software failure), the system may end up in an indeterminate state. Try, for example, inserting a spurious divide by zero somewhere in the **`DealWithKidnappers()`** method, and see what happens.

Running a Component Under MTS

Let's see what protection MTS gives. We'll take our **`SimpleNegotiator`** component, and set it up so that it runs under MTS. We do this by using the MTS Explorer. This has gone through a number of incarnations, and is now happily ensconced as a plug-in to the increasingly ubiquitous Microsoft Management Console.

Incidentally, if you haven't come across MMC before, take a look – we'll be writing our own component management plug-in later on in the book, when we covered managing, monitoring and control in Chapter 10.

This is a good point to take a look at Oleview (preferably using Expert View, and at the entries under the Automation Objects folder) at our Negotiator object. You should see that it is currently an in-process server with implementation path something like:

```
...\Chapter 5\SimpleNegotiator\Debug\SimpleNegotiator.dll
```

That will soon change...

Setting up a component to run under MTS is child's play. First of all, you need to define a **package**. Packages are groups of components that usually work together, and have a common security requirement. Defining a package (by right-clicking on the Packages Installed option) is basically a question of specifying that you want to create a brand new package and then giving it a name (say, Negotiator). You also need to specify which user identity the package is to run under; this should have just the minimum rights needed to carry out the negotiation process. This would mean having access rights to the `kidnap1` and `kidnap2` databases in SQL Server.

You now need to add your component to your new package. You can just drag the DLL to the right pane of MTS Explorer when Negotiator | Components is selected. Alternatively, you can right-click on Components, select New -> Components and ask the MTS Explorer to install or import a component.

Having done this, you should see your new component appear in the list of components for the `Negotiator` package:

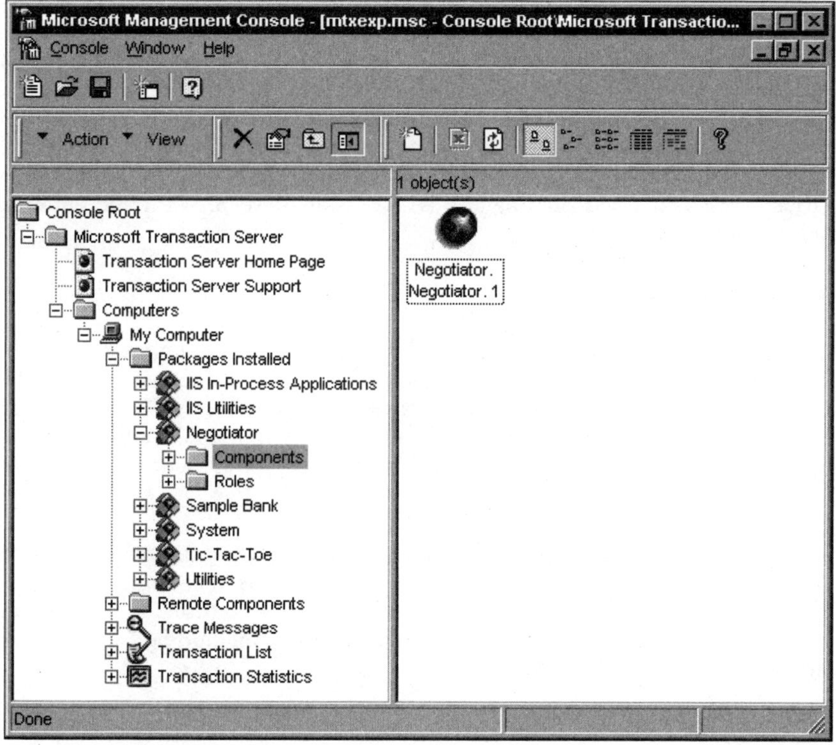

Keep an eye on that ball with the cross on it – it will play tricks later.

Back in Oleview, **`Negotiator`** has miraculously mutated from being an in-process server to a local server with this implementation path:

```
C:\WINNT\System32\mtx.exe /p:{EAE7E2CE-A7A5-11D1-B0F0-0040951082F7}
```

The UUID here is the UUID identifying the *package*, by the way.

All the components that have been registered with MTS run under the control of the transaction server proxy, **`mtx`**. It's **`mtx`** that requires that your components be part of a DLL, and use standard class factories and standard marshaling.

> *Strictly speaking, you don't have to use* **`mtx`**; *you can run your component in the client's process if you use the MTS Executive,* **`mtxex.dll`**, *as your proxy. However, we're interested in distributed systems here.*

OK, so we have now brought our component into the ambit of MTS. All we have to do now is tell MTS what to do about automatic transactions. If we look at the Transaction tab under Properties for the component, we see that we have four choices:

- Requires a transaction
- Requires a new transaction
- Supports transactions
- Does not support transactions

The second case is the most straightforward. If this is set, every time a component is instantiated, a new transaction is started. If the first choice is set, MTS ensures that the component is always running within the context of a transaction, but only creates a new one if necessary (in other words, if there isn't a context already available). In the third case, if there is a current transaction context, it is passed on to the component, but otherwise a new transaction isn't started. Finally, in the fourth case, the component is treated just as if it was running as a DLL outside of MTS. We'll find out more about transaction contexts in the next section.

We'll choose the first option for our component.

Having done this, let's try repeating some of the tests that we carried out on the component before we put it into MTS. You shouldn't see any difference, other than the amusing feature that whenever our component is instantiated, the ball with a cross on it starts to spin! It's actually quite a useful visual cue that something is going on. Once you've run the client a few times, take a look at the transaction statistics – you should see that for every test run you carried out, a transaction successfully completed.

We still haven't successfully managed to tie the two halves of our transaction together, however. If the second half fails, the first half still goes blindly ahead. So what is MTS doing for us here? (Apart from gathering statistics for us, that is.) Well, the fun starts if we put our divide by zero back into the **`DealWithKidnappers()`** method. Now look what happens: the method fails to complete, and an aborted transaction appears in our statistics!

What's more, if we take a look at the state of our databases after our attempted transaction, we'll find that no changes have taken place. So, even without putting any knowledge of the transaction into our component, we can see that MTS is providing a considerable degree of protection against software failure. It's just possible to think that, even without any fully-blown transaction content, you might consider bringing your components under MTS control anyway.

Transaction Context

Up to now, we've let MTS decide whether or not the transaction was successful. For more sophisticated applications, we really need to make that decision ourselves. How do we do this? The answer is all bound up with the **transaction context**. The transaction context is a COM object that maintains the continuity of the transaction across the many possible components of the transaction. The interface **IObjectContext** is used to control that context, of which more anon. Let's enhance our **SimpleNegotiator** object to take advantage of **IObjectContext**.

We'll start off by cloning our project into a new one called **TransNegotiator**. The first thing that we have to do is include another header file into our **Negotiator.cpp** file: **mtx.h**. Next, we need to make a few changes to the **DealWithKidnappers** method:

```
STDMETHODIMP CNegotiator::DealWithKidnappers(int amount,
                                             VARIANT_BOOL* pbFree)
{
   GetObjectContext(&m_spObjectContext);
   VARIANT_BOOL bCashThere = VARIANT_FALSE;

   HRESULT hResult = TakeCashFromAccount(amount, pbFree);
   if (FAILED (hResult))
   {
      m_spObjectContext->SetAbort();
      return hResult;
   }

   bCashThere = *pbFree;          // Was the cash there?

   hResult = ReleaseHostage(amount, pbFree);
   if (FAILED (hResult))
   {
      m_spObjectContext->SetAbort();
      return hResult;
   }

   if ((*pbFree == VARIANT_TRUE) && (bCashThere == VARIANT_TRUE))
   {
      *pbFree = VARIANT_TRUE;    // Return true to base client
      m_spObjectContext->SetComplete();
   }
   else
   {
      *pbFree = VARIANT_FALSE;   // Return false to base client
      m_spObjectContext->SetAbort();
   }
   return S_OK;
}
```

We start off by using the helper function **GetObjectContext()** to get hold of the object context interface. We pass in an **IObjectContext** pointer we add to **Negotiator.h**:

```
private:
   ...
   CComBSTR m_bstrHostage;
   CComBSTR m_bstrAccount;

   CComPtr<IObjectContext> m_spObjectContext;
```

Based on the result of our data manipulations, **pbFree** and **bCashThere**, we decide whether or not to commit the transaction, using those **SetCommit()** and **SetAbort()** methods. If we don't do this, MTS will make the decision for us, depending on whether or not the method runs to completion.

What is the result of all this? If we register this version with MTS, make sure the **Negotiator** object is set to Requires a Transaction and run the negotiator client, we can see that the component is now genuinely transactional. If the hostage is not freed (for whatever reason), and **IObjectContext::SetAbort()** gets called, no changes are made to either database. If, however, **IObjectContext::SetComplete()** is called, both changes go through.

> **If Requires a transaction or Requires a new transaction is not set in MTS, however, it will work in exactly the same way as the previous SimpleManager example – IObjectContext is not automatically associated with a transaction.**

But this seems too easy, and we've not really made use of the **IObjectContext** interface's methods. By the way, these are:

Method	Description
SetComplete()	Specifies that this object's transaction may complete and the object be deactivated, other things being equal.
SetAbort()	Abort the transaction, when the transaction manager asks, and deactivate the MTS object.
DisableCommit()	Your MTS object may maintain state while it's working; for instance, if it calls another object and waits for that to return, or if the client makes several calls during a transaction. The transaction mustn't commit in the meantime. However, MTS may reuse an MTS object for a different client – by default it assumes that the object carries no state between method calls. **DisableCommit()** guarantees that the client will get the same MTS object during a transaction.

Table Continued on Following Page

Method	Description
`EnableCommit()`	Re-enables the MTS object to commit if asked.
`CreateInstance()`	If your MTS object creates another MTS object as part of its work within a transaction, you don't want to lose that transaction's context information. If the second object fails, the calling object must know about it so that it rollback its changes.
`IsCallerInRole()`	Allows your MTS objects to check that their client has the right security clearance to continue. We'll be looking at MTS security in Chapter 9.

In the next section, we'll take a look at how we can share context between two objects. But before that, there's one more aspect of transaction context that I need to cover.

So far in this section, we have been talking about **automatic transactions**. In these transactions, it's MTS that decides when to initiate a transaction, based on the settings for the objects involved (Requires a new transaction etc.) It's also MTS that determines when the transaction is to be aborted or completed, based on our instructions to it via the object context (`SetComplete()` or `SetAbort()`). It's also possible in MTS to have **manual transactions**. With a manual transaction, the transaction comes under control of the client. How does this work?

In order to create our own transactions, we instantiate a `TransactionContextEx` object. This has the `ITransactionContextEx` interface, with the following methods:

Method	Description
`Abort()`	Aborts the current transaction.
`Commit()`	Commits the current transaction.
`CreateInstance()`	Create another object within this transaction context.

Let's imagine that our transaction involves a number of objects, each of which may commit or abort the transaction. We create all of our objects using the `CreateInstance()` method described here. Each of these objects can now get hold of their individual `IObjectContext` interfaces. (Notice the distinction between the two contexts: *transaction* context relates to the whole transaction, whereas *object* context just relates to a single object. Of course, that object might itself create instances of other objects within its own context.)

Each object then does all its work, and determines whether to invoke `SetComplete()` or `SetAbort()`. This, then determines whether or not the individual part of the transaction relating to that object is successful or not. Back at the top level, when we invoke our `Commit()` method on the *transaction* context, its success or otherwise depends on whether or not each of the individual components have committed or aborted. We won't be looking at manual transactions any more here, but you can quite easily adapt the examples here to use them instead of automatic ones. All you'll need to do is something like this in our Visual Basic application.

First of all, replace the line:

```
Set neg = New Negotiator
```

with,

```
Dim ctx as TransactionContext
Set ctx = CreateObject ("TxCtx.TransactionContext")

Set neg = ctx.CreateObject("Negotiator")
```

and then add this line at the end:

```
ctx.Commit
```

OK, let's get back to our object context.

Adding the Bank Clerk

The premise is this – the **`Negotiator`** needs to ask the **`BankClerk`**, on behalf of the base client, whether the ransom amount is in the account. The observant amongst you will realize that we're really just taking the code from the **`TakeCashFromAcount()`** method out of **`Negotiator`** and putting it into the **`BankClerk`**. Why? To demonstrate how MTS objects share context ... and to show off the ATL MTS support.

The **`BankClerk`** object has the following interface:

Method	Parameters	Description
`WithdrawCash`	**`[in] int amountNeeded,`** **`[in] BSTR account,`** **`[out, retal] VARIANT_BOOL* pIsCashThere`**	Find the account, check its balance against **`amountNeeded`** and fill out **`pIsCashThere`** accordingly

Because the **`BankClerk`** is a trustworthy sort, his word that the cash is there is quite enough for the **`Negotiator`** to keep working.

Let's insert this as a new ATL object into the **`TransNegotiator`** project, and this time, select the MS Transaction Server object. Fill out the class name as normal, but then look at the MTX tag:

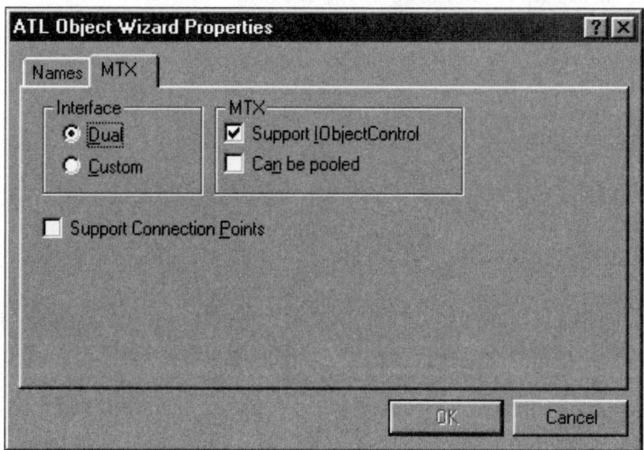

I've selected the Support IObjectControl checkbox, which is sufficient. This adds the **IObjectControl** interface to the **BankClerk** object, and includes **mtx.h** automatically. I've highlighted the relevant bits of the header file:

```
// BankClerk.h : Declaration of the CBankClerk

...

#include <mtx.h>

/////////////////////////////////////////////////////////////////////////////
CBankClerk
class ATL_NO_VTABLE CBankClerk :
   public CComObjectRootEx<CComSingleThreadModel>,
   public CComCoClass<CBankClerk, &CLSID_BankClerk>,
   public IObjectControl,
   public IDispatchImpl<IBankClerk, &IID_IBankClerk, &LIBID_TRANSNEGOTIATORLib>

...

// IObjectControl
public:
   STDMETHOD(Activate)();
   STDMETHOD_(BOOL, CanBePooled)();
   STDMETHOD_(void, Deactivate)();

   CComPtr<IObjectContext> m_spObjectContext;

...
```

The default implementations of the three methods of the interface look like this:

```
//////////////////////////////////////////////////////////////////////////////
// CBankClerk

HRESULT CBankClerk::Activate()
{
   HRESULT hr = GetObjectContext(&m_spObjectContext);
   if (SUCCEEDED(hr))
      return S_OK;
   return hr;
}

BOOL CBankClerk::CanBePooled()
{
   return FALSE;
}

void CBankClerk::Deactivate()
{
   m_spObjectContext->Release();
}
```

They'll do as they are. When the **BankClerk** object is created, the **Activate()** method is called first by the MTS environment. It gets the context object.

It's here that you'd call ***IObjectControl****'s* ***DisableCommit()*** *method, if you wanted the same MTS object to be used by a base client over multiple method calls.*

CanBePooled() *isn't implemented at the moment – the benefits of recycling object instances apparently aren't obvious, especially as resource managers like ODBC pool database connections, which are the time-consuming parts of object initialization.*

One thing you'll need to include in the Project | Settings... is the library **mtxguid.lib** for the value of **IID_IObjectControl**.

Because we're using the code from the **TakeCashFromAccount()** method in **BankClerk::WithdrawCash()**, we'll need copies of the **OpenDatabase()**, **FindRecordSet()** and the three **Log()** functions, and we'll need the ADO includes and library.

Back in the **Negotiator::TakeCashFromAccount()** method add the following code:

```
HRESULT CNegotiator::TakeCashFromAccount(int amount, VARIANT_BOOL* pbFree)
{
   // Create the BankClerk object using the Context object

   CComPtr<IBankClerk> pBankClerk;
   HRESULT hResult = m_spObjectContext->CreateInstance (CLSID_BankClerk,
                        IID_IBankClerk, reinterpret_cast<void**>(&pBankClerk));

   if (FAILED(hResult))
   {
      Log (hResult, "Creating Bank Clerk");
```

```
        return hResult;
    }

    // Ask the bank clerk to withdraw the cash

    hResult = pBankClerk->WithdrawCash(amount, m_bstrAccount, &pbFree);

    if (FAILED(hResult))
        Log (hResult, "Bank Clerk withdrawing cash");

    return hResult;
}
```

We create the **BankClerk** object using the **CreateInstance()** call, so that the Negotiator object's context information is passed down the line. A failure in either of the objects will result in both being rolled back.

We need to replace the components in the TransNegotiator package, set the **Negotiator** object to Requires a New Transaction and **BankClerk** to Requires a Transaction.... All should be ready for the recompiled Visual Basic client.

Resource Dispensers

There is a popular misconception that resource managers and resource dispensers are pretty much the same sort of thing, the only difference being that resource dispensers only deal with non-durable (i.e. memory-bound) data. However, if you have ever gone through the process of building your own resource manager and dispenser (as we all will, by the time we get to the end of Chapter 7), you will realize that they are different beasts altogether.

Here is the difference between the two:

- Resource managers are about managing the effect of transactions on resources.
- Resource dispensers are about making efficient use of a limited pool of resources.

The two often work hand in hand. Indeed, because of the way MTS is constructed, it's only resource dispensers that actually get access to the transaction context when the transaction is generated automatically by MTS. We'll leave the technicalities of this until Chapter 7, but for now, let's take another look at that ADO connection instantiation. Remember that ADO sits on top of ODBC? Well, it so happens that, within MTS, connections to ODBC are controlled by the ODBC Driver Manager, which is an MTS Resource Dispenser. So, when we instantiate our ADO connection object, we are actually getting hold of an ODBC connection resource. If we are operating within a transaction, the ODBC resource dispenser can get hold of the transaction context, and hence participate in the transaction commit process.

What else is the ODBC resource dispenser doing for us here? Let's say that our component is actually being used over and over again, very quickly. Do we really want the hassle of setting up the connection to SQL Server every time? No, what we'd really like would be to hang on to the connection, reset it and use it for the next invocation. This is what the ODBC resource dispenser does. Whenever a component drops a connection to a SQL Server database, the resource dispenser resets it, and sets a timer running. If the timer expires, it does indeed drop the connection to the database; however, if another component gets in before the timer expires, it simply picks up the existing connection.

This re-use of resources is a bit like the system on the Japanese underground where umbrellas are left around for commuters to pick up if they have forgotten theirs at home. It saves the hassle of buying another one, and – provided that the borrowed umbrellas are returned to the pool after use – it works admirably. The Dutch tried a similar system with white bicycles in Amsterdam in the sixties. However, most of the bicycles eventually ended up in the bottom of the canals – a sad comment, perhaps, on the ultimate comparative success of hippy idealism and Confucianism.

What else can resource dispensers be used for? If we want to share state between two instances of the same object for some reason, we can use a resource dispenser to control access to that shared area. The resource dispenser that handles this is called the Shared Property Manager, better known as SPM (pronounced "Spam").

SPM, SPM, Egg, Chips and SPM

The Shared Property Manager is basically a mechanism for accessing shared memory in a structured, controlled manner. Actually, calling it "shared memory" is stretching things a little, as we're talking about memory shared between individual instances within the same server, rather than the more enticing prospect of memory shared between different processes on the same machine. However, this isn't quite as restrictive as it might seem at first, as we shall see later on.

Shared properties are single, named or numbered **VARIANT**-type data items, grouped together in named, er, groups. The SPM is accessed by means of three COM interfaces:

- `ISharedPropertyGroupManager`
- `ISharedPropertyGroup`
- `ISharedProperty`

The names get shorter as you get near the action.

It's actually pretty simple to use. First of all, you get hold of an interface to the shared property group manager, `ISharedPropertyGroupManager`. This has the following methods:

Method	Parameters

`CreatePropertyGroup`	`[in] BSTR name,`
	`[in,out] LONG* plIsoMode,`
	`[in,out] LONG* plRelMode,`
	`[out] VARIANT_BOOL* pfExists,`
	`[out] ISharedPropertyGroup** ppGroup`

`get_Group`	`[in] BSTR name,` `[out] IsharedPropertyGroup** ppGroup`
`get__NewEnum`	`[out] IUnknown** ppEnumerator`

(Whilst we're at it, notice that `get__NewEnum()` interface – remember the enumerator we implemented in Chapter 1? They pop up all over the place...)

Using this, you can either create a new property group or get access to an existing one, in the form of an `ISharedPropertyGroup` interface. This has the following methods:

Method	Parameters

`CreateProperty`	`[in] BSTR name,`
	`[out] VARIANT_BOOL* pfExists,`
	`[out] ISharedProperty** ppProp`

`CreatePropertyByPosition`	`[in] INT index,`
	`[out] VARIANT_BOOL* pfExists,`
	`[out] ISharedProperty** ppProp`

`get_Property`	`[in] BSTR name,` `[out] ISharedProperty** ppProp`
`get_PropertyByPosition`	`[in] INT index,` `[out] ISharedProperty** ppProp`

This enables us to get access to the properties in the group. We can either create new properties, or get access to existing properties. These can either be named or numbered, according to taste. However, you can't get access to a named property by number, or a numbered property by name. Either way, what we end up with is an **`ISharedProperty`** interface. This has the following methods,

Method	Parameters
`get_Value`	`[out] VARIANT* pVal`
`put_Value`	`[in] VARIANT value`

which are pretty self-explanatory.

I must confess that I struggled a little to put together a decent application to demonstrate how SPM locks shared memory, in a way that could easily show what happened *without* SPM. What I wanted to do was generate an easily reproducible race condition that could be avoided by using SPM. What I ended up with was a very dull component that controls access to a simple flat file. Still, it will do the trick. We're going to develop a very simple component, called, not surprisingly, **`FlatFile`**. This has a very simple interface:

Method	Parameters	Description
`Write`	`[in] int value`	Write value, twice to the flat file **`"c:\race.txt"`**

Now, that's what I call a simple interface. This is the entire code for the object (in project **`NospamServer`**):

```
STDMETHODIMP CFlatFile::Write(int value)
{
    WriteToFile ("c:\\race.txt", value);
    WriteToFile ("c:\\race.txt", value);
```

```
    return S_OK;
}
```

```
void CFlatFile::WriteToFile (LPSTR lpszFile, int value)
{
    char szValue[128];
    sprintf (szValue, "%d\r\n", value);

    HANDLE hFile = CreateFile (lpszFile, GENERIC_WRITE, 0, NULL,
                              OPEN_ALWAYS, FILE_ATTRIBUTE_NORMAL +
                              FILE_FLAG_WRITE_THROUGH, NULL);

    SetFilePointer (hFile, 0, 0, FILE_END);

    ULONG nWritten;
    WriteFile (hFile, szValue, strlen (szValue), &nWritten, NULL);

    CloseHandle (hFile);
}
```

The Client

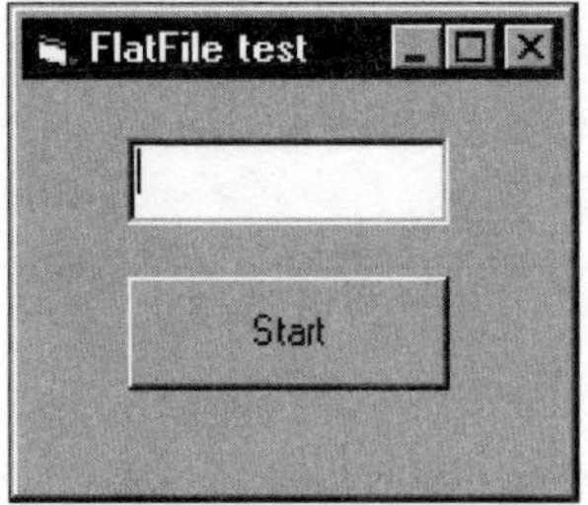

For our client, we'll use a very simple Visual Basic application, based around a form with one text box, one button and one timer. Here's the code:

```
Dim flat As FlatFile
Dim counter As Integer

Private Sub Form_Load()

    Timer1.Enabled = False
    Timer1.Interval = 1
    counter = 1000
    Set flat = New FlatFile

End Sub

Private Sub cmdStart_Click()

    Timer1.Enabled = True

End Sub
```

```
Private Sub Timer1_Timer()

    flat.Write (txtValue.Text)
    counter = counter - 1

    If (counter <= 0) Then
       MsgBox ("Finished!")
       Timer1.Enabled = False
    End If

End Sub
```

Let's see what happens if we set off a couple of EXE clients, both using this component to write to **`c:\race.txt`**. Our client will cycle around on a timer, writing the same number to the file 1000 times. If you try this out, not surprisingly you get a pretty random set of data in the output file. You'll see a whole load of 1s, then a couple of 2s, then a few pairs of 1s, then maybe a glut of 2s and so on. There is no consistent pattern to it at all – it's lumpy. This is simply because as soon as the first client is held up by the write to file, the second one grabs the CPU and has its go.

However, let's see what happens when we add some SPM-style locking. We'll create a clone of our project in the new project **`SpamServer`**. This is the new version of the **`Write`** method:

```
STDMETHODIMP CFlatFile::Write(int value)
{
   CComPtr<IObjectContext> pObjectContext = NULL;
   GetObjectContext (&pObjectContext);

   CComPtr<ISharedPropertyGroupManager> pSpamMgr;
   CComPtr<ISharedPropertyGroup> pSpamGroup;
   CComPtr<ISharedProperty> pSpamProp;

   if (pObjectContext)
   {
      pObjectContext->CreateInstance
                     (CLSID_SharedPropertyGroupManager,
                     IID_ISharedPropertyGroupManager,
                     reinterpret_cast(void**)&pSpamMgr);

      LONG lIsolationMode = LockMethod;
      LONG lReleaseMode = Process;
      VARIANT_BOOL bExists = VARIANT_FALSE;

      pSpamMgr->CreatePropertyGroup (L"LockGroup", &lIsolationMode,
                              &lReleaseMode, &bExists,
                              &pSpamGroup);
      pSpamGroup->CreateProperty (L"LockProperty", &bExists,
                           &pSpamProp);
   }

   WriteToFile ("c:\\race.txt", value);
   WriteToFile ("c:\\race.txt", value);

   return S_OK;
}
```

What are we doing here? We are instantiating the Shared Property Manager, creating a property group (called **LockGroup**), and creating a property within that (called **LockProperty**). If you try to create a property group or property, and it already exists, SPM treats the request as a **get_** type request – it will tell you that it already exists by setting the **bExists** flag.

Let's see what happens now. We install the component to run under MTS, as we did with **Negotiator**, except that don't need to specify anything about the component requiring a transaction. This is all we need to do to get a valid object context. We also need to change our clients to reference the **SpamServer** type library rather than the **NospamServer** one. This time, when we run two clients, we get a nice neat sequence of one or more pairs of 1s, then one or more pairs of 2s, then one or more pairs of 1s again. The creation of that shared property is acting as a *lock*. There is only one resource available here, and each client must wait its turn.

Where would we use this feature? We would use it wherever there is a need to share *state* between two separate instances of the same MTS object, in other words, where there was a need for some interaction between the two instances. The SPM can therefore be used to cache DBMS lookup tables and counters in order to avoid hot spots.

Other Resource Managers

SQL Server isn't of course the only resource manager available. Microsoft have been working hard at providing support for other databases, such as Oracle, by means of the industry-standard XA protocol. And in Chapter 7, as I have been trailing at every opportunity in this chapter, we're going to write our own. Next, however, we're going to look at a slightly unusual resource manager, in the form of Microsoft Message Queue. And if you're wondering how on earth something so intrinsically asynchronous as a guaranteed messaging system can get involved in transactions, read on...

6

Messaging and Loosely-Coupled Systems

"Is your name Marty McFly?"
"Yeah?"
"I've got something for you – a letter"
"A letter for me? That's impossible..."

Back to the Future, Part II

Late Delivery

Round my way, there's one thing you can guarantee every Christmas. I'm not talking about snow here by the way; I live in England after all, and the best we can hope for is a cold drizzle. No, the most regular feature here – more regular than door-to-door carol singers, arguments with relatives and plum pudding – is the story in the local newspaper about the Christmas card posted fifty years ago that has only just arrived. These stories are always good copy, because there are a lot of amusing angles to them. For instance, is there a whole pile of undelivered Paleolithic mail lying around in the corner of every sorting office, just waiting to be let out one item at a time? How many families have been torn apart by the apparent non-delivery of that one card? And do they charge extra for delivery because the postage rates have gone up in the meantime?

To me, however, the interesting question is this: should you be astounded at the incompetence of the postal authorities in failing to deliver the mail for so long, or should you be impressed with them for delivering it in the end, no matter how late? Obviously, the answer depends on the relative time-dependence of the item being posted. In the case of a Christmas card, if it's a month late, it might as well be thrown away, but if it's an important legal document, it doesn't matter so much if it's a bit late, as long as delivery is *guaranteed.*

Everything we've looked at so far in this book is to do with relatively closely-coupled systems, where, setting aside considerations of bandwidth, you can develop the software as if it was going to run on a single central server. Remember that phrase "location transparency"? Even when we talked about serializing our data for efficiency in Chapter 3, we made the assumption that the client and the server would both be running simultaneously, and would maintain good, if slow, communications with each other. But what if one of them wasn't running at all? Could we still write a system that made any sense?

The answer to this last question is, inevitably, yes. In the last chapter, we looked at how Microsoft is making transactions mainstream by absorbing them into the Windows operating system. In this chapter, we look at how they are making guaranteed messaging mainstream by absorbing that into the operating system too. The code name for Microsoft Transaction Server was Viper – a name that has all but disappeared from the lips of all but Redmond die-hards. The code for Microsoft Message Queue was Falcon, a name that you still see on documents. Well, would you rather be promoting a snake or a bird of prey?

The First Principle Of Data Conservation

When I get on a plane to Seattle (preferably the scenic route via Vancouver), I can state with a reasonable degree of certainty that I will get off at the other end at some point in the future. Moreover, I can guarantee that only one of me will get off at the other end, and that some strange clone of myself will not spontaneously materialize at another airport somewhere else in the world. Even if, heaven forbid, my plane blows up in mid-Atlantic, it will in theory be possible to recover all my atoms and prepare them for a decent burial (no flowers, please – donations to the home for distressed Netscape programmers).

All this is a direct consequence of the principle of conservation of mass. However convoluted the flight, you can't end up with more or less than you started with. (Having said that, I feel that I should point out that it is a well-known fact that aircraft *baggage* is subject to entirely different laws, in which chance has a significance that is usually only found at the subatomic level.)

At the risk of attempting to sound like a low-budget imitation of Nicholas Negroponte, when you start looking at *bits* rather than *atoms*, things get very different. I'll state something very obvious, which has an enormous impact on the design of loosely-coupled systems:

There is no principle of data conservation

If you send a packet of data over a wire, there is no earthly reason why, depending on the nature and quality of the systems at the other end, you may not end up with *two* copies of it, a *thousand* copies of it or indeed *none at all.* This principle (or lack of it) is, of course, the reason why digital systems are so amazingly cheap and powerful compared with physical ones, but it's also why they are so much more difficult to manage. If we are to develop loosely-coupled systems that work in a sensible, manageable way, we're going to have to make data behave more like a physical substance. And that's where guaranteed messaging systems come in.

Let's try a little falconry...

Know Your Queue

While the technology for Microsoft's Message Queue is well-tested and, dare I say it, stable, it is still a tad limited and not a bit confusing for the newcomer. So, to help at least partially demystify the terminology that MSMQ brings with it, I've jotted down its key terms below and documented my test setup for this chapter. This should help clarify the graphical representation of the system that we'll come across in MSMQ Explorer very shortly.

If you still haven't learnt as much as you would have liked about Message Queues by the end of this chapter, then there's another great Wrox Press book entitled *Professional MTS and MSMQ with VB and ASP* by Alex Homer and David Sussman (ISBN 1-861001-46-0) that you really should get hold of.

MSMQ Terminology

We'll start in the usual way, by defining a few terms.

The whole MSMQ network is referred to as an **enterprise**. This might comprise every single computer in a global organization (although each host has to have a different name, so you'll have to be careful with your naming convention) or maybe just one or two servers in selected key positions. An enterprise is divided up into **connected networks**, in which every computer communicates with every other one using the same protocol (TCP/IP or IPX/SPX for example). An enterprise is also subdivided into **sites**. All the computers in a site are assumed to be physically close, and connected by a LAN rather than a WAN, in similar fashion to an NT domain. A connected network may span more than one site; for example, it might include sites in Chicago, Seattle and Orlando.

This hierarchical topography is used by MSMQ in determining the most efficient route for each message.

One server is designated as the **Primary Enterprise Controller** (PEC), and this maintains the enterprise configuration database. Within each site, one server is designated as the **Primary Site Controller** (PSC); this maintains a local copy of the configuration. In a very small enterprise (like mine!) the PEC and PSC can be the same machine. There can also be one or more **Backup Site Controllers** (BSC). All Site Controllers and the PEC itself require a minimal installation of SQL Server to be installed prior to MSMQ in order to hold (copies of) the enterprise configuration database. In addition to this, other server machines can be designated as **Routing Servers**. The PEC, PSCs and BSCs are also de facto routing servers. The routing servers are responsible for passing messages through the enterprise. **Connector Servers** handle connections to foreign (in other words, non-Windows) systems, via systems like Level8's FalconMQ for Unix.

MSMQ clients are either **Dependent** or **Independent**. Dependent clients cannot function without a synchronous connection to a routing server, which carries out all the MSMQ operations on its behalf. Independent clients, on the other hand, can function whilst disconnected from the enterprise. Any messages that they send are saved until they next reconnect (which can put quite a substantial load on the system – particular if there's a lengthy server outage).

A **message queue** is a repository for messages. It resides on one machine only (which can either be a routing server or an independent client), and you can think of it in similar terms to a mailbox. However, it can be read by any machine in the network, provided that they have read access (we'll talk about security in general in Chapter 9). There can be many different queues in an enterprise, or indeed on a single machine.

So then, that's the theory. Now here's the practice.

MSMQ Set-Up

Some words of warning for those of you trying to install MSMQ for the first time.

- After installing the PEC on one machine, it is definitely a good idea to read the section in the MSMQ Administrator's Guide entitled 'Permissions and Rights Required to Install MSMQ'. This covers who has rights to install Message Queue clients and servers and the SQL Server minimum install that is required to host the enterprise and site controllers.
- Suppose, for example, that our Chicago office is setting up two MSMQ sites: One for Production and one for marketing. If one site contains the PEC and the other a PSC, then it should be noted that the PEC and PSC don't have to be in the same domain, but there has to be a trust relationship between the two. What happens is that applications trying to look at information on the PEC are doing so by attempting to establish an authenticated RPC connection to the PEC, which fails if the user in whose context the app is running is not trusted in the domain of the PEC. Incidentally, this restriction will likely be lifted with MSMQ 2.0 or perhaps even in NT Service Pack 4.

If you've got that, then here's how I set up my Messaging System. For my PEC, I've chosen my machine dipsy, which is running Windows NT4 Enterprise Edition. I've specified the name of my enterprise to be OverTheHills, and my local site to be FarAway. By definition, dipsy is also the PSC for this site. I've added one connected network, called Windmill. I've also got one independent client called tinky-winky. Let's take a look at this from the system administrator's point of view.

The administration tool for MSMQ is called the **MSMQ Explorer**. At the time of writing, it hasn't yet been incorporated into the Microsoft Management Console, but no doubt that will happen in time. If you start it up, you'll see something like this:

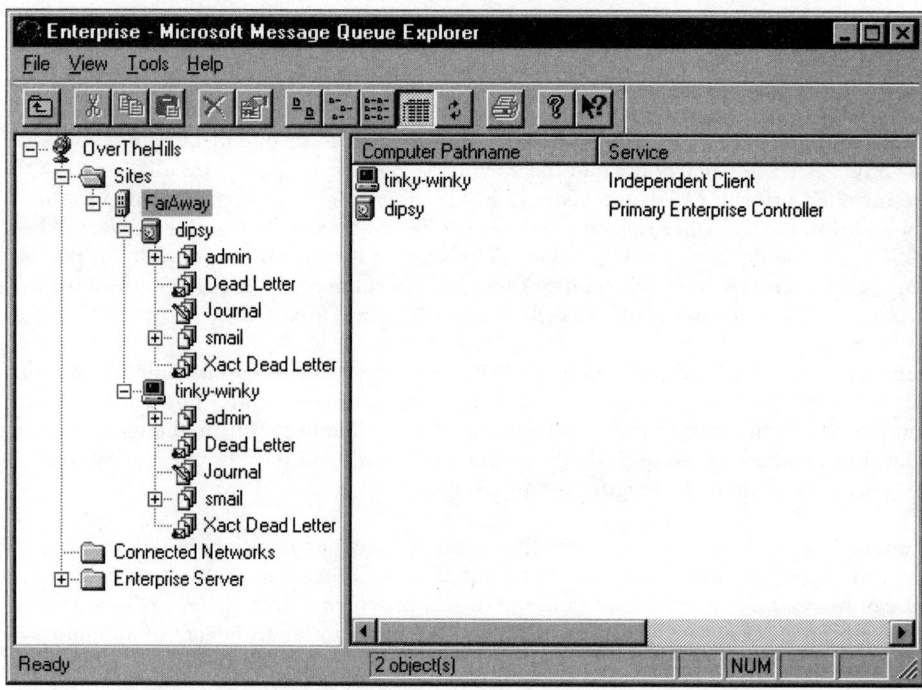

If you look at my enterprise (OverTheHills), you can see the site (Faraway), containing the two hosts dipsy and tinky-winky. I've defined two queues for each of these: admin and smail. We'll look at these queues in a little while, when we look at our first example.

You should also see three other queues: Dead Letter, Journal and Xact Dead Letter. These queues are set up automatically by MSMQ, and you can't change any of their properties or delete them.

The **Dead Letter queue** is the place where messages go when they can't be delivered. When you create a message, you have a number of choices about its lifetime. You can specify that it has infinite life – in other words, whatever happens to the enterprise, it will remain in the network until one way or other it manages to get delivered. Alternatively, you can specify that you're only prepared to wait a specific period until either it reaches the target queue or is read. If this timeout (whose default is a staggering 90 days) expires, the message is put in a dead letter queue. The actual dead letter queue chosen is the one on the machine that the message had reached at the point when the timer expired. Depending on circumstances, this could be the machine that sent the message, the target machine, or a routing machine somewhere in between the two.

You can specify that a message is also copied to a **Journal queue** on your own machine when it is sent. This is a bit like the facility in most e-mail systems where you can keep a copy of everything you send out; you'll notice a lot of e-mail analogies in MSMQ! We'll look at the **Transactional Dead Letter queue** later on in the chapter when we see how MSMQ integrates with MTS.

I think we're ready to try some MSMQ programming.

Do It Yourself E-mail

At first sight, MSMQ has much in common with an e-mail system, such as – say – Microsoft Exchange Server. For instance, there's an obvious correspondence between message queues and mailboxes. However, the crucial difference is that MSMQ is about *application to application* communication, and e-mail is about *person to person* communication. E-mail systems are optimized towards passing human-readable information between one or more humans. Messaging systems like MSMQ are pitched at a lower level, and are much more generic in scope.

Having said that, there's no reason why you can't build an e-mail system on *top* of MSMQ... MSMQ in fact has API functions built in for interconnecting with e-mail systems, using a subset of the standard MIME format.

Before we start, however, we have a choice between two APIs:

- The first is a standard C-type API, containing around forty functions with names that start off with the letters `MQ` (of which roughly half are for e-mail interconnectivity)
- The second one consists of a set of twenty-odd COM objects (of which – again – roughly half are for e-mail interconnectivity)

We won't be looking at e-mail interconnectivity here, but if you're interested all the API functions and objects are described in the MSMQ SDK help.

The second API was actually developed expressly for use by VB developers, and to be frank, it doesn't quite have the flexibility and depth of coverage of the C library. *However,* having tried both, I have to say that to seasoned COM heads such as ourselves, the COM one is actually nicer to use.

> *In case you're having trouble making up your mind, I've written this example in Visual C++ using MFC and both APIs. The* **`SimpleMail`** *project is the COM version, whilst the* **`NocomMail`** *project is, believe it or not, the no-COM version. Also, I think that the COM version is a pretty good demonstration of the power that the discipline of having to expose a good component interface gives to the API developer. Both of these projects are available to download from the Wrox Press website at http://www.wrox.com.*

Actually, now that we're a few pages into the chapter, you might be forgiven for wondering what MSMQ really has to do with DCOM. You might even be thinking that the only reason that I've mentioned the COM version of the MSMQ API in preference to the C version is just to work COM into it somehow. Nothing could be further from the truth. As we'll see later on in this chapter, there are two crucial areas where MSMQ is beginning to work in tandem with other COM technologies to add enormous value. The first of these is its role as a resource manager (which we'll look at later on in the chapter), and the second is as an alternative high-level transport for asynchronous "one-way" methods in DCOM (which we'll look at right at the end of the chapter).

Of course, we could do this first example without using COM at all, but – well, you can never get enough practice, can you? I'll go through the COM version of the project in some detail, and then I'll make some brief comparison with the no-COM version.

We'll start off by creating our e-mail message queues. We need one for each machine that we're sending messages to. For convenience, we'll give each of our queues the local name of smail. Each queue resides on one machine, and it can be referred to in a number of ways:

- Its pathname, for example dipsy\smail
- A user-friendly label, for example "Simplemail for dipsy"
- (And if you really insist) a UUID, **`58A4CE1C-A937-11D1-BA12-004095D103A0`** (the UUID is automatically generated by MSMQ when you create the queue)
- A format name, constructed out of the queue's pathname, or its UUID; for instance **`PUBLIC=<UUID>`** or **`DIRECT=OS:dipsy\MyQueue`**

The MSMQ 'C' API only uses format names, although the MSMQ component set can use any of these.

> *Pathnames and UUIDs are guaranteed to be unique, but labels aren't. This means that you can't use queue labels for operations like sending mail, because MSMQ can't necessarily tell unambiguously which queue you are talking about.*

As well as this, you can assign a type to each queue, so that you can search for queues of a particular type.

As well as our previously created smail queue, we'll create another one on each machine, called admin. This is going to be our queue for administration messages. This is a really neat feature. We can actually tell MSMQ to send us a message when something important has happened, like the message reaching the target queue, or if something bad has happened.

So that we can compare both the COM and no-COM versions, we'll build our mailer as a dialog-based MFC application. This is what our main dialog looks like:

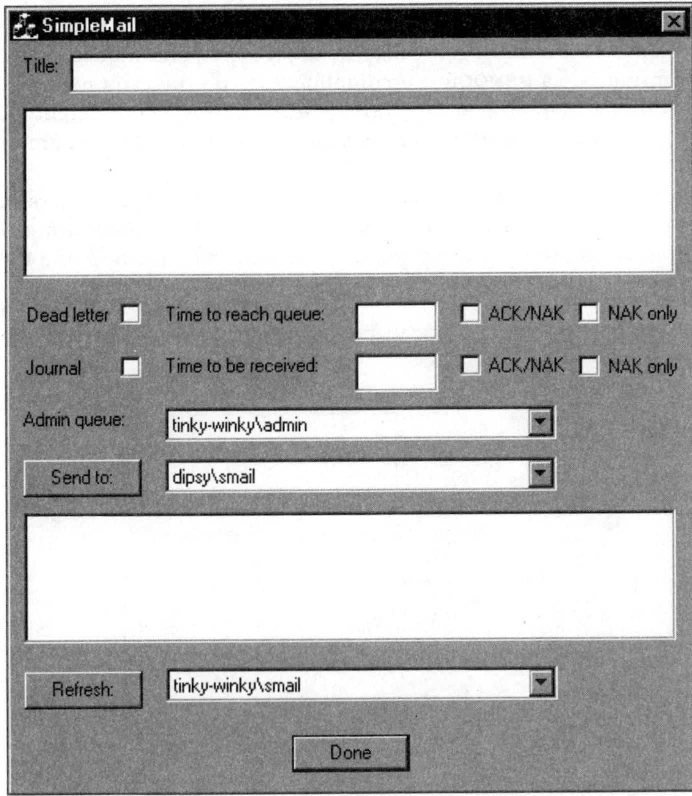

In this application, we're going to enter messages by specifying a title, some text, and two queues, one to send the message to and one to which administration messages are sent back. We're also going to set some options whenever we send a message. Take a look at these. We can:

- Specify whether or not the message is to be dumped into a dead letter queue if it fails to get through for whatever reason;
- Specify whether or not the message is to be copied to our local machine's journal file; (it is also possible to attach a separate journal queue to each queue, although this isn't demonstrated here)
- Override the standard default timeouts (in seconds) for reaching the destination queue and being read. Timeouts are specified in seconds
- Specify what kind of administration messages MSMQ is going to send us. For example, we can request that MSMQ gives us an acknowledgment (ACK) when a message is received (i.e. read) or a negative acknowledgement (NAK) if it isn't received, or perhaps a NAK only if the message fails to reach the destination queue.

We're also going to look out for messages coming back. We could, if we wanted, request asynchronous real-time notification. However, quite apart from the complications involved in getting MFC to accept events from COM objects, I think we're better off keeping it nice and simple at this stage. We'll see asynchronous notification in operation later on, anyway. For now, we'll content ourselves with polling the message queue whenever the user hits the Refresh button.

The MSMQ Component Set

The two most important components in the MSMQ set are **`MSMQMessage`** and **`MSMQQueue`**. Unsurprisingly, the former represents a message, whilst the latter represents a queue. As it happens though, you never actually instantiate a **`MSMQQueue`** component; to do this, you need to use one of the methods of the **`MSMQQueueInfo`** interface. The **`MSMQQueueInfo`** is a component that describes the static aspects of a queue, whereas the **`MSMQQueue`** component describes the dynamic aspects of it.

You can instantiate your own **`MSMQQueueInfo`** object, or you can get one by enumerating through a list by using a **`MSMQQueueInfos`** object. You can't, however, instantiate a **`MSMQQueueInfos`** object: the only way to get hold of one of these is by using the **`LookupQueue()`** method of a **`MSMQQuery`** object.

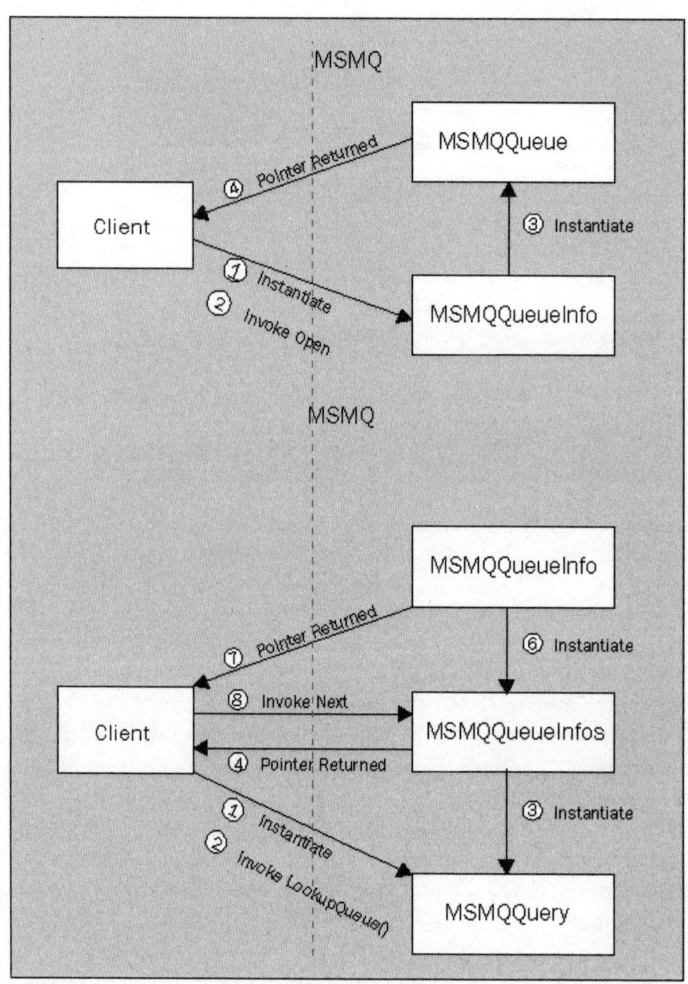

Confused? Don't worry – it's a lot more straightforward in practice. Let's put together our **SimpleMail** application. We'll start off by including the MSMQ header file at the top of the **SimpleMailDlg.h** file and – because we'll be using the Visual C++ compiler COM support classes – setting up a few smart pointer **typedef**s for the interfaces that we'll be using. (The MSMQ library and header files can be found in the **sdk** folder of your MSMQ installation directory):

```
#include <comdef.h>    // Compiler COM support classes
#define SMARTPTR_TYPEDEF(x)    \
   typedef _com_ptr_t<_com_IIID<x, &IID_##x> > x##Ptr;

#include <mqoai.h>    // MSMQ interfaces/GUIDs
SMARTPTR_TYPEDEF(IMSMQQueueInfos);
SMARTPTR_TYPEDEF(IMSMQQueueInfo);
SMARTPTR_TYPEDEF(IMSMQQueue);
SMARTPTR_TYPEDEF(IMSMQQuery);
SMARTPTR_TYPEDEF(IMSMQMessage);
```

To get the full definitions of the GUIDs from **mqoai.h**, we'll also need to **#include** this file in **StdAfx.cpp** after including **initguid.h**.

```
// Get the definitions of the MSMQ GUIDs (to avoid linker errors)
#include <initguid.h>
#include <mqoai.h>
```

The first change that we make is at the end of **OnInitDialog()**:

```
   SetIcon(m_hIcon, FALSE);       // Set small icon

   // Make sure COM has been initialized in CSimpleMailApp::InitInstance()
   // with a call to AfxOleInit()

   ShowQueues();
   OnRefresh();

   return TRUE;  // return TRUE  unless you set the focus to a control
}
```

Let's take a look at that **ShowQueues()** function; this is the piece of code that populates the three combo boxes that contain lists of the available queues.

```
void CSimpleMailDlg::ShowQueues()
{
   // Create query
   IMSMQQueryPtr pQuery;
   HRESULT hr = pQuery.CreateInstance(CLSID_MSMQQuery, NULL, CLSCTX_SERVER);
   if (FAILED(hr))
   {
      DisplayComError(_T("Failed to create message query"), hr);
      return;
   }

   // Get information on all queues
   VARIANT vEmpty;
   vEmpty.vt = VT_ERROR;
```

```
    IMSMQQueueInfosPtr pInfos;
    hr = pQuery->LookupQueue(&vEmpty, &vEmpty, &vEmpty, &vEmpty, &vEmpty,
                            &vEmpty, &vEmpty, &vEmpty, &vEmpty, &pInfos);
    if (FAILED(hr))
    {
       DisplayComError(_T("Failed to look up queues"), hr);
       return;
    }

    pInfos->Reset();

    CComboBox* pOutgoing = ComboPtr(IDC_OUTGOING); // ComboPtr() returns
    CComboBox* pIncoming = ComboPtr(IDC_INCOMING); // a CComboBox* when given
    CComboBox* pAdmin = ComboPtr(IDC_ADMIN);       // a resource ID

    pOutgoing->ResetContent();
    pIncoming->ResetContent();
    pAdmin->ResetContent();

    // Loop through queues, extracting path names
    while (1)
    {
       IMSMQQueueInfoPtr pInfo;
       pInfos->Next(&pInfo);

       if (pInfo == NULL)
          break;

       BSTR bstrQueue;
       pInfo->get_PathName(&bstrQueue);
       CString csQueue = bstrQueue;
       SysFreeString(bstrQueue);

       pOutgoing->AddString(csQueue);
       pIncoming->AddString(csQueue);
       pAdmin->AddString(csQueue);
    }

    pOutgoing->SetCurSel(0);
    pIncoming->SetCurSel(0);
    pAdmin->SetCurSel(0);
}
```

OK, that's how we get a list of the pathnames of all the available queues; how do we actually send a message to one of them?

Sending a Message

Here's the code that gets triggered when the user hits the Send button:

```
void CSimpleMailDlg::OnSend()
{
```

```
// Open up the outgoing queue
IMSMQQueuePtr pQueue = OpenQueue(IDC_OUTGOING, MQ_SEND_ACCESS);
if (pQueue == NULL)
   return;

// Create message and populate label and body
IMSMQMessagePtr pMessage;
HRESULT hr = pMessage.CreateInstance(CLSID_MSMQMessage, NULL,
                                     CLSCTX_SERVER);
if (FAILED(hr))
{
   DisplayComError(_T("Failed to create message"), hr);
   return;
}

pMessage->put_Label(GetDlgItemBSTR(IDC_TITLE));

CString csText;
GetDlgItemText(IDC_TEXT, csText);
pMessage->put_Body(_variant_t(csText));

// Set journal flag
int journal = MQMSG_JOURNAL_NONE;

if (GetDlgItemCheck(IDC_DEADLETTER))
   journal += MQMSG_DEADLETTER;

if (GetDlgItemCheck(IDC_JOURNAL))
   journal += MQMSG_JOURNAL;

pMessage->put_Journal(journal);

// Set up acknowledgement flag
int ack = MQMSG_ACKNOWLEDGMENT_NONE;

if (GetDlgItemCheck(IDC_FULLREACH))
   ack |= MQMSG_ACKNOWLEDGMENT_FULL_REACH_QUEUE;

if (GetDlgItemCheck(IDC_NAKREACH))
   ack |= MQMSG_ACKNOWLEDGMENT_NACK_REACH_QUEUE;

if (GetDlgItemCheck(IDC_FULLRECV))
   ack |= MQMSG_ACKNOWLEDGMENT_FULL_RECEIVE;

if (GetDlgItemCheck(IDC_NAKRECV))
   ack |= MQMSG_ACKNOWLEDGMENT_NACK_RECEIVE;

pMessage->put_Ack(ack);

// Set up timeouts for reaching queue and message receipt
int timeout = GetDlgItemInt(IDC_REACHTIME);
if (timeout)
   pMessage->put_MaxTimeToReachQueue(timeout);
```

```
    timeout = GetDlgItemInt(IDC_RECVTIME);
    if (timeout)
       pMessage->put_MaxTimeToReceive(timeout);

    // Define administration queue
    IMSMQQueueInfoPtr pInfo = GetInfoPtr(IDC_ADMIN);
    if (pInfo)
    {
       pInfo->Refresh();
       hr = pMessage->putref_AdminQueueInfo(pInfo);
    }

    // Send message
    hr = pMessage->Send(pQueue, &_variant_t());
    if (FAILED(hr))
    {
       DisplayComError(_T("Failed to send message"), hr);
       return;
    }
}
```

As you can see, sending a message is largely a question of creating the message object, populating whichever properties you want and then invoking the **`Send()`** method, specifying the queue you want to send the message to. One small item worth mentioning is that call to **`Refresh()`** on the administration queue **`MSMQQueueInfo`** object. We need this because we've instantiated the object, and set up the pathname (which is enough to identify it uniquely). However, we haven't filled in the rest of the object. That's what the call to **`Refresh()`** does.

Notice all those different options for returning an acknowledgement to us? If the **`MQMSG_ACKNOWLEDGMENT_FULL_XXX`** version is selected, we get told whatever happened. If only the **`MQMSG_ACKNOWLEDGMENT_NACK_XXX`** version is selected, we only get told if something goes wrong.

The work of actually opening up the queue is done by a helper function. Here it is :

```
IMSMQQueuePtr CSimpleMailDlg::OpenQueue(int nID, int mode)
{
    // Open queue specified in field
    IMSMQQueueInfoPtr pInfo = GetInfoPtr(nID);
    if (pInfo == NULL)
       return NULL;

    IMSMQQueuePtr pQueue;
    HRESULT hr = pInfo->Open(mode, NULL, &pQueue);
    if (FAILED(hr))
    {
       DisplayComError(_T("Failed to open message queue"), hr);
       return NULL;
    }

    return pQueue;
}
```

Notice that we don't open the queue directly; we use a **QueueInfo** object to get to it. This is the helper function that sets that up:

```
IMSMQQueueInfoPtr CSimpleMailDlg::GetInfoPtr(int nID)
{
   // Set up info object based on specified field
   IMSMQQueueInfoPtr pInfo;
   HRESULT hr = pInfo.CreateInstance(CLSID_MSMQQueueInfo, NULL,
                                      CLSCTX_SERVER);
   if (FAILED(hr))
   {
      DisplayComError(_T("Failed to create message queue info"), hr);
      return NULL;
   }

   pInfo->put_PathName(GetDlgItemBSTR(nID));
   return pInfo;
}
```

Notice that the only information necessary to specify the queue is its pathname – remember that this was unique? We get the pathname using another helper that we've created, **GetDlgItemBSTR()**, which works just like **GetDlgItemText()** except it returns a **_bstr_t** object.

We actually have three options available for opening a queue: **sending**, **receiving** or **peeking**. The last two are pretty similar, except that when you open a queue for peeking, you can't actually remove a message from it – we'll look at the peeking operation in a minute. We've already seen the sending operation in the **OnSend()** function above.

Once we've invoked the **Send()** method on the **MSMQMessage** object, it's up to MSMQ to handle the delivery of the message. It's out of our hands.

Receiving a Message

One of the things that strikes you as a trifle odd when you run this application is that you don't actually need two copies of it to try it out. You can simply use the same instance of the application to receive the message that you have just sent out. This is because, whilst queues do have a physical location, they can – security considerations aside – be read to and written from anywhere within the enterprise. You're not sending the message to a computer – you're sending it to a *queue*. In fact, as we'll see in the next example, it can be quite useful to have a queue that lots of different clients can read from.

So how do we get a list of the titles of all the outstanding messages on a queue? Here's how:

```
void CSimpleMailDlg::OnRefresh()
{
   // Open up the incoming queue
   IMSMQQueuePtr pQueue = OpenQueue(IDC_INCOMING, MQ_PEEK_ACCESS);
   if (pQueue == NULL)
      return;

   // Peek at the current (i.e. first) message
   _variant_t vTimeout(100L);
   _variant_t vFalse(false);
```

```
    IMSMQMessagePtr pMessage;
    HRESULT hr = pQueue->PeekCurrent(&vFalse, &vFalse, &vTimeout, &pMessage);
    if (FAILED(hr))
    {
       DisplayComError(_T("Failed to peek current"), hr);
       return;
    }

    CListBox* pMessages = ListPtr(IDC_MESSAGES);
    pMessages->ResetContent();

    // Get all the rest of the messages, outputting titles
    while (pMessage)
    {
       BSTR bstrTitle;
       pMessage->get_Label(&bstrTitle);
       CString csTitle = bstrTitle;
       SysFreeString(bstrTitle);
       pMessages->AddString(csTitle);

       pQueue->PeekNext(&vFalse, &vFalse, &vTimeout, &pMessage);
       if (FAILED(hr))
       {
          DisplayComError(_T("Failed to peek next"), hr);
          return;
       }
    }
}
```

What we're doing here is enumerating through the messages in the queue. We can optimize the peeking operation by specifying that we don't want the body of the message or the destination queue information set up – that's the reason for those two **vFalse** parameters. If you look at the no-COM version, you'll see that there is a whole load more flexibility about what information is actually extracted during a peek. However, in either case, the nature of the peek operation remains the same: nothing is actually removed from the queue.

There's one other point worth mentioning – the **vTimeout** parameter. Remember that we're dealing with a loosely-connected system, and that we might not be able to see the queue at all.

Having set up the list of messages in the queue, actually reading one is child's play. In this implementation, I've elected to enumerate all the messages in the queue until I come across one with the same title. I guess you could make this a little more sophisticated, but it's sufficient for our purposes:

```
void CSimpleMailDlg::OnDblclkMessages()
{
    // Get title of message to find
    CString csMessage;
    CListBox* pMessages = ListPtr(IDC_MESSAGES);
    int index = pMessages->GetCurSel();
    pMessages->GetText(index, csMessage);
```

```
// Open incoming queue
IMSMQQueuePtr pQueue = OpenQueue(IDC_INCOMING, MQ_RECEIVE_ACCESS);
if (pQueue == NULL)
   return;

_variant_t vTimeout(100L);
_variant_t vFalse(false);
_variant_t vTrue(true);

// Peek at current message
IMSMQMessagePtr pMessage;
HRESULT hr = pQueue->PeekCurrent(&vFalse, &vFalse, &vTimeout, &pMessage);
if (FAILED(hr))
{
   DisplayComError(_T("Failed to peek current"), hr);
   return;
}

// Go through messages, finding specified title
while (pMessage)
{
   BSTR bstrTitle;
   pMessage->get_Label(&bstrTitle);
   CString csTitle = bstrTitle;
   SysFreeString(bstrTitle);

   if (csTitle.Compare(csMessage) == 0)
   {
      // We've found it - take it off the queue
      hr = pQueue->ReceiveCurrent(&vFalse, &vFalse, &vTrue,
                                  &vTimeout, &pMessage);
      if (FAILED(hr))
      {
         DisplayComError(_T("Failed to receive current"), hr);
         return;
      }

      // Extract message status
      long msgClass;
      pMessage->get_Class(&msgClass);

      _variant_t vText;
      CString csText;

      switch (msgClass)
      {
         case MQMSG_CLASS_NORMAL:
            pMessage->get_Body(&vText);
            csText = vText.bstrVal;
            AfxMessageBox(csText);
            break;

         case MQMSG_CLASS_ACK_REACH_QUEUE:
            AfxMessageBox("Message has reached destination queue");
            break;
```

```
            case MQMSG_CLASS_ACK_RECEIVE:
               AfxMessageBox("Message has been received");
               break;

         case MQMSG_CLASS_NACK_REACH_QUEUE_TIMEOUT:
         AfxMessageBox("Message failed to reach destination queue in time");
               break;

            case MQMSG_CLASS_NACK_RECEIVE_TIMEOUT:
               AfxMessageBox("Message failed to be received in time");
               break;

            default:
               CString csError;
               csError.Format(_T("Message failed with error code %d"),
                              msgClass);
               AfxMessageBox(csError, msgClass);
               break;
         }
         OnRefresh();
         return;
      }

      pQueue->PeekNext(&vFalse, &vFalse, &vTimeout, &pMessage);
      if (FAILED(hr))
      {
         DisplayComError(_T("Failed to peek next"), hr);
         return;
      }
   }
}
```

The critical method call here is that one to **MSMQQueue**'s **ReceiveCurrent()**. This is similar to the call to **PeekCurrent()**, except that here, I'm actually asking for the body of the message. The other crucial difference, of course, is that once this method is invoked, the message is removed from the queue. Note the use of the **Class** property to determine whether the message being received is a standard one or an administration message telling us what happened to one that we sent previously.

Before we leave this example behind, here, as promised, is a fraction of this example re-implemented using the MSMQ API instead of the component set. Here's the function that opens up a queue:

```
QUEUEHANDLE CNocomMailDlg::OpenQueue(int nID, int mode)
{
   CString csError;
   USES_CONVERSION;

   CString csQueue;
   GetDlgItemText(nID, csQueue);

   WCHAR wszFormat[256];
   ULONG nChar = 256;

   MQPathNameToFormatName(T2W(csQueue), wszFormat, &nChar);
```

```
    QUEUEHANDLE hQueue;
    HRESULT hr = MQOpenQueue(wszFormat, mode, MQ_DENY_NONE, &hQueue);
    if (FAILED(hr))
    {
       csError.Format("Failed to open message queue, %x", hr);
       AfxMessageBox(csError);
       return NULL;
    }

    return hQueue;
}
```

The main difference is that in the straight API world, we're using handles to represent objects rather than interface pointers. There are also one or two other quirks; for example, we can't use the queue's pathname directly – we have to convert it to a format name first.

So that's our e-mail system. But what else can we do with MSMQ? Quite a lot as it turns out.

Messages and Transactions

I once wrote a foreign exchange order-passing system. The idea behind this system was that it should make orders for various foreign currencies available to a number of users worldwide in such a way as to ensure that, at any one time, only one small group of dealers actually had control of each order. At the end of each working day, the dealers would transfer their orders to one of their colleagues in another time zone. During the night, each outstanding order would make its weary way around the globe, until either it was executed, or it got back to the dealer who had it in the first place.

There were two important things that the system had to ensure: firstly, no orders could be lost, and secondly, no orders could be executed twice. Remember the discussion on the principles of conservation at the beginning of the chapter? Well, here's our principle of data conservation again. And let me tell you that this law was no simple matter to enforce, especially given that per-seat cost considerations meant that we couldn't consider using any off-the shelf message-oriented middleware packages. What I would have given for MSMQ...

Once a message is within MSMQ, we can trust the system to deliver it, or at least tell us that it failed to, so that we can take evasive action. So let's say that we have to take a record from one database and send it to another one using MSMQ – how can we ensure that this is completely safe? The answer is to make the message queue *transactional.* Now, I don't know about you, but I find the idea of incorporating something as asynchronous as a queue into a transaction ever so slightly counter-intuitive, so what are we really talking about here?

Let's go back to our aircraft analogy, and imagine now that instead of *us* making the trip to Seattle, it's our great aunt. She's going to see our long-lost distant cousin, the black sheep of the family, who it turns out has made a fortune in the coffee trade. Unfortunately, she's never been abroad before, and she's rather worried about making the trip. Apart from being slightly nervous about flying, all sorts of things might go wrong between leaving her apartment and actually getting on the plane. She's not even sure which terminal to go to.

Now, we're nice, helpful people, and we couldn't bear the thought of our poor great aunt struggling to the airport using public transport, so we offer to drive her. We pick her up at the apartment, and we take her all the way to the airport. We park the car, and carry her bags into the terminal. In fact, we don't let her out of our sight until she is safely through passport control – as far as we can go with her. Once she is through there, she is in the hands of the airport staff, and we can be pretty certain that she will end up in Seattle. Of course, when she eventually emerges at the other side of customs, we'll have to hope that our errant cousin deigns to turn up to greet her – he always was pretty unreliable.

What we've actually done here is turn the process of getting our great aunt on to the plane into a transaction. We have ensured that the two activities of "leave home" and "get on plane" both happen. If we had not intervened, "leave home" would have happened, but "get on plane" might not. Indeed, "get on wrong plane" might have happened instead. At the other end of the flight, a second transaction is poised ready to occur: the combination of "get off plane" and "go home with long-lost grandson".

What if the second transaction fails? What if our cousin fails to turn up? If this happens, we cannot proceed with the "get off plane" part of the transaction, and we might instead have to invoke a *compensating* transaction back at the other end, following a return flight. This would be the combination of "get off plane" and "go back home".

So this is where messages fit into the transaction environment. Once a message is on a queue – in our example, the plane – it's as good as being in another database. We don't worry about what happens when the message is received; that's part of *another* transaction.

It's time for another code example.

Using MSMQ With MTS

In this example (called `Collector`) , we're going to imagine that there's a group of us that are fanatical collectors of something that people scour the planet for. Something that you can buy in the shop for a few dollars and can subsequently change hands for thousands. As those of you out there with young daughters may already have guessed, I'm talking about Beanie Babies here. We have two conflicting requirements here: obviously, we want to avoid getting duplicates, but in order to build our collection as quickly as possible, we have to spread our team of buyers across the whole globe. Eagle-eyed readers may have already spotted that this is the foreign exchange order-passing system that I described above, albeit disguised a little.

Fortunately, all our buyers are armed with networked Windows NT machines running SQL Server, and, of course, MTS and MSMQ. So how are we going to configure this?

Let's say that each machine has a database containing a single table, **`checklist`**. This table has two fields: **`description`** and **`wanted`**. The first field is a **`varchar`** key. The second is a **`bit`** field, set up thus:

Key	Name	Datatype	Size	Default
✓	`description`	`varchar`	255	
	`wanted`	`bit`	1	0 (true)

For the purposes of this demonstration, we'll call the databases by the names of the computers themselves, in upper case. In turn, each server will access its local database through a SQL Server File DSN which we'll call **`WPSamples`**. Each database contains the items that the owner of that machine is currently looking for. There must be no duplication of items between databases, because that would mean that more than one buyer could be looking for the same Beanie Baby, and that's the situation that we're trying to avoid.

I won't go into the details of setting up the databases, as I covered this in the Kidnap Game example in the previous chapter.

As well as these databases, we'll need some queues. We'll set up one public queue per machine, named **`offered`**. This queue will be used by our clients to offer items for other buyers to look for. At the end of each day, a buyer might dump all the items in his or her outstanding want list onto this queue. Interested buyers in other parts of the globe could then scan this queue and take off any items that they think they stand a good chance of getting hold of. We'll make these queues **transactional**. Transactional messages can only be sent to transactional queues and non-transactional messages can only be sent to non-transactional queues (it is possible for a transactional queue to *receive* non-transactional messages from another local queue however). In general, the same holds for taking messages off queues, except that you *can* take a message off a transactional queue outside of a transaction, but *only* if it's a local queue.

The main difference between transactional and non-transactional queues is their behavior when it comes to dead letter queues. If a non-transactional message fails to be delivered, it will be dumped into the dead letter queue on the machine that it had reached at the point when it failed - but only if the dead letter option was specified when the message was created. If a transactional message fails to get delivered, the message is always dumped into the *transactional* dead letter queue on the machine that it was originally *sent* from.

So what ingredients do we need to build one of these clients? Well, we need some straight, non-transactional database manipulation, some straight, non-transactional message queuing and some transactional stuff to transfer messages between database and queue (and vice versa).

The Collector Client

I propose that we build a VB client that uses ADO for the ordinary database access and the MSMQ ActiveX objects for the message queuing, plus our own ATL-developed transactional object for the transfer. This is what our VB application's form looks like:

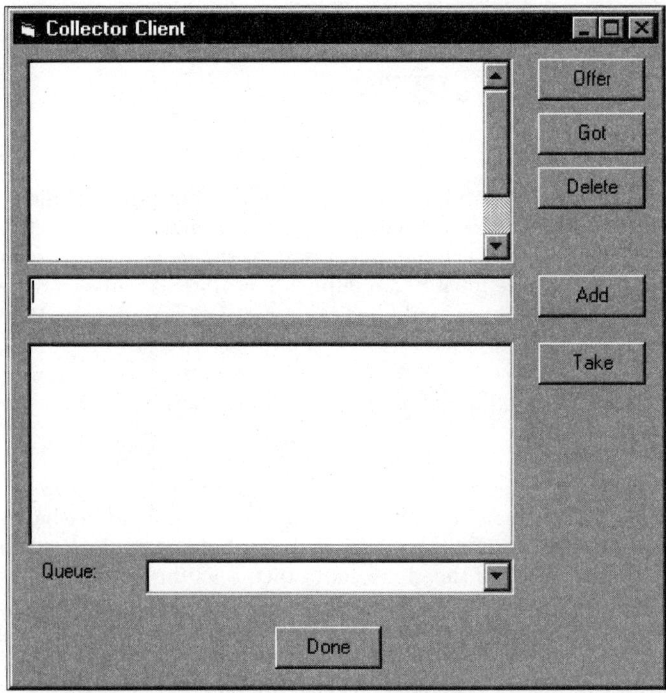

The top section of the form contains a list of all the Beanie Babies that this client is currently actively looking for. This is constructed by going through all the Beanie Babies in his or her database, and extracting the names of all those with the "wanted" bit set. If we're about to give up looking for one of them, we click on the Offer button, which adds it to the queue of those available for others to take over the search. If we actually *find* one of them, we click on the Got button. This clears the "Wanted" bit on the record, and it disappears from the list. If we made a mistake with one of the names, we can delete it altogether by clicking on the Delete button.

The text box in the middle, and the Add button are used to enter names for new Beanie Babies. These immediately become wanted, and are added to our list. There isn't, incidentally, a mechanism to ensure that the same Beanie Baby is added to several people's databases at the same time – a small flaw in the system.

The bottom section of the form is used if we want to take over the search for a Beanie Baby from someone else – say, for example, if we've just found a really good supplier that has got lots of really rare ones. We select a specific machine's queue to look at by means of the combo box at the bottom, and the list of Beanie Babies that are currently on that queue appears in the list box above. If we select one, and click on the Take button, it moves over to our database; this is the transactional stuff.

So, from the point of view of one node connected to the offered queue, this is where the information is moved from and to:

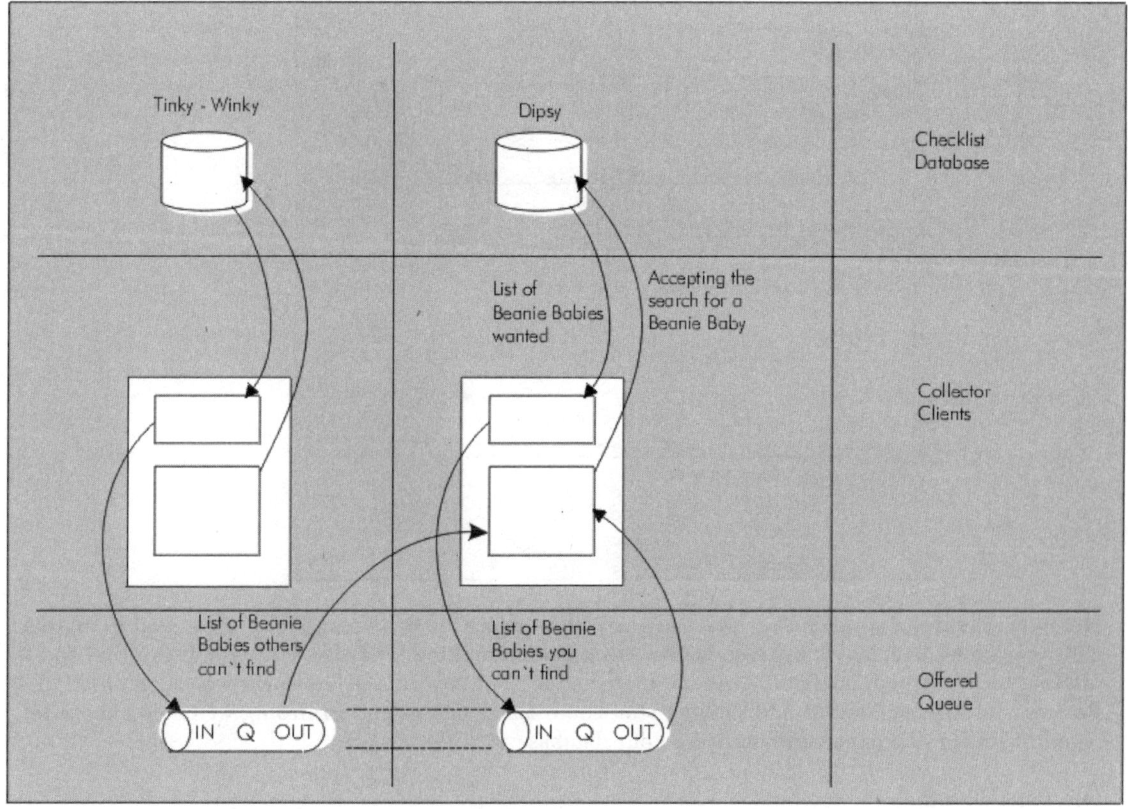

Here's an example in practice:

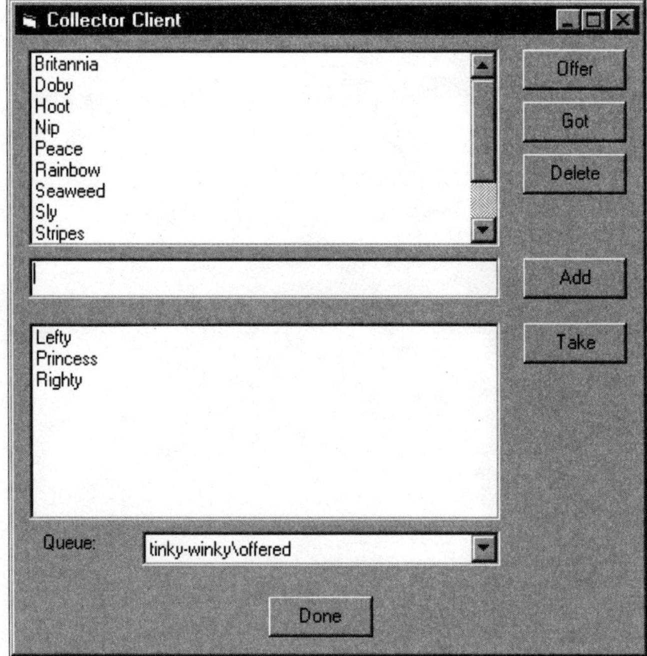

Here, our client (on node dipsy), is already actively looking for Britannia, Doby, Hoot and so on. Our colleague on node tinky-winky, meanwhile, has given up looking for Lefty, Righty and Princess and is offering the search opportunity to others. If we happen to know of a place where we can get hold of a Princess, for instance (and I'm not telling you where our daughter got *hers* from), we could choose to take Princess off the queue and put it into our database.

OK, what does the code look like?

This is the VB code for the routine that refreshes the "wanted" list:

```
Private Sub RefreshWanted()
    lstWanted.Clear

    Dim conn As ADODB.Connection
    Set conn = New Connection
    conn.Open dbopen

    Dim rs As ADOR.Recordset
    Set rs = New Recordset

    rs.Open "checklist", conn, adOpenForwardOnly, adLockPessimistic, _
            adCmdTable

    Dim fields As ADODB.fields
    Dim field As ADODB.field
```

```
    Dim name As String
    Dim want As Boolean

    Do While Not rs.EOF
        Set fields = rs.fields

        For Each field In fields
            If field.name = "description" Then
                name = field.Value
            ElseIf field.name = "wanted" Then
                want = field.Value
            End If
        Next field

        ' Only add wanted items to the list
        If want Then
            lstWanted.AddItem Trim(name)
        End If
        rs.MoveNext
    Loop

    Set fields = Nothing
    Set rs = Nothing
    Set conn = Nothing

End Sub
```

Notice how ADO makes walking sequentially through a database really very straightforward. Now let's see some of the message queue handling code. This is the bit that outputs the contents of a queue, when the combo box at the bottom is selected:

```
Private Sub cmbQueueList_Click()
    lstOffered.Clear

    Dim info As New MSMQQueueInfo
    info.PathName = cmbQueueList.Text

    Dim q As MSMQQueue
    Set q = info.Open(MSMQ.MQ_PEEK_ACCESS, MSMQ.MQ_DENY_NONE)

    Dim message As MSMQMessage
    Set message = q.PeekCurrent(, , 100)

    Do While Not message Is Nothing
        lstOffered.AddItem message.Label
        Set message = q.PeekNext(, , 100)
    Loop
End Sub
```

All of which bears a considerable resemblance to the MFC stuff in our earlier e-mail example (except ever so slightly *cleaner*). Once again, it's a question of peeking through our queue, picking off all the labels. Incidentally, our messages here have no body – they're just a label.

Now we get to the interesting bit. This is what happens when we click the Offer button:

```
Private Sub cmdOffer_Click()
    Dim count As Integer
    Dim index As Integer

    count = lstWanted.ListCount

    For index = 0 To count - 1
        If (lstWanted.Selected(index)) Then
            Dim item As String
            item = lstWanted.List(index)

            Dim xfer As Transfer
            Set xfer = New Transfer
            xfer.PutOnQueue item
        End If
    Next index

    RefreshWanted
End Sub
```

The critical part here is where we instantiate a **Transfer** object, and invoke the **PutOnQueue()** method. This **Transfer** object is running under MTS, so we're going to be doing some transactional maneuvers. This is where we get to do some ATL work (Ah! Real programming at last!). I won't show you the rest of the VB stuff here, but if you want it, it's available for download from www.wrox.com.

The Transfer Object

Our **Transfer** object has the following interface (called **ITransfer**):

Method	Parameters	Description
PutOnQueue	**[in] BSTR bstrItem**	Take selected item out of database, and put it on queue
TakeOffQueue	**[in] BSTR bstrQueue, [in] BSTR bstrItem**	Take selected item off queue and put into database

It's also got one property:

Property	Type	Description
DBName	**BSTR**	Connection string for database

Notice, incidentally, that this is a bona fide middle-tier object. There's no persistent data here; it's simply a component that gets called into action to carry out a specific job, following which it is destroyed.

Here is the code for the **PutOnQueue()** method. We start off by using some ADO calls to open up a connection to the database. Notice our old friend the object context making a reappearance. With this, we'll abort the transaction in case of any serious failure.

```
STDMETHODIMP CTransfer::PutOnQueue(BSTR bstrItem)
{
   CComPtr<IObjectContext> pContext;
   HRESULT hr = GetObjectContext(&pContext);
   if (FAILED(hr))
      return hr;

   CComPtr<ADOConnection> pConnection;
   pContext->CreateInstance(CLSID_CADOConnection,
                        IID_IADOConnection,
                        reinterpret_cast<void**>(&pConnection));

   CComBSTR bstrConnection;
   get_DBName(&bstrConnection);

   hr = pConnection->Open(bstrConnection, NULL, NULL, -1);
   if (FAILED(hr))
   {
      pContext->SetAbort();
      return hr;
   }
```

Now we find the required record.

```
   CComPtr<ADORecordset> pRecordset;
   pContext->CreateInstance(CLSID_CADORecordset,
                        IID_IADORecordset,
                        reinterpret_cast<void**>(&pRecordset));

   WCHAR szCommand[512];
   swprintf(szCommand, L"SELECT * FROM checklist WHERE description = '%s'",
         bstrItem);

   CComVariant vCommand(szCommand);
   CComVariant vConnection(pConnection);

   hr = pRecordset->Open(vCommand, vConnection, adOpenKeyset,
                        adLockPessimistic, adCmdText);
   if (FAILED(hr))
   {
      pContext->SetAbort();
      return hr;
   }
```

Now let's check to see if the Beanie Baby is currently wanted. If it isn't wanted, that means that we've already got it, so there's no point in offering it up for others to search for. In this case, we'll abort the transaction:

```
   CComPtr<ADOFields> pFields;
   pRecordset->get_Fields(&pFields);

   long count;
   pFields->get_Count(&count);
```

```
    for (long field = 0; field < count; field++)
    {
       CComVariant vField(field);
       CComPtr<ADOField> pField;
       pFields->get_Item(vField, &pField);

       CComBSTR bstrName;
       pField->get_Name(&bstrName);

       if (wcscmp(bstrName, L"wanted"))
          continue;

       CComVariant vValue;
       pField->get_Value(&vValue);
       if (vValue.boolVal == VARIANT_FALSE)
       {
          pContext->SetAbort();
          return S_OK;
       }
    }
```

If we get this far, it isn't in our collection, so let's delete it from our local database. No need to panic about rollback, because we're part of a transaction here.

```
    hr = pRecordset->Delete(adAffectCurrent);
    if (FAILED(hr))
    {
       pContext->SetAbort();
       return hr;
    }
```

OK, time for the message queue stuff. Let's find our outgoing queue, and open it up for sending.

```
    CComPtr<IMSMQQueueInfo> pInfo;
    pContext->CreateInstance(CLSID_MSMQQueueInfo,
                             IID_IMSMQQueueInfo,
                             reinterpret_cast<void**>(&pInfo));

    TCHAR szMachine[MAX_COMPUTERNAME_LENGTH + 1];
    ULONG length = MAX_COMPUTERNAME_LENGTH;
    GetComputerName(szMachine, &length);

    CComBSTR bstrMachine(szMachine);
    bstrMachine.Append("\\offered");
    pInfo->put_PathName(bstrMachine);

    CComPtr<IMSMQQueue> pQueue;
    hr = pInfo->Open(MQ_SEND_ACCESS, NULL, &pQueue);
    if (FAILED(hr))
    {
       pContext->SetAbort();
       return hr;
    }
```

Now we create the message:

```
    CComPtr<IMSMQMessage> pMessage;
    pContext->CreateInstance(CLSID_MSMQMessage,
                             IID_IMSMQMessage,
                             reinterpret_cast<void**>(&pMessage));

    pMessage->put_Label(bstrItem);

    VARIANT vTrans;
    V_VT(&vTrans) = VT_UI4;
    V_UI4(&vTrans) = MQ_MTS_TRANSACTION;

    hr = pMessage->Send(pQueue, &vTrans);
```

Hold on, what's this? We're setting the second parameter in the **Send()** to indicate that it's a transactional message. This is really the only thing that is seriously different about this use of the message queuing software:

OK, we've reached the point of no return. If the message has successfully been put on the queue, we can commit. Otherwise, let's abort and let MTS unwind us back to where we were before. (Incidentally, what sort of things can go wrong? Well, maybe we have a disconnected client or the local site server has gone down, and we can't see the queue configuration any more. Or perhaps we've failed to make the queue transactional – this is a neat way of testing whether or not the rollback is working, by the way.)

```
    if (FAILED(hr))
       pContext->SetAbort();
    else
       pContext->SetComplete();

    return hr;
}
```

The **TakeOffQueue()** method does pretty much the same sort of thing as **PutOnQueue()**, except the other way around, and I won't waste valuable trees by including it here. However, I will include the code that handles getting the property **DBName**:

```
STDMETHODIMP CTransfer::get_DBName(BSTR* pVal)
{
    TCHAR szMachine[MAX_COMPUTERNAME_LENGTH + 1];
    ULONG length = MAX_COMPUTERNAME_LENGTH;
    GetComputerName(szMachine, &length);

    for (ULONG iChar = 0; iChar < length; iChar++)
       if (szMachine[iChar] == '-')
          szMachine[iChar] = '_';

    CComBSTR bstrMachine(szMachine);
    WCHAR szName[128];
    swprintf(szName, L"FILEDSN=WPSamples;Database=%s;UID=sa;PWD=;",
                                                      bstrMachine);
    *pVal = SysAllocString(szName);
```

```
    return S_OK;
}
```

This constructs a database name that we can pass to the ADO **Connection Open()** method, based on the client's machine name. (Notice that SQL Server doesn't like hyphens!)

> **Don't forget to specify** Requires a new transaction **or** Requires a transaction **when you insert the component into MTS.**

So there we are. That's what transactional message queue operations look like, and frankly, they really aren't that much different from ordinary message queue operations.

What else can MTS do for us? I didn't include it in this example, but it's an interesting experiment to try sending two or more messages in the same transaction. If you do this, MSMQ is very fussy about preserving the order of the messages, and won't let you take them off the queue out of sequence. That's all I'm going to say about MSMQ and MTS – a pretty powerful twosome, if you ask me. What I'm sure you're dying to know more about is using MSMQ as a transport layer for DCOM. This is what Microsoft aims to do at some point in the future, in order to provide support for one-way asynchronous methods. However, we're impatient people, and we want it now. Remember the streaming and marshaling stuff back in Chapter 3? I think it's about time we finished it.

MSMQ as a Transport Layer

Back in Chapter 3, we looked at various ways of optimizing DCOM for use over a seriously wide area network. If you remember, we had an order entry system located in Tierra del Fuego, and a client base in Ulaanbaatar. What I'd like to explore now is how we could bring MSMQ to bear on the problem.

One of the problems with DCOM (as presently implemented) is that it is entirely synchronous. Every time your client in Ulaanbaatar invokes a method in Tierra del Fuego, it has to sit and wait until the method completes until it can move on to the next operation. Most of the time this is pretty acceptable; however, every now and then, we come across an application that can't wait – or perhaps doesn't even need to wait. So the connection between the client and the server has to become a little looser.

For once, we find here that our old friend and rival CORBA has got there ahead of us. In the CORBA IDL definition, we can specify a method to have the attribute **oneway**. If you specify a method as having this attribute, the client doesn't wait for the server to complete before moving on. A moment's thought will tell you that if you specify a method as being **oneway**, it can't have any **[out]** parameters, but that's OK, because we can get outputs back from the server as events. This looks suspiciously like re-inventing asynchronous programming, callbacks and all, and frankly, it is. The current buzzword to describe this is **Real-Enough Time**.

Just to recap, our orders are represented by **Order** objects, with – at the moment – a single interface, **IOrder**. This interface has five properties, all strings: **CustomerID**, **Title**, **Artist**, **Label** and **Price**. There is also a single method, **Submit()**, which actually enters the order into a "database" (actually a single-record file). What we're going to do is implement all the properties as local methods (so that all validation is carried out locally), and then make the **Submit()** method one-way asynchronous. We'll use MSMQ queues to communicate between the client and the server, so what we'll end up doing is serializing our orders somehow, encapsulating them as MSMQ messages, and then sending them over MSMQ to a queue located on the server. We'll also need to set up some kind of stub process sitting on the server machine to take the messages off the queue as and when they come in.

Now we could do all of this by means of custom marshalling. If we did this, we'd probably end up implementing **IOrder** in three places: in the COM server, in the proxy and also in the stub process. This ends up looking extremely inelegant, and there's actually a much better way of doing it. It turns out that MSMQ is rather good at sending and receiving objects.

This is what we're going to do. We'll start off by creating a standard queue on each machine, called *async*. We'll create a workspace called **AsyncOrder**, and add a project called **AsyncOrder** underneath it. This project will start off like the **SerialOrder** project that we had in Chapter 3. However, this time, it's implemented as a DLL. We'll also need to ensure that **IPersistStream::GetSizeMax()** is fully implemented, just as it was in the **MarshalOrder** project. We'll take this as our starting point and examine the changes that need to be made from this point on.

Later on, we'll create a second project in the workspace, called **AsyncOrderStub** and then we'll deal with the stub process. All of the code here can be downloaded from www.wrox.com. Right now, let's concentrate on the DLL.

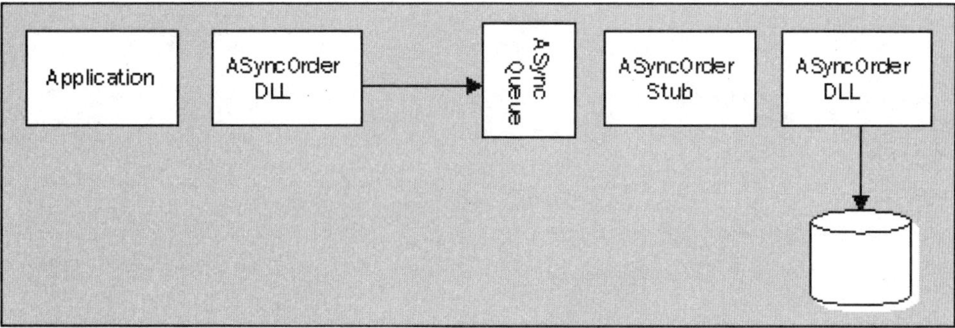

The Asynchronous DLL

Our first problem is that we haven't any way of telling our object which server to connect to. If we were using straight DCOM, we'd set **DCOMcnfg** accordingly. However, we can't do that, so for ease of implementation, we'll just add a second interface to our object (to avoid compromising the original **IOrder** interface definition). We'll call this interface **IAsync**, and give it a single **put_** property, **Destination**. We'll hold this in a **CComBSTR** member variable, **m_bstrDestination**, and while we're at it, we'll construct the queue pathname for this host as well, and hold this in **m_bstrDestPath**. We'll also add member variables for the local host name and queue pathname.

Here's the state of **Order.h** following our first round of changes:

```
class ATL_NO_VTABLE COrder :
   public CComObjectRootEx<CComSingleThreadModel>,
   public CComCoClass<COrder, &CLSID_Order>,
   public IDispatchImpl<IOrder, &IID_IOrder, &LIBID_ASYNCORDERLib>,
   public IDispatchImpl<IAsync, &IID_IAsync, &LIBID_ASYNCORDERLib>,
   public IPersistStreamInitImpl<COrder>,
   public CComControl<COrder>
{
private:
   HRESULT MandatoryAlphabetic(/*[in]*/ BSTR bstrValue);
   HRESULT OptionalAlphabetic(/*[in]*/ BSTR bstrValue);
   HRESULT MandatoryAlphanumeric(/*[in]*/ BSTR bstrValue);
   HRESULT OptionalAlphanumeric(/*[in]*/ BSTR bstrValue);
   HRESULT MandatoryPrice(/*[in]*/ BSTR bstrValue);
   void Write(/*[in]*/ IStorage* pStorage, /*[in]*/ LPOLESTR lpszField,
              /*[in]*/ CComBSTR& bstr);

   CComBSTR m_bstrCustomerID;
   CComBSTR m_bstrArtist;
   CComBSTR m_bstrTitle;
   CComBSTR m_bstrLabel;
   CComBSTR m_bstrPrice;

   // Data members for source and destination machine and queue names
   CComBSTR m_bstrSource;
   CComBSTR m_bstrSourcePath;
   CComBSTR m_bstrDestination;
   CComBSTR m_bstrDestPath;

   // SendOrder() sends the Order to a queue
   HRESULT SendOrder();

public:
   COrder()
   {
      TCHAR szMachine[MAX_COMPUTERNAME_LENGTH + 1] = {0};
      ULONG length = MAX_COMPUTERNAME_LENGTH;
      GetComputerName (szMachine, &length);
      _tcslwr(szMachine);
      m_bstrSource = szMachine;


      m_bstrSourcePath = m_bstrSource;
      m_bstrSourcePath.Append ("\\async");
   }

BEGIN_MSG_MAP(COrder)
END_MSG_MAP()

DECLARE_REGISTRY_RESOURCEID(IDR_ORDER)

BEGIN_COM_MAP(COrder)
   COM_INTERFACE_ENTRY(IOrder)
   COM_INTERFACE_ENTRY(IAsync)
   COM_INTERFACE_ENTRY2(IDispatch, IOrder)
```

```
   COM_INTERFACE_ENTRY_IMPL_IID(IID_IPersistStream, IPersistStreamInit)
END_COM_MAP()

BEGIN_PROPERTY_MAP(COrder)
   PROP_ENTRY("CustomerID", 1, CLSID_NULL)
   PROP_ENTRY("Artist", 2, CLSID_NULL)
   PROP_ENTRY("Title", 3, CLSID_NULL)
   PROP_ENTRY("Label", 4, CLSID_NULL)
   PROP_ENTRY("Price", 5, CLSID_NULL)
END_PROPERTY_MAP()

// IOrder
public:
   STDMETHOD(put_CustomerID)(/*[in]*/ BSTR newVal);
   STDMETHOD(get_CustomerID)(/*[out, retval]*/ BSTR *pVal);
   STDMETHOD(put_Artist)(/*[in]*/ BSTR newVal);
   STDMETHOD(get_Artist)(/*[out, retval]*/ BSTR *pVal);
   STDMETHOD(put_Title)(/*[in]*/ BSTR newVal);
   STDMETHOD(get_Title)(/*[out, retval]*/ BSTR *pVal);
   STDMETHOD(put_Label)(/*[in]*/ BSTR newVal);
   STDMETHOD(get_Label)(/*[out, retval]*/ BSTR *pVal);
   STDMETHOD(put_Price)(/*[in]*/ BSTR newVal);
   STDMETHOD(get_Price)(/*[out, retval]*/ BSTR *pVal);
   STDMETHOD(Submit)();

// IAsync
public:
   STDMETHOD(put_Destination)(/*[in]*/ BSTR newVal);

// IPersistStream
public:
   STDMETHOD(GetSizeMax)(ULARGE_INTEGER* pcbSize)
   {
      // Return size of data to be written to stream in bytes

      // ATL Version
      pcbSize->QuadPart = sizeof(DWORD);

      // User Data
      pcbSize->QuadPart +=
         SizeOfBSTR(m_bstrCustomerID) +
         SizeOfBSTR(m_bstrArtist) +
         SizeOfBSTR(m_bstrTitle) +
         SizeOfBSTR(m_bstrLabel) +
         SizeOfBSTR(m_bstrPrice);
      return S_OK;
   }
};
```

Here's the new method to handle the **Destination** property:

```
STDMETHODIMP COrder::put_Destination(BSTR newVal)
{
```

```
        m_bstrDestPath = m_bstrDestination = newVal;
        m_bstrDestPath.Append("\\async");
        return S_OK;
    }
```

Now, we're going to change our old **Submit()** method, so that – depending on whether it's being invoked on the client or the stub – it either sends an MSMQ message, or writes away the order as it used to. This is what the new version looks like:

```
    STDMETHODIMP COrder::Submit()
    {
        // If we have a destination machine,
        // and it's different from the the machine on which the Order
        // object is running,
        // then we call SendOrder() to put the Order object in the queue
        if (m_bstrDestination && wcsicmp(m_bstrDestination, m_bstrSource))
           return SendOrder();

        // Otherwise, save the order to file as before
        CComPtr<IStorage> pStorage;
        HRESULT hr = StgCreateDocfile(L"C:\\Order.dat",
                         STGM_SIMPLE| STGM_CREATE | STGM_READWRITE |
                         STGM_SHARE_EXCLUSIVE, 0, &pStorage);
        if (FAILED(hr))
           return hr;

        Write(pStorage, L"CustomerID", m_bstrCustomerID);
        Write(pStorage, L"Artist", m_bstrArtist);
        Write(pStorage, L"Title", m_bstrTitle);
        Write(pStorage, L"Label", m_bstrLabel);
        Write(pStorage, L"Price", m_bstrPrice);

        return S_OK;
    }
```

And here's the new **SendOrder()** member function:

```
    HRESULT COrder::SendOrder()
    {
        CComVariant vData(GetUnknown());

        CComPtr<IMSMQQueueInfo> pInfo;
        HRESULT hr = CoCreateInstance(CLSID_MSMQQueueInfo,
                                      NULL,
                                      CLSCTX_SERVER,
                                      IID_IMSMQQueueInfo,
                                      reinterpret_cast<void**>(&pInfo));

        if (FAILED(hr))
           return hr;

        pInfo->put_PathName(m_bstrDestPath);
```

```
    CComPtr<IMSMQQueue> pQueue;
    hr = pInfo->Open(MQ_SEND_ACCESS, NULL, &pQueue);
    if (FAILED(hr))
       return hr;

    CComPtr<IMSMQMessage> pMessage;
    hr = CoCreateInstance(CLSID_MSMQMessage,
                          NULL,
                          CLSCTX_SERVER,
                          IID_IMSMQMessage,
                          reinterpret_cast<void**>(&pMessage));

    if (FAILED(hr))
       return hr;

    WCHAR wszLabel[16];
    swprintf(wszLabel, L"%d", m_sequence++);
    CComBSTR bstrLabel(wszLabel);

    pMessage->put_Label(bstrLabel);
    pMessage->put_Body(vData);

    // To set a time limit on reaching the destination queue
    // uncomment the following line
    // pMessage->put_MaxTimeToReachQueue(30);

    // To set a time limit on message being received,
    // uncomment the following line
    // pMessage->put_MaxTimeToReceive(30);

    pInfo->put_PathName(m_bstrSourcePath);
    pInfo->Refresh();

    pMessage->putref_ResponseQueueInfo(pInfo);

    hr = pMessage->Send(pQueue, &CComVariant());
    return hr;
}
```

Now this is *really* cool. All the MSMQ stuff should look pretty familiar, except for one thing. Take a good look at what we're actually sending in the message. It's an **IUnknown** pointer to ourselves. Yes, MSMQ messages can actually send objects over the wire! But hang on a minute – what does that mean? If you think back to what we were doing in Chapter 3, you might have guessed by now that it's actually the persistent state of the object that we're talking about here. So how does MSMQ get hold of that? The answer is our old friend **IPersistStream**, which is the reason that we based this code on the **SerialOrder** code from Chapter 3.

Does this really work? Let's try it out. Obviously we won't have an application to receive the messages (because we haven't built that part yet), but we can take a look at the message using MSMQ Explorer. We'll need a client though, so we'll make yet another clone of our VB **OrderEntry** project from Chapter 3 – this time called **AsyncOrderEntry**. The only change we need to make, apart from changing the reference to use the **AsyncOrder** type library, is this:

```
Private Sub cmdConfirm_Click()

   ...

   Dim async As IAsync
   Set async = m_order
   async.Destination = "dipsy"

   m_order.Submit
   Unload Me
End Sub
```

We just use the new **`IAsync`** interface to set up our destination host before calling **`Submit()`**. OK, let's fire it up and see what MSMQ Explorer tells us. You should see something like this:

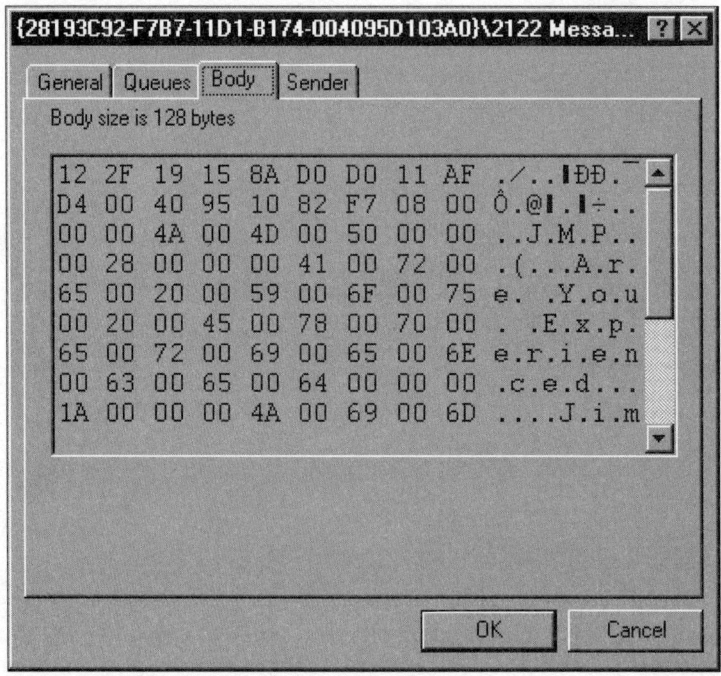

This looks pretty much what I entered in the order fields, prefaced by something that looks suspiciously like the Class ID for the **`Order`** object. Let's hope we can persuade the other end to understand this.

The Stub

So what sort of thing is our stub process? Well, it's going to spend most of its time sitting waiting for messages to come through. But wait one moment – up to now, we've polled our queues for messages. Do we really want our stub process thrashing around in a permanent loop? I don't think so. You can use **MSMQ events** to get notified whenever something happens but that entails revisiting connection points once more. If we go way back to Chapter 1, you might recall that connection points are pretty cool in VB, so-so in ATL, but pretty terrible in MFC so I think we'll duck out of MFC and use ATL to develop our stub instead

We'll create our stub as an executable ATL project. We need to define two objects: **`OrderStub`** (sole interface **`IOrderStub`**) and **`StubSink`** (sole interface **`IStubSink`**). The first of these is going to do all the set-up work, and the second is going to be hooked up to the MSMQ event connection point. The second one will be the one that handles all the incoming messages. How do we get started, then? We don't really want to have another client that only exists to kick the whole thing off, so let's make a small addition to our **`WinMain`** function to create an instance of our **`OrderStub`** object without client intervention:

```
if (bRun)
{
   hRes = _Module.RegisterClassObjects(CLSCTX_LOCAL_SERVER,
      REGCLS_MULTIPLEUSE);
   _ASSERTE(SUCCEEDED(hRes));

   CComObject<COrderStub>* pOrderStub;
   CComObject<COrderStub>::CreateInstance(&pOrderStub);

   hRes = pOrderStub->Initialize();
   _ASSERTE(SUCCEEDED(hRes));

   MSG msg;
   while (GetMessage(&msg, 0, 0, 0))
      DispatchMessage(&msg);

   pOrderStub->Uninitialize();
   pOrderStub->Release();

   _Module.RevokeClassObjects();
}
```

OK, let's take a look at the definition of our **`IOrderStub`** interface. We've got three methods, two of which we've just seen in use:

Method	Parameters	Description
`Initialize`	None	Initialize stub; hook up to connection point of local queue
`Uninitialize`	None	Uninitialize stub; unhook from connection point
`Enable`	None	Enable events on queue

Here's the code that implements this interface:

```
// OrderStub.cpp : Implementation of COrderStub
#include "stdafx.h"
#include "AsyncOrderStub.h"
#include "OrderStub.h"
#include "StubSink.h"
```

```
//////////////////////////////////////////////////////////////////////////////
// COrderStub

STDMETHODIMP COrderStub::Initialize()
{
   // Create queue info object
   CComPtr<IMSMQQueueInfo> pInfo;
   HRESULT hr = CoCreateInstance(CLSID_MSMQQueueInfo,
                                 NULL,
                                 CLSCTX_INPROC_SERVER,
                                 IID_IMSMQQueueInfo,
                                 reinterpret_cast<void**>(&pInfo));

   if (FAILED(hr))
      return hr;

   // Work out name of local queue, and populate info object
   TCHAR szMachine[MAX_COMPUTERNAME_LENGTH + 1];
   ULONG length = MAX_COMPUTERNAME_LENGTH;
   GetComputerName(szMachine, &length);
   _tcslwr(szMachine);

   CComBSTR bstrPath = szMachine;
   bstrPath.Append("\\async");
   pInfo->put_PathName(bstrPath);

   // Open up queue
   hr = pInfo->Open(MQ_RECEIVE_ACCESS, MQ_DENY_NONE, &m_pQueue);
   if (FAILED(hr))
      return hr;

   // Create event object
   hr = CoCreateInstance(CLSID_MSMQEvent,
                         NULL,
                         CLSCTX_INPROC_SERVER,
                         IID_IMSMQEvent,
                         reinterpret_cast<void**>(&m_pEvent));

   if (FAILED(hr))
      return hr;

   // Create sink object
   CComObject<CStubSink>* pSink = NULL;
   hr = CComObject<CStubSink>::CreateInstance(&pSink);
   if (FAILED(hr))
      return hr;

   pSink->put_OrderStub(this);

   hr = pSink->QueryInterface(IID_IDispatch,
                              reinterpret_cast<void**>(&m_pDispatch));
   if (FAILED(hr))
      return hr;
```

```
   // Attach to connection point of event object
   hr = AtlAdvise(m_pEvent, m_pDispatch, DIID__DMSMQEventEvents,
                  &m_dwCookie);
   if (FAILED(hr))
      return hr;

   return Enable();
}

STDMETHODIMP COrderStub::Uninitialize()
{
   AtlUnadvise(m_pDispatch, DIID__DMSMQEventEvents, m_dwCookie);
   return S_OK;
}

STDMETHODIMP COrderStub::Enable()
{
   // Enable notification for queue using event object
   CComVariant vtCursor(MQMSG_CURRENT, VT_I4);
   CComVariant vtTimeout(100000L);

   HRESULT hr = m_pQueue->EnableNotification(m_pEvent, &vtCursor,
                                             &vtTimeout);
   if (hr == MQ_INFORMATION_OPERATION_PENDING)
      hr = S_OK;

   return hr;
}
```

The code for opening the MSMQ queue should look familiar to you from earlier examples in this chapter. The connection point stuff should be familiar from Chapter 1. Notice that we pass a pointer to ourselves into the connection point; that's so it can get access to the **`Enable()`** method. This is because every time an event fires, the event object has to be re-enabled. Notice also that this is all very much in the usual MSMQ style: create two objects, one for the queue and one for the event, and then invoke a method on one of them to tie them together.

In this code, we've referenced one or two member variables, so we need to make some small changes to **`OrderStub.h`**:

```
class ATL_NO_VTABLE COrderStub :
   public CComObjectRootEx<CComSingleThreadModel>,
   public CComCoClass<COrderStub, &CLSID_OrderStub>,
   public IDispatchImpl<IOrderStub, &IID_IOrderStub,
                        &LIBID_ASYNCORDERSTUBLib>
{
private:
   CComPtr<IMSMQQueue> m_pQueue;
   CComPtr<IMSMQEvent> m_pEvent;
   CComPtr<IDispatch> m_pDispatch;
   DWORD m_dwCookie;

public:
   COrderStub()
```

```
    {
    }

DECLARE_REGISTRY_RESOURCEID(IDR_ORDERSTUB)

BEGIN_COM_MAP(COrderStub)
   COM_INTERFACE_ENTRY(IOrderStub)
   COM_INTERFACE_ENTRY(IDispatch)
END_COM_MAP()

// IOrderStub
public:
   STDMETHOD(Initialize)();
   STDMETHOD(Uninitialize)();
   STDMETHOD(Enable)();
};
```

OK, that's our main stub object completed. But what about our sink? We need to implement an interface that looks pretty much identical as the outgoing one from the MSMQ event object's connection point, and then do a little fiddle with the COM map to re-direct incoming methods on the connection point's interface onto our implementation.

This is the interface that we're going to have to implement:

Method	Parameters	Description
Arrived	**[in] IDispatch* Queue,** **[in] long Cursor**	There is a message in the queue
ArrivedError	**[in] IDispatch* Queue,** **[in] long ErrorCode,** **[in] long Cursor**	An error has occurred on the queue

This – I hope – all makes perfect sense. It's the kind of thing that you'd expect to see in an MSMQ event interface. I'll also add one property:

Property	Type	Description
OrderStub	**IOrderStub***	Pointer back to main object

Let's take a look at what our **StubSink.h** header file is going to look like:

```
// StubSink.h : Declaration of the CStubSink

#ifndef __STUBSINK_H_
#define __STUBSINK_H_

#include "resource.h"       // main symbols

#include "mqoai.h"
```

```
//////////////////////////////////////////////////////////////////////////////
// CStubSink
class ATL_NO_VTABLE CStubSink :
   public CComObjectRootEx<CComSingleThreadModel>,
   public CComCoClass<CStubSink, &CLSID_StubSink>,
   public IDispatchImpl<IStubSink, &IID_IStubSink, &LIBID_ASYNCORDERSTUBLib>
{
private:
   CComPtr<IOrderStub> m_pOrderStub;

public:
   CStubSink()
   {
   }

DECLARE_REGISTRY_RESOURCEID(IDR_STUBSINK)

BEGIN_COM_MAP(CStubSink)
   COM_INTERFACE_ENTRY_IID(DIID__DMSMQEventEvents,IStubSink)
   COM_INTERFACE_ENTRY(IStubSink)
   COM_INTERFACE_ENTRY(IDispatch)
END_COM_MAP()

// IStubSink
public:
   STDMETHOD(put_OrderStub)(/*[in]*/ IOrderStub* newVal);
   STDMETHOD(Arrived)(IDispatch* Queue, long Cursor);
   STDMETHOD(ArrivedError)(IDispatch* Queue, long ErrorCode, long Cursor);
};

#endif //__STUBSINK_H_
```

I've added one uncontroversial member variable, **m_pOrderStub**, which holds our local copy of the **OrderStub** property. I've also added that little fiddle to the COM map. Now, there's an important change to the IDL that we're going to have to make in order for this to work:

In order for COM_INTERFACE_ENTRY_IID to map one interface to another, you must make sure that the DISPIDs in both interfaces are identical with each other

The reason why I'm making a song and dance about this is that the default DISPIDs provided by the ATL Object Wizard (which start from 1) do *not* match those used by the MSMQ event connection point (which start from 0). As you may have guessed, I've been stung here myself! So let's make that change to our IDL:

```
interface IStubSink : IDispatch
{
   [id(0), helpstring("method Arrived")]
      HRESULT Arrived([in] IDispatch* Queue, [in] long Cursor);
```

```
    [id(1), helpstring("method ArrivedError")]
        HRESULT ArrivedError([in] IDispatch* Queue,
                    [in] long ErrorCode, [in] long Cursor);
    [propput, id(2), helpstring("property OrderStub")]
        HRESULT OrderStub([in] IOrderStub* newVal);
};
```

OK, we're ready to implement **IStubSink**. Here we go:

```
// StubSink.cpp : Implementation of CStubSink
#include "stdafx.h"
#include "mqoai.h"

#include "AsyncOrderStub.h"
#include "StubSink.h"

#include "..\AsyncOrder\AsyncOrder.h"
#include "..\AsyncOrder\AsyncOrder_i.c"

/////////////////////////////////////////////////////////////////////////////
// CStubSink

STDMETHODIMP CStubSink::Arrived(IDispatch* Queue, long Cursor)
{
   // Get hold of pointer to queue object
   CComPtr<IMSMQQueue> pQueue;
   HRESULT hr = Queue->QueryInterface(IID_IMSMQQueue,
                                   reinterpret_cast<void**>(&pQueue));
   if (FAILED(hr))
      return hr;

   CComVariant vTimeout(100L);
   CComVariant vFalse(false);
   CComVariant vTrue(true);

   // Get message from queue
   CComPtr<IMSMQMessage> pMessage;
   hr = pQueue->ReceiveCurrent(&vFalse, &vFalse, &vTrue, &vTimeout,
                              &pMessage);
   if (FAILED(hr))
      return hr;

   // Extract object from message
   CComVariant vData(static_cast<IUnknown*>(NULL));
   hr = pMessage->get_Body(&vData);
   if (FAILED(hr))
      return hr;
```

```
    // Get IOrder interface on new object
    CComPtr<IOrder> pOrder;
    hr = (vData.punkVal)->QueryInterface(IID_IOrder,
                                   reinterpret_cast<void**>(&pOrder));
    if (FAILED(hr))
       return hr;

    // Submit the order
    hr = pOrder->Submit();
    // Re-enable events
    if (m_pOrderStub)
       return m_pOrderStub->Enable();

    return hr;
}

STDMETHODIMP CStubSink::ArrivedError(IDispatch* Queue, long ErrorCode,
                                     long Cursor)
{
    if (m_pOrderStub)
       return m_pOrderStub->Enable();

    return S_OK;
}

STDMETHODIMP CStubSink::put_OrderStub(IOrderStub* newVal)
{
    m_pOrderStub = newVal;

    return S_OK;
}
```

Now I don't know about you, but I think that's rather beautiful. Did you check out the blink-if-you-missed-it way in which we took the object off the queue? Just one call to **get_Body()**, and there we have one instantiated, fully populated order object that we can go ahead and submit.

And that, ladies and gentlemen, is how to use MSMQ to implement one-way method calls.

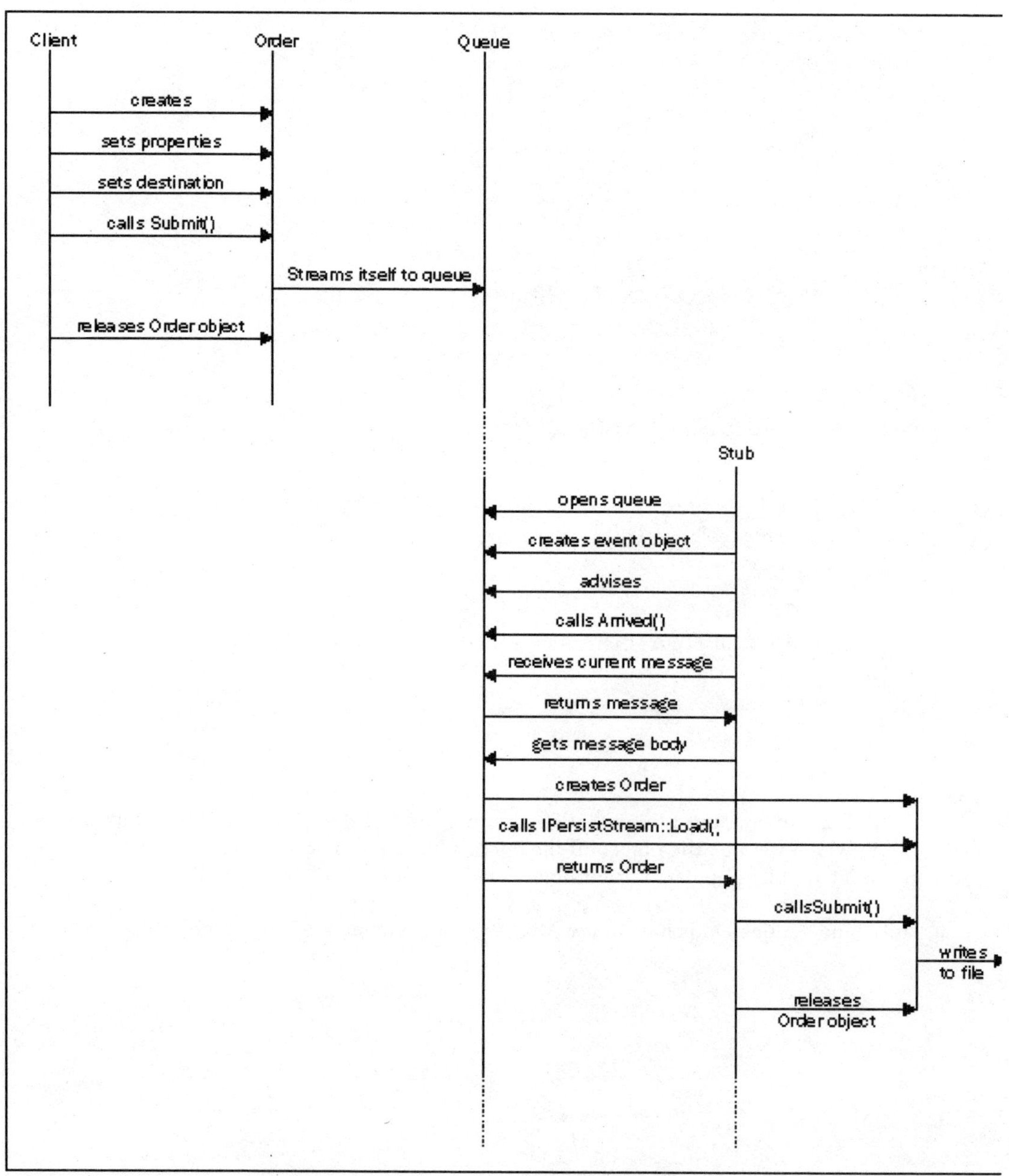

Client
Order
Queue
creates
sets properties
sets destination
calls Submit()
Streams itself to queue
releases Order object
Stub
opens queue
creates event object
advises
calls Arrived()
receives current message
returns message
gets message body
creates Order
calls IPersistStream::Load()
returns Order
callsSubmit()
writes to file
releases Order object

MSMQ and DCOM

Now, the question is: do you *still* think that MSMQ doesn't have much to do with DCOM? I think we know the answer now. MSMQ is an absolutely vital ingredient in the emerging infrastructure to support distributed COM programming. With MSMQ under our belts, we can put together some really powerful distributed systems, and when you put it together with MTS, it's pretty awesome.

In our next chapter, we're sticking with MTS, and we're going to scratch the surface a little and see what we can find underneath.

7

Building A Resource Manager

"Feel with your car; use all of your receptive senses and when you find out what it needs, seek the operation out and perform it with love.
The type of life your car contains differs from yours by time scale, logic level and conceptual anomalies but is "Life" nonetheless.
Its Karma depends on your desire to make and keep it – ALIVE!"

How to Keep Your Volkswagen Alive,
John Muir

Under The Hood

I've always been in two minds about this "looking under the hood" thing. A long time ago, I used to drive a Volkswagen Beetle. It was a great little car (if a little noisy), but the really good thing about it was that it wasn't that difficult (with the help of a few willing friends) to drop the engine out, carry it up two flights of stairs and spend the weekend stripping it down, fixing it and putting it back together again. I learnt a lot about what went on in the engine over those weekends, but I'm not entirely convinced that it made me a better driver.

These days, of course, the onset of marriage, kids and double basses (they came with the kids), has forced me towards middle-aged Volvo-dom. On those rare occasions when I look under the hood (usually to re-fill the screen washer reservoir), I have trouble telling what half the parts *are*, let alone how they work. Does this make me a worse driver? Of course it doesn't. So, when it comes to computer systems, I try to keep myself firmly on the applications side of the fence, working to a strict interface provided by the suppliers of the system. What goes on in the strange country on the other side of the interface is of no interest to me whatsoever. *Usually.*

Except, that is, when it comes to things like Microsoft Transaction Server. I'd tinkered with transactions before from time to time, but I'd never felt that I'd quite got to the bottom of what was really going on. What was two-phase commit really about, for example? What was the real difference between a resource manager and a resource dispenser? Did it matter?

So, one day when I was idly surfing www.microsoft.com and I came across a downloadable SDK for MTS, I was intrigued. I looked at the documentation that came with it, and discovered that it was an SDK for building your own resource managers and dispensers. Maybe, I thought, I could use this to dig a little deeper and find out what was going on underneath it all. As it turned out, I did find it useful. So, in the spirit of sharing the experience with you, the reader, I'd like to take you on a little tour through the internals of MTS. And, believe me, if MTS looks as poised and stately as a swan on the surface, underneath it's paddling away frantically. Just like a swan, in fact.

Actually, there's another reason for going through the exercise of building a resource manager. You might just want to do it in real life. What if you happened to have an old legacy system lying around that you wanted to incorporate into your transaction environment? If it happened to be XA-compliant, you could plug it straight in, but what if it was just any old system? Think about what you could do as we tunnel under MTS and see what we find ...

Travel Precautions

Before we get started, we're going to need the MTS SDK. This is now part of the Microsoft Platform SDK, which we've come across in other chapters. It's either available for download from `ftp://ftp.microsoft.com/bussys/viper/sdk/` or as one of the CDs in the MSDN kit. You'll have to make sure that the library and include directories for this get added to your Visual Studio, although the installation process should make this happen automatically.

When exploring unfamiliar territory, it's wise to know precisely where we are, and what is going on, so we're going to splatter our code with calls to event logging routines. The most straightforward way of logging events is simply to open a file, write a line to it, and close the file again. If all the various parts of the system use the same file, then we can get an idea of the exact sequence of events. For the purposes of building this system, we aren't interested in speed – we're on a reconnaissance mission here.

The Elements of Our System

We're going to have six interacting elements. Right at the top, we have our client, which is going to use a server to interact with a database in a transactional manner. This server is going to talk to a **resource dispenser**, which in turn is going to talk to a **resource manager**. Remember the rôles these last two played in Chapter 5:

- The resource dispenser controls access to a pool of limited resources, such as database connections
- The resource manager controls transaction enlistment and commitment.

The other key thing about a resource dispenser is that it generates transactions for us automatically. If we didn't have a resource dispenser, we'd have to create our own transactions within our server, which would remove much of the elegance of MTS from our system. As we'll see, our resource dispenser can pass details of the transaction on to the resource manager. An example of this in practice is the ODBC Resource Dispenser. As well as managing the pool of connections to an ODBC database, it passes transactions on to resource managers such as SQL Server, and enlists them in the two-phase commit process.

The remaining three elements are provided by MTS. The first of these is **DispMan**, the **Dispenser Manager**, which controls the pool of resources, in tandem with the various resource dispensers. The second is the **DTC Proxy Core Object**. This is the central object of the MTS **Distributed Transaction Coordinator**, or DTC, and it exposes all the interfaces that control transaction coordination. The last element, which is hovering just out of sight in the background most of the time, is the MTS **Transaction Manager**. The only time when we actually refer to this is when we export a transaction from the resource dispenser to the resource manager. Here are all our elements, with the main interfaces that they expose. As you see, there are quite a few.

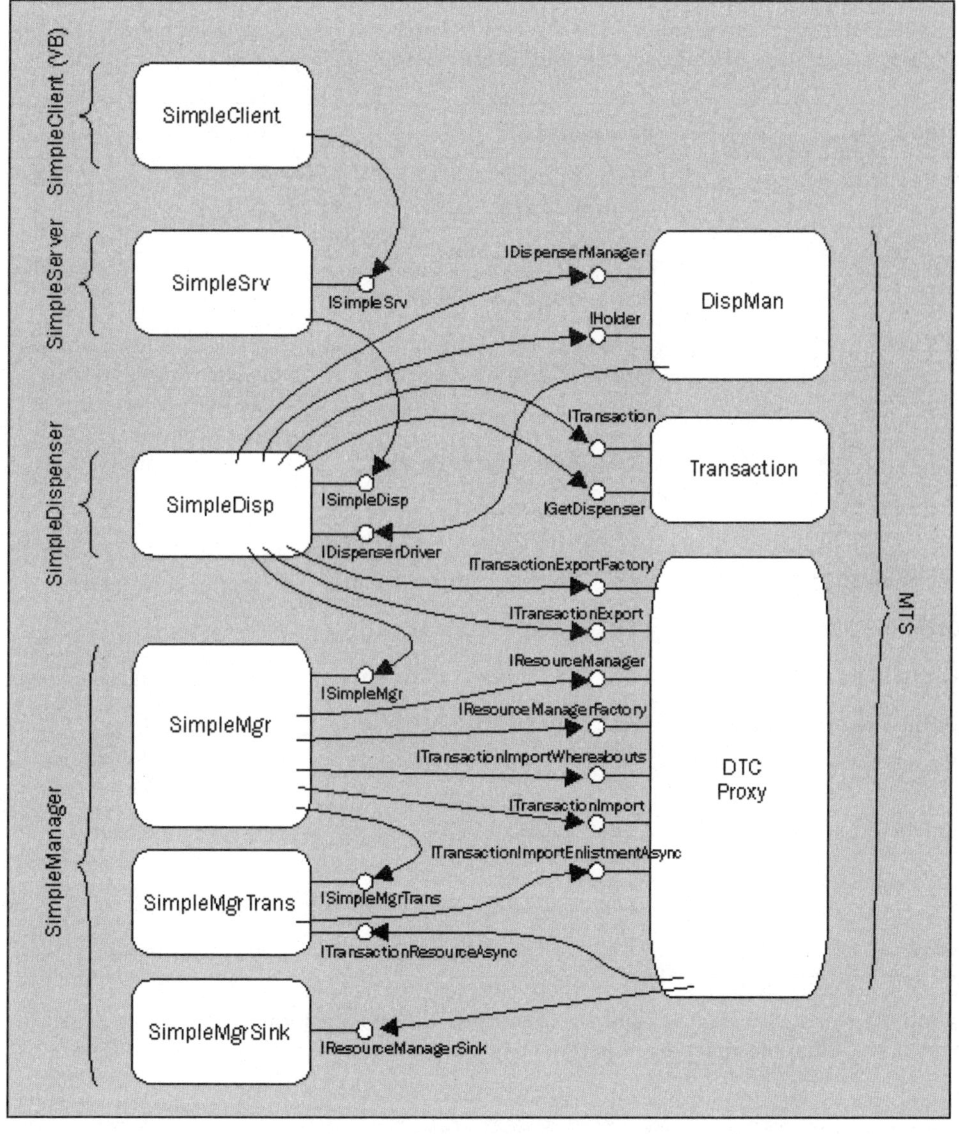

Don't panic about all those interfaces – we'll take them in nice easy stages. You may find it useful to refer back to the diagram now and then as we explore the software. Let's now take a more detailed look at each of the software elements that we're bringing to the party.

Resource Manager

At the bottom, we have our resource manager. This manages access to a database in a transactional manner. Our database isn't really a database at all – it consists of a number of files, each of which contains the textual representation of a floating point number. The files have names like **`data<n>.txt`**. Some database, huh? However, it will do very nicely for demonstration purposes, because if we want to see what a given value has been set to, we can simply pull up the file in Notepad.

The resource manager is implemented as a server, **`SimpleManager`**, and the main COM object class, **`SimpleMgr`**, has one interface, **`ISimpleMgr`**. Here is its definition:

Method	Parameters	Description
`PutValue()`	`[in] ULONG connection,` `[in] int index,` `[in] double value`	Set the data item with the specified index to the specified floating-point value; if value is negative, abort the transaction
`PutText()`	`[in] ULONG connection,` `[in] int index,` `[in] BSTR bstrValue`	Set the data item with the specified index to the specified string value; if the value is set to "ABORT", abort the transaction
`Connect()`	`[out] ULONG* connection`	Connect resource
`Disconnect()`	`[in] ULONG connection`	Disconnect resource
`Reset()`	`[in] ULONG connection`	Reset resource
`Initialize()`	`[in] IStream* pStream`	Initialize resource manager
`GetWhereabouts()`	`[out] VARIANT* pvWhere`	Get whereabouts of transaction manager for importing a transaction
`Enlist()`	`[in] ULONG connection,` `[in] VARIANT vCookie`	Enlist in transaction
`Unenlist()`	`[in] ULONG connection`	Unenlist from transaction

The abort logic is highly artificial, but I've put it into the specification so that we can see what happens if we attempt to make two operations in one transaction, and one of them fails.

There are also two other objects inside the **SimpleManager** server:

- **SimpleMgrTrans**
- **SimpleMgrSink**

The first of these is used by DTC when it wants to involve **SimpleManager** in a two-phase commit. It implements two interfaces: **ISimpleMgrTrans**, which is one of ours, and **ITransactionResourceAsync**, which is one of MTS's. Here are the methods for **ISimpleMgrTrans**:

Method	Parameters	Description
InitValue()	[in] IUnknown* pEnlistUnk, [in] int index, [in] double value	Set up the value, index and reference to **ITransactionEnlistmentAsync** interface on DTC proxy
InitText()	[in] IUnknown* pEnlistUnk, [in] int index, [in] BSTR bstrValue	Set up the string value, index and reference to **ITransactionEnlistmentAsync** interface on DTC proxy

As we shall see, this interface is mainly there to permit communication from **SimpleMgr** to **SimpleMgrTrans**. Again, don't worry too much about the details. The other interface that this object implements is **ITransactionResourceAsync**, which is the interface that the DTC Proxy uses to involve the resource manager in the two-phase commit process. Here are its methods:

Method	Parameters	Description
PrepareRequest()	[in] BOOL fRetaining, [in] DWORD grfRM, [in] BOOL fWantMoniker, [in] BOOL fSinglePhase	Prepare transaction
AbortRequest()	[in] BOID* pboidReason, [in] BOOL fRetaining, [in] XACTUOW* pNewUOW	Abort transaction
CommitRequest ()	[in] DWORD grfRM, [in] XACTUOW* pNewUOW	Commit transaction
TMDown ()		Transaction manager has gone down

The last object in **SimpleManager** is **SimpleMgrSink**, which is used by MTS to contact the resource manager if anything goes wrong. This just implements the MTS interface **IResourceManagerSink**, which has all of one method:

Method	Parameters	Description
`TMDown()`		Transaction manager has gone down

What's the point of this? And what's the difference between this **TMDown()** method and the one in **ITransactionResourceAsync**? Well, the **TMDown()** method in the **ITransactionResourceAsync** interface is used to inform one of the resources involved in the two-phase commit that the TM has gone down; this one is used to inform the whole resource manager.

Resource Dispenser

Still in the bottom tier, we have our resource dispenser, **SimpleDispenser**. This is implemented as an in-process DLL, containing a single object class with two interfaces. The first of these, **ISimpleDisp**, is one that we're providing. As well as this, it also supports the MTS interface **IDispenserDriver**. **ISimpleDisp** has the following methods:

Method	Parameters	Description
`PutValue()`	`[in] int index,` `[in] double value`	Set the data item with the specified index to the specified floating-point value
`PutText()`	`[in] int index,` `[in] BSTR bstrValue`	Set the data item with the specified index to the specified string value

The distinction between the two methods is – once again – pretty artificial, to be honest, but it will illustrate a point later on. As you might imagine, these are the methods that are invoked from the layer above to carry out the required operations on the data. The **IDispenserDriver** methods are all to do with managing resources. We'll discuss all these methods in much greater detail later, when we're looking at the code for the resource dispenser and at managing resources in particular, but I'll show them now for completeness.

Method	Parameters	Description

`CreateResource()`	`[in] const RESTYPID ResTypId,`
	`[out] RESID* pResId,`
	`[out] TIMEINSECS* pSecsFreeBeforeDestroy`
		Create resource of specified type

Method	Parameters	Description
`EnlistResource()`	`[in] const RESID ResId,` `[in] const TRANSID TransId`	Enlist resource in transaction
`ResetResource()`	`[in] const RESID ResId`	Reset resource
`DestroyResource()`	`[in] const RESID ResId`	Destroy resource
`DestroyResourceS()`	`[in] constSRESID SResId`	Destroy resource (using resource identifier as string)

Business Logic

In the all-important middle tier, we have our business logic. Remember the three-tier structure that we looked at in Chapter 5? Our business logic is contained within business objects, which are transient objects that are created specifically to perform a business task, before being thrown back into the pool. Our business objects here are represented by an in-process DLL, **`SimpleServer`**. This contains a single object class with a single interface, **`ISimpleSrv`**. This contains the following methods:

Method	Parameters	Description
`Commit2()`	`[in] BSTR bstrValue1, [in] BSTR bstrValue2`	Set two values, then commit the transaction
`Abort2()`	`[in] BSTR bstrValue1, [in] BSTR bstrValue2`	Set two values, then abort the transaction
`Auto2()`	`[in] BSTR bstrValue1, [in] BSTR bstrValue2`	Set two values, then finish, letting MTS commit the transaction automatically

This is a slightly arbitrary selection of operations, and you are welcome to add your own. However, this will at least test most of the possibilities, especially if we work it so that we can switch between **`PutValue()`** and **`PutText()`** according to whether or not, say, the first character is numeric.

User Interface

At the top tier, we have SimpleClient. This is a VB application that provides a rudimentary user interface to enable us to invoke our transactional components. This is what it looks like:

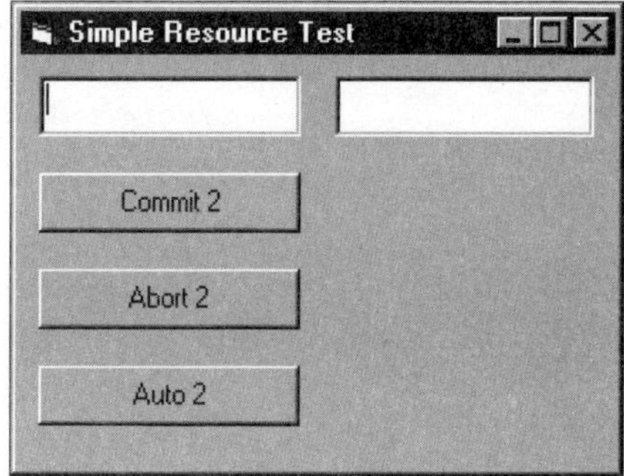

Here's the code:

```
Private Sub cmdCommit2_Click()

On Error GoTo failed

server.Commit2 txtValue1.Text, txtValue2.Text
MsgBox "Finished"

failed:
If (Err.Number = -2147164158) Then
    MsgBox ("Transaction aborted!")
Else
    MsgBox (Err.Description)
End If

End Sub

Private Sub cmdAbort2_Click()
Dim server As New SimpleSrv
server.Abort2 txtValue1.Text, txtValue2.Text
MsgBox ("Finished")
End Sub

Private Sub cmdAuto2_Click()
Dim server As New SimpleSrv
server.Auto2 txtValue1.Text, txtValue2.Text
MsgBox ("Finished")
End Sub
```

So as you can see, we're basically just passing all the logic on to our **SimpleSvr** object.

We'll see why we need to put that error handling code in towards the end of this chapter. Meanwhile, let's look at what MTS does for us.

MTS Components

Before we dive in and start developing our system, we'd better take a closer look at all those interfaces that are being exposed by the MTS components, **DispMan** and the **DTC Proxy Core object**. I won't be covering every single interface that they expose here – just the ones that we're going to be using. Equally, I won't list every single method in these interfaces; my intention is just to give a flavor of what they are about, so that when we meet them in anger, we won't be taken by surprise.

DispMan

First of all, let's look at the two interfaces from **DispMan** that we'll be using:

`IDispenserManager`	This interface is the one that resource dispensers use to connect themselves with **DispMan**.
`IHolder`	A **holder** is that part of **DispMan** that keeps an eye on the resources of a particular type. Each holder talks to its associated resource dispenser by using the **IDispenserDriver** interface that it exposes. The resource dispenser talks back to the holder by means of the **IHolder** interface.

DTC Proxy

We're using a grand total of eight of the interfaces exposed by the DTC Proxy. Here they all are:

`IGetDispenser`	This is actually an interface on a transaction object within the proxy, and is used to get hold of an interface on the Proxy Core Object; the resource dispenser uses it to find its way from the incoming transaction into the Proxy Core Object
`ITransactionExportFactory`	This interface is used to create a new transaction **export** object. A transaction can't just be passed on from resource dispenser to resource manager as a pointer to an **ITransaction** interface, because the Transaction Manager needs to know about what's going on with it. So the transaction has to be sent back to the Transaction Manager in a marshaled form first. The Resource Manager can pick it up from there.
`ITransactionExport`	This is an interface on a transaction export object, and this is what does the actual marshaling of the transaction object into an opaque **transaction cookie**. This cookie represents the whole of the transaction object – you can think of it as being a little like a moniker.
`IResourceManagerFactory`	This is the master interface on the DTC Proxy; it's the interface that we use for creating our local **resource manager object**. Confusingly, it's the resource manager object that represents the connection between the resource manager and the transaction manager.
`IResourceManager`	This is the main interface on the resource manager object. We use this to enlist in a transaction.
`ITransactionImportWhereabouts`	We use this interface to find out where we can get our incoming transaction object from.

ITransactionImport	We use this interface to actually get hold of our incoming transaction.
ITransactionEnlistmentAsync	We use this interface to report back when we have prepared, committed or aborted a transaction

Notice that I haven't mentioned **ITransaction***, which you might think was a serious omission. However, we don't actually use the* **ITransaction** *interface directly at all, although we pass a pointer to the interface around.*

Logging Routines

Before we dive into the code proper, let's take a quick look at the member functions that all of our Visual C++ software elements are going to use for logging. There are two main variations:

```
void CXXX::Log(HRESULT hResult, LPSTR lpszEvent)
{
   CHAR szEvent[128];
   if (FAILED (hResult))
   {
      LPSTR pMsgBuf;

      if (::FormatMessage(FORMAT_MESSAGE_ALLOCATE_BUFFER |
                          FORMAT_MESSAGE_FROM_SYSTEM,
                          NULL, hResult,
                          MAKELANGID(LANG_NEUTRAL,SUBLANG_DEFAULT),
                         (LPTSTR)&pMsgBuf, 0, NULL))
      {
         LPSTR lpszNewline = strchr (pMsgBuf, '\r');
         *lpszNewline = 0;

         sprintf(szEvent, "%s FAILED (%x, %s)", lpszEvent,
                                     hResult, (char*)pMsgBuf);
         LocalFree(pMsgBuf);
      }

      else
         sprintf(szEvent, "%s FAILED (%x)", lpszEvent, hResult);
   }

   else
      sprintf(szEvent, "%s OK", lpszEvent);

   Log(szEvent);
}

void CXXX::Log(LPSTR lpszEvent)
{
   SYSTEMTIME st;
   GetLocalTime(&st);
```

```
    HANDLE hFile = CreateFile("c:\\SimpleTX.txt", GENERIC_READ |
                        GENERIC_WRITE, 0, NULL, OPEN_ALWAYS, 0, NULL);
    SetFilePointer(hFile, 0, NULL, FILE_END);

    LPSTR str = new char[lstrlen(lpszEvent) + 25];
    wsprintf(str, "%02d:%02d:%02d DISPENSER:   %s\r\n",
               st.wHour, st.wMinute, st.wSecond, lpszEvent);
    DWORD written;
    WriteFile(hFile, str, lstrlen(str), &written, NULL);
    delete [] str;

    CloseHandle(hFile);
}
```

SimpleDisp has one extra, used for dumping out resource-related information:

```
void CSimpleDisp::Log(LPSTR lpszEvent, const RESID ResId)
{
    CHAR szEvent[128];
    sprintf(szEvent, "%s (resource identifier %x)",
                                    lpszEvent, ResId);

    Log(szEvent);
}
```

I think we're ready to set off now. We have a slight problem here, in that the three elements, **SimpleServer**, **SimpleDispenser** and **SimpleManager** are all constantly interacting with each other, and it's often quite difficult to discuss each one in splendid isolation from the others. So there may be several places where something completely incomprehensible happens, and we have to say, "Don't worry about that, it'll make sense later." The alternative would be to constantly flit between one element and another.

Inside the Code

SimpleServer

We've already got our VB client coded up, so let's put together our **SimpleServer** project. This is an ATL in-process DLL project, containing a single object, **SimpleSrv**, which has a single dual interface, **ISimpleSrv**. The interface definition includes the methods **Commit2()**, **Abort2()** and **Auto2()**, as shown in the table earlier. We'll also want to add some member functions, so make the following changes to the **SimpleSrv.h** header file:

```
// SimpleSrv.h : Declaration of the CSimpleSrv

#ifndef __SIMPLESRV_H_
#define __SIMPLESRV_H_

#include "resource.h"        // main symbols

interface ISimpleDisp;
```

```
/////////////////////////////////////////////////////////////////////////////
// CSimpleSrv
class ATL_NO_VTABLE CSimpleSrv :
   public CComObjectRootEx<CComSingleThreadModel>,
   public CComCoClass<CSimpleSrv, &CLSID_SimpleSrv>,
   public IDispatchImpl<ISimpleSrv, &IID_ISimpleSrv, &LIBID_SIMPLESERVERLib>
{
private:
   void Log (HRESULT hResult, LPSTR lpszEvent);
   void Log (LPSTR lpszEvent);
   HRESULT Put (ISimpleDisp* pDisp, int index, BSTR bstrValue);

public:
   CSimpleSrv()
   {
   }

DECLARE_REGISTRY_RESOURCEID(IDR_SIMPLESRV)

BEGIN_COM_MAP(CSimpleSrv)
   COM_INTERFACE_ENTRY(ISimpleSrv)
   COM_INTERFACE_ENTRY(IDispatch)
END_COM_MAP()

// ISimpleSrv
public:
   STDMETHOD(Commit2)(/*[in]*/ BSTR bstrValue1, /*[in]*/ BSTR bstrValue2);
   STDMETHOD(Abort2)(/*[in]*/ BSTR bstrValue1, /*[in]*/ BSTR bstrValue2);
   STDMETHOD(Auto2)(/*[in]*/ BSTR bstrValue1, /*[in]*/ BSTR bstrValue2);
};

#endif //__SIMPLESRV_H_
```

We'll also need to add an extra header file, **mtx.h** to our **SimpleSrv.cpp** source file:

```
#include "mtx.h"
```

Let's take a look at what happens when we carry out a *commit* type transaction. It all starts innocently enough, with the following code in the **Commit2()** method in **SimpleServer**. The full listing for this method is shown below:

```
STDMETHODIMP CSimpleSrv::Commit2(BSTR bstrValue1, BSTR bstrValue2)
{
   Log("Commit2 called");

   // Get context and create instance of dispenser

   CComPtr<IObjectContext> pObjectContext;
   HRESULT hResult = GetObjectContext(&pObjectContext);

   Log (hResult, "GetObjectContext");

   if (FAILED (hResult))
      return hResult;
```

```
    CComPtr<ISimpleDisp> pDisp;
    hResult = pObjectContext->CreateInstance (CLSID_SimpleDisp,
                              IID_ISimpleDisp, (void**)&pDisp);

    Log(hResult, "Created instance of dispenser");

    if (FAILED (hResult))
       return hResult;

    // Set up two values

    hResult = Put(pDisp, 1, bstrValue1);

    Log(hResult, "Put first value");

    hResult = Put(pDisp, 2, bstrValue2);

    Log(hResult, "Put second value");

    // Set transaction complete

    hResult = pObjectContext->SetComplete();

    Log(hResult, "Set complete");

    return S_OK;
}
```

*From now on, I'll leave out the calls to the event logging method, **`Log()`**, from all the code in this chapter, in order to cut down on the clutter.*

So, all we are doing here is instantiating the resource dispenser within the current transaction context, and then inserting two values (one for database 1 and one for database 2). Having done that, we commit the transaction with the call to **`SetComplete()`**, so that both of the database updates happen together.

Here's the member function, **`Put()`**, which simply calls the appropriate method on the resource dispenser:

```
HRESULT CSimpleSrv::Put (ISimpleDisp* pDisp, int index, BSTR bstrValue)
{
   // If starts with alphabetic, treat as text

   if (iswalpha (bstrValue[0]))
      return pDisp->PutText(index, bstrValue);

   // Otherwise, treat as value

   USES_CONVERSION;

   double value = atof(W2A(bstrValue));
   return pDisp->PutValue(index, value);
}
```

This method is determining which of the two alternative **Put()** methods to invoke on the resource dispenser object, depending on whether the user has entered textual or numeric data.

And that's it. All the really hard work's done in the layers below. So let's have a look at what the resource dispenser's doing.

SimpleDispenser

Object Definitions and Header Files

This is an ATL in-process DLL project, containing a single object, **SimpleDisp**, which has two interfaces, **ISimpleDisp** and **IDispenserDriver**. (Remember that we saw the definitions for the interfaces in the tables earlier in the chapter.) This object must have thread model "**both**", because it may get invoked from both multi-threaded and single-threaded apartments. We also need to aggregate in the free-threaded marshaler. Start off by creating an object with interface **ISimpleDisp** as specified above, and then make the following changes to the **SimpleDisp.h** header file:

```
// SimpleDisp.h : Declaration of the CSimpleDisp

#ifndef __SIMPLEDISP_H_
#define __SIMPLEDISP_H_

#include "resource.h"        // main symbols

interface ISimpleMgr;

typedef enum {
      VALUETYPE = 1,
      TEXTTYPE,
} SIMPLETYPE;

typedef struct {
   ULONG      m_connection;
   SIMPLETYPE   m_type;
} SIMPLERES;

/////////////////////////////////////////////////////////////////////////////
// CSimpleDisp
class ATL_NO_VTABLE CSimpleDisp :
   public CComObjectRootEx<CComMultiThreadModel>,
   public CComCoClass<CSimpleDisp, &CLSID_SimpleDisp>,
   public IDispatchImpl<ISimpleDisp, IID_ISimpleDisp,
                              &LIBIDSIMPLEDISPENSERLib>,
   public IDispenserDriver
{
private:
   CComPtr<IHolder> m_pHolder;
   CComPtr<ISimpleMgr> m_pManager;
   CComPtr<IStream> m_pStream;
   IUnknown* m_pFTM;

   void Log (HRESULT hResult, LPSTR lpszEvent);
   void Log (LPSTR lpszEvent, const RESID ResId);
```

```
    void Log (LPSTR lpszEvent);
    CComPtr<ISimpleMgr> GetSimpleMgr ();

public:
    CSimpleDisp()
    {
    }
    HRESULT FinalConstruct();
    void FinalRelease();

DECLARE_CLASSFACTORY_SINGLETON(CSimpleDisp);
DECLARE_PROTECT_FINAL_CONSTRUCT();

DECLARE_REGISTRY_RESOURCEID(IDR_SIMPLEDISP)

BEGIN_COM_MAP(CSimpleDisp)
    COM_INTERFACE_ENTRY(ISimpleDisp)
    COM_INTERFACE_ENTRY(IDispatch)
    COM_INTERFACE_ENTRY(IDispenserDriver)
    COM_INTERFACE_ENTRY_AGGREGATE(IID_IMarshal, m_pFTM)
END_COM_MAP()

// ISimpleDisp
public:
    STDMETHOD(PutText)(/*[in]*/ int index, /*[in]*/ BSTR bstrValue);
    STDMETHOD(PutValue)(/*[in]*/ int index, /*[in]*/ double value);

// IDispenserDriver
    STDMETHOD (CreateResource) (const RESTYPID ResTypId,
              RESID* pResId, TIMEINSECS* pSecsFreeBeforeDestroy);
    STDMETHOD (RateResource) (const RESTYPID ResTypId,
              const RESID ResId,
              const BOOL fRequiresTransactionEnlistment,
              RESOURCERATING* pRating);
    STDMETHOD (EnlistResource) (const RESID ResId,
              const TRANSID TransId);
    STDMETHOD (ResetResource) (const RESID ResId);
    STDMETHOD (DestroyResource) (const RESID ResId);
    STDMETHOD (DestroyResourceS) (constSRESID SResId);
};

#endif //__SIMPLEDISP_H_
```

We'll also need to add a couple of extra header files to our **SimpleDisp.cpp** source file:

```
#include "mtxdm.h"
#include "txdtc.h"
```

And to our **SimpleDispenser.cpp** source file:

```
#include "stdafx.h"
```

```
#include "mtxdm.h"

#include "resource.h"
#include "initguid.h"
#include "SimpleDispenser.h"

#include "txdtc.h"
#include "mtxdm_i.c"

#include "SimpleDispenser_i.c"
#include "SimpleDisp.h"
```

Let's take a look at the implementation code.

Initializing the Dispenser

You'll find the initialization for the dispenser object in the code inside the **FinalConstruct()** method of **CSimpleDisp**.

> *Why we should do this in a **FinalConstruct()** method, rather than the constructor itself? The simple answer is that we're doing a number of fairly complex things, any one of which might go wrong, and hence might give rise to a bad status return. We can't return a bad status from the constructor, but we **can** from **FinalConstruct()**.*

```
HRESULT CSimpleDisp::FinalConstruct()
{
   // Get hold of dispenser manager interface

   CComPtr<IDispenserManager> pDispMgr;
   HRESULT hResult = GetDispenserManager (&pDispMgr);

   if (FAILED (hResult))
      return hResult;

   IDispenserDriver *pDriver;    // NB Don't use smart pointer
   hResult = GetUnknown()->QueryInterface(IID_IDispenserDriver,
                                  reinterpret_cast<void**>(&pDriver));

   if (FAILED (hResult))
      return hResult;

   // Register with dispenser manager, getting holder interface

   hResult = pDispMgr->RegisterDispenser(pDriver,
                                          L"Simple Dispenser", &m_pHolder);

   if (FAILED (hResult))
      return hResult;

   // Create instance of resource manager

   hResult = CoCreateInstance(CLSID_SimpleMgr, NULL, CLSCTX_SERVER,
                              IID_ISimpleMgr, (void**)&m_pManager);
```

```
    if (FAILED (hResult))
       return hResult;

    // Initialize resource manager, passing stream for interface

    CreateStreamOnHGlobal(NULL, TRUE, &m_pStream);
    hResult = m_pManager->Initialize(m_pStream);

    if (FAILED (hResult))
       return hResult;

    hResult = CoCreateFreeThreadedMarshaler(GetUnknown(), &m_pFTM);

    return hResult;
}
```

OK, so what's going on here? We're using the helper function **`GetDispenserManager()`** to get hold of an interface to **`DispMan`**. Having got hold of this, we call one of its methods, **`RegisterDispenser()`**, to register ourselves. From this point on, the dispenser manager knows all about us, and knows how to call back to us as well. However, it's not just one way traffic, because it very generously gives us a pointer to one of its interfaces back – a pointer to **`IHolder`**, which we store in the private member variable **`m_pHolder`**. We'll need this interface later on.

*Notice that we don't release the **`IDispenserDriver`** interface. This is because there is a Microsoft-acknowledged bug in the implementation of **`RegisterDispenser()`**, in that it fails to **`AddRef()`** the pointer that we pass to it, and we have to treat it as a passed reference.*

We then create an instance of the resource manager, and initialize it. Notice that we first create a stream and pass it to the **`Initialize()`** method, but what is the stream for? This is a tricky one. It's all to do with **threading**. The problem is that once things get moving, the MTS environment is going to invoke the methods of our **`IDispenserDriver`** interface from various threads. Inside these methods, we're going to want to invoke some of the resource manager's methods. Unfortunately, we can't just use the **`m_pManager`** pointer that was returned by the original instantiation, because that has only been established for the current thread. If we try to use it in future on the wrong thread, we'll get an error return. If we're lucky, that is. If we're not, we'll just get one of those incomprehensible COM crashes.

So what can we do? Well, we can ask **`SimpleMgr`** to **marshal** the interface pointer into a stream. Then we can simply **unmarshal** the pointer from that stream every time we need one in future. That way, we can ensure that our code is thread-safe. Here's the member function that we'll be using to get hold of a pointer to the resource manager interface:

```
CComPtr<ISimpleMgr> CSimpleDisp::GetSimpleMgr ()
{
    LARGE_INTEGER offset;
    ULARGE_INTEGER newPosn;

    offset.LowPart = 0;
    offset.HighPart = 0;
```

```
    if (m_pStream == NULL)
       return NULL;

    m_pStream->Seek(offset, STREAM_SEEK_SET, &newPosn);

    CComPtr<ISimpleMgr> pManager;
    HRESULT hResult = CoUnmarshalInterface (m_pStream, IID_ISimpleMgr,
                           reinterpret_cast<void**>(&pManager));

    if (FAILED(hResult))
       return NULL;

    return pManager;
}
```

Inserting a Data Item

The next thing we're going to look at is what happens when our server actually makes a request to insert a value into our database. Remember that once it had created the instance of the resource dispenser, the server invoked either **PutValue()** or **PutText()**.

For the time being, we'll assume that we're dealing with textual data, and so we'll look at the **PutText()** routine in **SimpleDispenser**:

```
STDMETHODIMP CSimpleDisp::PutText(int index, BSTR bstrValue)
{
    CComPtr<ISimpleMgr> pManager = GetSimpleMgr();
    if (!pManager)
       return E_NOINTERFACE;

    // Ask holder for some resource

    RESID ResId;
    HRESULT hResult = m_pHolder->AllocResource((RESTYPID) TEXTTYPE,
                                               (RESID*) &ResId);

    // Use resource to pass data to resource manager

    SIMPLERES* pRes = reinterpret_cast<SIMPLERES*>(ResId);

    pManager->PutText(pRes->m_connection, index, bstrValue);

    // Free resource

    hResult = m_pHolder->FreeResource((RESID) ResId);

    return S_OK;
}
```

On the face of it, this looks innocuous enough. We allocate ourselves a resource, invoke the analogous **PutText()** method on the resource manager object, and then free the resource. The resource we're using doesn't actually contain much real data. We'll see what it looks like shortly, but its sole purpose as far as we're concerned is to enable us to enlist in a transaction. By requesting a resource, we trigger the automatic transaction mechanism.

In real life, our resources might be a whole load more scarce than that. So before we go any further, let's step back a little and consider what this resource management business is all about.

The Importance of Managing Resources

Why is resource management so important in transactions? The reason is that the key performance criterion in benchmarking transaction products is *throughput*, in other words, how many transactions per second the product can handle. And there's nothing that's going to slow down a transaction more than inefficient use of resources – initializing resources that don't need to be initialized, waiting for resources to be freed up before re-allocating them, hanging on to resources when you don't need them any more, and so on.

A resource, here, can be as basic as a large chunk of memory, or as complex as a connection to an SQL database (remember the ODBC resource dispenser?)

Resource Pooling

In order to make the most efficient use of these resources, they are put into a pool and managed by `DispMan`. The pool is divided up into four areas:

- Unenlisted inventory – this area contains resources that are not currently in use, and are not enlisted in a transaction (we'll look at enlistment in a little while)
- Enlisted inventory – this area contains resources that are not currently in use, but have been previously used in the current transaction
- Unenlisted in use – this area contains resources that are currently in use, but haven't yet been enlisted in a transaction
- Enlisted in use – this area contains resources that are currently in use, and have been enlisted in a transaction

How would a resource be in the pool, but not currently in use? Well, each resource has a timeout attached to it, so that once it's been freed, it hangs around for a while in case anyone else wants to pick it up and make use of it. This is particularly important if creating a resource is a complex process, but resetting an existing resource is more straightforward.

Remember that the holder (part of `DispMan`) communicates with the resource dispenser using its `IDispenserDriver` interface. This means that in order to allow `DispMan` to manage this pool of resources, we're going to have to implement all the methods of the `IDispenserDriver` interface, which we saw listed in a table earlier in the chapter. The next few sections will be focusing on these methods, namely:

- `CreateResource()`
- `RateResource()`
- `EnlistResource()`
- `ResetResource()`
- `DestroyResource()`

The process of allocating resources and enlisting in the transaction basically all happens during the `PutText()` function of the resource dispenser. Before we dive into the details of what is going on during these method calls, let's just take a quick look at the overall flow of events that take place during the allocation of resources.

- In the **PutText()** method, **SimpleDisp** calls **AllocResource()**, which is implemented by **DispMan**
- If there are no resources available, **DispMan** calls **CreateResource()** – this creates a resource and makes a connection to the manager object
- **DispMan** then calls **EnlistResource()** to enlist the new resource in the transaction – this constructs the transaction export object and tells the resource manager where it can find it
- After the corresponding **PutText()** method on the manager object is called, **SimpleDisp** calls the **FreeResource()** method of **DispMan**
- **DispMan** then calls **ResetResource()** so that we can clean up the resource

So what about **RateResource()** then? Well, this is called when **DispMan** does have resources available, and needs to decide which to use. We'll see more about this later. **DestroyResource()** is called by **DispMan** once the resource has timed out and should be removed from the pool.

Creating a Resource

OK, before we go ahead with creating our resource, let's see what's going to happen. We ask **DispMan** to provide us with a resource, using a call to the **AllocResource()** method on the **IHolder** interface (Remember that we saved a pointer to this interface back in the **SimpleDisp**'s **FinalConstruct()** method.). The holder in **DispMan** looks at the pool of available resources, and decides if it needs to allocate more resource. If it does, it invokes the **CreateResource()** method on our **IDispenserDriver** interface. The sequence of events is outlined in the diagram below:

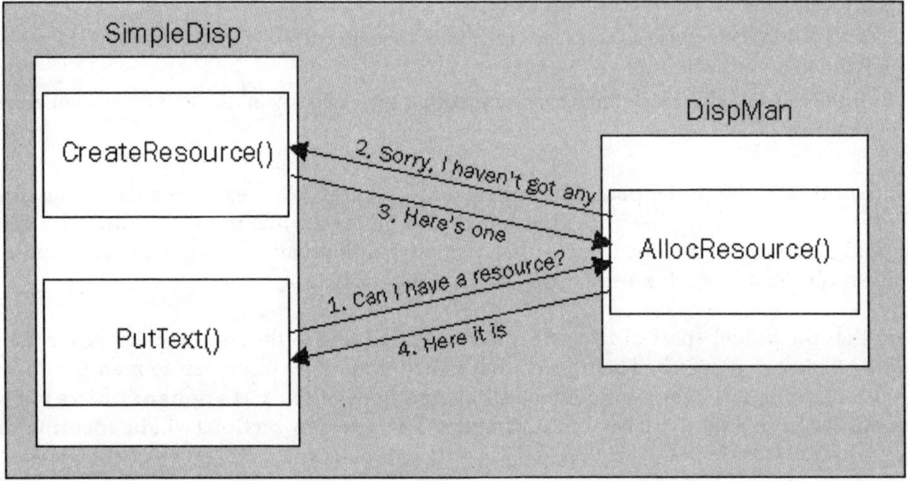

You might like to think of **DispMan** as being a bit like a bank. I ask the bank for some money from my account. If there's some there, they give me some. If there isn't, they might ask me to create some by transferring some in from another account. Or by going out and getting a proper job.

As it happens, because we're asking for a resource for the first time, there won't be any resource in the pool, so **CreateResource()** is going to be called. This is what our implementation looks like:

```
STDMETHODIMP CSimpleDisp::CreateResource (const RESTYPID ResTypId,
          RESID* pResId, TIMEINSECS* pSecsFreeBeforeDestroy)
{
```

```
    // Create resource and set its type

    SIMPLERES* pRes = new SIMPLERES;

    *pResId = reinterpret_cast<RESID>(pRes);

    pRes->m_type = (SIMPLETYPE) ResTypId;

    // Establish "connection" to resource manager

    CComPtr<ISimpleMgr> pManager = GetSimpleMgr();
    if (!pManager)
    {
       delete pRes;
       return E_NOINTERFACE;
    }

    HRESULT hResult = pManager->Connect(&pRes->m_connection);

    *pSecsFreeBeforeDestroy = 5;

    return hResult;
}
```

For the purposes of this demonstration program, I've created a dummy resource called **SIMPLERES**, which is just a simple structure, the definition of which is shown below. As you can see from the code above, creating the resource is pretty straightforward. It's a question of allocating an area of local dynamic memory, setting up the resource type (in this case **SIMPLERES**), establishing a new "connection" to the resource manager, by calling the resource manager's **Connect()** method, and saving the handle allocated. We'll see what this actually involves later on, when we look at the resource manager itself. As I said above, we're not actually going to use this resource for anything useful. It's only there to demonstrate how resources are managed. If you like, you can pretend that it's some really costly connection to a powerful back-end system.

The last thing that we do in our **CreateResource()** method in the resource dispenser is set ***pSecsFreeBeforeDestroy** to five seconds. This is effectively the expiry time of the resource. When five seconds have expired since the last time that it was returned to the inventory, **DispMan** will destroy the resource – we'll see what happens then further on in the chapter.

Here's the definition of the **SIMPLERES** structure:

```
typedef enum {
     VALUETYPE = 1,
     TEXTTYPE,
} SIMPLETYPE;

typedef struct {
     ULONG      m_connection;
     SIMPLETYPE m_type;
} SIMPLERES;
```

This structure basically carries a flag to indicate which sort of operation we're involved in (putting textual or value data), and a handle to a connection in the resource manager. You can imagine that in the case of, say, a database resource dispenser, the resource structure allocated for this might contain details of the database connection.

> *Incidentally, did you spot the use of the* **`GetSimpleMgr()`** *member function to unmarshal an interface pointer for us?*

Rating Existing Resources

We've just seen what happens if we ask **`DispMan`** to provide us with a resource, but there are none available. This won't always be the case, however. What if there were already some resources in the pool? Well, the first thing to say is that **`CreateResource()`** doesn't need to be called. But **`DispMan`** still has a problem, in that it doesn't know which one of the existing resources to choose. It solves this problem by asking us to give each one a rating, and it does that by invoking the **`RateResouce()`** method of the **`IDispenserDriver`** interface. This is illustrated in the diagram below:

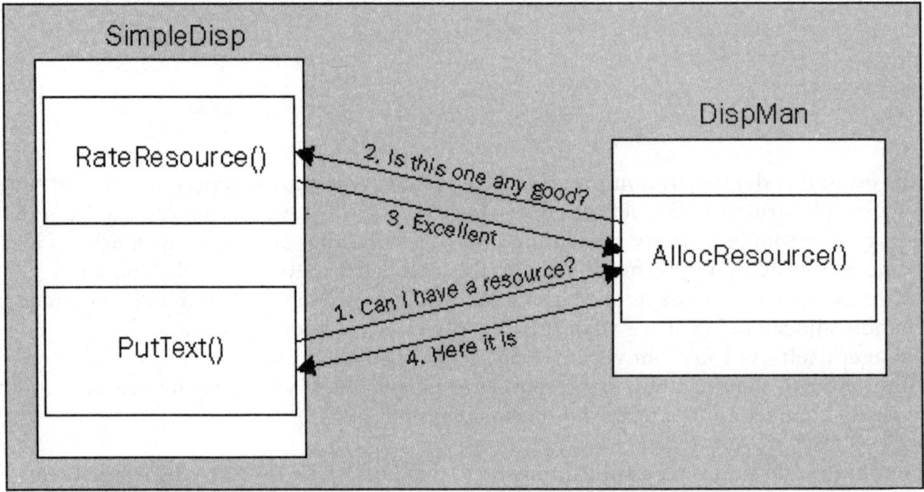

This is the method in **`IDispenserDriver`** that it invokes:

```
STDMETHODIMP CSimpleDisp::RateResource(const RESTYPID ResTypId,
        const RESID ResId, const BOOL fRequiresTransactionEnlistment,
        RESOURCERATING* pRating)
{
   SIMPLERES* pRes = reinterpret_cast<SIMPLERES*> ResId;

   if ((SIMPLETYPE) ResTypId != pRes->m_type)
      *pRating = 0;

   else
   {
      if (fRequiresTransactionEnlistment)
         *pRating = 50;
      else
```

```
            *pRating = 100;
    }

    return S_OK;
}
```

The rating we give the resource depends on whether or not it is the correct type, and, if so, whether or not it is already enlisted in the transaction. The ratings here are:

- **0** for a resource of the wrong type
- **50** for a resource of the right type, but not enlisted in the transaction
- **100** for a resource that is already enlisted

Resetting Resources

If we're going to use a second-hand resource, we want to make sure that it's been cleaned up properly. To do this, **DispMan** invokes our **ResetResource()** method after we've finished with it (signalled by us invoking the **FreeResource()** method on **IHolder**):

```
STDMETHODIMP CSimpleDisp::ResetResource (const RESID ResId)
{
    // Reset "connection" to resource manager

    SIMPLERES* pRes = reinterpret_cast<SIMPLERES*> ResId;

    CCom<ISimpleMgr> pManager = GetSimpleMgr();
    if (!pManager)
        return E_NOINTERFACE;

    HRESULT hResult = pManager->Reset(pRes->m_connection);

    return hResult;
}
```

Destroying a Resource

If our resource is still there unallocated when its timeout expires, **DispMan** frees it from the pool. But first, it invokes our **DestroyResource()** method:

```
STDMETHODIMP CSimpleDisp::DestroyResource (const RESID ResId)
{
    // Disconnect from resource manager

    SIMPLERES *pRes = reinterpret_cast<SIMPLERES*> ResId;

    CCom<ISimpleMgr> pManager = GetSimpleMgr();
    if (!pManager)
        return E_NOINTERFACE;

    HRESULT hResult = pManager->Disconnect(pRes->m_connection);

    delete pRes;
```

```
    return hResult;
}
```

There's another version of this method, **DestroyResourceS()**, which passes the resource identifier as a string, but we're going to return **E_NOTIMPL** to that.

And that's almost it as far as the resource dispenser's concerned, except ... did anyone mention transactions?

Enlisting Our Resource in a Transaction

OK, we've successfully allocated ourselves a resource. The next thing that's going to happen is that a transaction is going to appear on the scene. It's going to appear for two reasons:

- Our server has been registered with MTS as requiring a new transaction
- Our server has requested a resource from a dispenser that is registered with MTS

The transaction makes itself known to us as a parameter of the last method in the **IDispenserDriver** interface, **EnlistResource()**, which is invoked by the holder to enlist the resource in the transaction. This is what our implementation looks like:

```
STDMETHODIMP CSimpleDisp::EnlistResource (const RESID ResId,
                                          const TRANSID TransId)
{
    SIMPLERES* pRes = reinterpret_cast<SIMPLERES*> ResId;

    CCom<ISimpleMgr> pManager = GetSimpleMgr();
    if (!pManager)
        return E_NOINTERFACE;

    if (TransId == 0)
        return pManager->Unenlist(pRes->m_connection);

    CComPtr<ITransaction> pTrans = reinterpret_cast<ITransaction*> (TransId);

    // Get interface on DTC Proxy Core Object

    CComPtr<IGetDispenser> pDispenser;
    HRESULT hResult = pTrans->QueryInterface(IID_IGetDispenser,
                                             (void**) &pDispenser);

    if (FAILED(hResult))
        return hResult;

    // Get transaction export factory

    CComPtr<ITransactionExportFactory> pFactory;
    hResult = pDispenser->GetDispenser(IID_ITransactionExportFactory,
                                       (void**) &pFactory);

    if (FAILED(hResult))
        return hResult;
```

```
// Get whereabouts of transaction manager

CComVariant vWhere;
hResult = pManager->GetWhereabouts(&vWhere);

if (FAILED(hResult))
   return hResult;

// Construct transaction export object

SAFEARRAY* pArray = vWhere.parray;

long lBound;
SafeArrayGetLBound(pArray, 1, &lBound);

long uBound;
SafeArrayGetUBound(pArray, 1, &uBound);

ULONG cbSize = uBound - lBound + 1;

BYTE HUGEP* rgbWhere;
SafeArrayAccessData(pArray, reinterpret_cast<void HUGEP**> (&rgbWhere));

CComPtr<ITransactionExport> pExport;
hResult = pFactory->Create (cbSize, rgbWhere, &pExport);

SafeArrayUnaccessData(pArray);

if (FAILED(hResult))
   return hResult;

// Now export it to transaction manager

CComPtr<IUnknown> pUnkTrans;
pTrans->QueryInterface(IID_IUnknown,
                       reinterpret_cast<void**> (&pUnkTrans));

ULONG cbCookie;
hResult = pExport->Export(pUnkTrans, &cbCookie);

if (FAILED(hResult))
   return hResult;

// Get transaction cookie from transaction manager

SAFEARRAYBOUND rgsabound[1];
rgsabound[0].lLbound = 0;
rgsabound[0].cElements = cbCookie;

pArray = SafeArrayCreate(VT_UI1, 1, rgsabound);

BYTE* rgbCookie;
SafeArrayAccessData(pArray, (void HUGEP* FAR*)&rgbCookie);
```

```
    ULONG cbUsed;
    hResult = pExport->GetTransactionCookie(pUnkTrans, cbCookie,
                                            rgbCookie, &cbUsed);

    SafeArrayUnaccessData(pArray);

    if (FAILED(hResult))
       return hResult;

    // Pass the cookie to our resource manager

    CComVariant vCookie;
    vCookie.vt = VT_UI1 | VT_ARRAY;
    vCookie.parray = pArray;

    hResult = pManager->Enlist(pRes->m_connection, vCookie);

    return hResult;
}
```

Now, what's all this export stuff about?

Our problem is that we're really not that interested in the transaction within the resource dispenser; what we *really* want to do is pass it on to the resource manager. The trouble is that in order to do this, we have to go through the tedious rigmarole of *exporting* the transaction. But in order to pass it on, we need to know where to put it. This ensures that:

- The transaction manager knows about it
- The resource manager can pick it up again

This means that we've got to get hold of the whereabouts of the transaction manager, and the only part of the system that can find that is the resource manager itself.

Exporting the Transaction

The first step in exporting a transaction is to get hold of an interface to the DTC Proxy Core Object. In order to do this, we need to query for a different interface on the transaction object, **`IGetDispenser`**. We can use this to get hold of interfaces on the DTC Proxy, by invoking its **`GetDispenser()`** method. The interface that we actually want is **`ITransactionExportFactory`**, which is – unsurprisingly – an interface to the transaction export factory.

The next step is to find out the whereabouts of the transaction manager. Unfortunately, this information is something that only the resource manager itself can provide, as the address incorporates information about its own MTS environment (remember that it might well be running on a different machine!), so we have to ask the resource manager for its whereabouts. There isn't a standard method to invoke to find this out, so we'll have to implement one ourselves within the **`ISimpleMgr`** interface, called **`GetWhereabouts()`**. For safety, we'll pass the whereabouts details as a **`VARIANT`** array of bytes. That's what all the messing about with safe arrays is about.

So, we've got our transaction export factory, and we've got the whereabouts of the transaction manager. What next?

The next thing we do is create the transaction export object, using the **`Create()`** method on the export factory object, and then we export it using the export object's **`Export()`** method. However, we haven't finished yet, as we need to tell the resource manager how to get hold of the transaction details. We do this by invoking another method on the export object, **`GetTransactionCookie()`**. We wrap this up in another **`VARIANT`** array, and invoke one of the methods on the **`ISimpleMgr`** interface, **`Export()`**, to tell the resource manager about the transaction, passing in the cookie we've just obtained. We'll see what the resource manager does with this soon enough.

Notice, right at the start of the method, that if we get passed a transaction with a zero identifier, we're actually being asked to unenlist from the transaction. This doesn't happen in all the early versions of MTS: it does in the version supplied with NT4 Option Pack, but it doesn't in the Enterprise Edition version.

Odds and Ends

That's about it for the resource dispenser. However, just for the sake of completeness, I'll show you the last couple of routines. The first is the method **`PutValue()`**, which is very similar to **`PutText()`**:

```
STDMETHODIMP CSimpleDisp::PutValue(int index, double value)
{
   CComPtr<ISimpleMgr> pManager = GetSimpleMgr();

   if (!pManager)
      return E_NOINTERFACE;

   // Ask holder for some resource

   RESID ResId;
   HRESULT hResult = m_pHolder->AllocResource((RESTYPID) VALUETYPE,
                                          (RESID*) &ResId);

   // Use resource to pass data to resource manager

   SIMPLERES* pRes = reinterpret_cast<SIMPLERES*> (ResId);

   pManager->PutValue(pRes->m_connection, index, value);

   // Free resource

   hResult = m_pHolder->FreeResource((RESID) ResId);

   return hResult;
}
```

And here's our **`FinalRelease()`** method:

```
void CSimpleDisp::FinalRelease()
{
   // Close holder interface

   HRESULT hResult = m_pHolder->Close();
```

```
    // Release free-threaded marshaler

    hResult = m_pFTM->Release();
}
```

Now I think it's about time that we saw what the resource manager's up to.

SimpleManager

This is an executable server project, containing three objects:

- **SimpleMgr**
- **SimpleMgrTrans**
- **SimpleMgrSink**

Let's start by looking at the definitions of these objects.

Object Definitions and Header Files

The first of these, **SimpleMgr**, has a single interface, **ISimpleMgr.** Once more, we need to make a few small changes to the header file **SimpleMgr.h**:

```
// SimpleMgr.h : Declaration of the CSimpleMgr

#ifndef __SIMPLEMGR_H_
#define __SIMPLEMGR_H_

#include "resource.h"        // main symbols

interface IResourceManager;
interface ITransactionImportWhereabouts;
typedef struct {
   CComPtr<ITransaction> m_pTrans;
   char m_dummy[32];
} SIMPLECONN;

typedef SIMPLECONN* LPSIMPLECONN;

/////////////////////////////////////////////////////////////////////////////
// CSimpleMgr
class ATL_NO_VTABLE CSimpleMgr :
   public CComObjectRootEx<CComMultiThreadModel>,
   public CComCoClass<CSimpleMgr, &CLSID_SimpleMgr>,
   public ISimpleMgr
{
private:
   void Log (HRESULT hResult, LPSTR lpszEvent);
   void Log (LPSTR lpszEvent);

   CComPtr<IResourceManager> m_pResMgr;
   CComPtr<ITransactionImportWhereabouts> m_pWhereabouts;
```

```
public:
   CSimpleMgr()
   {
   }

   void FinalRelease()
   {
   }

DECLARE_REGISTRY_RESOURCEID(IDR_SIMPLEMGR)

BEGIN_COM_MAP(CSimpleMgr)
   COM_INTERFACE_ENTRY(ISimpleMgr)
END_COM_MAP()

// ISimpleMgr
public:
   STDMETHOD(Reset)(/*[in]*/ ULONG connection);
   STDMETHOD(Disconnect)(/*[in]*/ ULONG connection);
   STDMETHOD(Connect)(/*[out]*/ ULONG *connection);
   STDMETHOD(PutText)(/*[in]*/ ULONG connection, /*[in]*/ int index,
                      /*[in]*/ BSTR bstrValue);
   STDMETHOD(PutValue)(/*[in]*/ ULONG connection, /*[in]*/ int index,
                       /*[in]*/ double value);
   STDMETHOD(Unenlist)(/*[in]*/ ULONG connection);
   STDMETHOD(Enlist)(/*[in]*/ ULONG connection, /*[in]*/ VARIANT vCookie);
   STDMETHOD(Initialize)(/*[in]*/ IStream *pStream);
   STDMETHOD(GetWhereabouts)(/*[out]*/ VARIANT* pvWhere);
};

#endif //__SIMPLEMGR_H_
```

The next object, **SimpleMgrTrans** implements two interfaces, **ISimpleMgrTrans** and **ITransactionResourceAsync**. It should be created with a single interface **ISimpleMgrTrans**, as described above. Then we need to make some more changes to the header file to add the second interface:

```
// SimpleMgrTrans.h : Declaration of the CSimpleMgrTrans

#ifndef __SIMPLEMGRTRANS_H_
#define __SIMPLEMGRTRANS_H_

#include "resource.h"        // main symbols

/////////////////////////////////////////////////////////////////////////////
// CSimpleMgrTrans
class ATL_NO_VTABLE CSimpleMgrTrans :
   public CComObjectRootEx<CComSingleThreadModel>,
   public CComCoClass<CSimpleMgrTrans, &CLSID_SimpleMgrTrans>,
   public ISimpleMgrTrans,
   public ITransactionResourceAsync
{
private:
   void Log (HRESULT hResult, LPSTR lpszEvent);
   void Log (LPSTR lpszEvent);
```

```
    CComPtr<ITransactionEnlistmentAsync> m_pEnlist;
    int m_index;
    bool m_bValue;
    double m_value;
    char   m_szValue[32];
    HANDLE m_hFile;

public:
    CSimpleMgrTrans()
    {
    }

    void FinalRelease()
    {
    }

DECLARE_REGISTRY_RESOURCEID(IDR_SIMPLEMGRTRANS)
BEGIN_COM_MAP(CSimpleMgrTrans)
    COM_INTERFACE_ENTRY(ISimpleMgrTrans)
    COM_INTERFACE_ENTRY(ITransactionResourceAsync)
END_COM_MAP()

// ISimpleMgrTrans
public:
    STDMETHOD(InitValue)(/*[in]*/ IUnknown* pEnlistUnk, /*[in]*/ int index,
                    /*[in]*/ double value);
    STDMETHOD(InitText)(/*[in]*/ IUnknown* pEnlistUnk, /*[in]*/ int index,
                    /*[in]*/ BSTR bstrValue);

// ITransactionResourceAsync
public:
    STDMETHOD(PrepareRequest)(BOOL fRetaining, DWORD grfRM,
                         BOOL fWantMoniker, BOOL fSinglePhase);
    STDMETHOD(AbortRequest)(BOID* pboidReason, BOOL fRetaining,
                         XACTUOW* pNewUOW);
    STDMETHOD(CommitRequest)(DWORD grfRM, XACTUOW* pNewUOW);
    STDMETHOD(TMDown)();
};

#endif //__SIMPLEMGRTRANS_H_
```

Finally, there's the **SimpleMgrSink** object, which implements the two interfaces, **ISimpleMgrSink** and **IResourceManagerSink**. This should be created as an object with a blank interface **ISimpleMgrSink**. Once more, we have to change the header file:

```
// SimpleMgrSink.h : Declaration of the CSimpleMgrSink

#ifndef __SIMPLEMGRSINK_H_
#define __SIMPLEMGRSINK_H_

#include "resource.h"        // main symbols

/////////////////////////////////////////////////////////////////////////////
// CsimpleMgrSink
```

```
class ATL_NO_VTABLE CSimpleMgrSink :
   public CComObjectRootEx<CComSingleThreadModel>,
   public CComCoClass<CSimpleMgrSink, &CLSID_SimpleMgrSink>,
   public ISimpleMgrSink,
   public IResourceManagerSink
{
private:
   void Log(HRESULT hResult, LPSTR lpszEvent);
   void Log(LPSTR lpszEvent);

public:
   CSimpleMgrSink()
   {
   }

   void FinalRelease()
   {
   }

DECLARE_REGISTRY_RESOURCEID(IDR_SIMPLEMGRSINK)

BEGIN_COM_MAP(CSimpleMgrSink)
   COM_INTERFACE_ENTRY(ISimpleMgrSink)
   COM_INTERFACE_ENTRY(IResourceManagerSink)
END_COM_MAP()

// ISimpleMgrSink
public:

// IResourceManagerSink
public:
   STDMETHOD(TMDown) (void);
};

#endif //__SIMPLEMGRSINK_H_
```

We'll also need to add three extra header files to our **SimpleMgr.cpp** source file:

```
#include "xolehlp.h"
#include "txdtc.h"
#include "txcoord.h"
```

And one to our **SimpleMgrSink.cpp** source file:

```
#include "txdtc.h"
```

And one to our **SimpleMgrTrans.cpp** source file:

```
#include "txdtc.h"
```

Finally, we need to add these to our **SimpleDispenser.cpp** source file:

```
#include "stdafx.h"
#include "resource.h"
#include "initguid.h"

#include "xolehlp.h"
#include "txdtc.h"
#include "txcoord.h"

#include "SimpleManager.h"
#include "SimpleManager_i.c"
#include "SimpleMgr.h"
#include "SimpleMgrSink.h"
#include "SimpleMgrTrans.h"
```

Initializing the Resource Manager

If you look back at the **FinalConstruct()** method of the resource dispenser, you'll see that the last thing we did there was to instantiate the resource manager and then invoke its **Initialize()** method. Let's see what goes on there:

```
STDMETHODIMP CSimpleMgr::Initialize(IStream* pStream)
{
   // Get hold of resource manager factory

   CComPtr<IResourceManagerFactory> pFactory;
   HRESULT hResult = DtcGetTransactionManager(NULL, NULL,
                              IID_IResourceManagerFactory,
                              0, 0, 0,
                              reinterpret_cast<LPVOID*>(&pFactory));

   // Get hold of interface on transaction import whereabouts

   hResult = pFactory->QueryInterface
                           (IID_ITransactionImportWhereabouts,
                                    (void**) &m_pWhereabouts);

   if (FAILED (hResult))
      return hResult;

   // Create sink object

   CComObject<CSimpleMgrSink> *pSinkUnk;
   hResult = CComObject<CSimpleMgrSink>::CreateInstance(&pSinkUnk);

   if (FAILED (hResult))
      return hResult;

   CComPtr<IResourceManagerSink> pSink;
   hResult = pSinkUnk->QueryInterface(IID_IResourceManagerSink,
                                    reinterpret_cast<void**>(&pSink));

   if (FAILED (hResult))
   {
```

```
        pSinkObject->Addref();
        pSinkObject->Release();
        return hResult;
    }

    // Now register ourselves (creating resource manager object)

    hResult = pFactory->Create(&SimpleMgrGuid, "Simple Manager",
                               pSink, &m_pResMgr);

    if (FAILED (hResult))
        return hResult;

    // Marshal interface into stream for resource dispenser

    hResult = CoMarshalInterface (pStream, IID_ISimpleMgr,
                                  GetUnknown(), MSHCTX_LOCAL,
                                  NULL, MSHLFLAGS_TABLEWEAK);

    return hResult;
}
```

We start the method off by getting hold of a couple of interfaces into the MTS DTC proxy:

- **IResourceManagerFactory** – this will be used shortly to create our local resource manager object
- **ITransactionImportWhereabouts** – this will be used later on when we start export transactions; we'll store it locally for the time being in **m_pWhereabouts**

We create an object of type **SimpleMgrSink**, which we'll need to pass to the DTC Proxy when we register ourselves, because this is what the DTC Proxy uses to call back to us when there is a problem. It does this by invoking the sink's **TMDown()** method. (Remember that the **SimpleMgrSink** object implements the **IResourceManagerSink** interface, which has just one method, **TMDown()**).We'll take a look at the sink object in a minute.

Having created the sink object, we invoke the **Create()** method on the resource manager factory object. This effectively registers the resource manager with the DTC Proxy Core Object (just like the way that our resource dispenser registered itself with **DispMan**). Again, the resource manager factory generously responds by returning us a pointer to an **IResourceManager** interface. This is the interface that we'll use later on to actually enlist in transactions, so it's pretty important and we'll keep it safely in the member variable **m_pResMgr** until we need it. Notice that – not for the first time in COM – we identify the resource manager uniquely by using one of those ubiquitous UUID's. Ho hum.

We complete our resource manager initialization by marshaling our own **ISimpleMgr** interface into the stream that was passed as an argument when the function was called. This is the other side of marshaling from the side that we saw in Chapter 3, in that it's invoking **IMarshal** rather than implementing it.

Connecting to a Resource

Back in the resource dispenser's **PutText()** method, we allocated ourselves a resource. This caused **DispMan** to trigger **CreateResource()** in our **IDispenserDriver** implementation. Part of the resource creation process involved establishing some kind of connection to the resource manager. Here's the method in **ISimpleMgr** that actually got invoked:

```
STDMETHODIMP CSimpleMgr::Connect(ULONG* connection)
{
   // Allocate arbitrary connection array to resource

    *connection = reinterpret_cast<ULONG>(new SIMPLECON);

   return S_OK;
}
```

In real life, of course, the resource manager would be doing things like opening database connections or logging on to back-end mainframes. However, in this case, we're just going to grab enough memory to hold our connection structure and pretend that it's a very costly operation. I'll repeat the structure from the header file for you here:

```
typedef struct {
   CComPtr<ITransaction>    m_pTrans;
   char                     m_dummy[32];
} SIMPLECONN;
```

We'll be using our connection structure to keep track of the transaction that our resource is involved in. The dummy array is just to make it look as if we're doing something else as well.

For completeness, I'll also show you the two methods that get invoked when the resource is reset and destroyed, respectively:

```
STDMETHODIMP CSimpleMgr::Reset(ULONG connection)
{
   return S_OK;
}

STDMETHODIMP CSimpleMgr::Disconnect(ULONG connection)
{
   // Deallocate connection array from resource

   delete[] reinterpret_cast<char*>(connection);

   return S_OK;
}
```

Importing a Transaction

In the **SimpleDisp** object, we needed to implement the **EnlistResource()** method of the **IDispenserDriver** interface, because this method is called by **DispMan** in the resource allocation process. You'll remember that we saw this method when we looked at all that transaction export stuff.

Well, here's the other side of it. Our resource dispenser needed to find out the whereabouts of the transaction manager, and it did so by invoking the **GetWhereabouts()** method of the resource manager object. Here's the code for that method:

```
STDMETHODIMP CSimpleMgr::GetWhereabouts(VARIANT* pvWhere)
{
   ULONG cbSize;
   m_pWhereabouts->GetWhereaboutsSize(&cbSize);

   SAFEARRAYBOUND rgsabound[1];
   rgsabound[0].lLbound = 0;
   rgsabound[0].cElements = cbSize;

   SAFEARRAY* pArray = SafeArrayCreate(VT_UI1, 1, rgsabound);

   BYTE* rgbWhere;
   SafeArrayAccessData(pArray, (void HUGEP* FAR*)&rgbWhere);

   ULONG cbUsed;
   m_pWhereabouts->GetWhereabouts(cbSize, rgbWhere, &cbUsed);

   SafeArrayUnaccessData(pArray);

   V_VT(pvWhere) = VT_UI1 + VT_ARRAY;
   V_ARRAY(pvWhere) = pArray;

   return S_OK;
}
```

When we initialized the resource manager, we got hold of a pointer to the **ITransactionImportWhereabouts** interface on the MTS DTC proxy, and stored it **m_pWhereabouts**, and this is where we finally get to use it. There are two method invocations to make on this interface:

- **GetWhereaboutsSize()** – this finds out how big the whereabouts array is
- **GetWhereabouts()** – this actually gets it

The *last* thing that the resource dispenser did in its **EnlistResource()** method was to invoke the resource manager's **Enlist()** method. This is shown below:

```
STDMETHODIMP CSimpleMgr::Enlist(ULONG connection, VARIANT vCookie)
{
   LPSIMPLECONN pConn = reinterpret_cast<LPSIMPLECONN>(connection);

   // Extract transaction cookie from variant

   SAFEARRAY* pArray = vCookie.parray;

   long lBound;
   SafeArrayGetLBound(pArray, 1, &lBound);

   long uBound;
   SafeArrayGetUBound(pArray, 1, &uBound);
```

```
    ULONG cbSize = uBound - lBound + 1;

    BYTE HUGEP* rgbCookie;
    SafeArrayAccessData(pArray, (void HUGEP* FAR*)&rgbCookie);

    // Pass cookie to transaction manager to get transaction

    CComPtr<ITransactionImport> pImport;
    HRESULT hResult = m_pWhereabouts->QueryInterface
              (IID_ITransactionImport, (void**) &pImport);

    GUID riid = IID_ITransaction;
    hResult = pImport->Import(cbSize, rgbCookie, &riid, (void**) &m_pTrans);

    SafeArrayUnaccessData(pArray);

    return hResult;
}
```

Here, we're extracting the transaction cookie from the incoming variant array. Then we get hold of our transaction manager, and import the transaction from it by passing the cookie. Hey presto! One transaction object, loaded up and ready to use.

Enlisting in the Transaction

Having got its resource, our resource dispenser's **PutText()** method went on to invoke the resource manager's **PutText()** method. Here's what that does:

```
STDMETHODIMP CSimpleMgr::PutText(ULONG connection, int index, BSTR bstrValue)
{
    LPSIMPLECONN pConn = reinterpret_cast<LPSIMPLECONN>(connection);

    // Create async object

    CComObject<CSimpleMgrTrans>* pTransObj;
    HRESULT hResult =
          CComObject<CSimpleMgrTrans>::CreateInstance(&pTransObj);

    CComPtr<ISimpleMgrTrans> pSimpleTrans;
    hResult = pTransObj->QueryInterface(IID_ISimpleMgrTrans,
                   reinterpret_cast<void**>(&pSimpleTrans));

    if (FAILED(hResult))
       return hResult;

    CComPtr<ITransactionResourceAsync> pAsync;
    hResult = pTransObj->QueryInterface(IID_ITransactionResourceAsync,
                                       reinterpret_cast<void**>(&pAsync));

    if (FAILED(hResult))
    {
       pTransObj->AddRef();
```

```
        pTransObj->Release();
        return hResult;
    }

    // Enlist in transaction, passing interface to async object

    GUID uow;
    LONG isoLevel;
    CComPtr<ITransactionEnlistmentAsync> pEnlist;
    hResult = m_pResMgr->Enlist(pConn->m_pTrans, pAsync, &uow,
                               &isoLevel, &pEnlist);

    // Set up value in async object, plus pointer to enlist interface

    pSimpleTrans->InitText(pEnlist, index, bstrValue);

    return S_OK;
}
```

Here, we're creating a local **SimpleMgrTrans** object to receive asynchronous transaction notifications. This object, you may remember, implements two interfaces: one of our own, called **ISimpleMgrTrans**, and a standard one, **ITransactionResourceAsync**. So, having created our asynchronous transaction object, what do we do with it?

The resource manager enlists in the transaction. Remember that it contains the member, **m_pResMgr**, which points to an **IResourceManager** interface – we got this pointer back when we initialized the resource manager. Now, we actually get the chance to use it. When we enlist ourselves, what we pass in is a pointer to our local asynchronous transaction object. As usual, we get something back: this time it's a pointer, **pAsync**, to an interface on an asynchronous enlistment object, **ITransactionEnlistmentAsync**. We'll need this pointer shortly, during the transaction commitment process, so we need to store it in our asynchronous transaction object. We also need to pass it the value of the item that's being saved in the database; that's what the **InitText()** method call on **ISimpleMgrTrans** does.

And that's about all for **SimpleMgr**. Our text value is now sitting in a **SimpleMgrTrans** object, waiting for further instructions from DTC. What happens next – in our test system – is that the whole process is repeated for a second item of data. Thus we end up with two **SimpleMgrTrans** objects, both of which are enlisted in the same transaction. I think it's time to complete our tour by looking into the **SimpleMgrTrans** object.

Odds and Ends

But before we do that, just for completeness, here's the **PutValue()** method of **ISimpleMgr**:

```
STDMETHODIMP CSimpleMgr::PutValue(int index, double value)
{
    LPSIMPLECONN pConn = reinterpret_cast<LPSIMPLECONN>(connection);

    // Create async object

    CComObject<CSimpleMgrTrans>* pTransObj;
    HRESULT hResult =
         CComObject<CSimpleMgrTrans>::CreateInstance(&pTransObj);
```

```
    if (FAILED (hResult))
       return hResult;

    CComPtr<ISimpleMgrTrans> pSimpleTrans;
    hResult = pTransObj->QueryInterface(IID_ISimpleMgrTrans,
                     reinterpret_cast<void**>(&pSimpleTrans));

    if (FAILED(hResult))
    {
       pTransObj->AddRef();
       pTransObj->Release();
       return hResult;
    }

    CComPtr<ITransactionResourceAsync> pAsync;
    hResult = pTransObj->QueryInterface(IID_ITransactionResourceAsync,
                                    reinterpret_cast<void**>(&pAsync));

    if (FAILED(hResult))
       return hResult;

    // Enlist in transaction, passing interface to async object

    GUID uow;
    LONG isoLevel;
    CComPtr<ITransactionEnlistmentAsync> pEnlist;
    hResult = m_pResMgr->Enlist(pConn->m_pTrans, pAsync, &uow,
                          &isoLevel, &pEnlist);

    // Set up value in async object, plus pointer to enlist interface

    pSimpleTrans->InitValue(pEnlistUnk, index, value);

    return S_OK;
 }
```

As you can see, this is pretty similar to what goes on inside the **PutText()** method. Finally, here's what happens when we unenlist a resource from a transaction:

```
 STDMETHODIMP CSimpleMgr::Unenlist(ULONG connection)
 {
    LPSIMPLECONN pConn = reinterpret_cast<LPSIMPLECONN>(connection);

    if (pConn->m_pTrans)
    {
       pConn->m_pTrans->Release();
       pConn->m_pTrans = NULL;
    }

    return S_OK;
 }
```

The Asynchronous Transaction Object

In the **PutText()** method of the resource manager object, we stored the text from the first string entered by the user in an asynchronous transaction object, **SimpleMgrTrans**. We do this using the **InitText()** method, passing in the text to be stored as an argument:

```
STDMETHODIMP CSimpleMgrTrans::InitText(IUnknown* pEnlistUnk, int index,
                                       BSTR bstrValue)
{
   pEnlistUnk->QueryInterface(IID_ITransactionEnlistmentAsync,
                              (void**) &m_pEnlist);

   USES_CONVERSION;
   m_index = index;
   m_bValue = false;

   if (SysStringLen(bstrValue) < 32)
      lstrcpy(m_szValue, W2A(bstrValue));
   else
      m_szValue[0] = 0;

   m_hFile = NULL;

   return S_OK;
}
```

Here, we are making sure that we've got a local pointer to the **ITransactionEnlistmentAsync** interface. We also set up the data that we'll – eventually – insert in our database. For the sake of completeness, here's the equivalent method for value-type data items:

```
STDMETHODIMP CSimpleMgrTrans::InitValue(IUnknown* pEnlistUnk, int index,
                                        double value)

{
   pEnlistUnk->QueryInterface(IID_ITransactionEnlistmentAsync,
                              (void**) &m_pEnlist);

   m_index = index;
   m_bValue = true;
   m_value = value;
   m_hFile = NULL;

   return S_OK;
}
```

Now that we have both **SimpleMgrTrans** objects enlisted in the transaction and storing the relevant data, nothing is going to happen until the transaction is either aborted or committed.

Two-Phase Commit

I think it's time to explain what **two-phase commit** is all about. We're about to write some data away to a database. In fact, we're going to write two lots of data to different databases. We want to ensure that either both databases are written to or neither. Remember the ACID properties that we discussed in Chapter 5? However, unwinding a database operation is costly, so it would be nice if we could do things in two phases, that is, make absolutely sure that we're ready to commit the transaction before we start writing to the database.

The first phase **prepares** the operation. We have to get all the parties (that is, resource managers) involved in the transaction to agree that they are ready to go ahead. Not only does this trap many potential fatal errors before actually committing anything; it also ensures that the second phase is completed in the minimum time.

The second phase actually **commits** the operation, by requesting that all the resource managers commit themselves. Of course, the second phase could still fail, but the risk of having to do work to re-synchronize is substantially reduced. We'll explore what happens when things don't work out in the last section of this chapter.

This is a bit like how a symphony orchestra works. You'd never see the likes of Claudio Abbado stepping up to the podium and going "A-one, A-two, A-one-two-three-four ..." He'll raise the baton, and establish eye contact with *every single member* of the orchestra before he starts off. Because, after all, he needs every single member's commitment, and if – for example – the French horn player isn't quite ready, Bruckner's Fourth Symphony will have to wait until he is. And if he or she has been taken ill in the interval, the whole performance might have to be aborted.

Transaction commitment is triggered by the server process invoking the `SetComplete()` method on the object context.

> *Actually, if it doesn't commit itself, rest assured that MTS will do the job for it once the method invocation is over. Try calling `Auto2()` instead of `Commit2()`, and you'll observe identical behavior in the lower tiers. MTS will always force transaction commitment if the middle tier objects can't be bothered – too bad if they didn't read the small print.*

This call to `SetComplete()` is the signal that the MTS DTC proxy has been waiting for.

The MTS DTC proxy then goes through its list of asynchronous transaction objects and asks each one in turn whether or not it is ready to proceed. This takes the form of an invocation of the `PrepareRequest()` method on the `ITransactionResourceAsync` interface of each object:

```
STDMETHODIMP CSimpleMgrTrans::PrepareRequest (BOOL fRetaining,
                                              DWORD grfRM,
                                              BOOL fWantMoniker,
                                              BOOL fSinglePhase)
{
   // Check for abort conditions

   if ((m_bValue && (m_value < 0.0)) ||
      (!m_bValue && !strcmp(m_szValue, "ABORT")))
   {
      HRESULT hResult = m_pEnlist->PrepareRequestDone(E_FAIL, NULL, NULL);
      return S_OK;
   }

   // Prepare transaction by opening file
```

```
    char szFile[128];
    sprintf(szFile, "c:\\Data%d.txt", m_index);

    m_hFile = CreateFile(szFile, GENERIC_WRITE, 0, NULL, OPEN_ALWAYS,
                FILE_ATTRIBUTE_NORMAL + FILE_FLAG_WRITE_THROUGH, NULL);

    // Report success

    HRESULT hResult = m_pEnlist->PrepareRequestDone(S_OK, NULL, NULL);

    return S_OK;
}
```

I've arbitrarily decided that if a numerical data item is less than zero, or if a textual data item has the value **"ABORT"**, we'll abort the preparation, just to see what happens. In any other circumstances, we'll do our preparation work, and then invoke **PrepareRequestDone()** to give our consent. The amount of preparation work done here should be everything that we can do without actually doing anything that can't be undone in the event of having to abort. The idea is to ensure that the actual commitment of the transaction across all the parties involved is as close to simultaneity as possible. Remember that there may be other resource managers involved, and that they may be running on different machines – after all, the "D" in DTC stands for exactly the same word as it does in DCOM! In the case of our simple resource manager, the most that we can do is open the file that we are going to write to. In other circumstances, we might be preparing index updates, and checking for the availability of space – anything, in fact, that increases the speed of the second phase and ensures that the second phase does not fail.

Once all the resource managers involved have given their consent and are ready to continue, the DTC proceeds to the second phase, and invokes the **CommitRequest()** method:

```
STDMETHODIMP CSimpleMgrTrans::CommitRequest (DWORD grfRM, XACTUOW* pNewUOW)
{
    // Check for special cases

    char szValue[128];

    if (m_bValue)
        sprintf(szValue, "%f", m_value);
    else
        strcpy(szValue, m_szValue);

    if (!strcmp(szValue, "CRASH"))
    {
        HRESULT hResult = m_pEnlist->CommitRequestDone(E_FAIL);
        return S_OK;
    }

    if (!m_bValue && !strcmp(m_szValue, "DOUBT2"))
        return S_OK;

    // Write data to file

    ULONG nWritten;
    WriteFile(m_hFile, szValue, strlen (szValue), &nWritten, NULL);
```

```
    CloseHandle(m_hFile);

    // Report transaction complete

    HRESULT hResult = m_pEnlist->CommitRequestDone(S_OK);

    return S_OK;
}
```

Here, we actually carry out our write to file, and then report back success to the DTC by means of an invocation of **CommitRequestDone()**. I've added in a couple more special cases, to test what happens when something really catastrophic goes wrong – right in the middle of the second phase of the commit – so that we can try and recover from them later. I'll talk about recovery in a little while.

Of course, one of the other resource managers might fail the first phase of the commit, in which case, the whole thing has to be aborted. In this case, our **AbortRequest()** method gets invoked instead:

```
STDMETHODIMP CSimpleMgrTrans::AbortRequest (BOID* pboidReason,
                         BOOL fRetaining, XACTUOW* pNewUOW)
{
    // Close file

    CloseHandle(m_hFile);

    // Report transaction abort

    HRESULT hResult = m_pEnlist->AbortRequestDone(S_OK);

    return S_OK;
}
```

And that's pretty much it as far as the resource manager is concerned. So let's try it all out!

Transactions and Resources in Action

OK, let's create an MTS package called **SimplePackage**, and add our server and resource dispenser to it. We'll register **SimpleServer** as "requires a new transaction", and **SimpleDispenser** as "supports transactions".

Here's a printout of the log from a typical run of our simple client, requesting a **Commit2()** type operation, releasing all resources properly:

```
02:18:03 SERVER:     Commit2 called
02:18:03 SERVER:     GetObjectContext OK
02:18:03 DISPENSER: FinalConstruct called
02:18:03 DISPENSER: Get dispenser manager OK
02:18:03 DISPENSER: QI for local dispenser driver OK
02:18:03 DISPENSER: Register dispenser OK
02:18:04 DISPENSER: Create instance of RM OK
02:18:04 MANAGER:    Initialize called
02:18:04 MANAGER:    Get RM factory OK
```

```
02:18:04 MANAGER:    QI for whereabouts OK
02:18:04 MANAGER:    Create sink object OK
02:18:04 MANAGER:    QI for sink interface OK
02:18:04 MANAGER:    Create resource manager OK
02:18:04 MANAGER:    Marshalled interface OK
02:18:04 DISPENSER: Initialized RM OK
02:18:04 DISPENSER: Created FTM OK
02:18:04 SERVER:     Created instance of dispenser OK
02:18:04 DISPENSER: PutText called
02:18:04 DISPENSER: Unmarshal interface OK
02:18:04 DISPENSER: CreateResource called
02:18:04 DISPENSER: Text resource required
02:18:04 DISPENSER: Created resource (resource identifier a30ce0)
02:18:04 DISPENSER: Unmarshal interface OK
02:18:04 MANAGER:    Connect called
02:18:04 MANAGER:    Connection 9b0d10 allocated
02:18:04 DISPENSER: Connect to RM OK
02:18:04 DISPENSER: Unmarshal interface OK
02:18:04 DISPENSER: EnlistResource called (resource identifier a30ce0)
02:18:04 DISPENSER: QI for IGetDispenser interface OK
02:18:04 DISPENSER: Get transaction export factory OK
02:18:04 MANAGER:    GetWhereabouts called
02:18:04 MANAGER:    GetWhereaboutsSize OK
02:18:04 MANAGER:    GetWhereabouts OK
02:18:04 MANAGER:    Got whereabouts
02:18:04 DISPENSER: Get whereabouts OK
02:18:04 DISPENSER: Create export object OK
02:18:04 DISPENSER: Export transaction OK
02:18:04 DISPENSER: Get transaction cookie OK
02:18:04 MANAGER:    Enlist called for connection 9b0d10
02:18:04 MANAGER:    QI for transaction import OK
02:18:04 MANAGER:    Get transaction OK
02:18:04 DISPENSER: Export cookie OK
02:18:04 DISPENSER: Allocate resource OK
02:18:04 MANAGER:    PutText called for connection 9b0d10, index 1, value <first item>
02:18:04 MANAGER:    Create transaction async object OK
02:18:04 MANAGER:    QI for basic transaction async interface OK
02:18:04 MANAGER:    QI for transaction async interface OK
02:18:04 MANAGER:    Enlist transaction OK
02:18:04 DISPENSER: ResetResource called (resource identifier a30ce0)
02:18:04 DISPENSER: Unmarshal interface OK
02:18:04 MANAGER:    Reset called for connection 9b0d10
02:18:04 DISPENSER: Reset OK
02:18:04 DISPENSER: Free resource OK
02:18:04 SERVER:     Put first value OK
02:18:04 DISPENSER: PutText called
02:18:04 DISPENSER: Unmarshal interface OK
02:18:04 DISPENSER: RateResource called (resource identifier a30ce0)
02:18:04 DISPENSER: Incoming type = 2, resource type = 2, enlistment required = 0
02:18:04 DISPENSER: Rating set to 100
02:18:04 DISPENSER: Allocate resource OK
02:18:04 MANAGER:    PutText called for connection 9b0d10, index 2, value <second item>
02:18:04 MANAGER:    Create transaction async object OK
02:18:04 MANAGER:    QI for basic transaction async interface OK
02:18:04 MANAGER:    QI for transaction async interface OK
02:18:04 MANAGER:    Enlist transaction OK
02:18:04 DISPENSER: ResetResource called (resource identifier a30ce0)
02:18:04 DISPENSER: Unmarshal interface OK
02:18:04 MANAGER:    Reset called for connection 9b0d10
02:18:04 DISPENSER: Reset OK
02:18:04 DISPENSER: Free resource OK
02:18:04 SERVER:     Put second value OK
02:18:04 SERVER:     Set complete OK
```

```
02:18:04 MGR(TRANS):PrepareRequest called
02:18:04 MGR(TRANS):Writing to file <c:\Data1.txt>
02:18:04 MGR(TRANS):PrepareRequestDone (success) OK
02:18:04 MGR(TRANS):PrepareRequest called
02:18:04 MGR(TRANS):Writing to file <c:\Data2.txt>
02:18:04 MGR(TRANS):PrepareRequestDone (success) OK
02:18:04 MGR(TRANS):CommitRequest called
02:18:04 MGR(TRANS):Writing data <first item>
02:18:05 MGR(TRANS):FinalRelease called
02:18:05 MGR(TRANS):CommitRequestDone OK
02:18:05 MGR(TRANS):CommitRequest called
02:18:05 MGR(TRANS):Writing data <second item>
02:18:05 MGR(TRANS):FinalRelease called
02:18:05 MGR(TRANS):CommitRequestDone OK
02:18:19 DISPENSER: Unmarshal interface OK
02:18:19 DISPENSER: EnlistResource called (free) (resource identifier a30ce0)
02:18:19 MANAGER:   Unenlist called for connection 9b0d10
02:18:19 DISPENSER: DestroyResource called (resource identifier a30ce0)
02:18:19 DISPENSER: Unmarshal interface OK
02:18:19 MANAGER:   Disconnect called for connection 9b0d10
02:18:19 DISPENSER: Disconnect from RM OK
02:21:08 MANAGER:   FinalRelease called
02:21:08 MGR(SINK): FinalRelease called
02:21:08 DISPENSER: FinalRelease called
02:21:08 DISPENSER: Closed holder OK
02:21:08 DISPENSER: Released FTM OK
```

This should throw the sequence of events that we have been describing into perspective. Notice that the second time we got a resource, we didn't need to reallocate or re-enlist it, because it was already part of the transaction!

You can use this to find out what happens when you abort, or when you forget to commit, or what happens if you use differing resource types. It's entirely up to you. Experiment!

When Things Don't Work Out

First of all, what happens if the server doesn't call **`SetComplete()`** on the transaction after all, but reneges on the deal and calls **`SetAbort()`** instead? Well, this is pretty straightforward: inside the resource manager, we don't even get the **`PrepareRequest()`**. We're straight into an **`AbortRequest()`** invocation. There's no need to do anything at all here.

OK, so what if part of the transaction fails at the preparation stage? You can test this by setting the second input field to a negative number, or **`"ABORT"`**. In this case, **`PrepareRequest()`** is called for both items. The first one calls **`PrepareRequestDone()`** with an **`S_OK`** status, then the second calls with an **`E_FAIL`** status. Because the second part of the transaction has failed to prepare, the whole transaction must be aborted, so the DTC invokes **`AbortRequest()`** for the first part.

Incidentally, notice that in this case, the VB client application reports an error **`8004E002`**. If you hunt for this in the header files, you'll eventually find it in **`mtx.h`** (*not* **`winerror.h`**), with the name **`CONTEXT_E_ABORTED`**. No surprises there, except that you might expect it to be set as the return to the **`SetComplete()`** invocation. The trouble is, that invocation returned to the caller before the commit process started (take a look at the log file if you want to verify this). So it's actually the MTS surrogate that's returning the bad status to the client on our behalf. We pick this error up in the VB client, and output a message to the user to indicate that the transaction has been aborted.

What happens if the preparation goes fine for both parties, but one of the actual commits fails? Well, the outcome isn't entirely satisfactory, because the system as a whole thinks that everything has gone fine! What this emphasizes is the importance of making as sure as possible during the first phase of the commitment process that the second phase is going to go smoothly.

But what can our resource manager do to sort things out after this kind of problem? Presumably its commit failed for some transient reason; if there was a more fundamental reason, it should have been picked up during the first phase – at least by a well-behaved resource manager. So, the best thing to do is wait a decent interval, and then try again. Meanwhile, the resource manager shouldn't call **`CommitRequestDone()`** with a bad status; it shouldn't call it at all.

Recovery

What happens if the resource manager crashes during a transaction? We need some kind of recovery mechanism, and to this end, a well-behaved resource manager should keep a log of all **`PrepareRequests()`** and **`CommitRequests()`**. This is in contrast with other transaction processing systems, where it's the transaction manager that keeps the log.

On start-up, it should run through this log, and check for any unmatched **`PrepareRequests()`**. If it finds any, it needs to re-enlist in the transactions that caused those **`PrepareRequests()`** and establish whether or not it needs to commit or abort them according to the overall status of the transaction.

You may have observed that our **`SimpleManager()`** resource manager isn't well-behaved in this respect, and I leave it as an exercise to you, the reader, to rectify this. The kinds of things that you're going to have to do are as follows.

Add the following code to your **`PrepareRequest()`** implementation in the resource manager asynchronous transaction object:

```
CComPtr<IPrepareInfo> pPrepare;
m_pEnlist->QueryInterface(IID_IPrepareInfo,
                          reinterpret_cast<void**> (&pPrepare));

ULONG cbPrepare;
pPrepare->GetPrepareInfoSize(&cbPrepare);

BYTE prepInfo = new BYTE[cbPrepare];
pPrepare->GetPrepareInfo(prepInfo);
```

This code is getting hold of all the information needed to prepare the transaction for subsequent re-enlistment, following failure. It saves it in the byte array **`prepInfo`**.

You now need to write this away to a file, along with the details of the data item itself.

On start-up, the resource manager needs to read through this file and interrogate MTS to find out whether or not the overall transaction was successful. You can do this by means of the following code:

```
XACTSTAT xactStat;
hResult = m_pResMgr->Reenlist(prepInfo, cbPrepare, 100, &xactStat);
```

The **prepInfo** and **cbPrepare** values are read back from the file in turn, along with the required data to complete the transaction. The value of **xactStat** can take one of the following values:

- **XACTSTAT_COMMITTED** – the overall transaction was successful
- **XACTSTAT_ABORTED** – the transaction was aborted
- **XACTSTAT_NONE** – the request has timed out and MTS probably has no knowledge of the transaction

The last of these means that no recovery is necessary, and you probably shouldn't have presented the transaction for re-enlistment in the first place. In this case, the transaction hasn't happened. If you want to get around this, the best way is to write another record to the recovery file every time a successful transaction goes through.

If the overall transaction was successful, we should carry out the same procedure as we would have done in the **CommitRequest()** phase first time around. If the overall transaction aborted, we should carry out the same procedure as for **AbortRequest()**.

When we have finished recovering transactions, we simply make the following call:

```
m_pResMgr->ReenlistmentComplete()
```

This indicates that these transactions have been recovered successfully. We won't be able to try to recover them again, as the calls to **Reenlist()** will fail.

Note that you can't use this mechanism to find out the results of past transactions, because MTS forgets about transactions that have been completely committed or aborted; it's only the in-doubt ones that it hangs on to.

Journey's End

That's pretty much the end of our whirlwind tour of resource dispensers and managers. We've seen how the various elements interact with each other – generally by exchanging pointers to each other's interfaces. We have seen how **DispMan** keeps track of the resource inventory in the most efficient manner, how MTS DTC controls two-phase commit, and how we can recover from catastrophic failures. If you're still unsure as to how it all works, have a play with the samples – try different combinations of operations and see what happens. Try making it fail, and see how MTS copes.

In the next chapter we'll be investigating Microsoft Cluster Server and looking at how to use the cluster API to create cluster aware DCOM servers.

High Availability and Clustering

"I get knocked down,
But I get up again..."

- *"Tubthumping" (Chumbawamba)*

Howlin' Wolves

We've hissed with the Viper and flown with the Falcon. Now it's time to run with the Wolves. Wolfpack was Microsoft's codename for their cluster product, now re-christened Microsoft Clustering Services (MSCS). This is Microsoft's vehicle for attacking the market for high-availability systems – systems that can't be permitted to be down for any significant length of time. This is a market with diverse applications from banking to safety-critical environments such as nuclear reprocessing plants. Did I hear anyone say, "Not In My Backyard?" Shame on you...

So what is a cluster?

> *A cluster is a closely-coupled set of servers that appears to the rest of the world as a single entity. A cluster has access to a common set of resources such that if one of the servers fails, one of the others can take over the resources that were under its control.*

Hence the codename "Wolfpack". Or nearly, because in the release of MSCS current at the time of writing, the highest number of processors in any cluster is two. Mr and Mrs Wolf, perhaps

.

> *Actually, I'm being a little unfair here. Microsoft – and others – have successfully tested MSCS in clusters with more than two servers; however – to quote the Microsoft Clustering FAQ's – "... the algorithms and features in the current software must be extended and thoroughly tested on larger clusters before customers can reliably use a multi-node MSCS cluster for production work*

I should also point out that there is no permanent hierarchy of processors in a cluster – that is, there's no designated pack leader. The Wolves are an Equal Opportunity Household ("Stuff the ironing, I'm going out hunting, dear" "Hunting deer? Jolly good...").

Clusters have been around in some shape or form for years, so the concept isn't anything particularly new. Way back in the Seventies, Tandem were touting their *NonStop* systems using an ingenious selection of marketing gimmicks, from double-ended pens to two-handled coffee mugs. Several other manufacturers joined in, most notably Digital, with their *VaxClusters.* However, none of these systems was cheap, and they relied heavily on specialized, non-standard hardware. The crucial difference with Microsoft Clusters is that you can put one together with absolutely standard PCs and peripherals. The only slightly non-standard hardware required is the shared SCSI bus, of which more later. So, once again, we see Microsoft bringing the esoteric into the mainstream.

Unfortunately, Microsoft Clusters are not – yet – the complete solution for super-reliable computing. At the risk of dampening enthusiasms slightly, here are some of the things that MSCS doesn't do:

- It doesn't do load balancing
- It doesn't do file shadowing (although you can use RAID for that)
- It doesn't automatically log your client back on to the other server following a failover; your client must re-establish the session

Some of these are coming in Phase 2 – whether this means NT4 Service Pack 4 or NT5 is anyone's guess – and in fact there's an awful lot of Phase 2-itis about the whole thing. However, there's still plenty of functionality in Phase 1, and it's a good time to get to know the technology before it really takes off.

Before we go on, I should probably set all this into context. Clustering isn't a technology that has any great dependency on COM (let alone DCOM), so you might be forgiven for wondering what a chapter on the subject is doing in this book. Here's the reason. Microsoft Clusters are one more, highly significant, element in Microsoft's assault on the back office. If you're doing anything serious with DCOM or any of the other related technologies that we've been looking at, you're quite likely to come up against clusters at some point, and it's because DCOM works differently on clusters than on single machines that this chapter has been written. As we shall see, there are several changes that we may have to make to our components if they're going to run on a cluster–and you can't just take a standard single-node DCOM object and install it on a cluster and expect it to run perfectly.

Besides, clusters are *fun*!

Cluster Architectures

This is what a typical two-node Microsoft Cluster looks like:

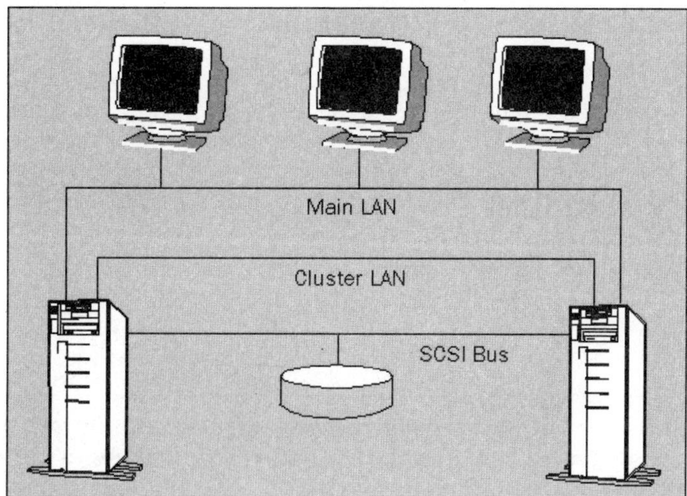

You'll probably notice the non-standard bit. It's that SCSI bus running between the two servers, with a disc hanging off it. I've only drawn one disc in, but in theory there can be any number of discs sitting on the SCSI bus. In practice, you'd probably use RAID to ensure full redundancy. These discs hold all the resources that are intended to be available to either processor. I'm choosing my words carefully here, because it's very tempting to fall into the trap of using the word "shared" to describe these resources. In the MSCS architecture, *nothing* is shared. Which brings me to a very important point.

There are basically two types of true clustering architecture: "shared disc" and "shared nothing". In the "shared disc" model, at any one time, all the servers have access to all the available resources. Clearly, if left unchecked, this would quickly become chaotic, so in this model, access to the resources is controlled by a *distributed lock manager* (DLM). VMS fans amongst you may recall that this is the model used in *VaxClusters.* The trouble with this is that it scales terribly – the DLM becomes a major bottleneck, and contention problems grow geometrically as you add more servers. Mr and Mrs Wolf can probably cope with sharing a single television, but when their ten cubs come along, you can imagine the fights over the remote control...

As it happens, MSCS *can* in theory support the "shared disc" architecture, although without a DLM, so it's liable to be somewhat anarchic. There are, moreover, no plans at present to introduce a DLM, so instead, the preferred Microsoft approach is to use "shared nothing". In this architecture, the resources are partitioned or replicated so that each server works with its own resources, without interfering with the others, until – that is – disaster strikes. So if Mrs Wolf is relaxing with the Style section of the Sunday paper, Mr Wolf is not allowed to read over her shoulder. Instead, he has to slink off with the Financial pages. Even if he doesn't understand a word of them.

Setting Up the Cluster

This is, of course, a software book, so I'm not going to go to great lengths describing how to set up a PC cluster. However, it is a little out of the ordinary, so in case your grasp of hardware is as good as mine (I'm the sort of person who needs to be told which end to hold the screwdriver), I'll offer you a few words of advice.

As you've probably worked out from the diagram in the preceding section, you'll need the following extra bits of kit:

- 2 SCSI host adapters (one for each PC)
- 1 SCSI drive
- 1 dual-ported external box to hold the drive
- 2 SCSI cables
- 4 network cards (2 per PC)

> **First of all, a quick word of warning about those adapters. The list of adapters that are supported is quite specific, so if you're looking to experiment, you're strongly advised to check with Microsoft's list before parting with any cash. You can find the list at `http://www.microsoft.com/NTServer/solutions/hardwarecomp/default.asp`. They're all PCI-based, so you won't find them at the cheap end of the price list, unfortunately. Make sure that you get good quality cables – you can waste a lot of time waiting for your disc drive to appear in your list of SCSI devices when all that's wrong is a kink in the cable.**

There aren't any restrictions on the network cards, apart from the fact that they are all supposed to be PCI (although I've managed to get MSCS going with ISA cards before now). If you're just doing experiments, you may be able to relax the configuration rules even more. For example, I've managed to get away with only one network card per server. In a production environment, you don't really want all your intra-cluster communications going out on your main network, so you would most definitely need the two cards.

If you haven't come across SCSI before, you'll find that the documentation probably makes no reference to configurations involving host adapters at both ends. Don't worry about this – they'll catch up eventually, and it doesn't mean that it won't work. Make sure that both your adapters are set to terminate the bus, and that your disc is set *not* to (this will probably differ from the default setting). Your documentation will probably recommend setting your adapters to have an ID of 7 - however, because you've got two on the same bus, you'll actually need to set one of them to be 6. Set your other disc(s) to be below this, in the range 0 to 5.

Connect it all together, and watch it all spring into life.

The next thing to do is install the clustering software on each node. At the time of writing, MSCS is only supported as part of the Enterprise Edition of Windows NT4. I won't go into the installation procedure here, because it's largely a question of following the instructions. The only part that may surprise you is the point where you are asked to enter an IP number for the cluster. When I first saw this, I was most confused and I ended up entering one of the IP numbers of the cluster servers. When this was rejected by the installation program, I entered a completely new one (in the same sub-address range), and, surprise, surprise, this was accepted. Once the installation process was over, I took a look at Network Neighborhood on my client machine and noticed that, as well as my two servers (MR-WOLF and MRS-WOLF), there was a new one, with the name of the cluster (MRANDMRSWOLF). I tried pinging the IP number that I had entered, and immediately got a response. So the cluster really is acting as a single server, with its own name and its own IP address. This was the point where I really got hooked...

Clustered DCOM

Before we start looking seriously into clustered resource management, let's try a little experiment to see if we really can treat the cluster as a single entity. First of all, make sure that the cluster is running on both machines. Your Cluster Administrator display should look something like this:

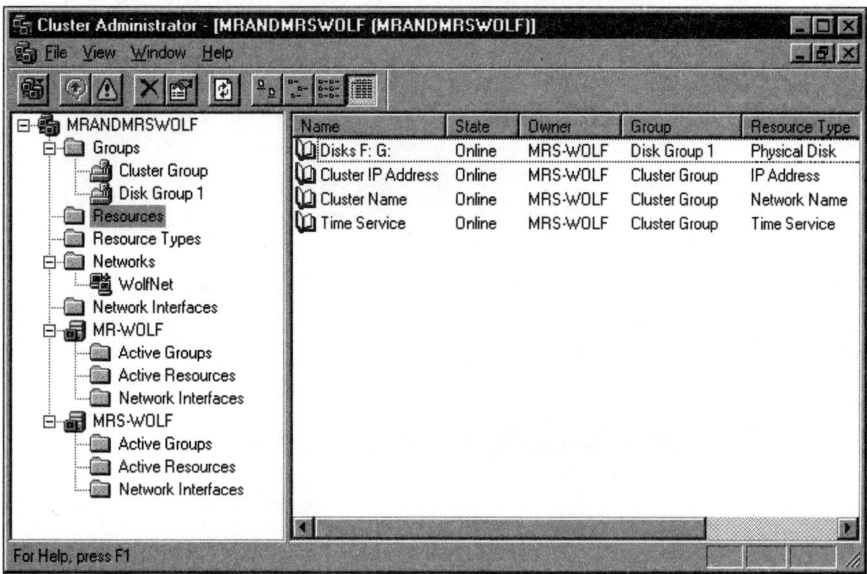

As we can see from this, both nodes are connected to the cluster, and MRS-WOLF currently has control of all the cluster's resources.

For our test server, we'll put together the bare bones of a component that we're going to develop later. This component, in an out-of-process EXE server called `GrannyServer`, is going to be called `Granny` (for reasons which may or may not become obvious later), with a single interface `IGranny`. For the time being, we'll leave `IGranny` with no properties or methods. Let's build `GrannyServer` as specified on our client machine. There's no reason why you couldn't build it on one of the cluster nodes, except that you'd then have to copy it to the client, and register it there.

Once you've built **GrannyServer**, copy it to both machines in the cluster and register it by running **GrannyServer/regserver** from either the command line or a DOS box. Note that it doesn't matter where your server resides. It doesn't have to be on the shared disc; in fact, that would be a positive disadvantage, as you'll notice that the shared disc currently isn't available at all on MR-WOLF. It doesn't have to be in the same place on each machine either.

Now go into DCOMCnfg on your client, and select Granny Class:

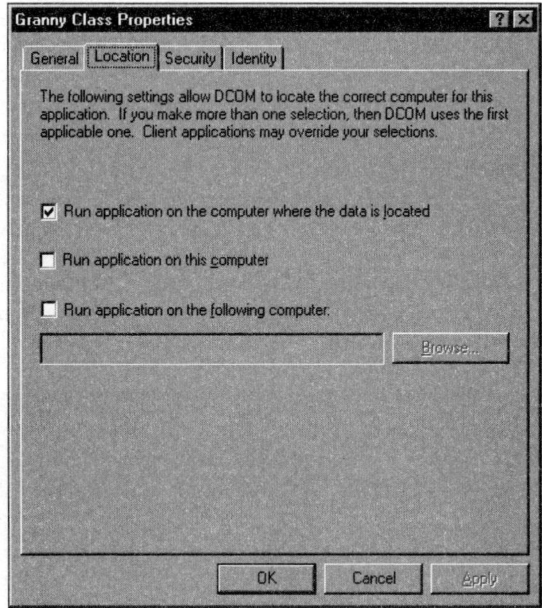

Elect to Run application on the following computer: and click on Browse... In the next dialog, select the domain containing your cluster. If you're running DCOM for Win95 as the client, the Browse... button won't have appeared. Simply type the cluster name into the box as //CLUSTERNAME instead. You'll see something like this:

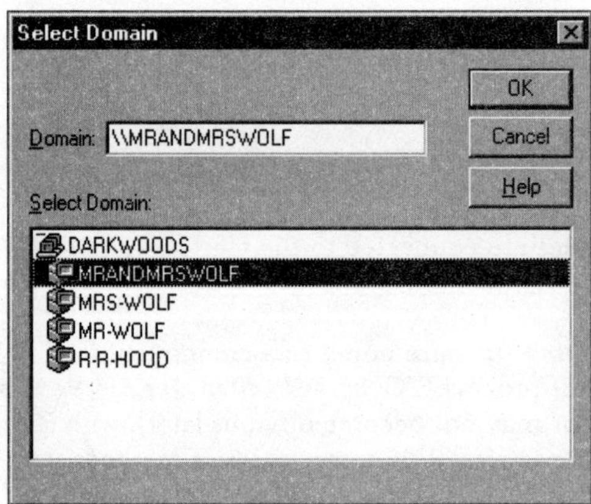

Notice that, as well as our cluster nodes (MR-WOLF and MRS-WOLF) and our client machine (R-R-HOOD), we do indeed have our cluster (MRANDMRSWOLF). Select this as our target host, and click on OK. We're ready to start our experiment.

Our client, **GrannyClient**, is a very simple Visual Basic application. Here's the code in its entirety:

```
Dim gran As Granny

Private Sub Form_Load()
   Set gran = New Granny
End Sub
```

There is no form to speak of, other than the default provided by VB. We do need to add the **GrannyServer** type library to our references, however.

We will be adding to this a little later. Not much, mind. However, please note that the version of **GrannyClient** included in the sample code is just a little more sophisticated, and will not run correctly against the version of **GrannyServer** that we have at this stage in the chapter.

Let's assume that the situation is exactly as shown above, in that all the resources are owned by MRS-WOLF. Open up the Task Manager window on MRS-WOLF, and take a look at it as you start up **GrannyClient**. You should see **GrannyServer** make an appearance. So what does this mean? We've used DCOMCnfg to configure the remote server to be MRANDMRSWOLF. The cluster, in turn, has mapped this on to MRS-WOLF, which is where the server has been started. Stop the client now, and you should see the server disappear from the Task Manager list.

OK, let's try something more interesting. We'll stop the cluster service on MRS-WOLF. This is simple enough to do – all you do is right-click on MRS-WOLF's entry in the left-hand pane of Cluster Administrator, and select Stop Cluster Service from the menu. You'll be asked to re-confirm, and then there will be a lot of disc activity, until eventually your display changes to something like this:

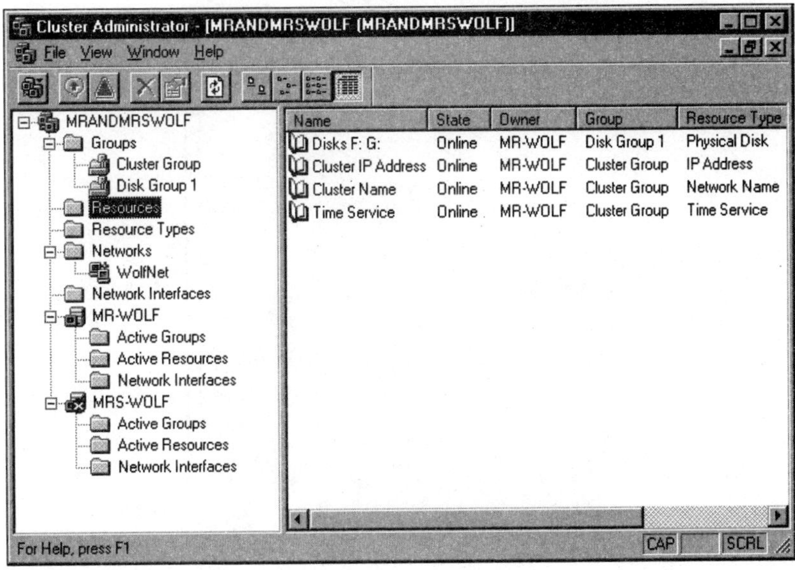

Notice that, as soon as MRS-WOLF's back is turned, MR-WOLF has grabbed all the resources. What's going to happen next time we try to run `GrannyClient`? OK, you've guessed already, but let's try it out anyway. Start up the client, whilst still keeping an eye on what's happening in MRS-WOLF's Task Manager window. The client starts up fine, but I bet you don't see the server starting up on MRS-WOLF. But if we take a look at MR-WOLF... well, as if by magic, there it is! And for my next trick, I shall need the assistance of an application from the audience. Ah! Thank you sir...

But before that, we need to take a look at resources in more detail.

Resources

Looking at the Cluster Administrator display above, we can see the list of resources configured by default – that is, the bare minimum that are set up by the installation process. We have one Physical Disc (partitioned into F: and G:), one IP Address, one Network Name and one Time Service. The physical disc resource is our SCSI device, by the way. All of these get transferred to another node in the event of a failure of the current owner. Let's take a quick look at some of the properties of these resources. You can access these by double-clicking on the resource in question. When you do this, a tabbed dialog comes up.

As you can see, there are three standard tabs for every resource, with an optional fourth tab which is a property page specific to the resource *type*. We'll look at the properties for the resource Cluster Name, which is of type Network Name. In the first one (General), the name of the resource is shown, along with its longer description and a list of the possible owners (which in a two-node cluster amounts to one or both). There is also a checkbox showing whether or not it is to be run in a separate Resource Monitor – we'll see what this means in a little while when we look at the internals of MSCS:

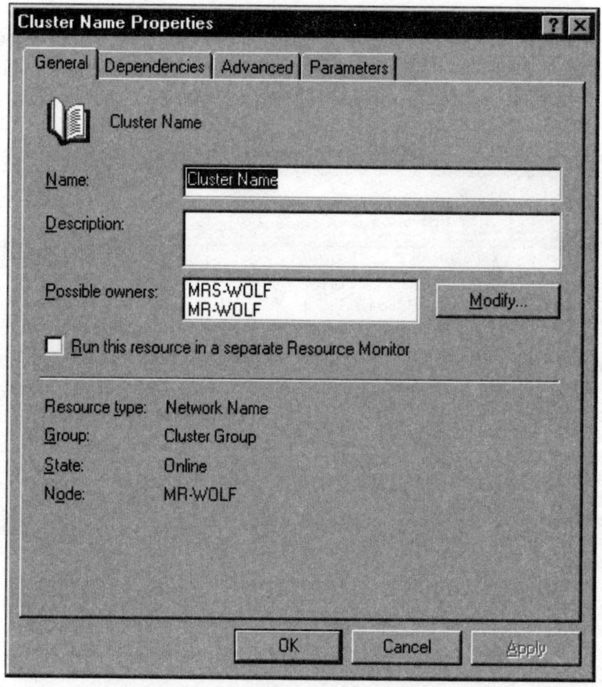

The next tab shows the Dependencies of the resource on other resources in the group. As you can see, the cluster name is dependent on the IP address – you can't change the owner of the IP address resource without moving the cluster name as well. Here's the tab:

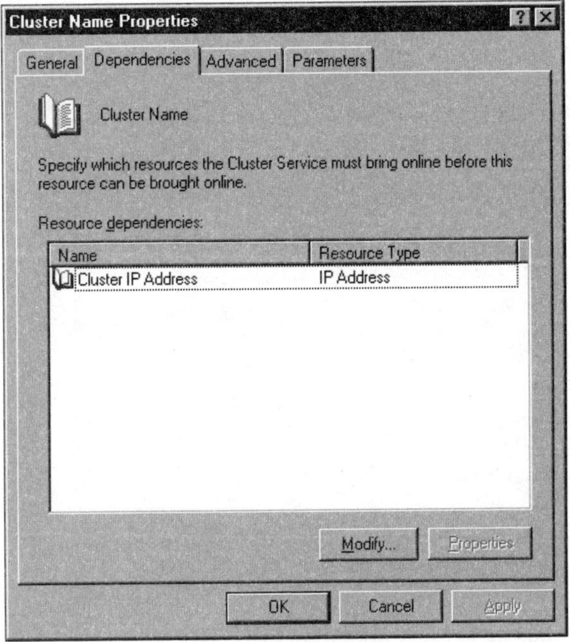

The Advanced tab, shown overleaf, describes how resource failure is to be handled. The first choice is between restarting and not restarting. Once we have decided to restart (the usual case), we have to decide at which point we want to failover to the other node. The way this works is that if a specified number of failures happens within a specified time threshold on one node, that node is deemed unsuitable, and the resource is failed over to the other. If the Affect the Group box is checked, then when the resource fails, so too do the other resources on which it is dependent. The cluster administrator will try first to bring back online these latter resources before the resource which relies upon them. In the case of the Cluster Name, the Cluster IP Address will also fail – this will also cause the entire cluster to fail, by the way.

The resource is polled every now and then to see if it's still alive. There are two types of poll: Looks Alive and Is Alive. These mean just what they say. The first basically looks at the resource and makes sure that it's still breathing, or at least hasn't started to stiffen yet. The second actually slaps it around the face and tries to get some sort of response. Maybe it's just me, but whenever I see this, I can't help inventing other status levels. You know the sort of thing: "Is Positively Breezy", "Seems A Bit Depressed", "Is Catatonic", "Smells a bit funny". OK, make up your own. We'll come back to the difference between being alive and looking alive later on when we develop our own resource.

The Pending timeout determines how long the system waits whilst the resource is in pending state before abandoning the attempt to bring it online.

Here's the tab anyway:

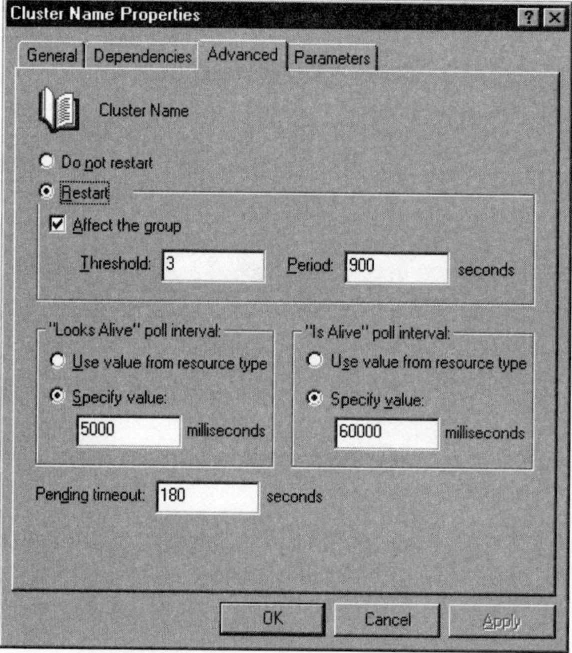

Incidentally, you can try out the failover policy by picking on any of the resources in the main display, right-clicking on it, and selecting Initiate Failure from the menu a few times. You'll see the resources go through four different states:

- Offline
- Online Pending
- Online
- Failed

The final tab is specific to the Network Name resource type, and, not surprisingly, it allows you to define the cluster name:

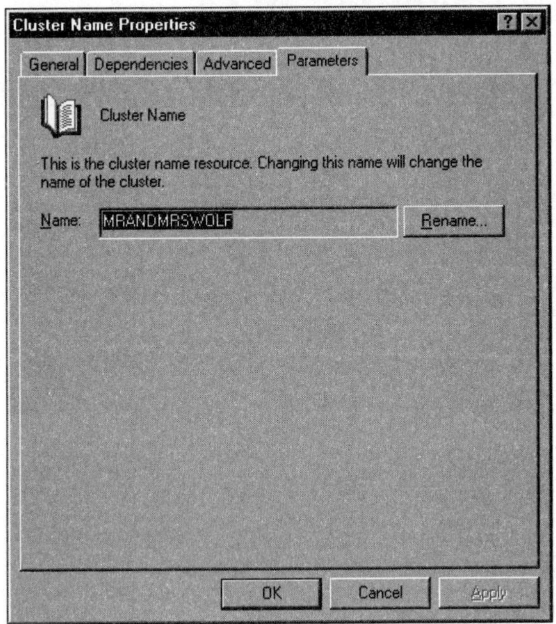

I won't go through the other cluster resources in as much detail, but it's worth pointing out one or two things. The Time Service resource is used to ensure that the cluster presents a consistent time to the rest of the world – in fact the answer to the popular playground question, "What's the time, Mr Wolf?" ("Dinner time!" I believe...)

The Discs F: G: are interesting. The first *physical* disc resource is treated slightly differently from the others (and because I've only got one SCSI disc device, all the discs in this example are treated this way). This resource is the **quorum resource** - it contains all the configuration data necessary to restart the cluster. The critical thing about the quorum disc is that, because it's a cluster resource, it can only be owned by one node in the cluster. This means that ownership of the quorum resource can be used to determine whether or not a node on its own is part of the cluster or not.

Without the quorum resource, you could get into strange situations if the network connection between the two nodes were to fail, in that both nodes might think that they were the only node left in the cluster. This would result in the cluster splitting into two factions, which would cause appalling problems if they were to come back together again. With the quorum resource, only one node retains control of the cluster, and the other must explicitly re-join. The cluster configuration is not compromised.

OK, we've looked at some resources – let's see how they fit into the cluster internal structure.

Cluster Internals and Resource DLLs

This is what a cluster looks like on the inside:

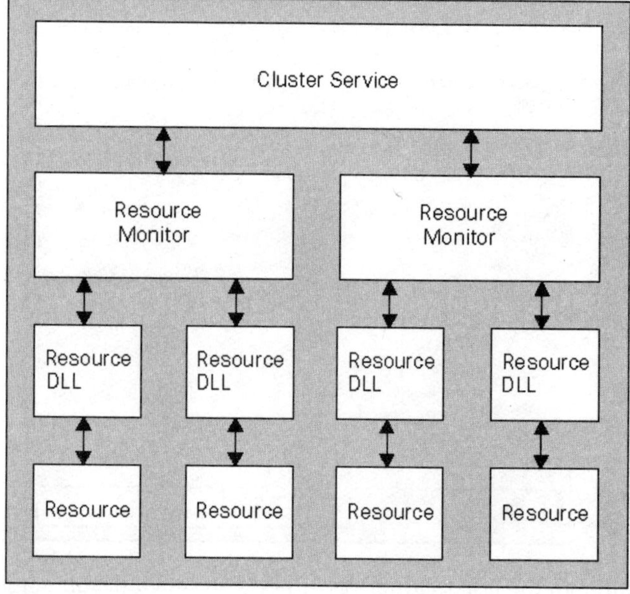

As you can see, the cluster service communicates with resources by means of one or more **Resource Monitors**. Usually, there will only be one of these per cluster, but when you create your resource, you can specify that it uses a separate resource monitor; you would normally only do this if your resource was particularly unusual (or unstable even) and you didn't want to risk affecting the other resources being monitored.

The resource monitors in turn control the resources by means of **Resource DLLs**. You can see a list of the resource DLLs in normal use by clicking on the Resource Types folder in the left-hand pane of the Cluster Adminstrator:

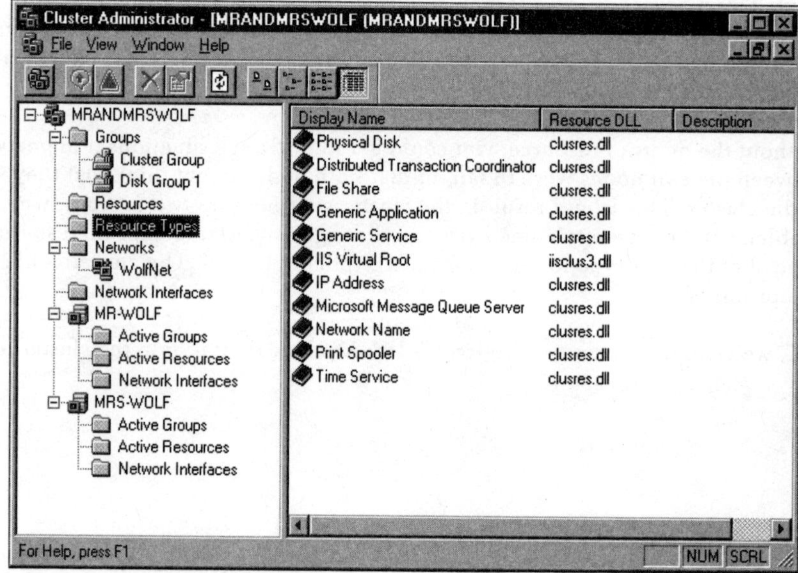

There aren't many resource DLLs in use, because there aren't really that many different things that you might want to do to a resource in a cluster. But there are a few circumstances where it is useful to write your own DLL, so we'll cover that in a little while.

However, I'm sure that what you're really itching to do is to add your own resource. So let's do just that.

Application Resources

Let's complete the definition of our sample application for this chapter. I put the words "Wolves" and "Nuclear reprocessing" (one of our possible target applications, remember) into my automatic scenario generator, and it came up with this:

> *Little Red Riding Hood on the way to see her Granny. Her Granny runs a nuclear reprocessing plant somewhere in the Dark Woods, so Little Red Riding Hood is taking with her a wheelbarrow full of spent fuel rods. At any point on the journey, she wants to be able to know how much Plutonium there is left, based on the half-life of the material.*

I know. I'm going to fix the thing, when I've got the time.

Let's translate this into terms that relate to the present subject. Granny's Plutonium is represented by the COM object **`Granny`** (interface **`IGranny`**). The current amount of material left is held in a file on the shared disc called **`AmountLeft.txt`**, and is adjusted at regular intervals by a process called **`Decay`**. We'll set this up as a cluster resource so that it will fail over if one of the nodes leaves the cluster.

We'll start off by trying **`Decay`** out as a Generic Application resource. Then we'll write a resource DLL to monitor and control it. Finally, we'll amend **`Granny`** to access the **`AmountLeft.txt`** file, so as to report back to our client how much material there is left whenever we want to know.

Decay

We start off by building **`Decay`** as an MFC EXE application – dialog-based will do, although we're not actually going to see any windows appear whilst it's working. We add the following line to the **`OnInitDialog()`** method of **`CDecayDlg`**:

```
SetIcon(m_hIcon, TRUE);          // Set big icon
SetIcon(m_hIcon, FALSE);        // Set small icon

SetTimer(1, 30000, NULL);

return TRUE;  // return TRUE  unless you set the focus to a control
```

Then we go into the Class Wizard and specify that we want to handle **WM_TIMER**. This is what we put in the **OnTimer()** method:

```
void CDecayDlg::OnTimer(UINT nIDEvent)
{
   char data[17];

   // This pathname should be changed to match the shared disc

   FILE *pFile = fopen("g:\\AmountLeft.txt", "r+w");

   if (pFile)
   {
      if (fgets (data, 16, pFile))
      {
         double value = atof (data);

         value /= 2.0;

         fseek(pFile, 0, SEEK_SET);

         fprintf(pFile, "%f", value);
      }

      fclose(pFile);
   }

   CDialog::OnTimer(nIDEvent);
}
```

Let's install it on one of our shared discs, say in the top level of disc G: (or which ever shared disc you're using). Now go into the Cluster Administrator on either one of our cluster nodes, and right click over the Resources folder in the left hand pane. Select New | Resource from the menu, and you should see something like this. Fill in the boxes as I've shown here:

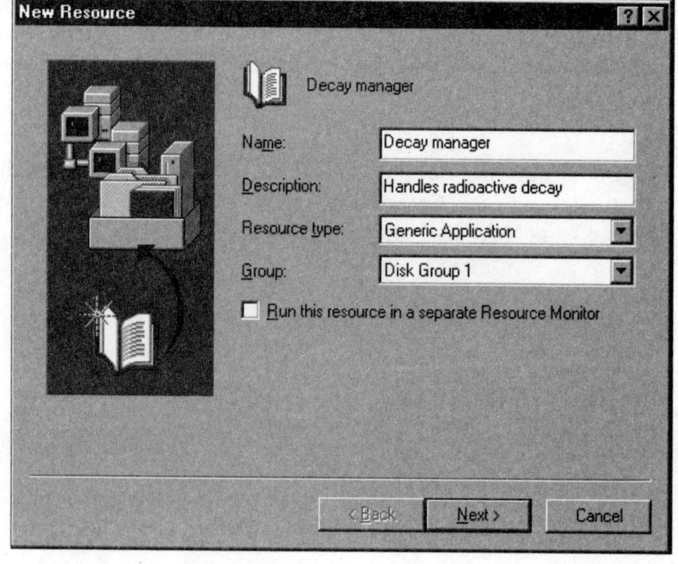

I've selected Disc Group 1 as the group, because we're going to have a dependency on disc G:, because that's where our data is. If you click on Next >, this is what you see:

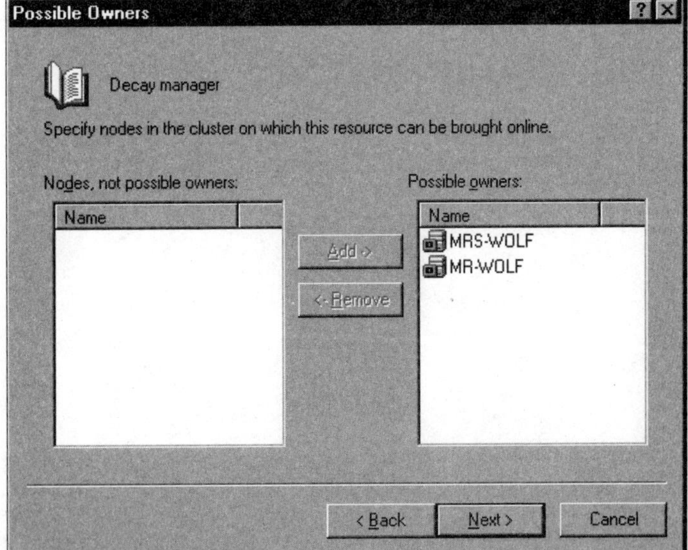

This is where we choose which machines can own our resource – obviously we select both, because it wouldn't be much of a cluster demonstration otherwise, would it? Click on Next > again...

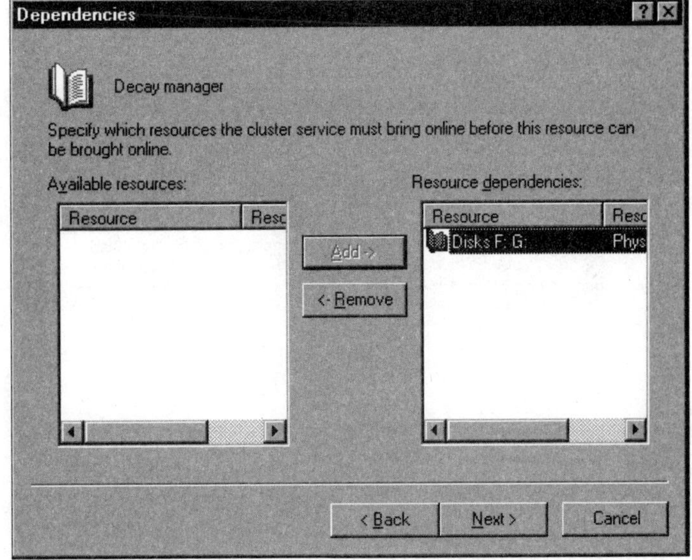

As I said above, we've got a major dependency on disc G:, so we move Discs F: G: from the left window to the right one. This means that we can't arbitrarily transfer ownership of Discs F: G: without moving **Decay** as well. Let's carry on...

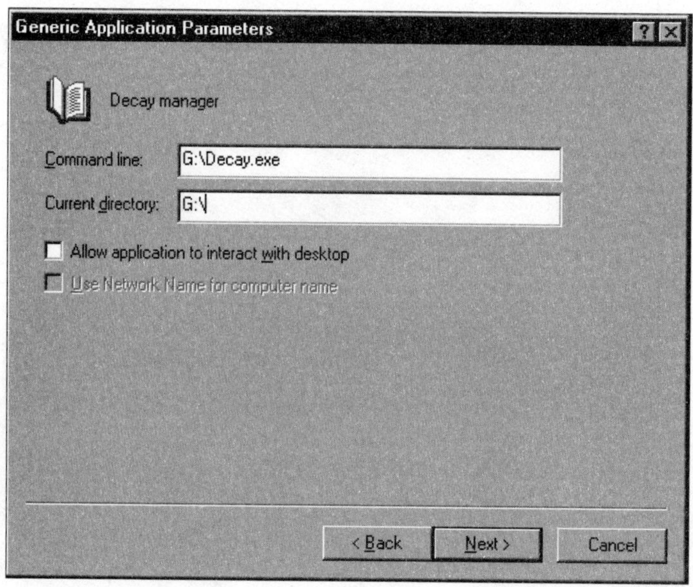

Here, we're specifying from which directory we're going to start the application. This is the first of two property pages that are specific to the Generic Application resource type. Let's see the next one:

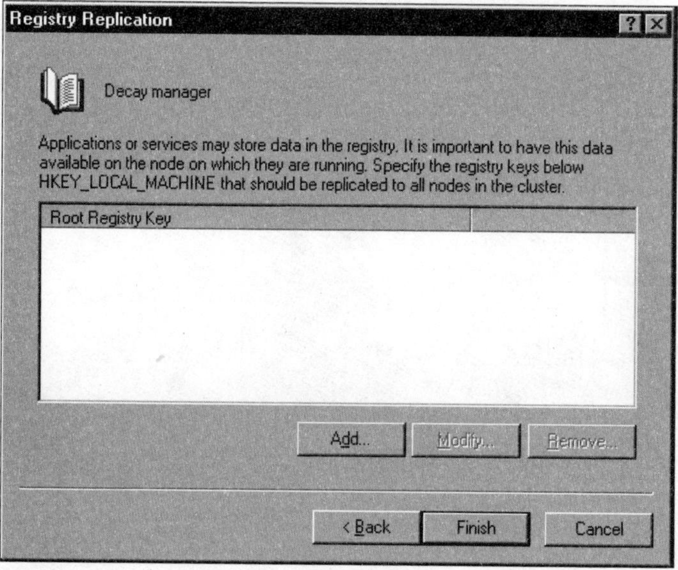

This is neat, because it allows us to specify anything in the registry that our application is going to be storing, so that it can be replicated on the other node. If ownership is transferred, we can pick up the registry where we left off. However, in this case, we aren't doing anything to the registry, so we leave it blank.

OK, we're done. Select Finish, the Cluster Administrator will confirm, and you'll see your new resource appear in the right hand pane, in Offline state. Before we go any further, just create a starter `AmountLeft.txt` file in the top-level directory on G:, with the number `10.0000` in it. Now bring our decay manager online, and see what happens. You should see it appear in the Task Manager window on the current owner, and you can check the text file from time to time to verify that it is actually reducing the amount left at regular intervals.

Next, try failing our resource. It'll pop back up for the first three times, but on the fourth, it will transfer over to the other node. You'll see that it isn't in the Task Manager window. You'll also notice that you can't look at the text file by its local pathname now, because ownership of the disc has also transferred. Time to go to the other machine, where you will find ... wow! It's running there now, same as before.

OK, that's all pretty cool, but I thought that it was a bit of a pain that we had to hard-code the text file name. Wouldn't it be nice if we could have a generic decay manager application that we could configure when we created the resource? Guess what we're going to do next...

Resource DLLs and Cluster Administration Extension DLLs

Having made the major step of acknowledging that we're dealing with a resource that's slightly out of the ordinary, our next move is to create a custom Resource DLL for it.

Generally, these go hand in hand with Cluster Administration DLLs, because you usually need something to handle the property pages for the new resource type. The good news is that the cluster people at Microsoft have put together an AppWizard that creates templates for both in one go. It's called the Cluster Resource Type AppWizard.

In order to make use of this, we'll have to make sure that we've got that ubiquitous Platform SDK installed on our machine. We've come across this in earlier chapters, but if you need to get hold of it, it's available for download from www.microsoft.com\msdn\sdk\winbase.htm as well as being on one of the CD's in the MSDN kit. You'll also need to install the Cluster Server SDK which is part of the Windows Base Services extension to the Build Environment of the Platform SDK. It is also available from www.microsoft.com\msdn\sdk\winbase.htm. Hidden away in this incredibly useful SDK is the aforementioned AppWizard. In order to access it, copy the contents of the `winbase\cluster\template` directory – most importantly the `.awx` files – into `..\DevStudio\SharedIDE\bin\ide` so that it will appear in the list offered by Visual Studio.

Let's take a look...

The Cluster Resource Type AppWizard

The first screen that you see is this one:

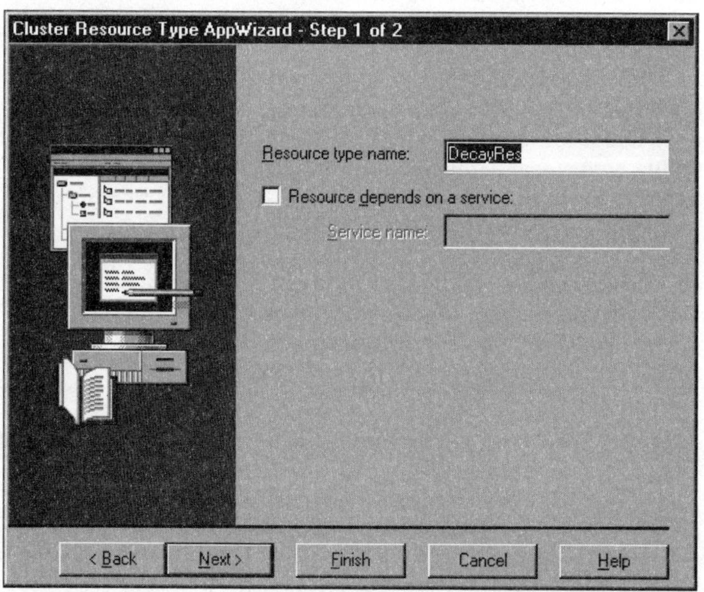

We aren't dependent on a service, so leave the check box blank, and move on to the second screen:

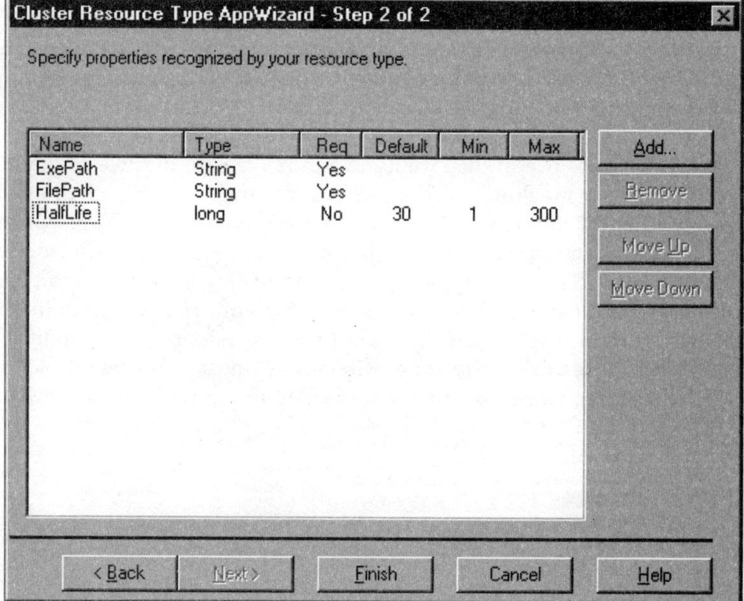

Notice that we've specified three properties: the pathnames of our executable file and the file that will contain the amount of our plutonium that is left. I've said that these are both required to bring the resource online – you can't do much without them. The third parameter is the half-life of the Plutonium, measured in seconds. This isn't mandatory, and it will take a default of 30 seconds. (Remember, this is a fairy story, right?)

When we've finished, we'll see that the AppWizard has created two projects, one for the Resource DLL, and one for the Cluster Adminstration Extension DLL. Each one contains a number of areas marked **`TODO`**, and we're going to look at those now.

The Cluster Administration Extension DLL

We can pass over **`DecayResEx`** very quickly, because it doesn't usually need any changes whatsoever! Just build it as it is. (Now *that's* what I call a Wizard...)

The Resource DLL

This is slightly more complicated, but it isn't that bad really. There are basically eight sections of code (marked as **`TODO:`**) that we can fill in if we want, as follows:

- Startup (which is invoked when the resource DLL is loaded)
- Bring online
- Take offline
- Terminate (which is invoked when a resource fails to respond to an attempt to take it offline)
- Looks alive
- Is alive
- Check interactions between properties
- Handle on-line changes to properties

In this case, because we've got a fairly simple resource, we're going to do the following:

- Startup – do nothing
- Bring online – start the application up
- Take offline – stop the application
- Terminate – same as take offline
- Looks alive – check that the application is running
- Is alive – same as looks alive
- Check interactions between properties – do nothing
- Handle on-line changes to properties – do nothing

In order to be able easily to close our resource down, we need to store the process handle in global memory, so we add this to the top of our **DecayRes.c** file:

```
.
.
//
// DecayRes resource read-write private properties.
//
RESUTIL_PROPERTY_ITEM
DecayResResourcePrivateProperties[] = {
    { PARAM_NAME__EXEPATH, NULL, CLUSPROP_FORMAT_SZ, 0, 0, 0,
RESUTIL_PROPITEM_REQUIRED, FIELD_OFFSET(DECAYRES_PARAMS,ExePath) },
    { PARAM_NAME__FILEPATH, NULL, CLUSPROP_FORMAT_SZ, 0, 0, 0,
RESUTIL_PROPITEM_REQUIRED, FIELD_OFFSET(DECAYRES_PARAMS,FilePath) },
    { PARAM_NAME__HALFLIFE, NULL, CLUSPROP_FORMAT_DWORD,
      (DWORD)PARAM_DEFAULT__HALFLIFE, (DWORD)PARAM_MIN__HALFLIFE,
      (DWORD)PARAM_MAX__HALFLIFE, RESUTIL_PROPITEM_SIGNED,
FIELD_OFFSET(DECAYRES_PARAMS,Halflife) },
    { 0 }
};

HANDLE hProcess;    //Handle of created process
DWORD dwProcessID;    //Identifier of created process

//
// Function prototypes.
//
.
.
```

Here's the code for bringing the resource online. Note that this is contained in **DecayResOnlineThread** and not **DecayResOnline** as you would think.:

```
DWORD
WINAPI
DecayResOnlineThread(
    PCLUS_WORKER WorkerPtr,
    IN PDECAYRES_RESOURCE ResourceEntry
    )

...

{
    RESOURCE_STATUS     resourceStatus;
    DWORD               status = ERROR_SUCCESS;
    LPWSTR              nameOfPropInError;
    WCHAR               szParams[128];
    PROCESS_INFORMATION processInfo;
    STARTUPINFO         startupInfo;
```

```
...

    //
    // Bring the resource online.
    //
    // TODO: Add code to bring your resource online.

    swprintf(szParams, L"%s %s~%d", ResourceEntry->Params.ExePath,
         ResourceEntry->Params.FilePath,
         ResourceEntry->Params.HalfLife);
    memset(&startupInfo, 0, sizeof (STARTUPINFO));

    CreateProcess(NULL, szParams, NULL, NULL, FALSE, 0,
                NULL, NULL, &startupInfo, &processInfo);

    hProcess = processInfo.hProcess;
    dwProcessId = processInfo.dwProcessId;

exit:

...
```

What we're doing here is creating a new process using the **ExePath** parameter from the resource set-up, passing it the values of **FilePath** and **HalfPath** as command-line parameters.

And this is what we do to the code in **DecayResOffline** to take it offline:

```
DWORD
WINAPI
DecayResOffline(
    IN RESID ResourceId
    )

...

// TODO: Offline code

    TerminateProcess(hProcess,0);

// NOTE: Offline should try to shut the resource down gracefully, whereas
// Terminate must shut the resource down immediately. If there are no

...
```

We need to make a similar change for termination in **DecayResDoTerminate**:

```
DWORD
DecayResDoTerminate(
    IN PDECAYRES_RESOURCE ResourceEntry
    )
```

```
...

//
// Terminate the resource.
//
// TODO: Add code to terminate your resource.

    TerminateProcess(hProcess, 0);

    if( status == ERROR_SUCCESS ) {
        ResourceEntry->State = ClusterResourceOffline;
    }

    return(status);

} // DecayResDoTerminate
```

Finally, this is what we do to see if the process is alive. In order to do this, I'm going to use a function from the SDK Platform library, which is part of the performance monitoring suite. In order to make use of this, I've added the following line to the top of the code:

```
#include <clusapi.h>
#include <resapi.h>
#include <stdio.h>
#include <psapi.h>
```

I've also included a reference to the library `psapi.lib` in the program settings. You'll need to amend your include and library pathnames to be able to find this and both `clusapi.h` and `clusapi.lib`. You also need to include the cluster SDK version of `Winerror.h` for these examples to work.

This is the code for checking whether or not the process is alive:

```
BOOL
DecayResCheckIsAlive(
   IN PDECAYRES_RESOURCE ResourceEntry
   )

...

{
   DWORD ids[1000];
   DWORD nSize;
   DWORD nId;
   DWORD id;
//
   // Check to see if the resource is alive.
   //
   // TODO: Add code to determine if your resource is alive.
```

```
   EnumProcesses(ids, 1000 * sizeof (DWORD), &nSize);

   nId = nSize / sizeof (DWORD);

   for (id = 0; id < nId; id++)
      if (ids[id] == dwProcessId)
         break;

   if (id == nId)
      return(FALSE);

   return(TRUE);

} // DecayResCheckIsAlive
```

Here, we're simply enumerating all the known processes, and checking the process identifier against the one that we saved when we created our process.

OK, let's build it.

Installation

Before we do anything else, let's get rid of our Decay Manager generic application resource. We now need to install our DLLs onto our cluster nodes. The first step is to copy both of them to the **\WinNT\cluster** directory on each machine. Once this is done, we can register the new resource type with the cluster. Don't do this until you have got the DLL in place on both machines, or you may find that it won't be recognised properly by the cluster until your next reboot. We register the new resource type using the command line **cluster** utility, like this:

```
cluster resourcetype DecayRes /create /dll:DecayRes.dll
```

You only need to do this on one machine, by the way, as the registry settings get synchronised. Incidentally, the resource name *is* case sensitive. You should see the new resource type magically appear in the Cluster Administrator window:

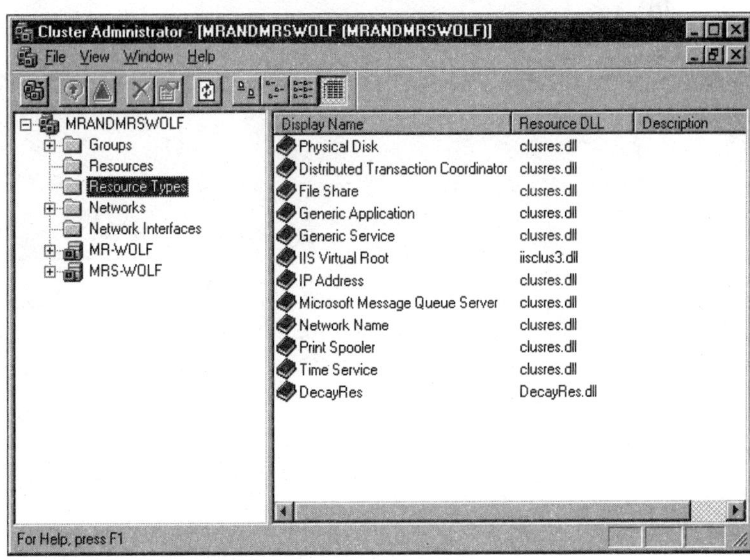

Lastly we need to register our Cluster Administration Extension DLL. Here's the command to do that:

```
RegClAdm DecayResEx.dll
```

Note that you'll either need to be in the same directory as the DLL or you'll have to supply **`RegClAdm`** with the full pathname of your DLL.

This is similar to the standard COM **`RegSvr32`** utility, except that it also triggers the specific self-registration code inside the DLL for connecting to the Cluster Administrator. OK, we're ready to re-create our resource with our new type.

Creating Our Resource

This goes exactly the same as before (except that we specify our resource as being of type **`DecayRes`**, instead of generic application), until we reach the fourth dialog of the set-up, which now looks like this:

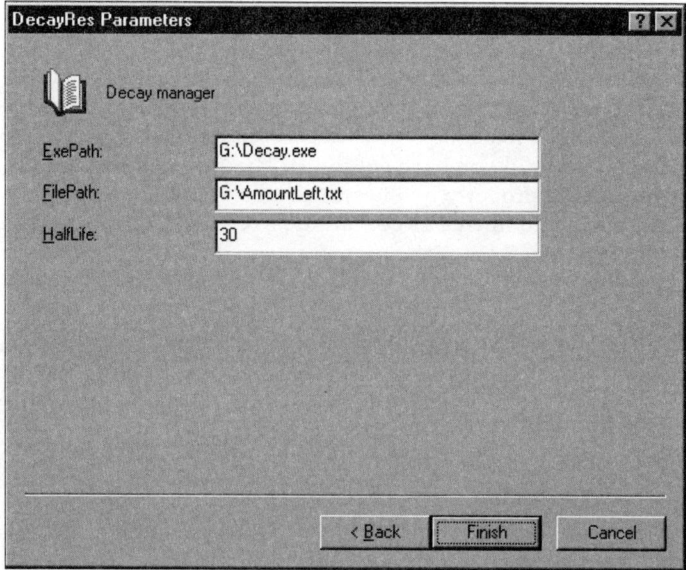

And there, in all their glory, are the properties that we specified when we went through the AppWizard. The Cluster Administration Extension DLL is doing its stuff, without us lifting a finger!

Completing the Application

What have we got left to do? Well, we need to make a small change to the **Decay.exe** process to extract the command line parameters. First of all, let's create a couple of public member variables in **CDecayDlg**:

```
// Construction
public:
    int m_halfLife;
    CString m_strFileName;
    CDecayDlg(CWnd* pParent = NULL);    // standard constructor
```

Now let's set them up in **CDecayApp::InitInstance()**:

```
#ifdef _AFXDLL
    Enable3dControls();          // Call this when using MFC in a shared DLL
#else
    Enable3dControlsStatic();    // Call this when linking to MFC statically
#endif

CCommandLineInfo cmdInfo;
ParseCommandLine(cmdInfo);

CDecayDlg dlg;

// Find our length of incoming command, and locate separator

int len = cmdInfo.m_strFileName.GetLength();
int sep = cmdInfo.m_strFileName.Find("~");

// Extract left part into file name string ...

dlg.m_strFileName = cmdInfo.m_strFileName.Left(sep);

// .. and right part into half life

dlg.m_halfLife = atoi(static_cast<LPCSTR>
            (cmdInfo.m_strFileName.Right (len - sep - 1)));

m_pMainWnd = &dlg;
int nResponse = dlg.DoModal();

...
```

And let's use them in **CDecayDlg::OnInitDialog()** by replacing the line:

```
    SetTimer(1,30000, NULL);
```

with

```
    SetTimer(1, 1000 * m_halfLife, NULL);
```

Similarly, in **`CDecayDlg::OnTimer()`**, we'll replace the line:

```
    FILE *pFile = fopen("x:\\AmountLeft2.txt", "r+w");
```

with

```
    FILE *pFile = fopen((LPCSTR) m_strFileName, "r+w");
```

OK, so that's the decay handling stuff sorted out. Now, we need to go back to our **`Granny`** component, and add a method to poll the amount left:

Method	Parameters	Description
`GetAmountLeft()`	**`[in] BSTR bstrFile,`** **`[out] double* dAmount`**	Get amount left in specified file

Here's the code for the method:

```
// Granny.cpp : Implementation of CGranny
#include "stdafx.h"
#include "GrannyServer.h"
#include "Granny.h"

#include <stdio.h>

//////////////////////////////////////////////////////////////////////////////
// CGranny


STDMETHODIMP CGranny::GetAmountLeft(BSTR bstrFile, double* dAmount)
{
    char szFile[129]={0};
    char data[17]={0};

    wcstombs(szFile, bstrFile, 128);
    FILE *pFile = fopen(szFile, "r");

    if (!pFile)
       return E_FAIL;
```

```
    if (!fgets(data, 16, pFile))
    {
       fclose(pFile);
       return E_FAIL;
    }

    *dAmount = atof(data);

    return S_OK;
}
```

Finally, we need to change our client. This is what the code looks like now:

```
Dim gran As Granny

Private Sub Form_Load()
Set gran = New Granny
End Sub

Private Sub cmdGetAmount_Click()
Dim pluto As Double
Call gran.GetAmountLeft("g:\AmountLeft.txt", pluto)
txtAmount.Text = pluto
End Sub
```

And our client form looks like this:

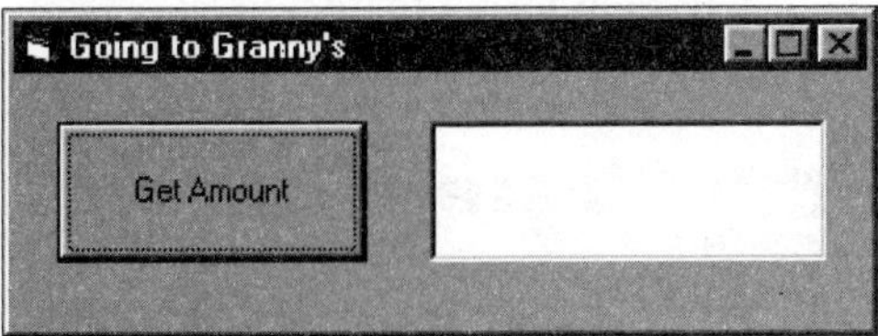

And that's pretty much it. We have a clustered COM server (**Granny**) that automatically fails over whenever the IP address flips, and a background resource that flips over under the control of our custom resource DLL.

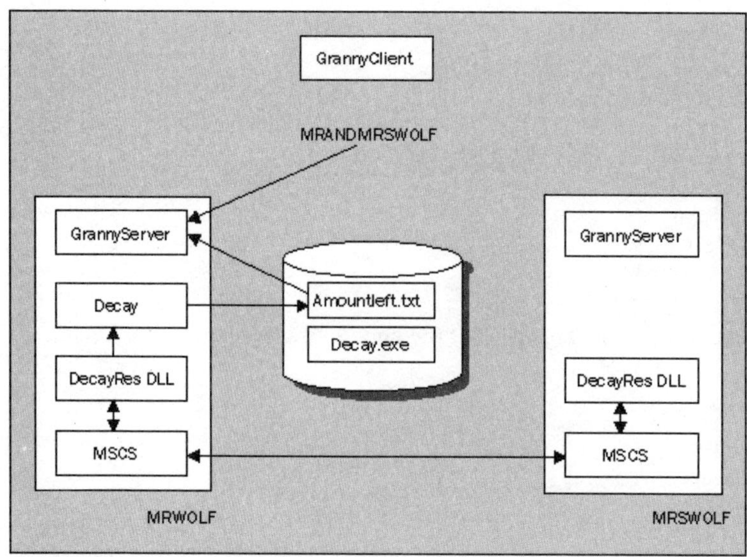

I should, perhaps, point out what we *haven't* got as well, just so that we don't get carried away. As I mentioned near the beginning of this chapter, interactive sessions don't fail over. If our client is holding an instance of an object on one node of the cluster, and that node fails over, the client will no longer be able to see the object. However, our client *will* be able to instantiate *new* objects. So how transparent the failover seems to the client really depends on whether they are holding references to remote objects at the time of failover. The ability to do a true DCOM-level transparent failover will probably appear in a future release (phase 2 again!), but it isn't there now.

Cluster Awareness and the Cluster API

There's only one more aspect to look into, and that's what we can do to make our server more "cluster-aware". Our server really ought to know when the resources that it is using are online or offline, so that it can report a bad status to the client. Wouldn't it be nice if the server could just interrogate the resource monitor and find out just that? Well, it just so happens that – as well as the APIs we've used (albeit without us really knowing)–for resource and cluster administration extension DLLs, there's a whole API that we can use for tapping into the cluster services. In fact, if we really wanted, we could use it to build our own administrator – it's that comprehensive.

Because of the sheer size of the Cluster API, I'm not going to go into it in any great detail – and to be honest, it's pretty straightforward to use. However, just to give you a flavor of what it's like, we're going to develop a small stand-alone program to search for cluster resources. Then I'll add a small bit of code to **`GrannyServer`** to check to see if our **`Decay`** resource is online.

Our cluster search application is a dialog-based MFC EXE, called **SearchCluster**, which enables the user to open a specified cluster, enumerate the resources, and then interrogate a given resource to determine its state. The dialog itself looks like this:

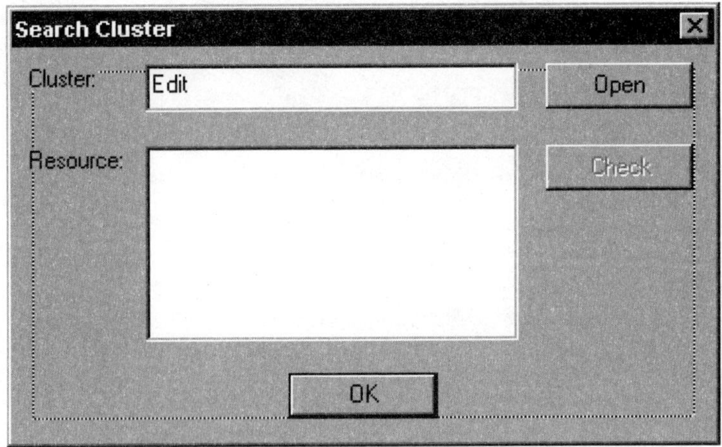

Before we touch any code at all don't forget to include a reference to **clusapi.lib** in the program settings and similarly to include **clusapi.h** within **SearchClusterDlg.h** as well. Not surprisingly, all hell breaks loose if you don't.

The **SearchCluster** routines below all use a cluster handle, **m_hCluster**, which we declare as a private variable in **SearchClusterDlg.h**, like so:

```
...
   //}}AFX_MSG
   DECLARE_MESSAGE_MAP()
private:
   HCLUSTER m_hCluster;
};

//{{AFX_INSERT_LOCATION}}

...
```

and then initialise in **OnInitDialog()**.

```
...
   SetIcon(m_hIcon, FALSE);       // Set small icon

   // TODO: Add extra initialization here
   m_hCluster = NULL;

   return TRUE;  // return TRUE  unless you set the focus to a control
}
```

So that's the prelims dealt with – here's the code for the **OnOpen()** method:

```
void CSearchClusterDlg::OnOpen()
{
   if (m_hCluster)
      CloseCluster(m_hCluster);

   CEdit* pCluster = reinterpret_cast<CEdit*>
                        (GetDlgItem (IDC_CLUSTER));
   CString csCluster;
   pCluster->GetWindowText(csCluster);
```

Here we get a handle to the cluster:

```
   if (csCluster.IsEmpty ())
      m_hCluster = OpenCluster(NULL);
   else
      m_hCluster = OpenCluster(csCluster.AllocSysString());

   if (!m_hCluster)
   {
      AfxMessageBox("Failed to open cluster");
      GotoDlgCtrl(pCluster);
      return;
   }

   if (csCluster.IsEmpty ())
   {
      WCHAR szCluster[129];
      DWORD dwCluster = 128;

      GetClusterInformation(m_hCluster, szCluster, &dwCluster,
                            NULL);

      CString csCluster = szCluster;
      pCluster->SetWindowText(csCluster);
   }
```

Having done that, we need to get an enumerator for the resources:

```
   HCLUSENUM hEnum = ClusterOpenEnum(m_hCluster,
                              CLUSTER_ENUM_RESOURCE);

   if (!hEnum)
   {
      AfxMessageBox("Failed to enumerate resources");
      GotoDlgCtrl(pCluster);
      return;
   }
```

```
    CListBox* pResources = reinterpret_cast<CListBox*>
                        (GetDlgItem (IDC_RESOURCES));
    pResources->ResetContent();
```

And now we do the enumeration (one of the easier enumerators in all of the Windows APIs!):

```
    for (DWORD dwIndex = 0;; dwIndex++)
    {
       DWORD dwCount = 128;
       WCHAR szName[129];
       DWORD dwType;

       DWORD dwReturn = ClusterEnum(hEnum, dwIndex, &dwType,
                                    szName, &dwCount);

       if (dwReturn == ERROR_NO_MORE_ITEMS)
          break;

       CString csName = szName;
       pResources->AddString(csName);
    }

    CButton* pCheck = reinterpret_cast<CButton*>
                            (GetDlgItem (IDC_CHECK));
    pCheck->EnableWindow(dwIndex > 0);
 }
```

OK, that's cool. Here's the method that gets invoked when the user requests to check a resource for its status:

```
 void CSearchClusterDlg::OnCheck()
 {
    CListBox* pResources = reinterpret_cast<CListBox*>
                                (GetDlgItem (IDC_RESOURCES));
    int index = pResources->GetCurSel();

    CString csResource;
    pResources->GetText(index, csResource);
```

First we get a handle to the resource:

```
HRESOURCE hResource = OpenClusterResource(m_hCluster,
                              csResource.AllocSysString ());

if (!hResource)
{
   AfxMessageBox("Failed to open resource");
   GotoDlgCtrl(pResources);
   return;
}

WCHAR szNode[129];
DWORD dwNode = 128;
WCHAR szGroup[129];
DWORD dwGroup = 128;
```

And then we ask for its state:

```
CLUSTER_RESOURCE_STATE state = GetClusterResourceState(hResource,
                                   szNode, &dwNode,
                                   szGroup, &dwGroup);

CString csState;

switch (state)
{
   case ClusterResourceInitializing:
      csState = "Initializing";
      break;
   case ClusterResourceOnline:
      csState = "Online";
      break;
   case ClusterResourceOffline:
      csState = "Offline";
      break;
   case ClusterResourceFailed:
      csState = "Failed";
      break;
   case ClusterResourcePending:
      csState = "Pending";
      break;
   case ClusterResourceOnlinePending:
      csState = "Online Pending";
      break;
   case ClusterResourceOfflinePending:
      csState = "Offline Pending";
      break;
   default:
      csState = "Unknown";
      break;
}
```

```
    CString csNode = szNode;
    CString csGroup = szGroup;

    CString csStatus;
    csStatus.Format("Resource is in state %s, in group %s on node %s",
                 static_cast<LPCSTR> (csState),
                 static_cast<LPCSTR> (csGroup),
                 static_cast<LPCSTR> (csNode));
    AfxMessageBox(csStatus);

    CloseClusterResource(hResource);
}
```

And that's pretty much it, apart from making sure that the cluster handle gets released on exit:

```
void CSearchClusterDlg::OnOK()
{
    if (m_hCluster)
       CloseCluster(m_hCluster);

    CDialog::OnOK();
}
```

Let's try it out and see if it works. This is what we see when we run it:

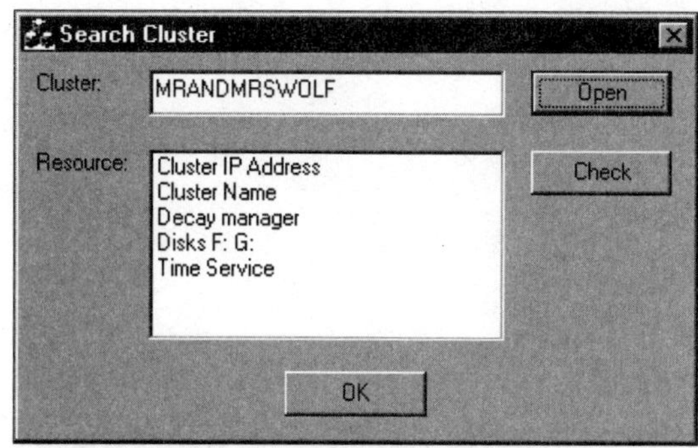

This comes as no great surprise, as it's the same list that we've seen in the Cluster Administrator. If we select Decay manager and click on Check, this is what we get:

Which tallies with what we know from Cluster Administrator.

OK, we're ready for the last piece of the jigsaw. Let's go back to **GrannyServer**, include **clusapi.h** in **Granny.cpp** and add a reference to **clusapi.lib** in our project settings. Now we're able to add a last new Boolean property, **Running**. Here's the code for the **get_Running()** method:

```
STDMETHODIMP CGranny::get_Running(BOOL * pVal)
{
   HCLUSTER hCluster = OpenCluster (NULL);

   if (!hCluster)
      return E_FAIL;

   HRESOURCE hResource = OpenClusterResource(hCluster,
                                    L"Decay manager");

   if (!hResource)
      return E_FAIL;

   WCHAR szNode[129] = {0};
   DWORD dwNode = 128;
   WCHAR szGroup[129] = {0};
   DWORD dwGroup = 128;

   CLUSTER_RESOURCE_STATE state = GetClusterResourceState(hResource,
                              szNode, &dwNode,
                              szGroup, &dwGroup);

   if (state == ClusterResourceOnline)
      *pVal = VARIANT_TRUE;
   else
      *pVal = VARIANT_FALSE;

   return S_OK;
}
```

This is pretty much a condensed version of our cluster search program. All we need to do now is add another button to our Visual Basic client to look like this:

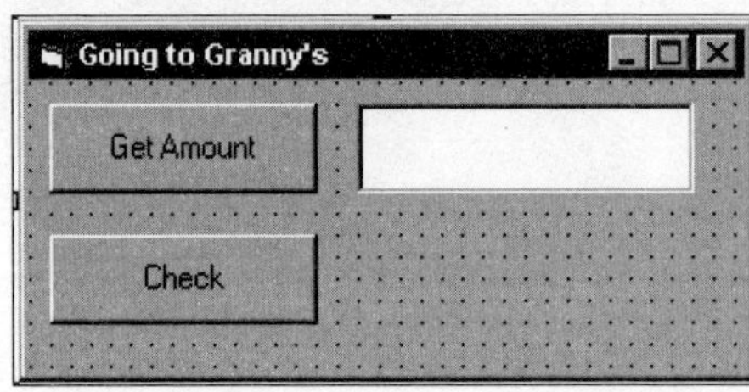

and some code to go with it:

```
Private Sub cmdCheck_Click()
Dim fRunning As Boolean
fRunning = gran.running
If (fRunning) Then
    MsgBox("Still working")
Else
    MsgBox("Stopped working")
End If
End Sub
```

We now have a fully cluster-aware DCOM server.

Cluster Futures

At the time of writing, Microsoft Clusters are pretty primitive things, but keep an eye on them. They are going to be very big. Watch out for clusters involving more than two nodes. Imagine how you're going to develop cluster-aware software that runs effectively in the middle of that. Exciting, isn't it?

In the next chapter, we're going to move away from high availability systems to systems that go out of their way to be unavailable. Unless, that is, you're one of the select few who are allowed in. Security is next on the agenda.

9

Security

"He'd learnt that humans in the Store had their names on little badges because – he'd been told – they were so stupid that they wouldn't remember them otherwise. This man had his name on his hat. Masklin squinted and made out the shape of the letters: S ... E ... C ... U ... R ... I ... T ... Y. He had a white moustache."

"Truckers" (Terry Pratchett)

Stopping People from Doing Things

Now we come to a subject that I can never work up quite so much enthusiasm for as all the others. My problem is that I like to write software that enables – nay, *empowers* – people to do exciting new things, and it just doesn't seem fair to deny other people the opportunity. Then again, of course, there are many occasions when the only way in which you *can* actually offer a service to your target user community is by denying it to all others outside that community, so perhaps I'm being a little naïve here. In any case, in any attempt to cover all the issues involved in DCOM application development, there is no possible way that we can avoid it. In the words of the song, we can't go round it, we can't go over it, so we've got to go through it...

Security is a curious subject. There is a vast infrastructure designed to enforce it, but, to a large extent, provided that you don't try to do anything that you're not supposed to do, you don't notice that it's there at all. It's completely transparent to you. This is, of course, a bit like real life. In any democratic country, there are a large number of men and women devoted to keeping law and order, but, provided that you're not of a criminal disposition, you tend not to come across them. (At least, that's how it's supposed to work.)

If you want to get a flavour of some of the things that are bubbling under the surface in Windows NT security, I can do no better than refer you once again to Dr Richard Grimes' Professional DCOM book – in particular, Chapter 7. There's also plenty of good information in Sing Li and Panos Economopoulos' Professional ActiveX/COM Control Programming. I won't attempt to short-change you by repeating this material here, although I will go over some of the ground that they cover from a slightly different angle. This is one subject where the more angles you approach it from, the nearer you're going to get to making sense of it. A bit like COM itself, really.

Why do we need security? There are two principal reasons. First of all, if I'm doing something that involves the transfer of money, or sensitive information, for example, I would like to know who I am dealing with, and I'd like them to prove this to me beyond all shadow of a doubt. This is the process known as **authentication**. Next, having established who they are, I need to know if they are allowed to do what they want to do. This is the process known as **authorization**. (Incidentally, this is why, when programming security, you should never have any variable names with just the letters **`auth`** in them. It's got to be **`authn`** or **`authz`**!)

The two aspects of security that we have highlighted are basically two parts of the Anastasia question. If someone that we'd previously known as Anna Anderson comes to us claiming to be Princess Anastasia, the first thing that we have to do is *authenticate* her credentials and establish whether or not she is indeed the last of the Romanovs. If we did manage to prove this beyond all doubt, the next stage would be to see if she was *authorized* to get her hands on all their loot. Although, as it turned out...

There are several further aspects to security. If I have produced something, I need to be sure that its integrity is not compromised by some third party. For example, I might have just sent the CEO a report on how to increase our profits by 300% in just two months (well, it surprised me too, I can tell you). The last thing I want is one of my rivals sneaking in and changing the accompanying e-mail so that it starts "Dear Lardface". I want the security system to ensure the **integrity** of my data. As well as this, I want to be sure that if someone happens to be listening in to my conversations, they won't be able to understand a word of it: I need **encryption**.

All these requirements are beginning to be met by Windows NT.

DCOM and the NT Security Architecture

Before we dive in and play with DCOM security, I'll give you a little bit of background. This should lessen the weirdness of some of the things that you're going to see, and show you where we are currently on the evolutionary path. Part of the problem in making sense of Windows NT security is that there are quite a few hooks exposed for things that haven't been implemented yet, in the mainstream at least, and it isn't at all obvious what works now and what isn't going to work until sometime in the future.

Once we have done that, I'll take you through standard NT4 security and how it relates to DCOM, before mapping out the exciting future offered by NT5 and Kerberos.

The standard picture of the Windows NT security architecture – or at least the part that concerns us – looks like this:

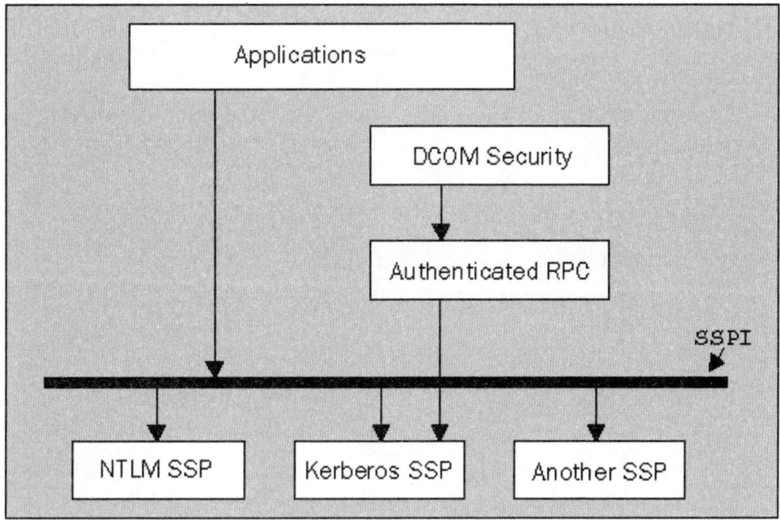

The clever part is the **Security Support Provider Interface** (SSPI). This interface isolates everything that the user sees from the systems that actually handle security. These are developed as plug-in modules, called **Security Support Providers** (SSPs). The existence of a fixed SSPI means that increasingly sophisticated security mechanisms can be bolted on to Windows NT as time goes by, without necessitating a complete re-write of the system.

We won't be building our own SSP in this book (although, as you would expect, there are a number of well-documented APIs for doing just that), but it's useful to keep the architecture in mind.

Take a look at those boxes underneath the SSPI line. NTLM stands for NT LAN Manager – this provides the security support that we know and love in Windows NT4. As we'll see soon, it has a number of shortcomings, and in NT5, further SSPs will be added – most notably that for Kerberos.

If you look above the line, the key thing to note is that DCOM applications don't talk directly to the SSPI. This is excellent news. It gets better because, as things turn out, there are only two DCOM interfaces that handle security: `IClientSecurity` and `IServerSecurity`. Piece of cake, eh?

Security Blankets and Impersonation

The collection of parameters that govern how security is handled between a client and a server is known as the **security blanket**. This is one of the more bizarre terms in Windows. I imagine that it's supposed to give the impression of an all-embracing entity surrounding everything that you do; however, to me a security blanket is the thing that kids like Linus in the Peanuts cartoons drag around after them. Whenever I see the term, an image comes into my head of a snotty-nosed little COM object with a permanent sniff.

Back to security blankets.

A security blanket basically consists of the following parameters:

- Authentication service
- Authentication level
- Authentication identity
- Authorization service
- Authorization level
- Impersonation level
- Server principal name

Let's first take a look at the server side.

The Server

In order to do anything, we need to get hold of the blanket, and the way to do that is via the `IServerSecurity` interface. We get hold of that by means of a call to `CoGetCallContext()` (don't worry – we'll see an example of this soon enough). You do not implement the `IServerSecurity` interface, and you do not write the call context object: the system does all that for you. Once we've got hold of the interface, getting hold of the blanket is simple enough.

Here's the specification of the `IServerSecurity` interface:

Method	Parameters	Description

`QueryBlanket`	`[out] DWORD* pAuthnSvc,`
	`[out] DWORD* pAuthzSvc,`
	`[out] OLECHAR** pServerPrincName,`
	`[out] DWORD* pAuthnLevel,`
	`[out] DWORD* pImpLevel,`
	`[out] RPC_AUTHZ_HANDLE* pPrivs,`
	`[out] DWORD** pCapabilities`
		This method finds out the details of the security blanket for the user on the current thread.

Table Continued on Following Page

Method	Parameters	Description
`ImpersonateClient`		This method enables us to impersonate the client for the rest of the current method call
`RevertToSelf`		This method restores our own identity following an impersonation (like the impressionist always says at the end of the show "... and this is me!")
`IsImpersonating`		This method tells us whether or not we are currently impersonating a client

As you can see, this is mostly about *impersonation.* Let's take a look at what this is all about. You, a warm-blooded human being, are sitting at a workstation somewhere attached to a network. You run a program that makes a DCOM call to some disembodied server on a machine somewhere else on the network. That server is now your representative within the network. To what extent are you prepared for it to act on your behalf? To use another metaphor, an ambassador to some foreign country may be authorized to gather intelligence on that country, and to provide assistance to expatriates living there, but, one assumes, he or she is not to be authorized to declare war.

The following levels of impersonation are available:

Level	Description
`RPC_C_IMP_LEVEL_ANONYMOUS`	(Not currently supported) The client is anonymous to the server – the server can't even find out who the client is.
`RPC_C_IMP_LEVEL_IDENTIFY`	The server can find out who the client is, and can impersonate the client for **access control list** checking, but it can't access system objects as if it were the client
`RPC_C_IMP_LEVEL_IMPERSONATE`	The server can impersonate the client completely locally and can access system objects as if it were the client.
`RPC_C_IMP_LEVEL_DELEGATE`	(NT5 only) The server can impersonate the client locally; it can also make outgoing calls to other servers on behalf of the client.

So that really covers everything that the server can do as far as security is concerned. It can find out who's calling, under what blanket arrangements, and then decide whether or not to impersonate them up to the permitted level.

What about the client?

The Client

First of all, the client has to get hold of the ubiquitous security blanket. It does this by querying for **`IClientSecurity`** on the interface that it's using for the DCOM call. (Again, you will never have to implement this interface yourself, it is provided by the system as part of a proxy object used in marshaling an interface.)

What can it do then? Well, here are the methods available to it:

Method	Parameters	Description

`QueryBlanket`	`[in] void* pProxy,`
	`[out] DWORD* pAuthnSvc,`
	`[out] DWORD* pAuthzSvc,`
	`[out] OLECHAR** pServerPrincName,`
	`[out] DWORD* pAuthnLevel,`
	`[out] DWORD* pImpLevel,`
	`[out] RPC_AUTH_IDENTITY_HANDLE** ppAuthInfo,`
	`[out] DWORD** pCapabilities`
		This method finds out the details of the current security blanket.

`SetBlanket`	`[in] void* pProxy,`
	`[in] DWORD dwAuthnSvc,`
	`[in] DWORD dwAuthzSvc,`
	`[in] WCHAR* pServerPrincName,`
	`[in] DWORD dwAuthnLevel,`
	`[in] DWORD dwImpLevel,`
	`[in] RPC_AUTH_IDENTITY_HANDLE* pAuthInfo,`
	`[in] DWORD dwCapabilities`
		This method changes the blanket for the current DCOM proxy – it does this for every user of the interface in this apartment

`CopyProxy`	`[in] IUnknown* punkProxy,` `[out] IUnknown** ppunkCopy`	This makes a local copy of the proxy, so that the client can call SetBlanket without affecting other users

So this is all about changing the security blanket (maybe for a warmer one). Why would a client want to do this? Perhaps the client would be particularly keen to raise the level of authentication during a secure credit card transaction. Note that the call to **`SetBlanket`** changes the blanket for all users of that DCOM proxy in an apartment. If you don't want to affect all code that uses this proxy, you should make a local copy of the proxy first, using **`CopyProxy`**.

Anyway, that's about it for the client. So you see, there isn't much to DCOM security... Let's try it out. First of all, we need to configure DCOM correctly.

DCOM Configuration

We've come across **`DCOMCnfg`** before, of course, but so far in this book we've steered clear of all the tabs except the ones marked Location and Identity. It's time now to look at the others.

The first thing to point out about **`DCOMCnfg`** is one which is actually very easy to miss at first, but which is very, very important if we are to make any headway in understanding how to use it.

> ***`DCOMCnfg`*** *is actually two separate programs rolled into one. There is a* client ***`DCOMCnfg`*** *and a* server ***`DCOMCnfg`****.*

Once you realize this, lots of things start to make sense. The client part of **`DCOMCnfg`** purely handles the problem of finding the server. The server part handles all the security issues. A further confusion arises from the fact that some parts of it aren't implemented at all yet. I'll highlight these as we go on.

There's a nice easy way of demonstrating this in action, and we're going to try it out now. In fact, just one simple client and server pair will show us almost everything we need to know about NTLM-style security.

> **In the worked example that follows, both client and server are Windows NT4 machines. NTLM security behaves slightly differently when Windows 95 clients are involved, and I'll highlight the differences as we go along.**

Let's kick off with the server.

If we want to investigate how the server handles security, the neatest way to do it is write a component that we can interrogate to tell us what it knows about the security blanket. This object is in an EXE server called **`SecQuery`**. We'll call the component **`QuerySecurity`**, and give it a single **`dual`** interface **`IQuerySecurity`**.

This interface has two read-only properties:

Property	**Type**	**Description**
`Privs`	**`BSTR`**	String identifying client
`AuthnLevel`	**`BSTR`**	Authorization level

Note that we don't bother returning the impersonation level: this is because the parameter that would return this is currently unsupported by **`IServerSecurity::QueryBlanket()`**.

Here's the code for our component:

```
// QuerySecurity.cpp : Implementation of CQuerySecurity
#include "stdafx.h"
#include "SecQuery.h"
#include "QuerySecurity.h"

/////////////////////////////////////////////////////////////////////////////
// CQuerySecurity

STDMETHODIMP CQuerySecurity::get_Privs(BSTR* pVal)
{
    // Get hold of the current security context
    CComPtr<IServerSecurity> pSecurity;
    HRESULT hr = CoGetCallContext(IID_IServerSecurity,

    reinterpret_cast<void**>(&pSecurity));
    if (FAILED(hr))
        return hr;

    // Query the security blanket for the string identifying the client
    LPWSTR pPrivs;
    hr = pSecurity->QueryBlanket(NULL, NULL, NULL, NULL, NULL,
                        reinterpret_cast<void**>(&pPrivs), NULL);
    if (FAILED(hr))
        return hr;

    // Return string to caller
    *pVal = SysAllocString(pPrivs);

    // Free the string returned from QueryBlanket()
    CoTaskMemFree(pPrivs);

    return S_OK;
}

STDMETHODIMP CQuerySecurity::get_AuthnLevel(BSTR* pVal)
{
    // Get hold of the current security context
    CComPtr<IServerSecurity> pSecurity;
    HRESULT hr = CoGetCallContext(IID_IServerSecurity,

    reinterpret_cast<void**>(&pSecurity));
    if (FAILED(hr))
        return hr;
```

```
    // Query the security blanket for the authentication level
    DWORD dwAuthnLevel;
    hr = pSecurity->QueryBlanket(NULL, NULL, NULL, &dwAuthnLevel, NULL,
                                              NULL, NULL);
    if (FAILED(hr))
          return hr;

    // Return string representing level to caller
    switch (dwAuthnLevel)
    {
          case RPC_C_AUTHN_LEVEL_NONE:
                *pVal = SysAllocString(L"None");
                break;
          case RPC_C_AUTHN_LEVEL_CONNECT:
                *pVal = SysAllocString(L"Connect");
                break;
          case RPC_C_AUTHN_LEVEL_CALL:
                *pVal = SysAllocString(L"Call");
                break;
          case RPC_C_AUTHN_LEVEL_PKT:
                *pVal = SysAllocString(L"Packet");
                break;
          case RPC_C_AUTHN_LEVEL_PKT_INTEGRITY:
                *pVal = SysAllocString(L"Packet Integrity");
                break;
          case RPC_C_AUTHN_LEVEL_PKT_PRIVACY:
                *pVal = SysAllocString(L"Packet Privacy");
                break;
          default:
                *pVal = SysAllocString(L"Unknown");
                break;
    }

    return S_OK;
}
```

Let's try this out with a simple Visual Basic client application for starters. This is what our form looks like:

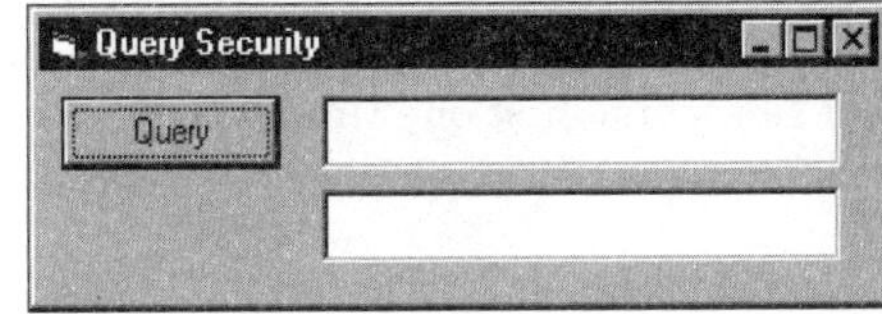

And here's the code:

```
Private Sub cmdQuery_Click()

   Dim qs As QuerySecurity
   Set qs = New QuerySecurity

   txtPrivs.Text = qs.Privs
   txtAuthnLevel.Text = qs.AuthnLevel

End Sub
```

This should provide no problems running locally, but to get a real feel for security we will want to run the object on another machine. So let's copy the server there, and register it in the usual manner by running it with the /RegServer switch. (Note that you'll be using `DCOMCnfg` lots on the server, so log in as Administrator.)

Back on the client machine, off we go to the Location tab of `DCOMCnfg` (you have to be logged on as Administrator to run this):

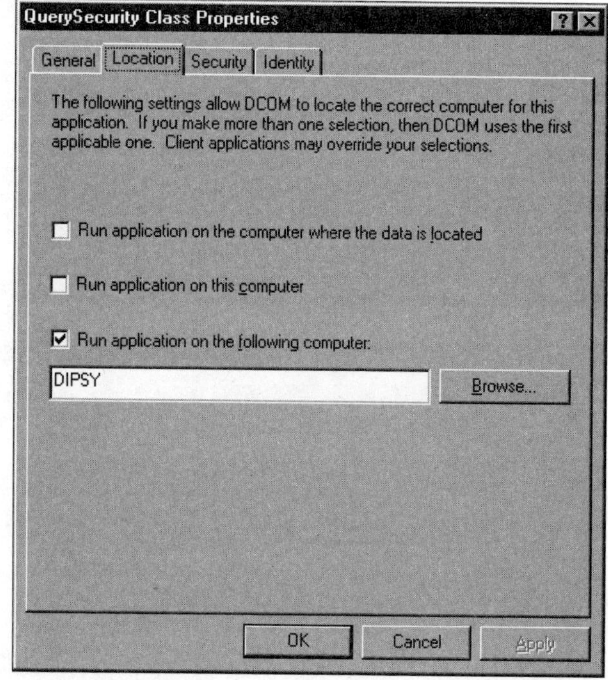

and there's nothing particularly unusual in that. Don't touch anything else: that's *server* stuff.

So let's go to the server. Again, let's assume that we've got our component set up to run locally. This time, when we go into `DCOMCnfg`, we stay clear of the Location tab altogether, because that's *client* stuff. (By the way, you might imagine that you could configure a component on a server to run on a second server so that the first one simply acted as a transparent gateway. Dream on, DCOM ain't that simple – it's there to cut down on network traffic.)

Before we try anything else, let's run our application on the client machine. Log on as yourself and, assuming that your account isn't an administrator, you should see one of these:

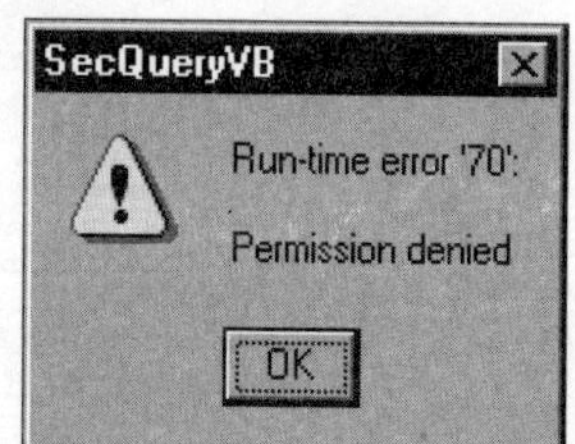

So far, so good. Security is working just fine.

Let's add our user to the list of those permitted to launch the component. We do this in the Security tab of the **`QuerySecurity`** entry on the **`DCOMCnfg`** on the server:

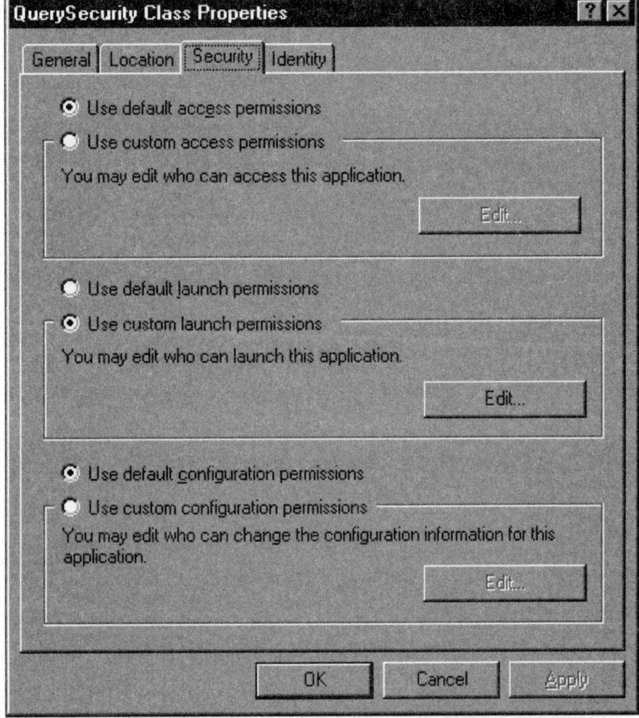

Click on Edit...:

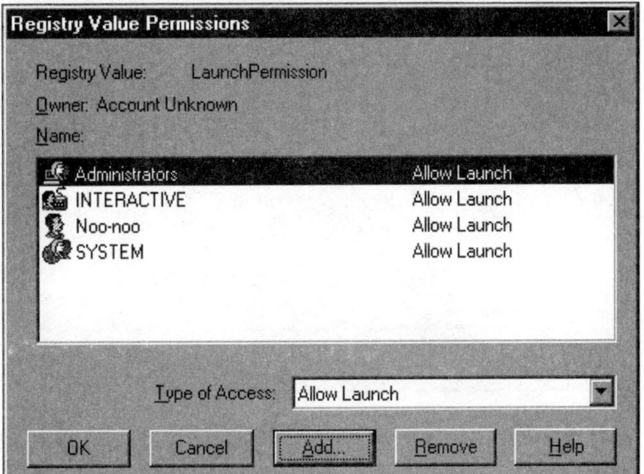

Our user (Noo-noo) is now enabled to launch `QuerySecurity()`, however, to be able to ask it to do something you must also give it *access permissions* too. Once you have allowed Noo-noo to have access to the `QuerySecurity` *server*, let's try running our client again. This is what happens this time:

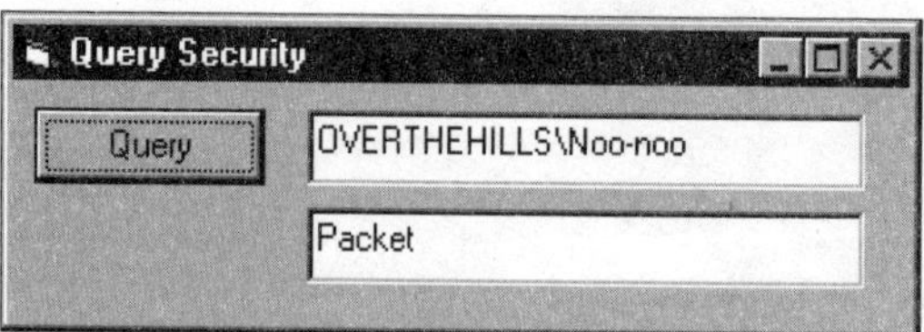

Now there's something a little curious going on here: the default authentication level specified for DCOM is Connect, not Packet. Let's have a play with this. We can change the setting by means of the Default Properties tab in `DCOMCnfg` on the server:

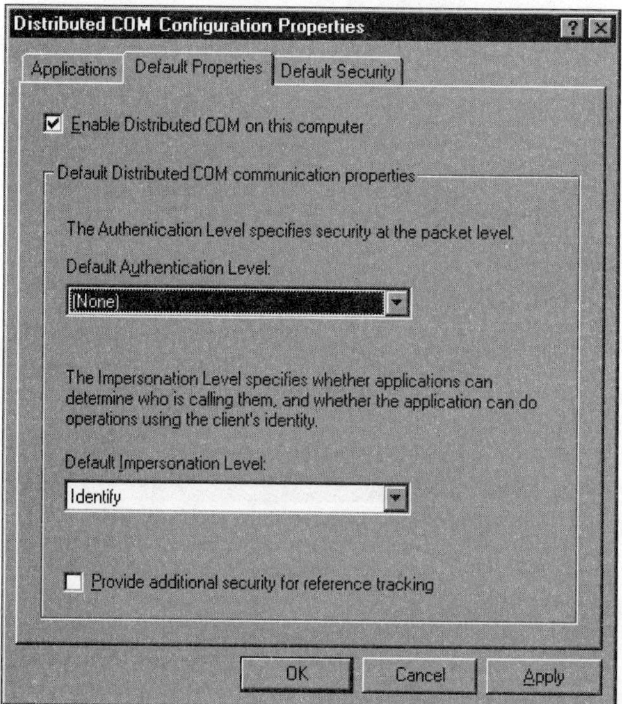

If we try setting the level to (None), Call, Connect or Default, then, as far as the blanket is concerned, it's Packet. However, if we try Packet Integrity this happens:

Similarly, if we were to change the setting to Packet Privacy, the blanket would get changed as well.

What do these authentication levels mean anyway? Here's the full list:

Authentication level	Description
`RPC_C_AUTHN_LEVEL_NONE`	No authentication
`RPC_C_AUTHN_LEVEL_CONNECT`	Authenticates only when client establishes a relationship with the server
`RPC_C_AUTHN_LEVEL_CALL`	Authenticates only at the beginning of each remote procedure call
`RPC_C_AUTHN_LEVEL_PKT`	Authenticates every packet
`RPC_C_AUTHN_LEVEL_PKT_INTEGRITY`	Authenticates every packet, and verifies that none of the data has been modified
`RPC_C_AUTHN_LEVEL_PKT_PRIVACY`	Authenticates every packet, verifies that none of the data has been modified, and encrypts the argument values in each remote procedure call

So what we're seeing is that standard DCOM doesn't have any truck with anything below authentication of *every* packet. Which is the least we'd expect, really.

This is one area where Windows 95 security differs from NT. Because Windows 95 can only use TCP as its underlying protocol, DCOM will accept lower levels of authentication from a Windows 95 client. Once you've got two TCP sockets safely hooked up to each other, packet-level authentication won't usually add much more value. The packet-level default for NT-NT communication reflects the use of a connectionless protocol, UDP.

We've seen how we can use `DCOMCnfg` on the server to alter the settings of the security blanket. However, what can we do at the client end?

Negotiating the Security Blanket

To look into this further, we'll need another program. I've designed this around a simple MFC dialog, and basically the idea is this. There are two functions available: `Query()` and `Set()`. The `Query()` function is similar to our VB client, except that as well as querying the server view of the security blanket, it queries the local proxy as well. The `Set()` function actually sets the security blanket to our specification before doing the querying.

Here is the dialog:

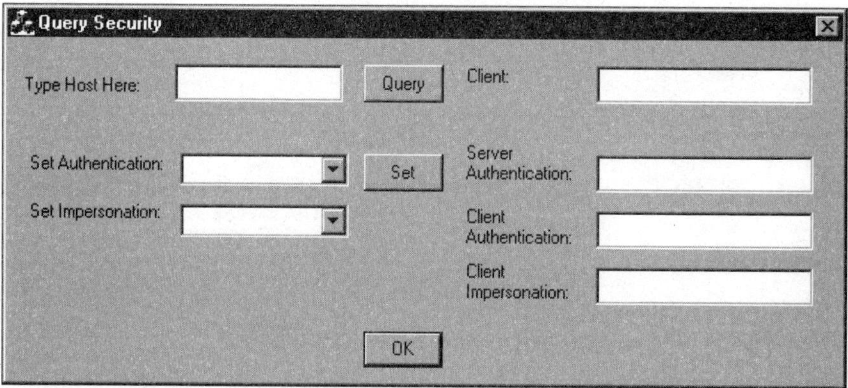

Here's the code to handle the query function. We start off by creating an instance of the **QuerySecurity** component:

```
void CSecClientExDlg::OnQuery()
{
    // Declare _bstr_t variable just for ANSI to Unicode conversion
    // The server name is set by the user
    _bstr_t bstrName(GetDlgItemBSTR(IDC_HOST));

    // Initialize the COSERVERINFO to zero and set the server name
    COSERVERINFO serverInfo = {0};
    serverInfo.pwszName =  bstrName;

    // Set the MULTI_QI structure to query for IQuerySecurity
    MULTI_QI qis[1] = {0};
    qis[0].pIID = &IID_IQuerySecurity;

    HRESULT hr = CoCreateInstanceEx(CLSID_QuerySecurity, NULL,
                    CLSCTX_REMOTE_SERVER, &serverInfo, 1, qis);
    if (FAILED (hr))
    {
        DisplayComError(_T("Failed to create instance"), hr);
        return;
    }

    // Construct a smart pointer based on returned interface
    // without a call to AddRef()
    IQuerySecurityPtr pQuery(static_cast<IQuerySecurity*>(qis[0].pItf),
                                                                false);

    DisplayQuerySecurityProperties(pQuery);
```

```
        // Get the IClientSecurity interface from the QuerySecurity object
        IClientSecurityPtr pSecurity;
        hr = pQuery->QueryInterface(IID_IClientSecurity,
                   reinterpret_cast<void**>(&pSecurity));
        if (FAILED (hr))
        {
              DisplayComError(_T("Failed to QI for IClientSecurity"), hr);
              return;
        }

        DisplayClientSecurityProperties(pSecurity, pQuery);
  }
```

As a recap, the smart pointer definition for **IQuerySecurityPtr** follows (**IClientSecurityPtr** is already defined in **comdef.h**):

```
  // SecClientExDlg.h : header file
  //

  ...

  #include <comdef.h>
  #define SMARTPTR_TYPEDEF(x) \
        typedef _com_ptr_t<_com_IIID<x, &IID_##x> > x##Ptr;

  #include "..\SecQuery\SecQuery.h"
  SMARTPTR_TYPEDEF(IQuerySecurity);
```

We get the server view of the blanket, using the helper function **DisplayQuerySecurityProperties()**:

```
  void CSecClientExDlg::DisplayQuerySecurityProperties(IQuerySecurityPtr& pQuery)
  {
        // Get the Privs property and display it to the user
        BSTR bstrPrivs;
        pQuery->get_Privs(&bstrPrivs);
        CString csPrivs = bstrPrivs;
        SysFreeString(bstrPrivs);
        SetDlgItemText(IDC_PRIVS, csPrivs);

        // Get the AuthnLevel property and display it to the user
        BSTR bstrAuthnLevel;
        pQuery->get_AuthnLevel(&bstrAuthnLevel);
        CString csAuthnLevel = bstrAuthnLevel;
        SysFreeString(bstrAuthnLevel);
        SetDlgItemText(IDC_AUTHN_OUT, csAuthnLevel);
  }
```

The client view comes through **DisplayClientSecurityProperties()**:

```
HRESULT CSecClientExDlg::DisplayClientSecurityProperties(IClientSecurityPtr&
pSecurity, IUnknown* pProxy)
{
      // Get current authentication and impersonation levels from blanket
      DWORD dwAuthnLevel;
      DWORD dwImpLevel;
      HRESULT hr = pSecurity->QueryBlanket(pProxy, NULL, NULL, NULL,
                              &dwAuthnLevel, &dwImpLevel, NULL, NULL);
      if (FAILED(hr))
      {
            DisplayComError(_T("Failed to query blanket"), hr);
            return hr;
      }

      // Output authentication level
      switch (dwAuthnLevel)
      {
            case RPC_C_AUTHN_LEVEL_NONE:
                  SetDlgItemText(IDC_AUTHN_CLIENT, _T("None"));
                  break;
            case RPC_C_AUTHN_LEVEL_CONNECT:
                  SetDlgItemText(IDC_AUTHN_CLIENT, _T("Connect"));
                  break;
            case RPC_C_AUTHN_LEVEL_CALL:
                  SetDlgItemText(IDC_AUTHN_CLIENT, _T("Call"));
                  break;
            case RPC_C_AUTHN_LEVEL_PKT:
                  SetDlgItemText(IDC_AUTHN_CLIENT, _T("Packet"));
                  break;
            case RPC_C_AUTHN_LEVEL_PKT_INTEGRITY:
                  SetDlgItemText(IDC_AUTHN_CLIENT, _T("Packet Integrity"));
                  break;
            case RPC_C_AUTHN_LEVEL_PKT_PRIVACY:
                  SetDlgItemText(IDC_AUTHN_CLIENT, _T("Packet Privacy"));
                  break;
            default:
                  SetDlgItemText(IDC_AUTHN_CLIENT, _T("Unknown"));
                  break;
      }
      // Output impersonation level
      switch (dwImpLevel)
      {
            case RPC_C_IMP_LEVEL_ANONYMOUS:
                  SetDlgItemText(IDC_IMP_CLIENT, _T("Anonymous"));
                  break;
            case RPC_C_IMP_LEVEL_IDENTIFY:
                  SetDlgItemText(IDC_IMP_CLIENT, _T("Identify"));
                  break;
            case RPC_C_IMP_LEVEL_IMPERSONATE:
                  SetDlgItemText(IDC_IMP_CLIENT, _T("Impersonate"));
                  break;
```

```
        case RPC_C_IMP_LEVEL_DELEGATE:
            SetDlgItemText(IDC_IMP_CLIENT, _T("Delegate"));
            break;
        default:
            SetDlgItemText(IDC_IMP_CLIENT, _T("Unknown"));
            break;
    }

    return hr;
}
```

The code for the **Set()** function is similar, except that this time, instead of querying the security blanket, we set it to the specified levels:

```
void CSecClientExDlg::OnSet()
{
    // Declare _bstr_t variable just for ANSI to Unicode conversion
    // The server name is set by the user
    _bstr_t bstrName(GetDlgItemBSTR(IDC_HOST));

    // Initialize the COSERVERINFO to zero and set the server name
    COSERVERINFO serverInfo = {0};
    serverInfo.pwszName =  bstrName;

    // Set the MULTI_QI structure to query for IQuerySecurity
    MULTI_QI qis[1] = {0};
    qis[0].pIID = &IID_IQuerySecurity;

    HRESULT hr = CoCreateInstanceEx(CLSID_QuerySecurity, NULL,
                    CLSCTX_REMOTE_SERVER, &serverInfo, 1, qis);
    if (FAILED(hr))
    {
        DisplayComError(_T("Failed to create instance"), hr);
        return;
    }

    // Construct a smart pointer based on returned interface
    // without a call to AddRef()
    IQuerySecurityPtr pQuery(static_cast<IQuerySecurity*>(qis[0].pItf), false);
    // Get the IClientSecurity interface from the QuerySecurity object
    IClientSecurityPtr pSecurity;
    hr = pQuery->QueryInterface(IID_IClientSecurity,
                   reinterpret_cast<void**>(&pSecurity));
    if (FAILED (hr))
    {
        DisplayComError(_T("Failed to QI for IClientSecurity"), hr);
        return;
    }
```

```
    // Get new client security settings from user
    CString csAuthn;
    GetDlgItemText(IDC_AUTHN_IN, csAuthn);

    CString csImp;
    GetDlgItemText(IDC_IMP_IN, csImp);

    // Convert settings to DWORDs
    DWORD dwAuthnLevel;
    DWORD dwImpLevel;

    if (csAuthn == _T("None"))
          dwAuthnLevel = RPC_C_AUTHN_LEVEL_NONE;
    else if (csAuthn == _T("Connect"))
          dwAuthnLevel = RPC_C_AUTHN_LEVEL_CONNECT;
    else if (csAuthn == _T("Call"))
          dwAuthnLevel = RPC_C_AUTHN_LEVEL_CALL;
    else if (csAuthn == _T("Packet"))
          dwAuthnLevel = RPC_C_AUTHN_LEVEL_PKT;
    else if (csAuthn == _T("Packet Integrity"))
          dwAuthnLevel = RPC_C_AUTHN_LEVEL_PKT_INTEGRITY;
    else if (csAuthn == _T("Packet Privacy"))
          dwAuthnLevel = RPC_C_AUTHN_LEVEL_PKT_PRIVACY;

    if (csImp == _T("Anonymous"))
          dwImpLevel = RPC_C_IMP_LEVEL_ANONYMOUS;
    else if (csImp == _T("Identify"))
          dwImpLevel = RPC_C_IMP_LEVEL_IDENTIFY;
    else if (csImp == _T("Impersonate"))
          dwImpLevel = RPC_C_IMP_LEVEL_IMPERSONATE;
    else if (csImp == _T("Delegate"))
          dwImpLevel = RPC_C_IMP_LEVEL_DELEGATE;

    // Set security blanket to required levels
    hr = pSecurity->SetBlanket(pQuery, RPC_C_AUTHN_WINNT, RPC_C_AUTHZ_NONE,
                               NULL, dwAuthnLevel, dwImpLevel, NULL, NULL);

    if (FAILED(hr))
    {
          DisplayComError(_T("Failed to set blanket"), hr);
          return;
    }
    // Now get the settings again to see what really happened
    DisplayQuerySecurityProperties(pQuery);
    DisplayClientSecurityProperties(pSecurity, pQuery);
}
```

In the last two lines of the project, we carry out another query.

Let's see this in action. First of all, let's issue a query, taking over from where we left off with our Visual Basic client (authentication level set to Packet Integrity at the server):

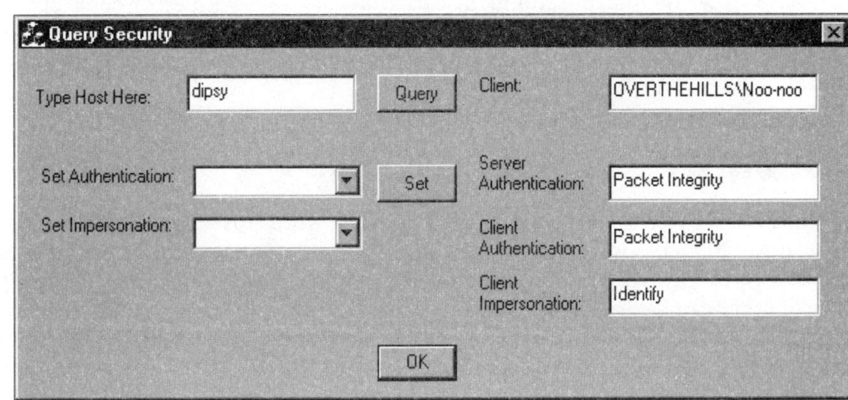

Which is pretty much what we would expect – it's at least reassuring to know that the proxy on the client shares the same view of the security blanket as the server!

Now, before we try setting the security blanket, let's try something else. Let's go into **`DCOMCnfg`** on the server again and try setting the impersonation level, say to Impersonate. What happens is that the client security blanket reports that nothing has changed, and that it's still set to Identify as far as the client is concerned. What does this mean? What it means is that the selection of impersonation level is entirely up to the client, and the server really doesn't have anything to do with it – and why should it? It's up to the client to decide! (So why is there that combo box in **`DCOMCnfg`**? It's there to specify the default impersonation level used by clients if they don't explicitly set an impersonation level.)

OK, we're ready to try changing the security blanket. Let's go for Packet Privacy authentication and Impersonate impersonation level. So we're asking to raise the authentication up to RPC argument value encryption level, and we're asking the server to impersonate us as far as it can.

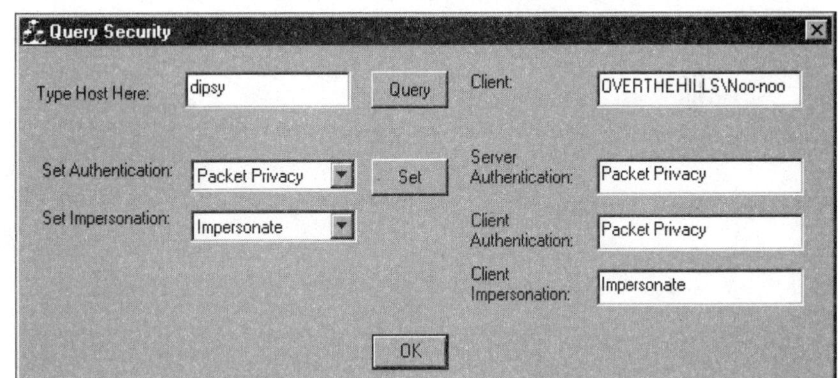

And so it goes. The only mildly unusual thing that happens is when we try to set the authentication level to None. If we do this, the call to **SetBlanket()** fails with error code 800706d2, which means The binding does not contain any authentication information . Well, I knew that – but the point is that DCOM requires at least *some* level of authentication to work. You can't cut it out altogether.

MTS Security

Before we leave DCOM security, I'd just like to say a word or two about Microsoft Transaction Server security. MTS has introduced a new level of subtlety into security, with the addition of the concept of a **rôle**. Any MTS package can have a number of different rôles defined for it, and any user or group of users can be assigned to a given rôle. Within your component, you can find out from the object context which rôle your current user is in, and change your behavior accordingly. Let's take a quick look at how this works out in practice.

The easiest thing to do is take our transactional Kidnap Game server from Chapter 5, **TransNegotiator**, and add some security support to it. Let's define two possible rôles for our component: **Negotiator** and **Super negotiator**. A super negotiator is authorized to offer whatever he or she feels is appropriate in order to secure the release of our hostage, whereas an ordinary negotiator is only permitted to offer up to $100000. To add a rôle to the **TransNegotiator** package, right click on the Roles folder and click New -> Role.

What changes do we need to make to our code to support this? This is what we do. In our **DealWithKidnappers** method, we need to add the following code near the start:

```
STDMETHODIMP CNegotiator::DealWithKidnappers(int amount, VARIANT_BOOL*
pbFree)
{
   GetObjectContext(&m_spObjectContext);

   // If security not enabled, bomb out
   if (!m_spObjectContext->IsSecurityEnabled ())
      return E_FAIL;

   // If super negotiator, let through unconditionally
   BOOL fPermitted = FALSE;

   HRESULT hResult = m_spObjectContext->IsCallerInRole
                        (L"Super negotiator", &fPermitted);

   if (FAILED (hResult))
      return hResult;

   if (!fPermitted)
   {
      // If ordinary negotiator, check amount against permitted level
      hResult = m_spObjectContext->IsCallerInRole (L"Negotiator",
                                                         &fPermitted);
```

```
        if (FAILED (hResult))
           return hResult;

        if (fPermitted && (amount > 100000))
           fPermitted = FALSE;
     }

     if (!fPermitted)
        return E_FAIL;

     VARIANT_BOOL bCashThere = VARIANT_FALSE;

     HRESULT hResult = TakeCashFromAccount(amount, pbFree);
     if (FAILED (hResult))
     {
        m_spObjectContext->SetAbort();
        return hResult;
     }

     bCashThere = *pbFree;          // Was the cash there?

     hResult = ReleaseHostage(amount, pbFree);
     if (FAILED (hResult))
     {
        m_spObjectContext->SetAbort();
        return hResult;
     }

     if ((*pbFree == VARIANT_TRUE) && (bCashThere == VARIANT_TRUE))
     {
        *pbFree = VARIANT_TRUE;     // Return true to base client
        m_spObjectContext->SetComplete();
     }
     else
     {
        *pbFree = VARIANT_FALSE;    // Return false to base client
        m_spObjectContext->SetAbort();
     }

     return S_OK;
  }
```

In the highlighted code, our first step is to establish whether or not MTS security is actually operational – that is, whether the object is running in the server process or not. Next, we check to see if our user is a super negotiator – if he or she is, we let them through. If not, we check for the combination of ordinary negotiator and an amount less than the threshold. And that's about it. Build this new DLL and replace the objects in the **`TransNegotiator`** package.

But hold on a minute – how do we configure the user as a Negotiator or Super negotiator? In MTS Explorer, expand your Roles folder and the two roles you've defined, and you'll see you can add Users to each role:

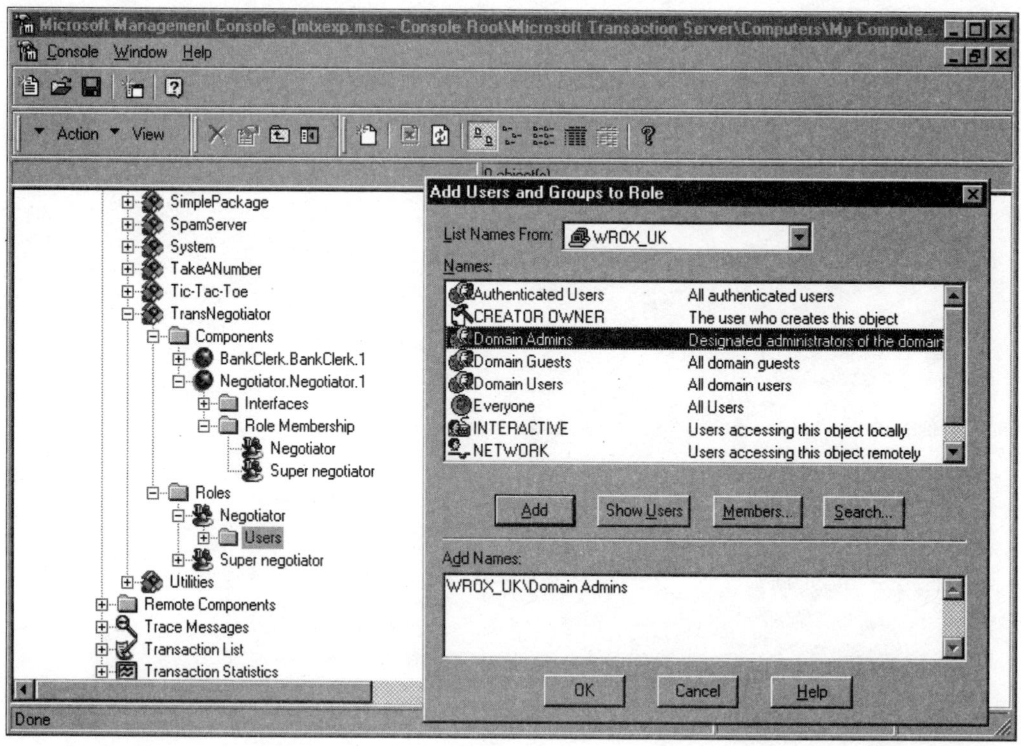

> *If we really wanted, there is another MTS interface,* **`ISecurityProperty`***, which gives us access to the real nitty-gritty security information in the lower levels of NTLM. I'm not going to cover any of that here, but if you're interested, I refer you to both Chapter 7 and Chapter 10 of Richard Grimes'* Professional DCOM *book.*

That's about it for our tour of NT4 DCOM and MTS security. I've tried to keep it very much focused on what you can do purely from the DCOM and MTS point of view. Which isn't, as you will have seen, all that much.

Security in NT is just beginning to get a whole load more interesting, however, and the rest of this chapter looks at the developments that are just beginning to emerge at the time of writing.

Cryptography for Beginners

Once we begin to dig into things like authentication and encryption, we can't go far without running into security keys. So, before we go any further, here's a quick introduction. I'll assume nothing, so apologies if this goes a little slowly. I will, however, spare you any of the mathematics involved. It's all fascinating stuff, but it isn't really relevant to the discussion in hand. You'll have to trust me that it works.

Secret Keys

Security keys are the basis of encryption. The idea is that – like the 007 code sets that we played with as kids – you apply a transformation one way to your message to make it unreadable to untrusted third parties. The transformation uses some mathematical technique, parameterised by a key. To go back to our kids' coding set, our transformation technology might be the one where you write down a magic word underneath the first few letters of the alphabet, and then fill in the ones left after it. The magic word is our key. For instance, if we used the word "CARIBOU" as our key, we'd end up with something like this:

A	B	C	D	E	F	G	H	I	J	K	L	M
C	A	R	I	B	O	U	D	E	F	G	H	J

N	O	P	Q	R	S	T	U	V	W	X	Y	Z
K	L	M	N	P	Q	S	T	V	W	X	Y	Z

To encrypt a message, we just read off the equivalent letter from the bottom row. To decrypt it, we do the exact opposite. Dlw calts sdcs, sdbk? (And my spell-checker's just thrown in the towel...)

Once you've encrypted your message using the key, you send it to your intended destination. Your recipient also knows the key, and can decrypt by checking against the table. If we didn't know that the key was CARIBOU, it would take us a while to decode this one. Of course, it wouldn't be that much of a challenge to Alan Turing's bunch at Bletchley Park in World War II, let alone the kind of machines available these days, so our techniques have become somewhat more sophisticated. However, the principles remain the same.

Public and Private Keys

The technique that I've just described is based on a *secret* key. A secret is something that is shared between two or more parties. This is a very useful mechanism to use when both parties are known to each other and are in regular contact. However, if contact is occasional or not pre-planned, we have a problem, because the second party won't necessarily know the first party's secret key.

On the other hand, a *private* key is one that is known to no-one except the owner. On the face of it, this is about as much use as a write-only memory, but when used in combination with a corresponding *public* key, it's an extremely powerful authentication mechanism. How does this work?

Secret keys are a *symmetric* encryption technique. You use exactly the same key to decrypt the message as was used to encrypt it. Public key encryption, however, is *asymmetric.* A pair of keys are mathematically generated, one public and one private. The two are completely different. Each pair is unique, so that one half of one pair can never be used to decrypt a message encoded using half of a totally different pair.

Here's how public key encryption works. Imagine you've got a whole load of strongboxes, each fitted with copies of the same sophisticated lock. There are two keys for this type of lock, one of which (key C) can only close it and one of which (key O) can only open it. You give everyone an open box, plus key C. They take the box, put whatever they want to send to you in it, and lock it with the key. Now no one can open it unless they have key O. And the only person who has key O is *you.*

As an example of this in action, let's imagine that we are running some sort of operation that relies on our clients being assured of confidentiality. Maybe we're operating an enterprise-wide hotline for reporting bullying by senior staff (never happens, I know). How can we assure the poor harassed underlings that what they say can't be intercepted by Big Brother? Well, what we do is publish a public key that the staff can use to encrypt all their lurid tales. We keep the private key to ourselves, so that we are the *only* people who can decrypt them (and a sorry story it makes, I can tell you). More conventionally, you might use this technique to ensure secure e-commerce; this is how your friendly neighborhood e-mall can take your credit card number without the risk of it falling into the wrong hands.

Thinking back to NT for a moment, you can see how this might form part of the security blanket negotiation. A client initiates a connection to a server, and the server offers a default level of authentication – maybe just "Packet integrity". At this point, the client interjects, "Hey! I've got your public key! Let's have a little privacy, shall we?" – and sets the security blanket authentication level to "Packet privacy" with authentication type set to "Public key". The next step might be to use public key encryption to exchange a secret key. Having done that, the two parties could switch to secret key authentication. The advantage of doing this is that secret key authentication carries a much lower computational overhead than public key – public key requires some *serious* mathematics.

Actually, public and private keys are an astonishingly powerful mechanism. Not only can you use them for encryption, but you can also use them for authentication. Here's how.

Digital Signatures

Let's go back to the Anna Anderson/Anastasia Romanov problem, and how it was solved – albeit after her death. The riddle was solved by carrying out DNA analysis: she was just plain Anna Anderson, after all. The thing about DNA is that it's unique (setting aside considerations of identical twins), and it can't be faked. I carry my DNA around with me wherever I go, and if ever I were called upon to prove who I was, I could – in theory – produce a sample. (This isn't quite so far fetched as it sounds. I recently saw an invitation to tender for a *very* secure machine room which – in all seriousness – was suggesting that those responding might like to consider DNA verification as a technique for permitting access. This led to some ribald speculation as to how it might be collected from the males present, as you may imagine.)

My DNA, then, is my body's *signature.* By analysing it, using publicly available techniques, anyone – or at least anyone with a fully equipped lab at their disposal – can verify who I am. However, the only person who can produce any of it is me. Inside every cell of my body, there are the instructions for producing my DNA, but they are entirely private to me. No-one else can steal them and generate someone with the same DNA.

> *Actually, most of the foregoing discussion should probably be prefaced with "at the time of writing". Dolly the sheep would, after all, disagree. Baa!*

So how does this relate to computer authentication?

Well, let's go back to public key encryption, and this time we're going to turn it on its head. This time, we're going to use the *private* key to encrypt our message, and the rest of the world is going to use the *public* key to decrypt it. Don't worry, we're not interested in secrecy here – we're interested in authentication.

What's the point of encrypting our message with our private key? Well, it's because no-one else can. If we send our message in plain text along with our private-key encrypted version of it, the recipient can decrypt our second version and compare it with the first. If the two are identical, then it must have come from us. No-one, but *no-one* else could have generated an encrypted version that could be read with our public key (remember, each pair of keys is unique and inseparable). In actual fact, it's a little bandwidth-intensive to encrypt our entire message to send along with our clear text message, so we'd probably use some kind of **hashing mechanism** instead. (A hash of a message is simply a number constructed from the message by applying a formula to the numeric codes of the letters, so that the chances of two different messages producing the same number is very small.)

If we think in terms of strongboxes again, this time we've a whole load of boxes that only we can lock shut (although everyone else can open). We put a copy of our message in the box, lock it tight and send it along with the original of our message to our destination. The recipient sees that the box has arrived sealed, and so knows that only we could have sent it. They open the box and verify that the two messages are the same.

Incidentally, did you notice something else that we're getting here, for free? Yes, we're getting message *integrity.* If anyone wanted to tamper with the clear text version of the message, they'd have to make the same changes to the encrypted version, and they can't do that without our private key! Equally, if they made some random change to the encrypted version, it won't decrypt properly, and so it won't match the clear text. This is great, because it means that our recipient can be assured that not only does it come from us, but that it looks exactly as we intended it to look.

This process is called digital signing, for obvious reasons. By encrypting our message with a hash based on our private key, we are adding our signature to it in just the same way as we sign that credit card slip. Actually, it's a whole load more secure than that.

OK, this is all fine and dandy when we are dealing with someone that we've dealt with before, and whose public key we've come to know and love. But where do we get that public key from in the first place? Do we write to them and get it through the post? Or can we do it electronically?

Digital Certificates

How can I tell who I am dealing with? OK, I can see their signature, but how do I know that it's *really* their signature if I'm seeing it for the first time?

If you want someone to prove who they are (maybe the man who comes to read the gas meter), you can ask them to show some kind of identification. This will be signed by someone else. If you don't happen to know or trust that person, you can call them up and ask who can vouch for *them.* And so on, all the way up the line until eventually you get to someone who you'll believe. Paranoid? Moi?

Digital certificates work in the same way. A digital certificate is essentially a message digitally signed by a third party to establish that whoever is presenting it is indeed who they say they are. That third party may themselves require certification from a more trusted certificate authority (CA) higher up the chain, until you eventually arrive at a super-CA like the VeriSign Corporation, whose public key is well known.

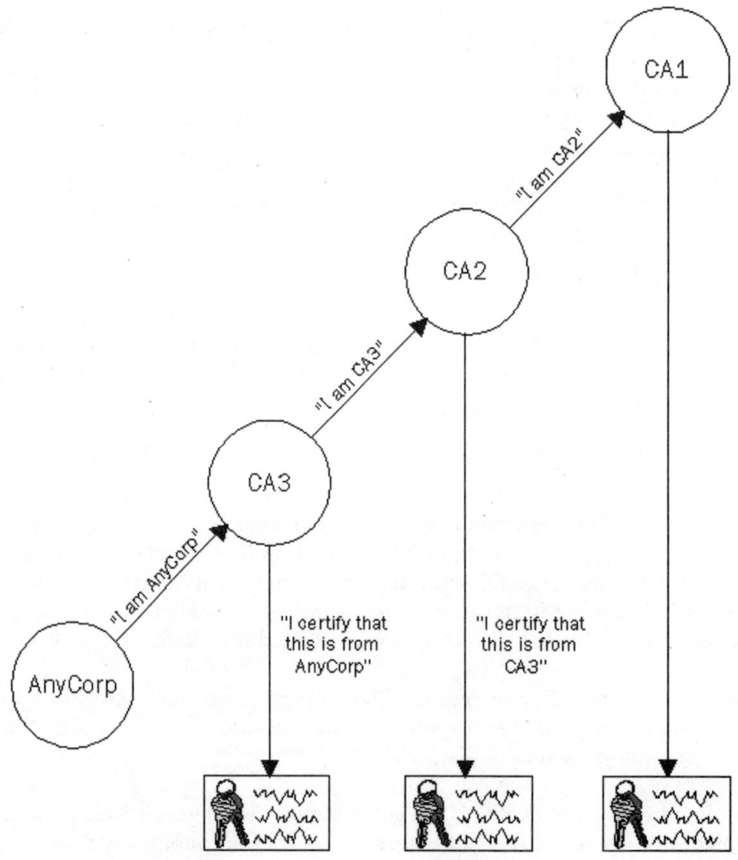

So, we've taken a quick spin around the various technologies involved in advanced security. I hope I've whetted your appetite to read on and find out where they are finding their way into Windows NT.

Certificate Server

Let's start off with something that's available right now: Microsoft Certificate Server. Version 1.0 of this appeared as part of Microsoft Internet Information Server Version 4.0. Certificate Server is Microsoft's system for generating certificates on demand. The neat thing about Microsoft's Certificate Server is that there is – inevitably – an API with it. This permits you to specify policies for granting certificates according to the quality of the initial request. For example, one policy might be to grant certain privileges only if the requester turns up in person. Others might be granted if the enquirer is using a client that is connected via a secure DCOM connection.

What might we use such a certificate for? What would it hold? As we have seen already, the certificate establishes who we are. It might also hold details of what we're allowed to do. Perhaps we'd present our certificate when the client that we're using connects to its COM server. In this case, the certificate would hold highly application-specific permission information. The really cool thing about this is that the permissions are held on the certificate, not in some central database that has to be managed. Our certificate would be like a kind of digital smart card.

You've probably seen digital certificates in use on the Internet. The most frequent manifestation of them is a dialog that looks like, well, a certificate, the one that pops up whenever you access a web page that requires an ActiveX control to be downloaded. The check is triggered by Microsoft's Authenticode technology, which checks the digital certificate bound into the software to be downloaded and pops up a dialog, telling you which certificate authority has authenticated the signature on the code.

However, what the example above shows is that digital certificates aren't restricted to the Internet. They have a place on the enterprise intranet as well.

The Limits of NTLM

Time to meet another member of the menagerie. The vipers, falcons and wolves are about to be joined by a three-headed mythological dog, **Kerberos**. You may recall that Kerberos was the dog that guarded Hades, although this is a slightly confused metaphor. After all, a computer security system is designed to keep the bad guys out. The dog's job was to make sure that the bad guys stayed *in.*

We're definitely well into NT5 territory here. At the time of writing, the Kerberos Security Support Provider is only just beginning to emerge in all its glory in the NT5 beta program. But what is it?

Kerberos Version 5 is a well-established standard authentication service, described in Internet RFC 1510 (dated September 1993). Did I say standard? Well, here's just one more example of Microsoft abandoning its proprietary model when its time is up. As I said back in Chapter 4 when we looked at LDAP, bet on Windows and COM being around for a while yet. But whenever there's a decent non-proprietary standard available, Microsoft will move to that.

But why does NT5 need it to replace NT LAN Manager? What's the problem with it? The key problems are *scaling* and *secure internetworking.*

Let's imagine that we've got a very large global network, some nodes of which are linked to each other by highly secure, highly localized connections and some of which are linked by looser arrangements.

In fact, some parts of the network are in parts of the world where we suspect that they're not too fussy about security anyway, and we'd really rather not have them connected to us at all. Whether this is actually true, or pure prejudice on our part doesn't really matter – security is about perception as much as fact.

How would we set up such a network if we were to use NTLM security?

First of all, we'd carve the world up into **domains**. You've probably come across domains before; in NT networking, you're either part of a **workgroup** or a domain. A workgroup is simply a collection of machines connected by a network; if you want to gain access to another machine, you need access to an account on that machine. This is nice and easy if your current user name and password happen to match an account on the other machine, but generally it's a pain. A domain, on the other hand, has a common authentication policy across all the nodes in the network. User account information is held on a **Primary Domain Controller** (PDC), and, optionally, a **Backup Domain Controller** (BDC). Once you have gained access to one machine in the domain, you can go anywhere you like, subject to the authorizations applied to your account.

So we have a whole series of domains scattered around the world. The next thing we want to do is set up some trust relationships between them, so that users attached to the domain in Tristan da Cunha can access information in London, and vice versa. Of course, the people in London want to share information with Paris, so we set up a trust relationship between those domains as well. Does this mean that Tristan da Cunha can access information from Paris? Well, no. We'd have to set up explicit relationships between those two as well. NTLM domain trust relationships are not **transitive**. There are good reasons for this: the good people of Tristan da Cunha have heard all sorts of rumours about dodgy dealings in the City of London, and the last thing they really want to do is give London carte blanche to pass on access to their domain to anyone they choose. But look at what's happening to our network. As more and more domains are added to it, the whole web of trusts is beginning to look like a cat's cradle. Before long, it's going to be completely unmanageable.

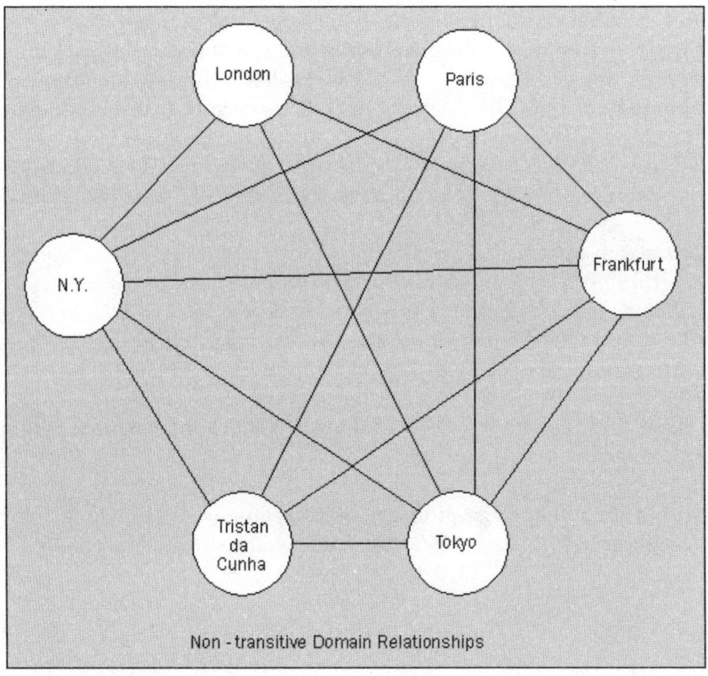

Non -transitive Domain Relationships

We need something that's more secure than this, so that we can feel comfortable in setting up transitive trust relationships. That something is Kerberos.

Beware of the Dog

Kerberos works in a very similar way to the certificates that we saw earlier. However, the Kerberos term for the token that lets you gain access to a part of the network is a **ticket**. Excellent term – so far, so good. Unfortunately, that's the high point, and it isn't too long in the standard explanation of Kerberos before you reach the term TGT, which stands for **ticket-granting ticket**. This is usually the point at which I start to froth at the mouth. So before we launch into Kerberos in any depth, I'd like to walk through a little analogy.

Imagine that we own a company that has somehow managed to acquire several of England's historic monuments. Our principal aim in doing this was, of course, to ensure their continued preservation as national treasures, but we'd actually like to make loads of money out of them as well. We're also very keen on making loads of money without having too many staff to pay, so we've installed an ultra-efficient ticketing system. This is how it works.

First of all, you go along to the ticketing center. This is where you hand over your money in exchange for a rover ticket that allows you to go to any three sites within three days. The whole of this area is devoted to the very simple task of taking your money for one fixed item. Very efficient.

Next, you take this ticket next door to the validation center. This is where you choose which three attractions you're going to visit. There may be complications: for example, one of your chosen sites might be closed for repairs. This area is devoted to sorting all that out, and issuing tickets for the required attractions accordingly. It is completely unsullied by financial exchanges, as payment has already been sorted out.

Finally, you take your ticket along to each site in turn. Your tickets are valid for three days, so you can come and go as you please. Enjoy! (Actually, the weather was terrible, and the kids hated everything apart from the Stonehenge Adventure Playground Experience...)

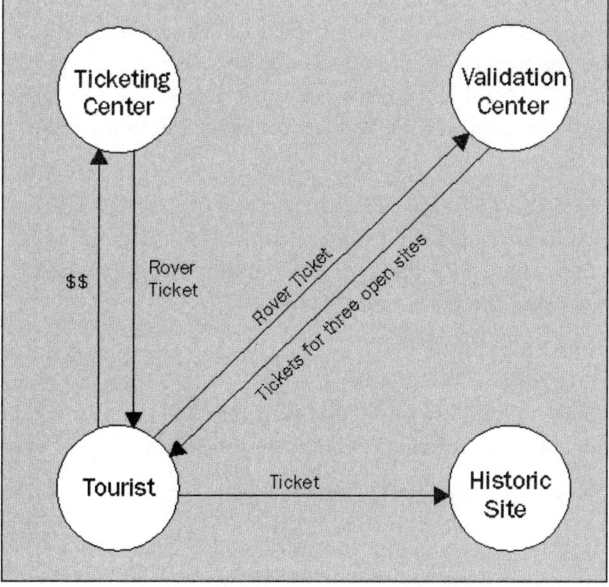

Of course, in Kerberos, it's just a little more complicated, as we've got some serious encryption involved as well. It's all secret key encryption, using the DES standard. (DES, by the way, stands for Data Encryption Standard. What else?) The Kerberos protocol involves at least two servers, the AS (**Authentication Server**), and at least one TGS (**Ticket-Granting Server**). The AS and the TGS can physically be hosted in the same machine. This is, of course, apart from the server machine that the client ultimately requires access to. We'll refer to this as the ultimate server, or US.

Here's what goes on between the client and the various servers:

1. In the first stage of the authentication process, the client goes to the AS and requests a ticket to the local TGS in plain text. This message contains the user name, plus the name of the required TGS. The AS checks that the client's user exists, and then generates a session key to be used between the user and the TGS. It then sends a message back to the client. The first part of the message contains the session key encrypted using the user's secret key (which is known only to the user and the AS). The second part contains a TGT (yup, a ticket-granting ticket), encrypted in the TGS's secret key (which is known only to the TGS and the AS). The TGT contains the session key, plus the user's name and address.

2. We've finished with the AS now. Next, the client decrypts the first part of the message and retrieves the session key. It then constructs an authenticator consisting of the user's name and address, plus a timestamp. This is encrypted with the session key. It then sends a message to the TGS consisting of the TGT plus the authenticator and the name of the US. Remember that the TGT was encrypted with the TGS's secret key, and the authenticator is encrypted using the session key.

3. The TGS decrypts the first part of the message using its secret key, and gets the TGT. From the TGT, it extracts the session key. Great! The client and the TGS both know their session key now. Let's talk. The TGS extracts the authenticator from the second half of the message and decrypts it using the session key. It compares the user name and address with that found in the TGT and the timestamp with the current time. If everything matches, it generates a new session key for use between the client and the US (and if you're beginning to get a sense of déjà vu, good). The TGS then sends a message back to the client. The first part of the message is the new session key, encrypted in the old session key. The second part is the ticket for the US, encrypted in the US's secret key (which is known only to the US and the TGS). The ticket contains the usual stuff (the user's name and address and timestamp), plus an expiry time for the ticket.

4. OK, we've finished with the TGS now. The client decrypts the new session key from the first message, and uses that to encrypt a new authenticator. It extracts the ticket from the second message, and sends that, along with the encrypted authenticator, to the US. (Remember that the ticket is encrypted using the US's secret key.)

5. The US decrypts the first part of the message using its secret key, and extracts the ticket. From the ticket, it extracts the session key (getting a really strong feeling of déjà vu now ...). So now the client and the US are talking the same language. The US extracts the authenticator from the second half of the message and decrypts it using the session key. If everything matches, we're off!

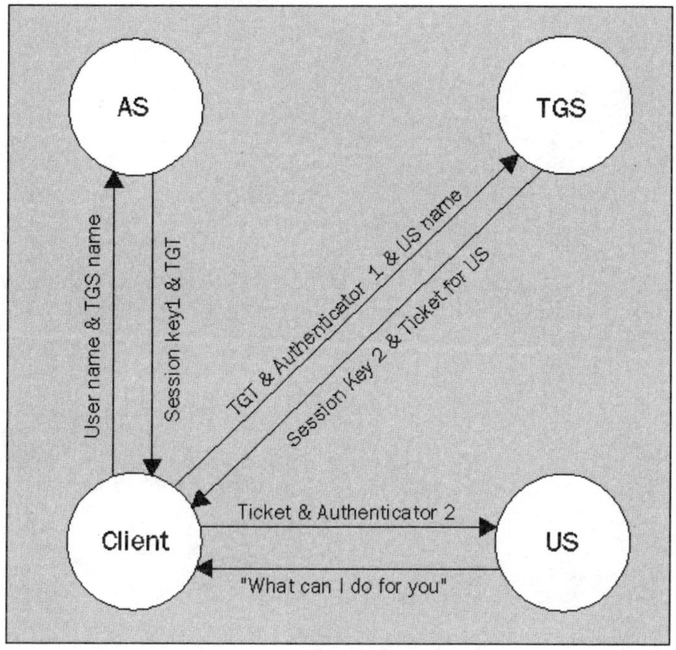

What Else?

Security features are creeping into NT elsewhere as well. For example, NT5 is featuring an encrypted file system, or EFS. This NT5 feature uses public key encryption to ensure that files can only be accessed through the NT file system. The files are encrypted using the public key, but only NT can decrypt them, on behalf of authorized users. If I steal the server, trash the operating system and attempt to recover the files from the raw data, I'll fail miserably because I don't have the private key.

Security is one enormous subject, and I've only given you a flavour of some of the developments that are under way. I hardly need to add that it's very important to understand, and it's getting more important with every new feature that gets added.

Next, we're going to move on from securing our system to managing, monitoring and controlling it.

10

Management, Monitoring and Control

'I don't hear any music,' said Milo.
'That's right,' said Alec; 'you don't listen to this concert –
you watch it. Now, pay attention.'
As the conductor waved his arms, he moulded the air like handfuls of soft clay,
and the musicians carefully followed his every direction.
'What are they playing?' asked Tock, looking up inquisitively at Alec.
'The sunset, of course. They play it every evening, about this time.'

"The Phantom Tollbooth" (Norton Juster)

How the Other Half Sees Things

Anyone who has spent any time in any enterprise that develops and uses software to any extent will know that there are basically two views of life. There is the *optimistic* view, better known as the *developer's* view. The software is perfect. Nothing will go wrong. The job is complete once the last line of code has been written. Sorry, *tested.* Any optimists out there? Yup. Me too.

Then there is the *pessimistic* view, better known as the *support* view. The software is flawed. Whatever can go wrong will go wrong. Users will do stupid things. The job *starts* once the roll-out begins. I would guess that, given that this is a book for developers, this view is slightly less popular, which is unfortunate, because it's probably the more accurate one. It also tends to be the view held by management in most successful organisations...

So here's a suggestion. If you DCOM gurus out *really* want to impress the management of your enterprise, don't tell them how quick and cheap your software development is going to be. Anyone can develop quick and cheap software. Tell them how cheap your system is going to be to *manage*. Tell them you're going to provide them with the tools to monitor and control your system, so that they aren't going to get beaten up every week by *their* bosses because it has ground to a halt yet again.

Believe me, *this* is the really important stuff.

A Management and Monitoring Framework

So let's think about how we can set up a framework for managing and monitoring our object network. I should point out before we start that there are many different ways of doing this. You'll almost certainly look at my suggestions and say to yourself, "That'd be no use in my system" or "I could do better than that". Great! Do it. The whole point of this exercise is to start you thinking about it. For the first part of this chapter, we're not even going to look at any new technologies. Later on, we're going to have a play with the MMC SDK, so if you're a gadget freak, skip on to there. I'll catch up with you later, OK?

Meanwhile, let's decide what we need to know about our distributed components. Well, I'd like to :

- Have some idea of which components are being invoked on each host.
- Know what errors each components have raised.
- Be able to get some idea of how well they are performing.

Building Our Framework

What, then, do we need to set up our monitoring framework?

The Monitor Service

First of all, we need to have something running on every PC that monitors our components. I suggest that the most appropriate vehicle for this–at least in an NT environment–is a *service*. Apart from the mild novelty value of the fact that we haven't done one yet in this book, it's just right for this sort of requirement. You could make it part of the standard server build in your enterprise.

I think that we can handle all three of our requirements with just three COM interfaces. The first one, `IMonitor`, will be implemented by our monitor service, and invoked by our components. The second one, `IPing`, will be implemented by our components and invoked by the monitor service. The third one, `IObjectList`, will be implemented by the monitor service, and will be invoked by management workstations wishing to get access to the list of known objects. We're actually going to be using DCOM to manage DCOM!

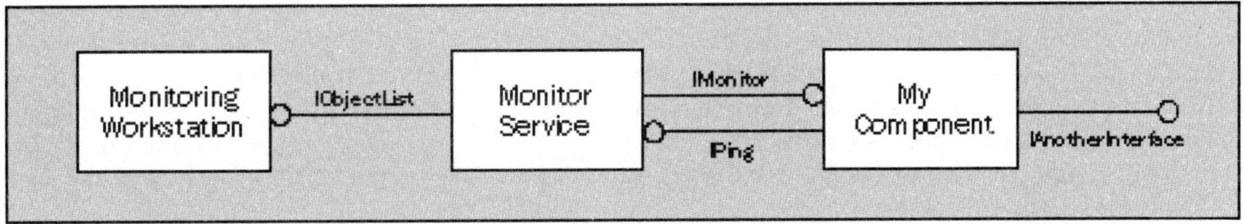

The use of **IMonitor** will handle our first two requirements of knowing which components have been invoked on which host, and what errors they have raised.

The use of **IPing** will handle our last requirement of knowing how well our components are performing.

The Interfaces

Let's make a first cut at defining the **IMonitor** interface:

Method	Parameters	Description
`Connect`	`[in] REFCLSID rclsid,` `[in] BSTR bstrName`	Connect to monitor service

`LogError`	`[in] int severity,`
	`[in] BSTR bstrShort,`
	`[in] BSTR bstrLong`
		Log error condition (with short description and long description)

How are we going to use this? Well, I propose that we create our monitoring component inside the **FinalConstruct()** method of each of our components, and invoke the **Connect()** method to pass in our **CLSID** and name. We'll release our reference in our **FinalRelease()** method. Note that, because I've decided to pass the **CLSID** as a **REFCLSID**, rather than a **BSTR**, **IMonitor** is going to have to be a pure vtable interface. We could if we wanted to, implement a dispatch version as well, in case we have any VB COM objects to monitor.

And here's the **IPing** interface:

Method	Parameters	Description
`Ping`	None	Ping interface for response

Actually, there's even less to it than meets the eye. But we'll come on to that later. I won't define **IObjectList** yet, either, because we won't need it for a while.

Developer Support

We'll also need to make it straightforward for our developers to use `IMonitor` and implement `IPing` (because we don't want to give them any excuses not to!) This basically means providing them with an IDL file that they can import into the ones for their own components, and a corresponding header file. You'll have come across these headers all over the place wherever you've developed something outside the core of COM – we'll meet another pair later on this chapter, in fact, in the shape of `mmc.idl` and `mmc.h`.

The Monitoring Program

Last of all, we'll need the monitoring program itself. This will only run on privileged PCs. It will use the `IObjectList` interface on the monitoring services in each server to find out which components are installed where, and the `IPing` interface to find out the status of each.

Time for some coding. Let's start with the monitoring service.

The Monitoring Service

If you've never implemented a COM object as a service, don't worry. It's a piece of cake. Our project is going to be called `MonitorService`, and as you may have guessed by now, is available for download along with the rest of the code for this chapter in the source code area of the Wrox Press website at `http://www.wrox.com`. When you create the project, and you specify the ATL wizard, you're presented with three options, like this:

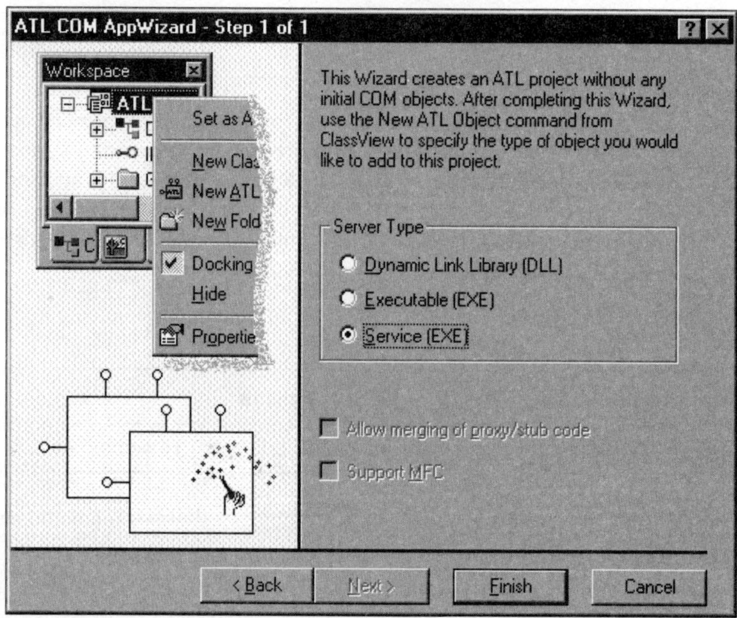

Normally, we're used to selecting one of the first two. This time, we'll take the third option. Then we just sit back and let the wizard do the rest. If you're that way inclined, take a look at the stuff that the wizard produces – there's some familiar stuff and some other stuff that you won't have seen before. If you're keen to find out what it's all about, I strongly recommend Chapter 8 of *Professional DCOM Programming* by Richard Grimes, which covers NT services in great detail.

Once you've done this, you can basically forget that you're dealing with a service at all, because adding the COM objects to it is just the same as for DLLs and EXEs. We can go right ahead and implement our **IMonitor** interface. Let's create a **Monitor** object, with the single *custom* interface **IMonitor**, in the standard way using the ATL Object Wizard. We've got one small addition to make to the header file **Monitor.h**:

```
.
.
.

/////////////////////////////////////////////////////////////////////////////
// CMonitor
class ATL_NO_VTABLE CMonitor :
   public CComObjectRootEx<CComSingleThreadModel>,
   public CComCoClass<CMonitor, &CLSID_Monitor>,
   public IMonitor
{

private:
   CComBSTR m_bstrName;

public:
   CMonitor()
   {
   }
```

This member variable will hold the name of the object that's connected to us.

Connecting to the Service

In our **Connect()** method, we update a file containing details of the objects that have connected at some time. We'll need this stored in a persistent format, so that if we stop and start the service, we don't lose all knowledge of objects that have connected in the past. I've chosen to use the object name as the key, and the class identifier as data. This is not ideal, as the class identifier is the only thing that's guaranteed to be unique. Unfortunately, if we render this as a string, it's too long for a stream name![1] So in "real life" (whatever that is), we'd probably use some other file mechanism – perhaps the registry.

Anyway, for the purposes of this example, we're going to store all our object details in a file called **c:\monitor.dat**, like this:

```
STDMETHODIMP CMonitor::Connect(REFCLSID rclsid, BSTR bstrName)
{
   // Save object name

   m_bstrName = bstrName;

   // Store object details in monitor file ...

   CComPtr<IStorage> pStorage;
```

[1] No this isn't documented, it's just a conclusion from years of experience.

```
    HRESULT hResult = StgOpenStorage (L"c:\\monitor.dat", NULL,
                      STGM_READWRITE | STGM_SHARE_EXCLUSIVE,
                          NULL, 0, &pStorage);

    if (FAILED (hResult))
    {
       hResult = StgCreateDocfile (L"c:\\monitor.dat", STGM_CREATE |
             STGM_READWRITE | STGM_SHARE_EXCLUSIVE, 0, &pStorage);

       if (FAILED (hResult))
          return hResult;
    }

    // Use object name as stream name ...

    CComPtr<IStream> pStream;
    hResult = pStorage->OpenStream(bstrName, NULL, STGM_READWRITE |
                               STGM_SHARE_EXCLUSIVE, 0, &pStream);

    if (FAILED (hResult))
    {
       hResult = pStorage->CreateStream(bstrName, STGM_READWRITE |
                           STGM_SHARE_EXCLUSIVE, 0, 0, &pStream);

       if (FAILED (hResult))
          return hResult;
    }

    // ... and store Class ID as data

    hResult = pStream->Write (&rclsid, sizeof (CLSID), NULL);

    return hResult;

}
```

Logging Errors

The error logging method is similar, except that we've got one file per object now. We've also effectively abandoned keys, in that we're just appending all our error details to the end of a single stream, called "**`Errors`**". For convenience in enumerating the error list, we'll add a second stream, called "**`Count`**", which just holds a count of the number of errors logged. (In this implementation, we'll let the list grow indefinitely; in a real implementation, of course, you'd have to worry about when to roll the log over, but that's outside the scope of this example...)

```
STDMETHODIMP CMonitor::LogError(int severity, BSTR bstrShort, BSTR bstrLong)
{
   // Set up path to this object's log file

   WCHAR szPath[256];
   swprintf(szPath, L"c:\\monitor\\%s.dat", m_bstrName);

   // Open up the log file

   CComPtr<IStorage> pStorage;
   HRESULT hResult = StgOpenStorage(szPath, NULL, STGM_READWRITE |
                        STGM_SHARE_EXCLUSIVE, NULL, 0, &pStorage);

   if (FAILED (hResult))
   {
      hResult = StgCreateDocfile(szPath, STGM_CREATE | STGM_READWRITE |
                              STGM_SHARE_EXCLUSIVE, 0, &pStorage);

      if (FAILED (hResult))
         return hResult;
   }

   // Open error stream

   CComPtr<IStream> pStream;
   hResult = pStorage->OpenStream(L"Errors", NULL, STGM_READWRITE |
                           STGM_SHARE_EXCLUSIVE, 0, &pStream);

   if (FAILED (hResult))
   {
      hResult = pStorage->CreateStream(L"Errors", STGM_READWRITE |
                        STGM_SHARE_EXCLUSIVE, 0, 0, &pStream);

      if (FAILED (hResult))
         return hResult;
   }

   // Go to end of stream

   LARGE_INTEGER offset;

   offset.LowPart = 0;
   offset.HighPart = 0;

   pStream->Seek(offset, STREAM_SEEK_END, NULL);

   // Write details of error

   CComVariant vSeverity(severity);
   CComBSTR cbstrShort = bstrShort;
   CComBSTR cbstrLong = bstrLong;
```

```
    vSeverity.WriteToStream(pStream);
    cbstrShort.WriteToStream(pStream);
    cbstrLong.WriteToStream(pStream);

    // Read current error count

    CComVariant vCount(0);
    pStream = NULL;
    hResult = pStorage->OpenStream(L"Count", NULL, STGM_READWRITE |
                                  STGM_SHARE_EXCLUSIVE, 0, &pStream);

    if (FAILED (hResult))
    {
       hResult = pStorage->CreateStream(L"Count", STGM_READWRITE |
                                 STGM_SHARE_EXCLUSIVE, 0, 0, &pStream);

       if (FAILED(hResult))
          return hResult;
    }

    else
    {
       hResult = vCount.ReadFromStream(pStream);

       if (FAILED (hResult))
          return hResult;
    }

    // Increment it and write back

    vCount.lVal++;

    pStream->Seek(offset, STREAM_SEEK_SET, NULL);
    vCount.WriteToStream(pStream);

    return S_OK;
}
```

Because our object has a vtable interface, we'll need to build the proxy/stub DLL and we also need to tell the compiler to register our project as a service, so you should make sure that the following lines are added to the custom build settings for the project:

```
"$(TargetPath)" /Service
echo Service Registration done
nmake -f MonitorServiceps.mk
regsvr32 /s MonitorServiceps.dll
```

The presence of **wchar** in **LogError** also implies we should include **wchar.h** in our project as well, so don't forget to add the relevant **include** statement at the top of **monitor.cpp**. The last thing we need to do is give our service a nice name. The service name is held in the string table, part of the **MonitorService** resource file, under **IDS_SERVICENAME**. Let's change this to "**Object monitor**". Since you are changing the name of the service, you also need to change how it is registered, so open **MonitorService.cpp** and edit the **RegisterServer()** method. Change this line,

```
if (bService)
{
   key.SetValue(_T("MonitorService"), _T("LocalService"));
   key.SetValue(_T("-Service"), _T("ServiceParameters"));
   Install();
}
```

to,

```
if (bService)
{
   key.SetValue(_T("Object monitor"), _T("LocalService"));
   key.SetValue(_T("-Service"), _T("ServiceParameters"));
   Install();
}
```

You have to do this because when you create one of the objects served by this service COM will need to know how to start the server (if it hasn't already started). These values tells COM that it should start a service called **Object monitor**.

OK, that'll do for our service for now. Let's take a look at the other side of things. How do we make it easy to hook this into our developers' objects?

Constructing Importable IDL and Header files

We can do most of the work involved in constructing our importable IDL file and header using the standard ATL wizards. However, there's a small amount of trickery involved, so keep your eyes peeled. We'll start by developing a typical out-of-process server (as a **.exe** file) that we might want to monitor. We'll call it **MyServer**. This contains a single object, **MyObject**, which implements two interfaces: **IMyObject** and **IPing**. We won't worry about the details of **IMyObject** for the time being. Instead, let's use **MyObject** as a vehicle for setting up **IPing**. We'll create the **MyObject** object with **IPing** as its only interface. We'll then add the method **Ping()** to **IPing**. This is the **IDL** produced:

```
// MyServer.idl : IDL source for MyServer.dll
//

// This file will be processed by the MIDL tool to
// produce the type library (MyServer.tlb) and marshalling code.
```

```
import "oaidl.idl";
import "ocidl.idl";
    [
        object,
        uuid(16DC0C9D-CD8D-11D1-B12B-0040951082F7),
        dual,
        helpstring("IPing Interface"),
        pointer_default(unique)
    ]
    interface IPing : IDispatch
    {
        [id(1), helpstring("method Ping")] HRESULT Ping();
    };
[
    uuid(16DC0C90-CD8D-11D1-B12B-0040951082F7),
    version(1.0),
    helpstring("MyServer 1.0 Type Library")
]
library MYSERVERLib
{
    importlib("stdole32.tlb");
    importlib("stdole2.tlb");

    [
        uuid(69C423C3-3021-11D1-A95A-00A0C9308FE4),
        helpstring("MyObject Class")
    ]
    coclass MyObject
    {
        [default] interface IPing;
    };
};
```

Before we do anything else, let's compile the IDL file. This creates our server's header file **MyServer.h**. Don't worry if you can't see it in the Visual Studio file list. It isn't actually part of our project. We'll need this file in a minute.

Now let's extract the IDL for **IPing** into a separate file, **SimpleMonitor.idl**:

```
[
    object,
    uuid(16DC0C9D-CD8D-11D1-B12B-0040951082F7),
    dual,
    helpstring("IPing Interface"),
    pointer_default(unique)
]
interface IPing : IDispatch
{
    [id(1), helpstring("method Ping")] HRESULT Ping();
};
```

We replace this with an **import** statement in the original **MyServer.idl**:

```
import "oaidl.idl";
import "ocidl.idl";
import "SimpleMonitor.idl";

[
   uuid(16DC0C90-CD8D-11D1-B12B-0040951082F7),
   version(1.0),
   helpstring("MyServer 1.0 Type Library")
]
library MYSERVERLib
{
   importlib("stdole32.tlb");
   importlib("stdole2.tlb");

   [
      uuid(69C423C3-3021-11D1-A95A-00A0C9308FE4),
      helpstring("MyObject Class")
   ]
   coclass MyObject
   {
      [default] interface IPing;
   };
};
```

Don't compile it yet! Sorry about that, but this is important. If you compile the **IDL** file now, the **MyServer.h** file will be replaced by another one that contains the statement:

```
#include "SimpleMonitor.h"
```

but doesn't contain anything about **IPing**! All that will have been lost. So, before we go ahead, we need to extract everything concerning **IPing** from the existing **MyServer.h** into a new file called **SimpleMonitor.h**. (I said to keep your eyes peeled, didn't I?)

So, let's copy **MyServer.h** into **SimpleMonitor.h**. Remove the section of the file between the lines,

```
#ifndef __MyObject_FWD_DEFINED__
#define __MyObject_FWD_DEFINED__
```

and,

```
#endif    /* __MyObject_FWD_DEFINED__ */
```

Now remove the last section of the file, between the lines,

```
#ifndef __MYSERVERLib_LIBRARY_DEFINED__
#define __MYSERVERLib_LIBRARY_DEFINED__
```

and,

```
#endif /* __MYSERVERLib_LIBRARY_DEFINED__ */
```

Now change the two references to **__MyServer_h__** to **__SimpleMonitor_h__**.

If we were to build the server now, we'd find that **IID_IPing** came up as an undefined reference. So we need to make sure that this is defined in **SimpleMonitor.h** as well. So look for the line,

```
EXTERN_C const IID IID_IPing;
```

and replace it with:

```
DEFINE_GUID(IID_IPing, 0x16DC0C9D, 0xCD8D, 0x11D1, 0xB1, 0x2B, 0x00, 0x40,
0x95, 0x10, 0x82, 0xF7);
```

where the GUID is the one that you'll find for **IID_IPing** in the file **MyServer_i.c**. This macro makes sure that **IID_IPing** is defined in the module where **initguid.h** is included, and referenced as an external everywhere else. OK, *now* you can compile **MyServer.idl**. This should work fine.

So we have the beginnings of an importable **IDL** file and header file for our monitoring interfaces, in **SimpleMonitor.idl** and **SimpleMonitor.h**.

Whilst we're at it, we might as well add the definitions of the methods for **IMonitor** into **SimpleMonitor.h** as well. This involves copying and pasting from the **MonitorService.h** file from our previous project. First of all, copy the lines:

```
#ifndef __IMonitor_FWD_DEFINED__
#define __IMonitor_FWD_DEFINED__
typedef interface IMonitor IMonitor;
#endif     /* __IMonitor_FWD_DEFINED__ */
```

into the "**forward declarations**" section. Then, copy everything between the lines,

```
#ifndef __IMonitor_INTERFACE_DEFINED__
#define __IMonitor_INTERFACE_DEFINED__
```

and,

```
#endif     /* __IMonitor_INTERFACE_DEFINED__ */
```

into the space just before the analogous area for **IPing**. What else do we need to do? We need to do the same as we did for **IID_IPing**, namely replace the line:

```
EXTERN_C const IID IID_IMonitor;
```

with

```
DEFINE_GUID(IID_IMonitor, 0x13092DBE, 0xBE45, 0x11D1, 0xB1, 0x1A, 0x00, 0x40,
0x95, 0x10, 0x82, 0xF7);
```

(or whatever GUID appears in **MonitorService_i.c**). We also need to define **CLSID_Monitor**, by inserting the following line after that for **IID_IMonitor**:

```
DEFINE_GUID(CLSID_Monitor, 0x13092DBF, 0xBE45, 0x11D1, 0xB1, 0x1A, 0x00,
0x40, 0x95, 0x10, 0x82, 0xF7);
```

Building a Test Server

Now we can start to add some meat to our test server. The best way to do this is to throw away everything we've done so far, apart from **SimpleMonitor.idl** and **SimpleMonitor.h**, and create a new **MyServer** project from scratch. This time, when we create the **MyObject** component, leave the default interface as **IMyObject**. Add two methods, **DoSomething()** and **DoSomethingWrong()**.

Now let's hook into the **SimpleMonitor** environment. First of all, let's implement the **IPing** interface. Change the declaration of **CMyObject** in **MyObject.h** as follows:

```
//////////////////////////////////////////////////////////////////////////////
// CMyObject
class ATL_NO_VTABLE CMyObject :
   public CComObjectRootEx<CComSingleThreadModel>,
   public CComCoClass<CMyObject, &CLSID_MyObject>,
   public IDispatchImpl<IMyObject, &IID_IMyObject, &LIBID_MYSERVERLib>,
   public IDispatchImpl<IPing, &IID_IPing, &LIBID_MYSERVERLib>
{
private:
   IMonitor* m_pMonitor;

public:
   CMyObject()
   {
   }
   HRESULT FinalConstruct();
   void FinalRelease();

DECLARE_REGISTRY_RESOURCEID(IDR_MYOBJECT)

BEGIN_COM_MAP(CMyObject)
   COM_INTERFACE_ENTRY(IMyObject)
   COM_INTERFACE_ENTRY(IPing)
   COM_INTERFACE_ENTRY2(IDispatch,IMyObject)
END_COM_MAP()
```

```
// IMyObject
public:
   STDMETHOD(DoSomethingWrong)();
   STDMETHOD(DoSomething)();

// IPing
public:
   STDMETHOD(Ping)();
};
```

Notice that we've also added a private member variable to hold our pointer to the monitor interface. Next, import **SimpleMonitor.idl** into **MyServer.idl**, and add a reference to **IPing** into the type library section:

```
import "oaidl.idl";
import "ocidl.idl";
import "SimpleMonitor.idl";

   [
      object,
      uuid(7EB6B23D-CD96-11D1-B12B-0040951082F7),
      dual,
      helpstring("IMyObject Interface"),
      pointer_default(unique)
   ]
   interface IMyObject : IDispatch
   {
      [id(1), helpstring("method DoSomething")] HRESULT DoSomething();
      [id(2), helpstring("method DoSomethingWrong")]
                                          HRESULT DoSomethingWrong();
   };
[
   uuid(7EB6B230-CD96-11D1-B12B-0040951082F7),
   version(1.0),
   helpstring("MyServer 1.0 Type Library")
]
library MYSERVERLib
{
   importlib("stdole32.tlb");
   importlib("stdole2.tlb");

   [
      uuid(69C423C3-3021-11D1-A95A-00A0C9308FE4),
      helpstring("MyObject Class")
   ]
   coclass MyObject
   {
      [default] interface IMyObject;
      interface IPing;
   };
};
```

Finally, add a blank **`Ping()`** method to the **`CMyObject`** class:

```
STDMETHODIMP CMyObject::Ping()
{
   return S_OK;
}
```

Yup, **`Ping()`** doesn't actually do anything at all in this implementation. It doesn't need to. All we're going to do with it is use it to check that you can obtain a reference to an interface and invoke a method without it timing out or crashing. You could argue that **`AddRef()`** on **`IUnknown()`** would be an equally good way of doing this, but that's missing the point. I've specified a very simple **`IPing`** interface here to keep the example straightforward; however, in practice, you might want to specify a much more complex diagnostic interrogation interface, which would still have to be implemented by every component that you are going to allow on your network.

Now let's add some references to **`IMonitor`** in **`MyServer`**. We'll override the **`FinalConstruct()`** and **`FinalRelease()`** methods and create an instance of **`IMonitor`**, connecting in the former and releasing it in the latter. We'll also log an error whenever the method **`DoSomethingWrong()`** is invoked. This is what our code now looks like:

```
// MyObject.cpp : Implementation of CMyObject
#include "stdafx.h"
#include "MyServer.h"
#include "MyObject.h"

/////////////////////////////////////////////////////////////////////////////
// CMyObject


STDMETHODIMP CMyObject::DoSomething()
{
   return S_OK;
}

STDMETHODIMP CMyObject::DoSomethingWrong()
{
   m_pMonitor->LogError (1, CComBSTR("Error"), CComBSTR("Did something
                                                         wrong"));
   return S_OK;
}

STDMETHODIMP CMyObject::Ping()
{
   return S_OK;
}

HRESULT CMyObject::FinalConstruct()
{
   CoCreateInstance(CLSID_Monitor, NULL, CLSCTX_LOCAL_SERVER,
                    IID_IMonitor, reinterpret_cast<void**> (&m_pMonitor));
```

```
    m_pMonitor->Connect(CLSID_MyObject, L"My object");

    return S_OK;
}
void CMyObject::FinalRelease()
{
    m_pMonitor->Release();
}
```

Where did **CLSID_Monitor** and **IID_IMonitor** come from, by the way? Well, we imported **SimpleMonitor.idl** into our **MyServer.idl** file. If you compile **MyServer.idl** and take a look at the **MyServer.h** header file that the MIDL compiler has generated for us, you'll see these lines in the middle of it:

```
/* header files for imported files */
#include "oaidl.h"
#include "ocidl.h"
#include "SimpleMonitor.h"
```

Hey! That's our header file in there! That's the file that we created earlier, when we created **SimpleMonitor.idl**, and it's that file that contains the Class ID for the **Monitor** object and the Interface ID for the **IMonitor** interface.

Starting Up Our Service

I think we're ready to take this for a drive. Let's build our monitor service, start it up and try it out. After building, **MonitorService** should have registered itself as a service, so if you go into the Control Panel, and select Services, you should see something like this:

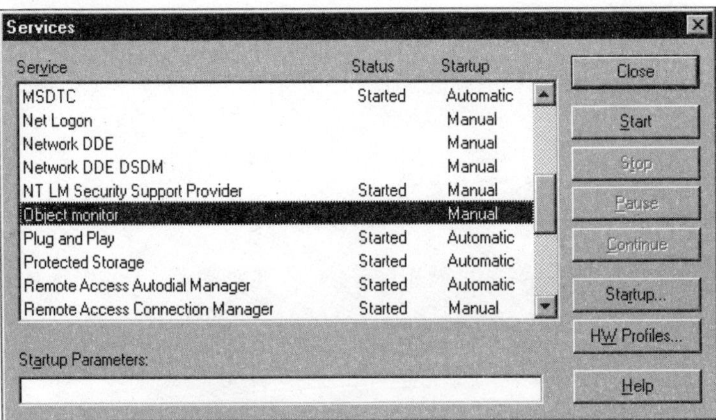

As you can see, this is set to Manual – in other words, it doesn't yet start up automatically when the PC boots. We'll change this when we're happy with the service. For now, just click on the Start button. You should see a dialog like this pop up:

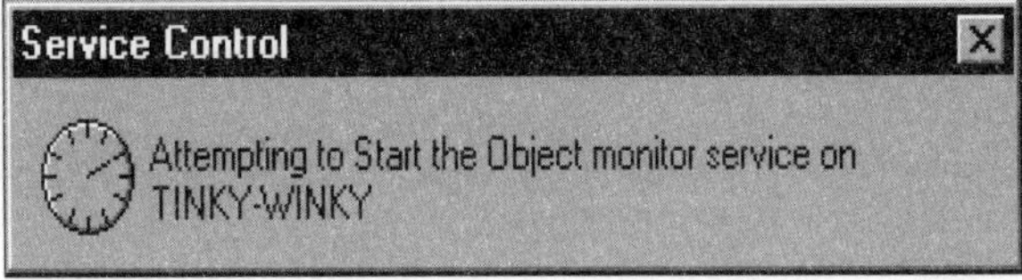

And we're off!

Let's put together a very simple VB client to test this out. Here's our form:

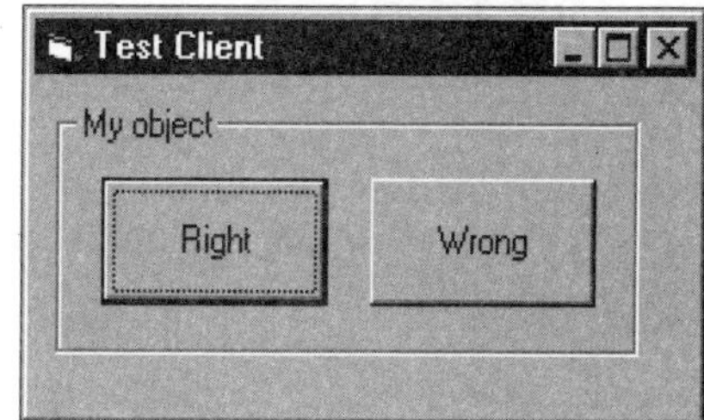

And here's the code:

```
Private Sub cmdRight_Click()
Dim obj As New MyObject
obj.DoSomething
End Sub

Private Sub cmdWrong_Click()
Dim obj As New MyObject
obj.DoSomethingWrong
End Sub
```

We'll need to add the **MyServer** type library to our references, but apart from that, we're ready to go.

If you try running this, and click on the Right button, you should notice that a **c:\monitor.dat** file appears. Let's use **dfview** to take a look at what there is inside it:

which looks suspiciously like our Class ID.

Moreover, if you create a **c:\monitor** directory and click on the Wrong button, you should also see a **Myobject.dat** file appear. If we check the **Errors** stream inside this file, this is what we see:

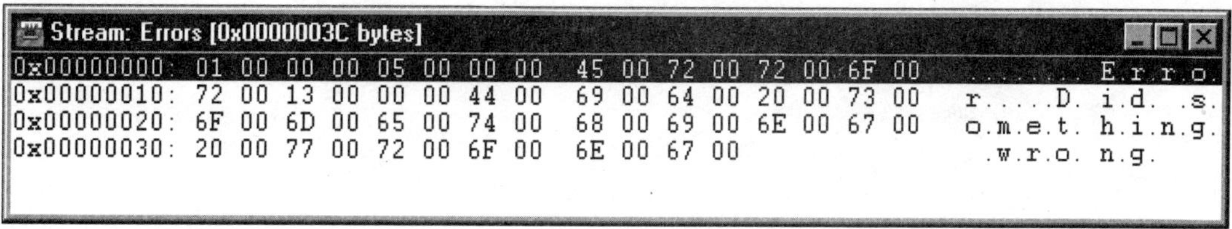

Great. Now we need to add another interface or two to enable our monitoring service to get at all this information. We need one interface to give us a list of objects, and another to give us a list of errors for a given object. Sounds like enumeration to me...

Enumerating the Objects

Yes, **IObjectList** is another enumeration interface. Remember how we did this back in Chapter 1? We have to include two "**get**" properties in our interface specification: **Count** (**long**) and **_NewEnum** (**LPUNKNOWN**) so that Visual Basic will treat it as a collection. As well as this, we need one more objects to represent each enumerated object, and we'll call this **MonObject**. We'll look at this in more detail in a little while.

Here's the code for the object list interface. Note how **IStorage** helps us here, by providing an enumerator for every stream in the storage object.

```
// ObjectList.cpp : Implementation of CObjectList
#include "stdafx.h"
#include "MonitorService.h"
#include "ObjectList.h"
#include "MonObject.h"

/////////////////////////////////////////////////////////////////////////////
// CObjectList


STDMETHODIMP CObjectList::get_Count(long* pVal)
{
   CComPtr<IStorage> pStorage;
   HRESULT hResult = StgOpenStorage (L"c:\\monitor.dat", NULL,
         STGM_READWRITE | STGM_SHARE_EXCLUSIVE, NULL, 0,
         &pStorage);

   if (FAILED (hResult))
      return hResult;

   CComPtr<IEnumSTATSTG> pEnum;
   pStorage->EnumElements (0, NULL, 0, &pEnum);

   long count;

   for (count = 0;; count++)
   {
      STATSTG stat;
      ULONG found = 0;

      pEnum->Next (1, &stat, &found);

      // enumerator allocated this for us, so we need to free it
      CoTaskMemFree(stat.pwcsName);

      if (found < 1)
         break;
   }

   *pVal = count;

   return S_OK;
}
```

Note that the enumerator returns a **STATSTG** structure in the call to **Next()**. It will use the task allocator to create a buffer to hold the name of the item and it is our responsibility to free this buffer, hence the call to **CoTaskMemFree()**.

```
STDMETHODIMP CObjectList::get__NewEnum(LPUNKNOWN* pVal)
{
   HRESULT hResult;
   long lItems;
   *pVal = NULL;
   hResult = get_Count(&lItems);
   if (FAILED(hResult))
      return hResult;

   CComPtr<IStorage> pStorage;
   CComPtr<IEnumSTATSTG> pEnum;

   // open the compound file
   hResult = StgOpenStorage (L"c:\\monitor.dat", NULL,
      STGM_READWRITE | STGM_SHARE_EXCLUSIVE, NULL, 0, &pStorage);

   if (FAILED (hResult))
      return hResult;

   pStorage->EnumElements (0, NULL, 0, &pEnum);

   // create the enumerator
   typedef CComObject< CComEnum< IEnumVARIANT, &IID_IEnumVARIANT,
                                 VARIANT, _Copy<VARIANT> > > Enum;
   Enum* pEnumObjs;
   Enum::CreateInstance(&pEnumObjs);
   long index;

   //create the MonObjects and put them in an array
   VARIANT* pVar = new VARIANT[lItems];
   for (index = 0; index < lItems; index++)
   {
      STATSTG stat;
      ULONG found = 0;

         // Use storage enumerator

      pEnum->Next (1, &stat, &found);

         // Open next stream and extract class ID

      CComPtr<IStream> pStream;
      pStorage->OpenStream (stat.pwcsName, NULL,
         STGM_READ | STGM_SHARE_EXCLUSIVE, 0, &pStream);

      CLSID clsid;
      ULONG nRead;

      pStream->Read (&clsid, sizeof (CLSID), &nRead);
```

```
      // Convert class ID into readable form
      LPOLESTR lpszClsid;
      StringFromCLSID (clsid, &lpszClsid);

      CComBSTR bstrName = stat.pwcsName;
      CoTaskMemFree(stat.pwcsName);
      CComBSTR bstrClsid = lpszClsid;
      CoTaskMemFree(lpszClsid);

         // now create the MonObject
      CComObject<CMonObject>* pObj;
      CComObject<CMonObject>::CreateInstance(&pObj);
      pObj->put_Name (bstrName);
      pObj->put_CLSID (bstrClsid);
      pVar[index].vt = VT_DISPATCH;
      pObj->QueryInterface(IID_IDispatch,
         reinterpret_cast<void**>(&(pVar[index].pdispVal)));
   }

   //put the data into the enumerator, make a copy
   pEnumObjs->Init(&pVar[0], &pVar[lItems], NULL, AtlFlagCopy);

   //get rid of our copy of the list items
   for (index = 0; index < lItems; index++)
   {
      VariantClear(&pVar[index]);
   }

   delete [] pVar;

   return pEnumObjs->QueryInterface(IID_IUnknown,
      reinterpret_cast<void**>(pVal));

}
```

You will recognize the code to create the enumerator from a **CComEnum<>** object from Chapter 1. This implements the standard interface **IEnumVARIANT**, and returns the object descriptions as objects of type **MonObject**. Note again how the standard enumeration helps us here.

Finally, we need to define our enumerated item object (an enumerated object object, in fact). We'll give it a single interface, **IMonObject**, with two **BSTR** properties, **CLSID** and **Name**. Here's the header file:

```
// MonObject.h : Declaration of the CMonObject

#ifndef __MONOBJECT_H_
#define __MONOBJECT_H_

#include "resource.h"        // main symbols
```

```
//////////////////////////////////////////////////////////////////////////
// CMonObject
class ATL_NO_VTABLE CMonObject :
   public CComObjectRootEx<CComSingleThreadModel>,
   public CComCoClass<CMonObject, &CLSID_MonObject>,
   public IDispatchImpl<IMonObject, &IID_IMonObject,
                                    &LIBID_MONITORSERVICELib>
{

private:
   CComBSTR m_bstrName;
   CComBSTR m_bstrCLSID;

public:
   CMonObject()
   {
   }

DECLARE_REGISTRY_RESOURCEID(IDR_MONOBJECT)

BEGIN_COM_MAP(CMonObject)
   COM_INTERFACE_ENTRY(IMonObject)
   COM_INTERFACE_ENTRY(IDispatch)
END_COM_MAP()

// IMonObject
public:
   STDMETHOD(get_CLSID)(/*[out, retval]*/ BSTR *pVal);
   STDMETHOD(put_CLSID)(/*[in]*/ BSTR newVal);
   STDMETHOD(get_Name)(/*[out, retval]*/ BSTR *pVal);
   STDMETHOD(put_Name)(/*[in]*/ BSTR newVal);
};

#endif //__MONOBJECT_H_
```

And here's what the implementation looks like:

```
// MonObject.cpp : Implementation of CMonObject
#include "stdafx.h"
#include "MonitorService.h"
#include "MonObject.h"

//////////////////////////////////////////////////////////////////////////
// CMonObject


STDMETHODIMP CMonObject::get_Name(BSTR* pVal)
{
   *pVal = m_bstrName.Copy();

   return S_OK;
}
```

```
STDMETHODIMP CMonObject::put_Name(BSTR newVal)
{
   m_bstrName = newVal;

   return S_OK;
}
STDMETHODIMP CMonObject::get_CLSID(BSTR* pVal)
{
   *pVal = m_bstrCLSID.Copy();

   return S_OK;
}

STDMETHODIMP CMonObject::put_CLSID(BSTR newVal)
{
   m_bstrCLSID = newVal;

   return S_OK;
}
```

A pretty simple object, then.

Enumerating the Errors

The code for the interface **IErrorList** that enumerates through the errors for a given object is similar to **IObjectList**, except that we can't use the **IStorage** enumerator to help us because we're storing all the errors in a single sequential stream. We need to add one property, **Name,** to enable the calling application to specify for which object errors are to be fetched. We'll store this in a private member variable:

```
// ErrorList.h : Declaration of the CErrorList

#ifndef __ERRORLIST_H_
#define __ERRORLIST_H_

#include "resource.h"        // main symbols

/////////////////////////////////////////////////////////////////////////////
// CErrorList
class ATL_NO_VTABLE CErrorList :
   public CComObjectRootEx<CComSingleThreadModel>,
   public CComCoClass<CErrorList, &CLSID_ErrorList>,
   public IDispatchImpl<IErrorList, &IID_IErrorList,
                        &LIBID_MONITORSERVICELib>
{
private:
   CComBSTR m_bstrName;

public:
   CErrorList()
   {
   }

DECLARE_REGISTRY_RESOURCEID(IDR_ERRORLIST)
```

```
BEGIN_COM_MAP(CErrorList)
   COM_INTERFACE_ENTRY(IErrorList)
   COM_INTERFACE_ENTRY(IDispatch)
END_COM_MAP()
// IErrorList
public:
   STDMETHOD(put_Name)(/*[in]*/ BSTR newVal);
   STDMETHOD(get__NewEnum)(/*[out, retval]*/ LPUNKNOWN *pVal);
   STDMETHOD(get_Count)(/*[out, retval]*/ long *pVal);
};

#endif //__ERRORLIST_H_
```

Here's the implementation code for the **ErrorList** object:

```
// ErrorList.cpp : Implementation of CErrorList
#include "stdafx.h"
#include "MonitorService.h"
#include "ErrorList.h"
#include "Error.h"

#include <wchar.h>

/////////////////////////////////////////////////////////////////////////////
// CErrorList

STDMETHODIMP CErrorList::get_Count(long* pVal)
{
   // Open object-specific error file

   WCHAR szPath[256];
   swprintf (szPath, L"c:\\monitor\\%s.dat", m_bstrName);

   CComPtr<IStorage> pStorage;
   HRESULT hResult = StgOpenStorage (szPath, NULL,
                     STGM_READWRITE | STGM_SHARE_EXCLUSIVE,
                     NULL, 0, &pStorage);

   if (FAILED (hResult))
      return hResult;

   // Open up error count stream

   CComPtr<IStream> pStream;
   hResult = pStorage->OpenStream (L"Count", NULL,
                     STGM_READWRITE | STGM_SHARE_EXCLUSIVE, 0,
                     &pStream);

   if (FAILED (hResult))
      return hResult;

   // Read count from stream
```

```
    CComVariant vCount;
    vCount.ReadFromStream (pStream);

    *pVal = vCount.lVal;

    return S_OK;
}


STDMETHODIMP CErrorList::put_Name(BSTR newVal)
{

    m_bstrName = newVal;

    return S_OK;
}
```

Notice that this time around, we have to read our count of items from the file. This is what **get__NewEnum()** looks like:

```
STDMETHODIMP CErrorList::get__NewEnum(LPUNKNOWN * pVal)
{
    HRESULT hResult;
    long lItems;
    *pVal = NULL;
    if (m_bstrName.Length() == 0)
       return E_FAIL;
    hResult = get_Count(&lItems);
    if (FAILED(hResult))
       return hResult;

    WCHAR szPath[256];
    swprintf (szPath, L"c:\\monitor\\%s.dat", m_bstrName);

    CComPtr<IStorage> pStorage;
    hResult = StgOpenStorage (szPath, NULL,
       STGM_READWRITE | STGM_SHARE_EXCLUSIVE, NULL, 0, &pStorage);

    if (FAILED (hResult))
       return hResult;

    CComPtr<IStream> pStream;
    hResult = pStorage->OpenStream (L"Errors", NULL,
       STGM_READ | STGM_SHARE_EXCLUSIVE, 0, &pStream);

    if (FAILED (hResult))
       return hResult;

    // create the enumerator
    typedef CComObject< CComEnum< IEnumVARIANT, &IID_IEnumVARIANT,
                                  VARIANT, _Copy<VARIANT> > > Enum;
    Enum* pEnumErrs;
    Enum::CreateInstance(&pEnumErrs);
    long index;
```

```
    // create the MonObjects and put them in an array
    VARIANT* pVar = new VARIANT[lItems];
    for (index = 0; index < lItems; index++)
    {
         // Read severity code from stream

       CComVariant vSeverity;
       vSeverity.ReadFromStream (pStream);

         // Read short description

       CComBSTR bstrShort;
       bstrShort.ReadFromStream (pStream);

         // Read long description

       CComBSTR bstrLong;
       bstrLong.ReadFromStream (pStream);

         // Construct enumerated object

       CComObject<CError>* pError;
       CComObject<CError>::CreateInstance(&pError);

       pError->put_Severity (vSeverity.iVal);
       pError->put_Short (bstrShort);
       pError->put_Long (bstrLong);

       pVar[index].vt = VT_DISPATCH;
       pError->QueryInterface(IID_IDispatch,
          reinterpret_cast<void**>(&(pVar[index].pdispVal)));
    }

    //put the data into the enumerator, make a copy
    pEnumErrs->Init(&pVar[0], &pVar[lItems], NULL, AtlFlagCopy);

    //get rid of our copy of the list items
    for (index = 0; index < lItems; index++)
    {
       VariantClear(&pVar[index]);
    }
    delete [] pVar;

    return pEnumErrs->QueryInterface(IID_IUnknown,
       reinterpret_cast<void**>(pVal));
}
```

Note the differences between this one and the object enumerator – here, we're reading along one stream of errors, whereas previously we enumerated a number of discrete streams.

I won't reproduce the code for the enumerated **Error** object here, as it's very similar to the rather tedious little **MonObject** object above. It's got a single interface, **IError**, with three properties, **Severity** (**long**), **Short** (**BSTR**) and **Long** (**BSTR**).

More Changes to SimpleMonitor.h

Before we go on we need to add the interface definitions and GUIDs for the **IObjectList**, **IMonObject**, **IErrorList** and **IError** as you did for the **IMonitor** interface and **Monitor** object.

Testing the Monitor Service

With the **IObjectList** and **IErrorList** interfaces, we now have the technology to interrogate the monitoring service on a given server for a list of known objects and a log of errors raised by them. I've put together a small VB application to verify this, **MonitorClient**. We could also do with another object to test, so I've cloned **MyServer** into another project called–wait for it–**MyOtherServer**. I've also extended the test client that we used earlier to permit us to call the **DoSomething()** and **DoSomethingWrong()** methods of **IMyObject**, so that we can do the same on **IMyOtherObject**. I won't waste space by showing you that either.

However, at this point we probably do need a diagram showing what connects to what. This is where we are. This is basically a refinement of our earlier object diagram:

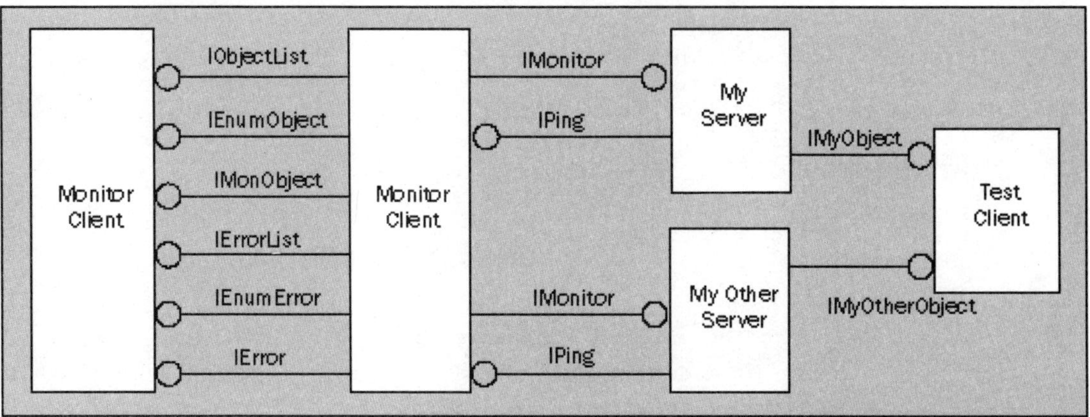

Let's just take a quick look at our VB **MonitorClient** application, then we can test the system. Here's the form:

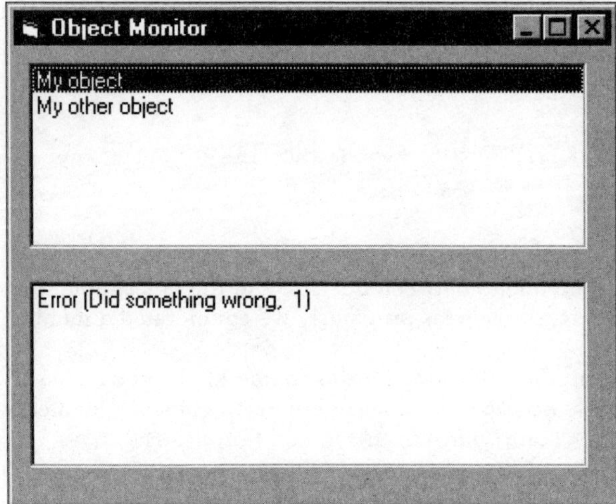

The idea is that the upper list box shows all the known objects, whilst the lower one shows the error log for the selected object. Here's the code:

```
Private Sub Form_Load()
   Dim list As New ObjectList
   Dim obj As MonObject
   For Each obj In list
      lstObjects.AddItem (obj.Name)
   Next obj
End Sub

Private Sub lstObjects_Click()
   lstErrors.Clear
   On Error GoTo finish
   Dim list As New ErrorList
   list.Name = lstObjects.Text
   Dim err As Error
   For Each err In list
      lstErrors.AddItem (err.Short + " (" + err.Long + ", " +
                          Str(err.severity) + ")")
   Next err
   finish:
End Sub
```

Well, it works, but that's about all you can say about it.

I think we need something a little slicker. It's time to play with the Microsoft Management Console...

The Microsoft Management Console

It's unlikely that you will have got this far with trying out the examples in this book without encountering the MMC at some point. It is rapidly becoming the Windows standard user interface for management and monitoring – to the extent that all new third-party products will soon be required to support it if they want to have an official "BackOffice" badge. This all makes excellent sense of course. The more uniformity in the management interface there is, the more manageable the system is likely to be.

The other good thing is that the MMC is extendable, by means of user-written modules called "snap-ins". I have to say right from the start that writing a snap-in isn't entirely intuitive, but it's worth getting to grips with. After all, you've done all the hard infrastructure work, but no-one's going to appreciate that if you don't provide a decent user interface.

MMC snap-ins are in-process COM servers that use a set of standard interfaces to communicate with the MMC itself; they are also required to implement some other interfaces. As so often with Windows plug-in modules, the relationship between the MMC and its snap-ins is a kind of "I'll expose my interface to you if you'll expose your interface to me" type of thing. We've come across this before – for example, when we wrote our MTS resource manager and dispenser. It's a pretty slick way of doing things, even if the tangle of interrelationships gets a little messy at times. And, believe me, MMC snap-ins can get *very* complex. The one that we're going to develop is pretty straightforward by comparison with some of the things that you can do...

This is what our MMC snap-in is going to look like when it's running:

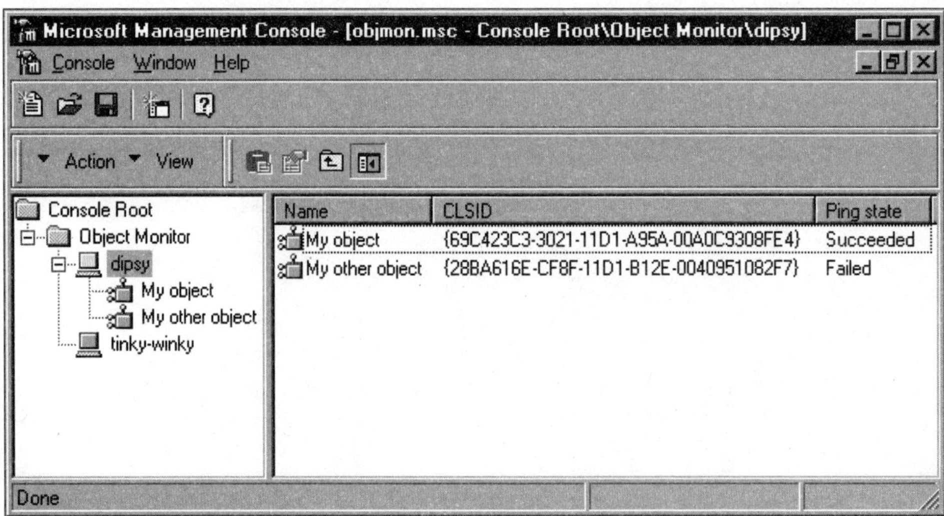

As you can see, there are two panes of information: the **scope** pane (on the left) and the **result** pane on the right. The scope pane is basically used for walking down a tree to the piece of information that you want (very much like Windows Explorer), and the result pane is used for showing the information in full. Each item in the scope pane is called a **node**. We have three node types in our implementation: *root*, *computer* and *object*. You can see examples of all three in the screenshot above. Object Monitor is the root node, dipsy is a computer, and My Object is an object.

The MMC Interfaces

The MMC API specifies a *lot* of interfaces, and we're not going to be able to cover all of them in this chapter. However, we will be able to look at most of the interesting ones. We'll be developing four COM objects, each of which exposes one or more of these interfaces.

Our first object is `ComponentData`, which exposes `IComponentData` and `IPersistStorage`. This controls the display of all the items in the scope pane.

Our second one is `Component`, which exposes `IComponent`. This controls the display of a single item in the result pane.

The third one is `DataObject`, which exposes `IDataObject`; this is a generic, non-MMC-specific interface that handles data transfer and notification of changes in data. I've also added one of my own to the object, called `IMyDataObject`, for reasons which will become clear later on. Each DataObject object represents one node in the scope pane.

The last object is `ExtendContextMenu`, which exposes `IExtendContextMenu`. This controls extensions to the context menu. I've also added an interface of my own, called `IMyExtendContextMenu` – again, the reasons will become clear in due course.

In this example, I've chosen not to implement the following interfaces:

`IExtendControlbar`	This would enable us to add custom control bars
`IExtendPropertySheet`	This would enable us to pages to a property sheet
`ISnapinAbout`	This would enable us to provide a custom About... property page

We'll be using the following MMC interfaces:

`IConsole`	This enables our snap-in to communicate with the console
`IConsoleNameSpace`	This enables our snap-in to add or delete items from the scope pane
`IConsoleVerb`	This enables our snap-in to adjust the state of standard console verbs, or menu commands
`IContextMenuCallback`	This enables our snap-in to add items to a context menu
`IContextMenuProvider`	This enables our snap-in to manipulate context menus
`IHeaderCtrl`	This enables our snap-in to manipulate columns in the result pane
`IImageList`	This enables our snap-in to add images as icons in either pane
`IResultData`	This enables our snap-in to manipulate the result pane

We won't, however, be using these:

`IControlBar`	This would enable our snap-in to create, attach and detach toolbars and other controls
`IMenuButton`	This would enable our snap-in to manipulate menu buttons
`IPropertySheetCallback`	This would enable our snap-in to add property pages to a property sheet
`IPropertySheetProvider`	This would enable our snap-in to manipulate custom property sheets
`IResultDataCompare`	This would enable our snap-in to override standard sorting in the result pane
`IResultOwnerData`	This would enable our snap-in to use virtual lists (i.e. massive lists with no storage) in the result pane
`IToolbar`	This would enable our snap-in to manipulate toolbars

So let's take a quick look at how our implementation is going to look in a lollipop diagram:

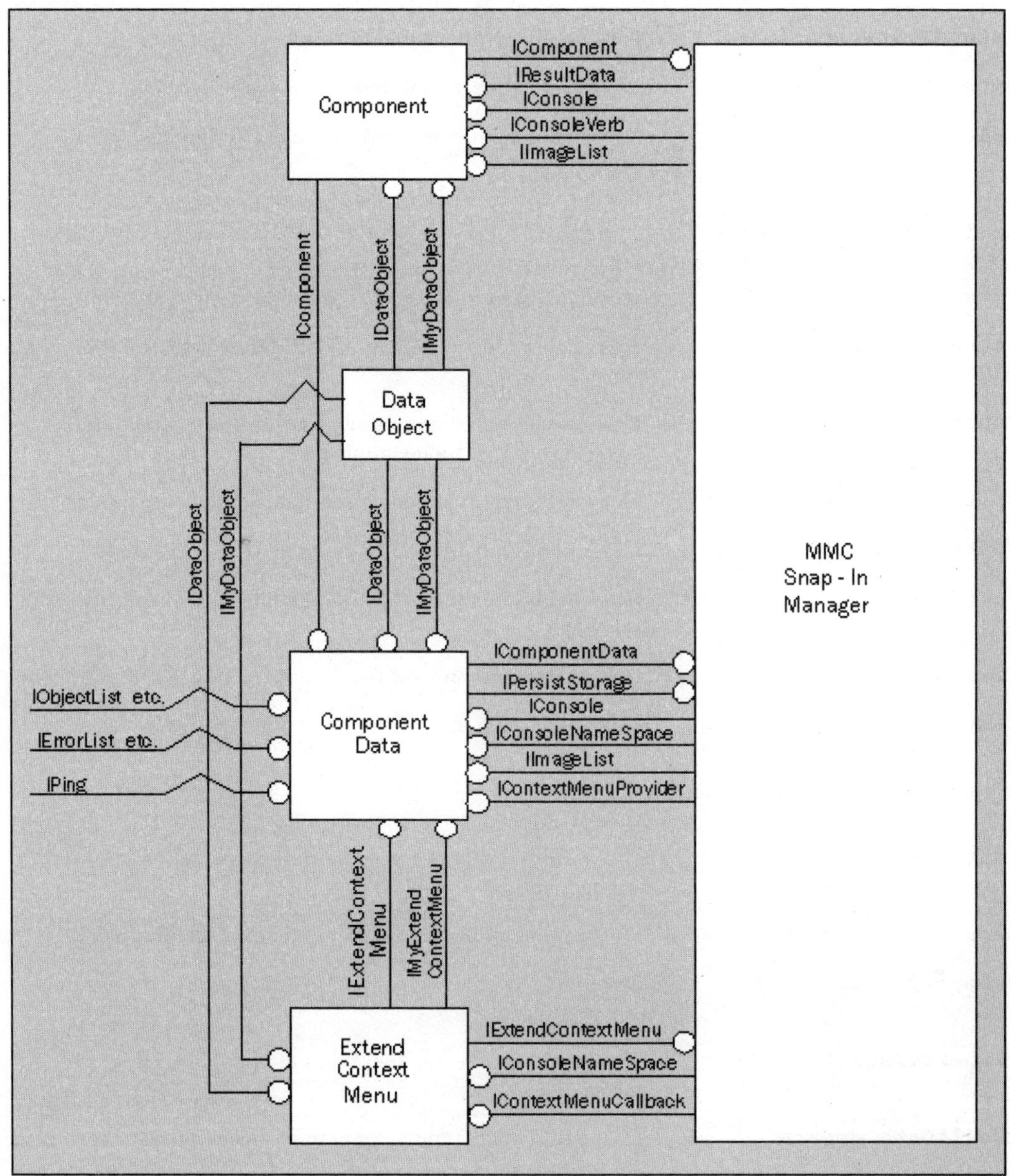

Excited? Me, I can't wait ...

Creating Our Objects

The first stage of the development process, as ever, is to create our ATL project – this time it's an in-process DLL, which I'm calling **ObjectMonitor**.

Next, we'll create our objects using the ATL object wizard in the usual manner. We'll start off by creating the following objects: **Component**, **ComponentData**, **DataObject** and **ExtendContextMenu** – these should all have custom interfaces. (Don't worry about adding any methods or properties to them – we can do that by hand.) This will generate our header files, source stubs and IDL. We'll have to make a few changes to the IDL file. First of all, remove the **IComponent** and **IComponentData** interface definitions altogether. Then make the following changes:

```
// ObjectMonitor.idl : IDL source for ObjectMonitor.dll
//

// This file will be processed by the MIDL tool to
// produce the type library (ObjectMonitor.tlb) and marshalling code.

import "oaidl.idl";
import "ocidl.idl";
import "mmc.idl";

   [
      uuid(0621BEB0-CEC6-11d1-B12D-0040951082F7),

      helpstring("IMyDataObject Interface"),
      pointer_default(unique)
   ]
   interface IMyDataObject : IUnknown
   {
      [propget, id(1), helpstring("property Cookie")]
                  HRESULT Cookie([out, retval] long *pVal);
      [propput, id(1), helpstring("property Cookie")]
                  HRESULT Cookie([in] long newVal);
   };

   [
      uuid(92643790-CEC4-11d1-B12D-0040951082F7),

      helpstring("IMyExtendContextMenu Interface"),
      pointer_default(unique)
   ]
   interface IMyExtendContextMenu : IUnknown
   {
      [propput, id(1), helpstring("property Console")]
                  HRESULT Console([in] LPUNKNOWN newVal);
   };

[
   uuid(82DB1FE0-CE1D-11D1-B12C-0040951082F7),
   version(1.0),
```

```
      helpstring("ObjectMonitor 1.0 Type Library")
   ]
   library OBJECTMONITORLib
   {
      importlib("stdole32.tlb");
      importlib("stdole2.tlb");

      [
         uuid(37842E90-CE2C-11d1-B12C-0040951082F7),
         helpstring("ComponentData Class")
      ]
      coclass ComponentData
      {
         [default] interface IComponentData;
         interface IPersistStorage;
      };
      [
         uuid(4332A080-CE2C-11d1-B12C-0040951082F7),
         helpstring("DataObject Class")
      ]
      coclass DataObject
      {
         [default] interface IDataObject;
         interface IMyDataObject;
      };
      [
         uuid(50420EC0-CE2C-11d1-B12C-0040951082F7),
         helpstring("Component Class")
      ]
      coclass Component
      {
         [default] interface IComponent;
      };
      [
         uuid(5CA65800-CE2C-11d1-B12C-0040951082F7),
         helpstring("ExtendContextMenu Class")
      ]
      coclass ExtendContextMenu
      {
         [default] interface IExtendContextMenu;
         interface IMyExtendContextMenu;
      };
   };
```

What we're doing here is defining our two new interfaces, **IMyDataObject** and **IMyExtendContextMenu**, and ensuring that we are picking up the standard MMC definitions for all the other interfaces.

Incidentally, in order for your Visual Studio to see that **mmc.idl** file, you'll need to have the Platform SDK installed on your machine, and the library and include paths extended accordingly. As I've mentioned previously, this is available either for download from **http://www.microsoft.com/msdn/sdk/bldenv.htm** or on one of the MSDN CDs.

ComponentData

Not surprisingly, this is going to have some knock-on effects in the header files for each of our object classes. Whilst we're at it, we've got a few member variables to add, so let's get them all sorted out. We'll start with **ComponentData.h**:

```
// ComponentData.h : Declaration of the CComponentData

#ifndef __COMPONENTDATA_H_
#define __COMPONENTDATA_H_

#include "resource.h"        // main symbols

class CItem;

/////////////////////////////////////////////////////////////////////////////
// CComponentData
class ATL_NO_VTABLE CComponentData :
   public CComObjectRootEx<CComSingleThreadModel>,
   public CComCoClass<CComponentData, &CLSID_ComponentData>,
   public IComponentData,
   public IPersistStorage
{
private:
   IConsoleNameSpace* m_pConsoleNameSpace;
   IContextMenuProvider* m_pContextMenuProvider;
   IExtendContextMenu* m_pExtendContextMenu;
   CItem* m_pRoot;

public:
   CComponentData()
   {
      m_pContextMenuProvider = NULL;
      m_pRoot = NULL;
   }

DECLARE_REGISTRY_RESOURCEID(IDR_COMPONENTDATA)

BEGIN_COM_MAP(CComponentData)
   COM_INTERFACE_ENTRY(IComponentData)
   COM_INTERFACE_ENTRY(IPersistStorage)
END_COM_MAP()

// IComponentData
public:
   STDMETHOD(CompareObjects)(LPDATAOBJECT lpDataObjectA,
                   LPDATAOBJECT lpDataObjectB);
   STDMETHOD(GetDisplayInfo)(LPSCOPEDATAITEM pItem);
   STDMETHOD(QueryDataObject)(long cookie, DATA_OBJECT_TYPES type,
                   LPDATAOBJECT* ppDataObject);
   STDMETHOD(Notify)(LPDATAOBJECT lpDataObject,
         MMC_NOTIFY_TYPE event, long arg, long param);
```

```
    STDMETHOD(CreateComponent)(LPCOMPONENT* ppComponent);
    STDMETHOD(Initialize)(LPUNKNOWN pUnknown);
    STDMETHOD(Destroy)();
// IPersistStorage
public:
    STDMETHOD(GetClassID)(CLSID* pClsid);
    STDMETHOD(IsDirty)();
    STDMETHOD(InitNew)(IStorage* pStorage);
    STDMETHOD(Load)(IStorage* pStorage);
    STDMETHOD(Save)(IStorage* pStorage, BOOL fSameAsLoad);
    STDMETHOD(SaveCompleted)(IStorage* pStorage);
    STDMETHOD(HandsOffStorage)();
};

#endif //__COMPONENTDATA_H_
```

Both the interfaces we've got here are already defined for us: **IComponentData** by MMC, and **IPersistStorage** by standard COM. (Remember those **IPersist** interfaces, by the way? You can't get away from them!) Notice also the reference to **CItem**; this is an entirely local non-COM class that we're going to use to hold details of each of our monitored items. We'll define it in a little while.

The **IComponentData** interface is used to control the display of data in the scope pane, whilst **IPersistStorage** is used to write away the current settings to a file.

DataObject

Next up is the header file **DataObject.h**:

```
// DataObject.h : Declaration of the CDataObject

#ifndef __DATAOBJECT_H_
#define __DATAOBJECT_H_

#include "resource.h"        // main symbols

const UUID UUIDRootNode = /* 7393A460-CE20-11d1-B12C-0040951082F7 */
{
    0x7393A460,
    0xCE20,
    0x11d1,
    {0xB1, 0x26, 0x00, 0x40, 0x95, 0x10, 0x82, 0xF7}
};

const UUID UUIDComputerNode = /* DE3EA740-CF8B-11d1-B12E-0040951082F7 */
{
    0xDE3EA740,
    0xCF8B,
    0x11d1,
    {0xB1, 0x2E, 0x00, 0x40, 0x95, 0x10, 0x82, 0xF7}
};
```

```
const UUID UUIDObjectNode = /* FE495DC0-CF8B-11d1-B12E-0040951082F7 */
{
   0xFE495DC0,
   0xCF8B,
   0x11d1,
   {0xB1, 0x2E, 0x00, 0x40, 0x95, 0x10, 0x82, 0xF7}
};

/////////////////////////////////////////////////////////////////////////////
// CDataObject
class ATL_NO_VTABLE CDataObject :
   public CComObjectRootEx<CComSingleThreadModel>,
   public CComCoClass<CDataObject, &CLSID_DataObject>,
   public IDataObject,
   public IMyDataObject
{
private:
   static UINT s_cfDisplayName;
   static UINT s_cfNodeType;
   static UINT s_cfSnapinClsid;

   long m_cookie;

   void WriteDisplayName (IStream* pStream);
   void WriteNodeType (IStream* pStream);
   void WriteClsid (IStream* pStream);

public:
   CDataObject()
   {
      s_cfDisplayName = RegisterClipboardFormat(CCF_DISPLAY_NAME);
      s_cfNodeType = RegisterClipboardFormat(CCF_NODETYPE);
      s_cfSnapinClsid =
            RegisterClipboardFormat(CCF_SNAPIN_CLASSID);
   }

DECLARE_REGISTRY_RESOURCEID(IDR_DATAOBJECT)

BEGIN_COM_MAP(CDataObject)
   COM_INTERFACE_ENTRY(IDataObject)
   COM_INTERFACE_ENTRY(IMyDataObject)
END_COM_MAP()

// IDataObject
public:
   STDMETHOD(GetDataHere)(FORMATETC* pformatetc, STGMEDIUM* pmedium);
   STDMETHOD(GetData)(LPFORMATETC lpFormatetcIn,
            LPSTGMEDIUM lpMedium);
   STDMETHOD(EnumFormatEtc)(DWORD dwDirection,
            LPENUMFORMATETC* ppEnumFormatEtc);
   STDMETHOD(QueryGetData)(LPFORMATETC lpFormatetc);
   STDMETHOD(GetCanonicalFormatEtc)(LPFORMATETC lpFormatetcIn,
            LPFORMATETC lpFormatetcOut);
```

```
    STDMETHOD(SetData)(LPFORMATETC lpFormatetc, LPSTGMEDIUM lpMedium,
                BOOL bRelease);
    STDMETHOD(DAdvise)(LPFORMATETC lpFormatetc, DWORD advf,
                LPADVISESINK pAdvSink, LPDWORD pdwConnection);
    STDMETHOD(DUnadvise)(DWORD dwConnection);
    STDMETHOD(EnumDAdvise)(LPENUMSTATDATA* ppEnumAdvise);
// IMyDataObject
public:
    STDMETHOD(get_Cookie)(/*[out, retval]*/ long* pVal);
    STDMETHOD(put_Cookie)(/*[in]*/ long newVal);
};

#endif //__DATAOBJECT_H_
```

There's some interesting stuff in here, for sure. **IDataObject** is basically an OLE data transfer interface, which is why it talks about things like clipboard formats. We're using it here to provide information to MMC about any one of the nodes in the display. When we implement it, we have to say in which formats we're prepared to transfer information about our data items back to MMC, which is the reason for the registration procedure in the constructor. Note that the parameters to **RegisterClipboardFormat()** (eg **CCF_DISPLAY_NAME**) are UNICODE strings defined in **mmc.h**.

The UUIDs are there to be returned to the MMC if it asks for information in node type format – as we'll see shortly, each of these UUIDs represents a different node type.

The cookie is a unique number identifying the node represented by this instance of the object. The interface that I've added, **IMyDataObject**, simply exposes this number as a property in order to make it simple to set up and retrieve. You could, if you wanted to, simply define your own clipboard format in order to get at the cookie (in fact that's what one of the Microsoft samples does), but personally I think that it's neater to add a second interface.

Component

Our third header is **Component.h**:

```
// Component.h : Declaration of the CComponent

#ifndef __COMPONENT_H_
#define __COMPONENT_H_

#include "resource.h"        // main symbols

/////////////////////////////////////////////////////////////////////////////
// CComponent
class ATL_NO_VTABLE CComponent :
   public CComObjectRootEx<CComSingleThreadModel>,
   public CComCoClass<CComponent, &CLSID_Component>,
   public IComponent
{
```

```
private:
   LPRESULTDATA m_pResultData;
   LPCONSOLEVERB m_pConsoleVerb;
   LPHEADERCTRL m_pHeaderCtrl;
   LPIMAGELIST m_pImageResult;
   HBITMAP m_hBmp16x16;
   HBITMAP m_hBmp32x32;

   void DoAddImages (LPDATAOBJECT lpDataObject);
   void DoSelect (LPDATAOBJECT lpDataObject, long arg);
   void DoShow (LPDATAOBJECT lpDataObject);

public:
   CComponent()
   {
   }

DECLARE_REGISTRY_RESOURCEID(IDR_COMPONENT)

BEGIN_COM_MAP(CComponent)
   COM_INTERFACE_ENTRY(IComponent)
END_COM_MAP()

// IComponent
public:
   STDMETHOD(Initialize)(LPCONSOLE lpConsole);
   STDMETHOD(Notify)(LPDATAOBJECT lpDataObject,
               MMC_NOTIFY_TYPE event, long arg, long param);
   STDMETHOD(Destroy)(long cookie);
   STDMETHOD(GetResultViewType)(long cookie,  LPOLESTR* ppViewType,
               long* pViewOptions);
   STDMETHOD(QueryDataObject)(long cookie, DATA_OBJECT_TYPES type,
               LPDATAOBJECT* ppDataObject);
   STDMETHOD(GetDisplayInfo)(RESULTDATAITEM*  pResultDataItem);
   STDMETHOD(CompareObjects)(LPDATAOBJECT lpDataObjectA,
               LPDATAOBJECT lpDataObjectB);
};

#endif //__COMPONENT_H_
```

This one isn't particularly exciting – I'll cover the private member functions and variables in due course. The interface is a standard MMC one, and is used to control one data item in the results pane.

ExtendContextMenu

Our last header is **ExtendContextMenu.h**:

```
// ExtendContextMenu.h : Declaration of the CExtendContextMenu

#ifndef __EXTENDCONTEXTMENU_H_
#define __EXTENDCONTEXTMENU_H_

#include "resource.h"       // main symbols
```

```
///////////////////////////////////////////////////////////////////////////
// CExtendContextMenu
class ATL_NO_VTABLE CExtendContextMenu :
   public CComObjectRootEx<CComSingleThreadModel>,
   public CComCoClass<CExtendContextMenu, &CLSID_ExtendContextMenu>,
   public IExtendContextMenu,
   public IMyExtendContextMenu
{
private:
   IConsoleNameSpace* m_pConsoleNameSpace;

   void DoErrors (LPDATAOBJECT pDataObject);
   void DoNew (LPDATAOBJECT pDataObject);
   void DoPing (LPDATAOBJECT pDataObject);

public:
   CExtendContextMenu()
   {
      m_pConsoleNameSpace = NULL;
   }

   void FinalRelease()
   {
      if (m_pConsoleNameSpace)
         m_pConsoleNameSpace->Release();
   }

DECLARE_REGISTRY_RESOURCEID(IDR_EXTENDCONTEXTMENU)

BEGIN_COM_MAP(CExtendContextMenu)
   COM_INTERFACE_ENTRY(IExtendContextMenu)
   COM_INTERFACE_ENTRY(IMyExtendContextMenu)
END_COM_MAP()

// IExtendContextMenu
public:
   STDMETHOD(AddMenuItems)(LPDATAOBJECT pDataObject,
               LPCONTEXTMENUCALLBACK piCallback,
               long* pInsertionAllowed);
   STDMETHOD(Command)(long lCommandID, LPDATAOBJECT pDataObject);

// IMyExtendContextMenu
public:
   STDMETHOD(put_Console)(/*[in]*/ LPUNKNOWN newVal);
};

#endif //__EXTENDCONTEXTMENU_H_
```

This interface is used to deal with extensions to the context menu (the one that appears if you right-click on an item or click the Action button). It needs access to the console name space interface, so I've created a second interface in order to pass that in as a property – like we did with the cookie in **DataObject**. The main interface, **IExtendContextMenu**, is standard MMC.

CItem

Inside our **ComponentData** object, we maintain a list of data items in a tree, represented locally by objects of type **CItem**. This isn't a COM object class – it's just an ordinary C++ class that's a convenient way of storing a local tree of data. Here's the header file:

```
// Item.h : Declaration of the CItem

#include "mmc.h"

#ifndef __ITEM_H_
#define __ITEM_H_

class CItem;
typedef CItem* LPITEM;

class CItem
{
private:
   LPOLESTR m_lpszName;
   LPOLESTR m_lpszClsid;
   int m_level;
   int m_nSub;
   LPITEM *m_pSubs;
   HSCOPEITEM m_hScopeItem;
   LPITEM m_lpParent;
   int m_ping;

public:
   CItem ();
   CItem (ULONG indent, LPOLESTR lpszName, LPOLESTR lpszData,
         LPITEM lpParent);
   ~CItem();

   LPOLESTR GetName ();
   LPOLESTR GetClsid ();
   int GetCount ();
   LPITEM GetSubItem (int sub);
   LPITEM AddItem (LPOLESTR lpszName, LPOLESTR lpszData);
   void SetScopeItem (HSCOPEITEM hScopeItem);
   HSCOPEITEM GetScopeItem ();
   int GetLevel ();
   void Ping ();
   LPOLESTR GetPing ();
   void ListErrors ();
};

#endif //__ITEM_H_
```

The key to understanding this object is the pair of member variables **m_nSub** and **m_pSubs**. These define an array of pointers to items in the next level down. This enables us to represent a tree of nodes locally. We'll see later on how we use this object to communicate with our monitor service and our objects that are being monitored (remember the whole point of this exercise?!)

For the time being however, now that we've defined our header files, we really need to understand the interconnections between each of them and their corresponding **.cpp** files. We're going to be moving at a pretty fast pace from now on and it's best if we have a solid foundation for us to start on. The following diagram shows which **.cpp** files include which **.h** files besides **ObjectMonitor.h** and **stdafx.h**:

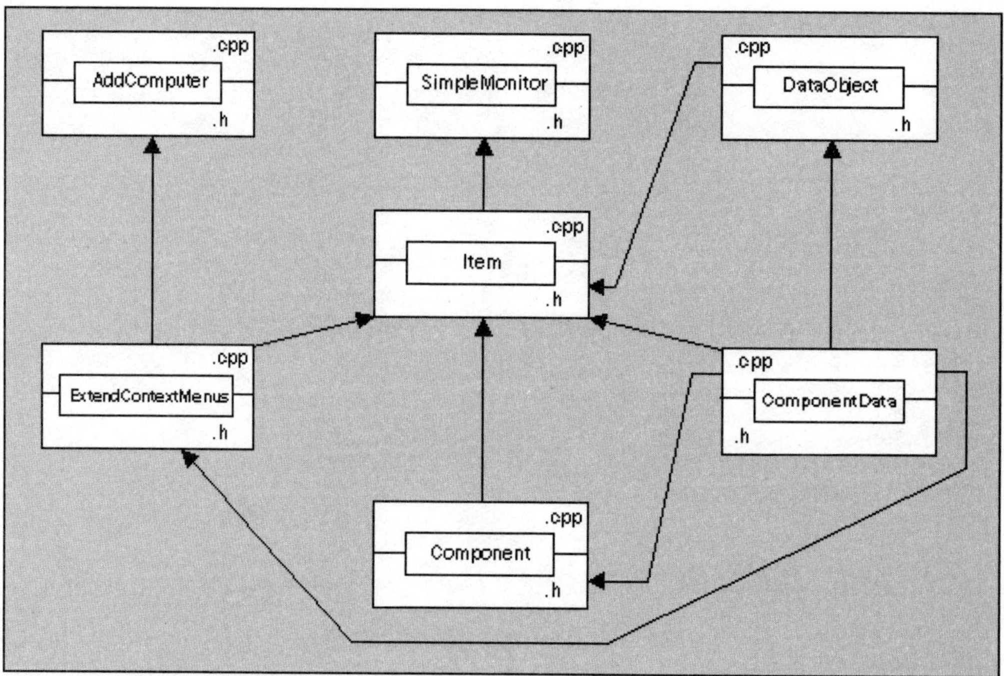

MMC and the Registry

The critical interface that we're going to have to implement is **IComponentData**; as I've said above, this is used to represent the data in the scope pane. This is the interface that the MMC queries for in our snap-in in order to set the whole ball rolling. But how does it know which object to get hold of? The answer is in the registry. Let's have a look at the registry settings that we're going to have to set up, and take a walk through the code that gets invoked inside the **DllRegisterServer** routine in our DLL. The routine below is called from the standard routine **DllRegisterServer** and is added to **ObjectMonitor.cpp** just after the object map declaration.

There's an area of the registry devoted to snap-ins, and we need to add our details to it. Note the highlighted UUID: this is the class ID of the object that implements **IComponentData**, as allocated by the ATL object wizard (you can verify this by looking at the **ComponentData** coclass in the IDL file above).

```
void RegisterSnapin ()
{
   HKEY hMmcParentKey;
   RegOpenKey (HKEY_LOCAL_MACHINE,
              L"Software\\Microsoft\\MMC\\SnapIns",
              &hMmcParentKey);
     HKEY hObjMonParentKey;
   RegCreateKey (hMmcParentKey,
                L"{37842E90-CE2C-11d1-B12C-0040951082F7}",
          &hObjMonParentKey);
```

Now we have to give it a name and identify the root node type. Recall that we're going to have three types of node in our snap-in: the root, computers and objects. Each represents a lower level in the scope pane tree. The node types are all defined below. The UUIDs are simply obtained by using the UUIDGEN tool in Visual Studio.

```
   RegSetValueEx (hObjMonParentKey,
                  L"NameString", 0, REG_SZ,
                  (LPBYTE)L"Object Monitor SnapIn",
                  sizeof(L"Object Monitor SnapIn"));

   RegSetValueEx (hObjMonParentKey, L"NodeType", 0, REG_SZ,
           (LPBYTE)L"{7393A460-CE20-11d1-B12C-0040951082F7}",
           sizeof(L"{7393A460-CE20-11d1-B12C-0040951082F7}"));

   HKEY hStandAloneKey;
   RegCreateKey (hObjMonParentKey, L"StandAlone", &hStandAloneKey);
   RegCloseKey (hStandAloneKey);

   HKEY hNodeTypesKey;
   RegCreateKey (hObjMonParentKey, L"NodeTypes", &hNodeTypesKey);

   HKEY hNodeKey;
   RegCreateKey (hNodeTypesKey,
          L"{7393A460-CE20-11d1-B12C-0040951082F7}", &hNodeKey);

   RegSetValueEx (hNodeKey, NULL, 0, REG_SZ,
           (LPBYTE)L"Root Node", sizeof(L"Root Node"));

   RegCloseKey (hNodeKey);

   RegCreateKey(hNodeTypesKey,
           L"{DE3EA740-CF8B-11d1-B12E-0040951082F7}",
           &hNodeKey);

   RegSetValueEx (hNodeKey,
           NULL, 0, REG_SZ,
           (LPBYTE)L"Computer Node",
           sizeof(L"Computer Node"));

   RegCloseKey (hNodeKey);
   RegCreateKey (hNodeTypesKey,
           L"{FE495DC0-CF8B-11d1-B12E-0040951082F7}",
           &hNodeKey);
```

```
    RegSetValueEx (hNodeKey,
            NULL, 0, REG_SZ,
            (LPBYTE)L"Object Node",
            sizeof(L"Object Node"));
    RegCloseKey (hNodeKey);
    RegCloseKey (hNodeTypesKey);
    RegCloseKey (hObjMonParentKey);
    RegCloseKey (hMmcParentKey);
}
```

Why do we need to specify all the UUIDs for these node types? As it happens, for a stand-alone snap-in like the one we're developing, we could get away with only defining the root node. All we have to do is make it unique, so that MMC doesn't treat us as an extension to an existing node type. However, we might as well define them all, for the sake of completeness – we might wish to support extensions to our snap-in at some point in the future. We mustn't forget either that it's always a good idea to define a method to unregister our snap-in as well and we'll do that in **`ObjectMonitor.cpp`** as well:

```
void UnregisterSnapin ()
{
    HKEY hMmcParentKey;
    RegOpenKey (HKEY_LOCAL_MACHINE,
            L"Software\\Microsoft\\MMC\\SnapIns",
            &hMmcParentKey);

    HKEY hObjMonParentKey;
    RegOpenKey (hMmcParentKey,
            L"{F3A462B0-CE1F-11d1-B12C-0040951082F7}",
            &hObjMonParentKey);

    HKEY hNodeTypesKey;
    RegOpenKey (hObjMonParentKey,
            L"NodeTypes",
            &hNodeTypesKey);

    RegDeleteKey (hNodeTypesKey,
            L"{7393A460-CE20-11d1-B12C-0040951082F7}");
    RegDeleteKey (hNodeTypesKey,
            L"{DE3EA740-CF8B-11d1-B12E-0040951082F7}");
    RegDeleteKey (hNodeTypesKey,
            L"{FE495DC0-CF8B-11d1-B12E-0040951082F7}");
    RegCloseKey (hNodeTypesKey);

    RegDeleteKey (hObjMonParentKey, L"NodeTypes");
    RegDeleteKey (hObjMonParentKey, L"StandAlone");
    RegCloseKey (hObjMonParentKey);
    RegDeleteKey (hMmcParentKey,
            L"{F3A462B0-CE1F-11d1-B12C-0040951082F7}");
    RegCloseKey (hMmcParentKey);
}
```

Note also the fact that we're using Unicode strings throughout. We do this because later on we'll see that MMC forces us to build this as a Unicode project.

A Walk Through MMC

Initializing Our Snap-in

OK, we're ready to take a stroll through our snap-in code. As I said above, the `IComponentData` interface is the point of entry to the snap-in. If you take a look at the sample code, you'll notice that the `ComponentData` object implements the `IPersistStorage` interface as well; we'll come back to that a little later. From here on in, things will get a little complex, as we'll have to do a little bit of dodging and weaving from one of our objects to another. However, the good thing is that, for once, we're dealing with a program that has a visual interface, so we can actually see the effect of our code without going to the trouble of writing endless Visual Basic test apps.

Let's imagine that we've built our snap-in, and it has never been run before. We start up MMC, by simply running it as `mmc` from the Run... command box. If we ask to add a snap-in, we see something like this appears:

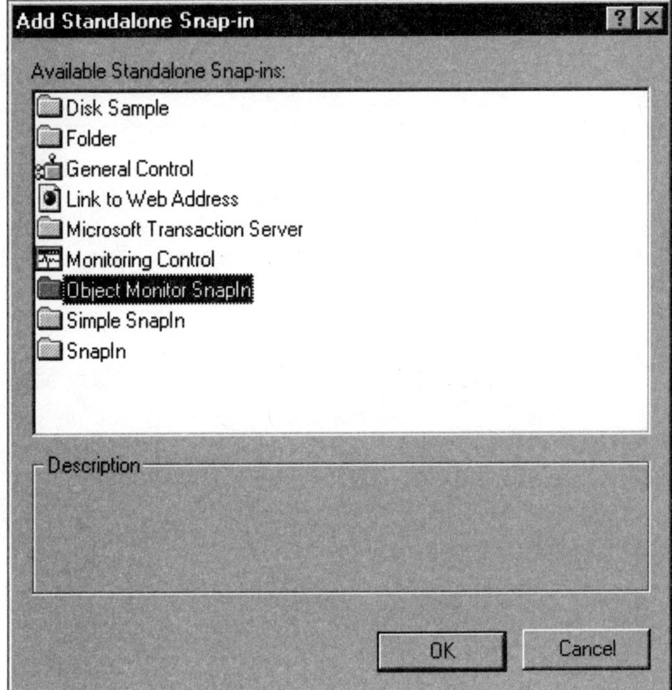

Here we see that our object monitor snap-in is known to MMC, which is a good sign. If we select it, we now see something like this:

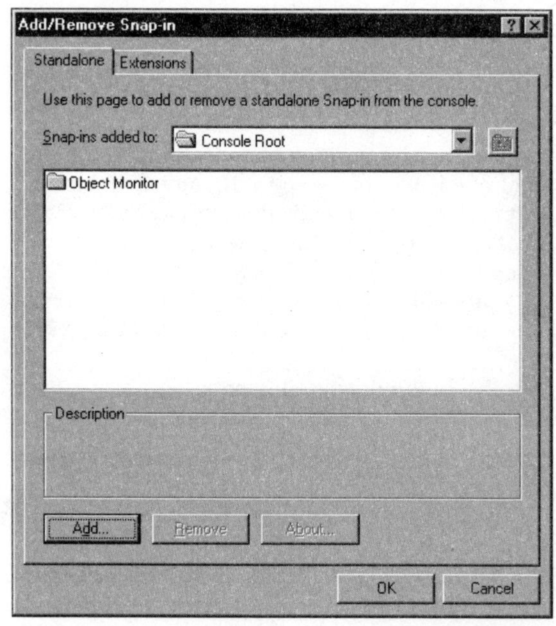

Now, at this point, MMC has already started invoking our code. Let's see what it's done. Curiously, it hasn't invoked the `Initialize()` method of `IComponentData`. Instead, it's gone straight for `QueryDataObject()`. So, we shouldn't take it for granted that `Initialize()` is always the first method called! Having said that, if we start our explanation of `IComponentData` anywhere other than with `Initialize()`, we'll get tied into all sorts of knots, so I won't say any more about it for now.

If we now click on the OK button, our MMC display comes back, with our root item ("Object Monitor") duly shown in the tree:

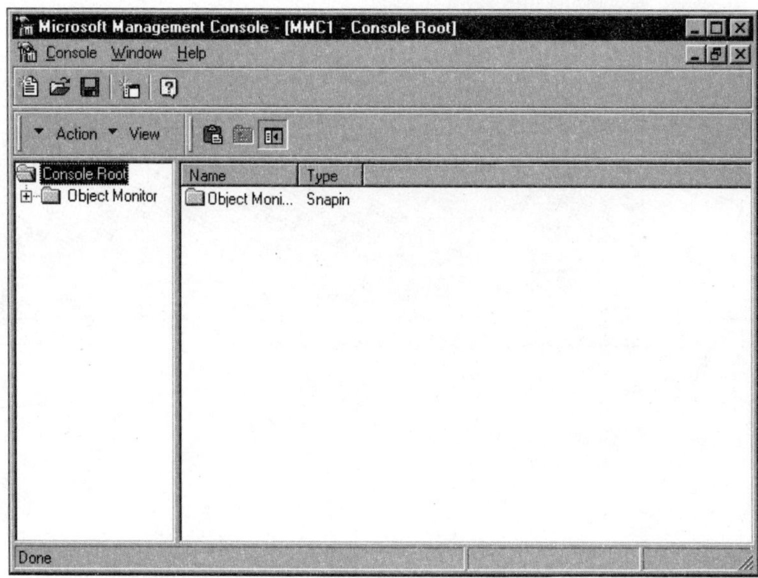

Several interactions have taken place in order for this to happen. The first is the invocation of **Initialize()** (at last!). This is what it looks like. We start off by creating our root item:

```
STDMETHODIMP CComponentData::Initialize (LPUNKNOWN pUnknown)
{
    m_pRoot = new CItem();
```

Remember that **CItem** is a local non-COM object created purely for my own convenience, to hold details about every node in the tree. Depending on which level we are in the tree, it will be used to hold data about the root node, a computer, an object or a logged error. It's simple, but versatile. When first created, the root item is completely empty. Let's carry on the initialization. The next thing we do is get hold of some other interfaces from the incoming console **IUnknown**. We'll need them later.

```
    pUnknown->QueryInterface (IID_IConsoleNameSpace,
        (void**)(&m_pConsoleNameSpace));
    pUnknown->QueryInterface (IID_IContextMenuProvider,
        (void**)(&m_pContextMenuProvider));
```

Next, we need to set up an object to manage extensions to the context menu (That's the little thing that pops up when you right-click over one of the items in the tree.) In order to do that, we'll use our extra **IMyExtendContextMenu** interface to pass a pointer to the console namespace interface into the context menu extension object.

We'll see what happens when we actually extend the menu later on.

```
    CComObject<CExtendContextMenu> *pExtendContextMenu;
    CComObject<CExtendContextMenu>::CreateInstance(&pExtendContextMenu);

    pExtendContextMenu->QueryInterface (IID_IExtendContextMenu,
        (void**) &m_pExtendContextMenu);

    IMyExtendContextMenu* pMyExtendContextMenu;
    pExtendContextMenu->QueryInterface (IID_IMyExtendContextMenu,
        (void**) &pMyExtendContextMenu);

    pMyExtendContextMenu->put_Console (pUnknown);
    pMyExtendContextMenu->Release ();
```

Finally, we set up the strip of icons to be used when displaying items in the scope pane. I've used four icons in this example – two sets of two (one for a computer, one for an object, one for selected, one for unselected). We'll see how they are selected in a little while. We use an **external HINSTANCE** variable called **ghInst** declared in both **ComponentData.cpp** and **Component.cpp** to handle the bitmaps.

```
    LPCONSOLE lpConsole;
    pUnknown->QueryInterface (IID_IConsole, (void**)(&lpConsole));

    LPIMAGELIST lpImageScope;
    lpConsole->QueryScopeImageList (&lpImageScope);
    lpConsole->Release();
```

```
    HBITMAP hBmp16x16 = LoadBitmap (ghInst,
                          MAKEINTRESOURCE (IDB_16x16));
    HBITMAP hBmp32x32 = LoadBitmap (ghInst,
                          MAKEINTRESOURCE (IDB_32x32));

    lpImageScope->ImageListSetStrip
               (reinterpret_cast<LONG*> (hBmp16x16),
               reinterpret_cast<LONG*> (hBmp32x32),
               0, RGB (0,255,0));
    lpImageScope->Release();

    return S_OK;
}
```

As you can see, the snap-in caches interface pointers during initialization. These are released when the snap-in is destroyed:

```
STDMETHODIMP CComponentData::Destroy()
{
    if (m_pConsoleNameSpace)
       m_pConsoleNameSpace->Release();
    if (m_pContextMenuProvider)
       m_pContextMenuProvider->Release();
    if (m_pExtendContextMenu)
       m_pExtendContextMenu->Release();
    if (m_pRoot)
       delete m_pRoot;
    return S_OK;
}
```

OK, so that's our snap-in duly initialized. Next, MMC asks us for details of the root item, by invoking the **QueryDataObject()** method – still on our **IComponentData** interface. In this, we start off by creating an object with interface **IDataObject** to represent the item in the display:

```
STDMETHODIMP CComponentData::QueryDataObject (long cookie,
          DATA_OBJECT_TYPES type, LPDATAOBJECT* ppDataObject)
{
    CComObject<CDataObject>* pDataObject;
    CComObject<CDataObject>::CreateInstance(&pDataObject);
```

As I mentioned earlier, this is a standard OLE interface that is used for data transfer – it's not an MMC special. Our implementation of the interface is in fact pretty minimal, as we'll see shortly. As with the context menu, we'll use our extra interface **IMyDataObject** to initialize the object:

```
    IMyDataObject* pMyObject;
    pDataObject->QueryInterface (IID_IMyDataObject,
                          (void**) &pMyObject);

    if (cookie)
       pMyObject->put_Cookie (cookie);
    else
       pMyObject->put_Cookie (reinterpret_cast<long> (m_pRoot));
```

What's this cookie? The cookie is a reference to our own local data representing the item in the tree. Once we start moving down the tree, the cookie passed into us will be non-zero (of which more later), but this time it's zero, so we'll use the pointer to our root item instead. Notice that the **`Cookie`** property is part of our additional interface, so that we can pass the cookie into our **`DataObject`** object – we'll see why it needs it soon.

Finally, we pass the pointer to the **`IDataObject`** interface back to the MMC, and set up our extensions to the context menu:

```
    pDataObject->QueryInterface(IID_IDataObject,
       reinterpret_cast<void**>(ppDataObject));

    pMyObject->Release();

    if (m_pContextMenuProvider)
       m_pContextMenuProvider->AddPrimaryExtensionItems
                    (m_pExtendContextMenu, *ppDataObject);

    return S_OK;
}
```

How does the menu get extended? What happens next is that the MMC invokes the **`AddMenuItems()`** method on our **`IExtendContextMenu`** interface. What we do in response depends on two things: what we are allowed to do by MMC, and what level we are at in the tree. To find out what level we are at in the tree, we need to get hold of the local **`CItem`** object that corresponds to the **`DataObject`** that we've been passed a pointer to. There's a one-to-one correspondence between our local **`CItem`** objects and the **`DataObject()`** COM objects that MMC deals with; each one represents a single node in the tree. The link between the two is the cookie, and the next code segment shows how we get from the cookie to the local **`CItem`** object.

You'll see the section of code that gets the local data item in several places, so it's quite important to spend a little while making sure that you understand exactly what it's doing:

```
STDMETHODIMP CExtendContextMenu::AddMenuItems (LPDATAOBJECT pDataObject,
                        LPCONTEXTMENUCALLBACK pCallback,
                        long* pInsertionAllowed)
{
   // Get local data item
```

```
IMyDataObject* pMyObject;
pDataObject->QueryInterface (IID_IMyDataObject, (void**) &pMyObject);

long cookie;
pMyObject->get_Cookie (&cookie);
pMyObject->Release ();

LPITEM lpItem = reinterpret_cast<LPITEM> (cookie);

if (!lpItem)
   return S_OK;

// Find out level in node tree

int level = lpItem->GetLevel ();

CONTEXTMENUITEM cmi;
memset (&cmi, 0, sizeof (CONTEXTMENUITEM));
```

The **GetLevel()** method on the **CItem** object finds out at what level in the tree of items we're at. If we're at level –1, our item represents the root of the tree. If we're at level 0, our item represents a computer. Finally, if we're at level 1, our item represents a monitored object. We'll look at the **CItem** code later on.

If we're dealing with an object in the tree, we're going to add an option to the top of the menu to allow the user to re-request the error log for this object:

```
// Level 1 (objects)

if ((*pInsertionAllowed & CCM_INSERTIONALLOWED_TOP) &&
   (level == 1))
{
   cmi.strName = L"Error Log";
   cmi.lCommandID = 0x1;
   cmi.lInsertionPointID = CCM_INSERTIONPOINTID_PRIMARY_TOP;

   pCallback->AddItem (&cmi);
}
```

If we're at the root of the tree, we're going to extend the new menu to let the user add a computer to the list:

```
// Level -1 (root)

if ((*pInsertionAllowed & CCM_INSERTIONALLOWED_NEW) &&
   (level == -1))
{
   cmi.strName = L"Computer";
   cmi.lCommandID = 0x2;
   cmi.lInsertionPointID = CCM_INSERTIONPOINTID_PRIMARY_NEW;
```

```
        pCallback->AddItem (&cmi);
    }
```

If we're dealing with an object, we're going to extend the task menu to let the user ping the object:

```
    // Level 1 (objects)

    if ((*pInsertionAllowed & CCM_INSERTIONALLOWED_TASK) &&
        (level == 1))
    {
        cmi.strName = L"Ping";
        cmi.lCommandID = 0x3;
        cmi.lInsertionPointID = CCM_INSERTIONPOINTID_PRIMARY_TASK;
        pCallback->AddItem (&cmi);
    }

    return S_OK;
}
```

We'll see what happens when we add a new computer in a minute, but first let's complete this first round of interactions by looking at what the MMC does with the **IDataObject** interface that we passed back in the **QueryDataObject()** call. It invokes the **GetDataHere()** method:

```
STDMETHODIMP CDataObject::GetDataHere (LPFORMATETC lpFormatEtc,
                                       LPSTGMEDIUM lpMedium)
{
    // Overlay global data with stream

    IStream* pStream;
    CreateStreamOnHGlobal (lpMedium->hGlobal, FALSE, &pStream);

    CLIPFORMAT cf = lpFormatEtc->cfFormat;

    // Handle correct clipboard format
    if (cf == s_cfDisplayName)
        WriteDisplayName (pStream);
    else if (cf == s_cfNodeType)
        WriteNodeType (pStream);
    else if (cf == s_cfSnapinClsid)
        WriteClsid (pStream);

    pStream->Release ();

    return S_OK;
}
```

Remember those clipboard formats that we registered in the constructor for **CDataObject**? Well, we've declared them in **DataObject.cpp** and now we get to use them. We are required to support all three of these in our snap-in, although MMC doesn't actually make much use of them. As far as I have been able to ascertain, MMC only ever asks us for the node type (and if you leave it blank, it doesn't seem to care!) and the display name. The only display name that it asks us for is that for the root.

Here are the private member functions that do the actual work for us here:

```
void CDataObject::WriteNodeType (IStream* pStream)
{
   // If no cookie defined, bomb out

   if (!m_cookie)
      return;

   // Get level from local object

   LPITEM lpItem = reinterpret_cast<LPITEM> (m_cookie);
   int level = lpItem->GetLevel ();

   // Write UUID for correct node type to stream

   switch (level)
   {
      case -1:
         pStream->Write (&UUIDRootNode, sizeof (UUID), NULL);
         break;

      case 0:
         pStream->Write (&UUIDComputerNode, sizeof (UUID), NULL);
         break;

      case 1:
         pStream->Write (&UUIDObjectNode, sizeof (UUID), NULL);
         break;
   }
}

void CDataObject::WriteDisplayName (IStream* pStream)
{
   pStream->Write (L"Object Monitor", sizeof (L"Object Monitor"),
            NULL);
}

void CDataObject::WriteClsid (IStream* pStream)
{
   pStream->Write (&CLSID_ComponentData,
            sizeof(CLSID_ComponentData), NULL);
}
```

Apart from `GetDataHere()`, I've left all the methods in `IDataObject` as returning `E_NOTIMPL`. In this relatively simple snap-in, they just aren't necessary. Unfortunately, we can't get away from using `IDataObject`, because–as we shall see–this is the vehicle of choice for all data to be passed between MMC and the snap-in. In our snap-in, however, it's basically an encapsulation of our local `CItem`, thinly disguised as the `Cookie` property. We've finished with the code for `DataObject`, so you can cross that one off your list.

The last method of `IComponentData` that gets invoked is `CreateComponent()`. This sets up an item for the result pane, and we'll discuss this further later.

Adding a New Computer

What happens when the user clicks on the extension to the New context menu that requests a new computer to be added? This is where the fun starts. The **Command()** method of our **IExtendContextMenu** interface gets invoked by MMC:

```
STDMETHODIMP CExtendContextMenu::Command (long lCommandID,
                                         LPDATAOBJECT pDataObject)
{
   switch (lCommandID)
   {
      case 0x01:
         DoErrors (pDataObject);
         break;

      case 0x02:
         DoNew (pDataObject);
         break;

      case 0x03:
         DoPing (pDataObject);
         break;
   }

   return S_OK;
}
```

When we added the Computer extension to the New menu, we specified **0x02** as the identifier of the menu choice, so the **DoNew()** private member function gets invoked (notice, incidentally, that the current item in the menu is identified by its **IDataObject** interface). Inside this, the first thing that happens is that a small dialog gets popped up to get the name of the new computer:

```
void CExtendContextMenu::DoNew (LPDATAOBJECT pDataObject)
{
   if (!m_pConsoleNameSpace)
      return;

   // Get name of new computer

   CAddComputer add;
   if (add.DoModal () == IDCANCEL)
      return;
```

Here's what the dialog looks like:

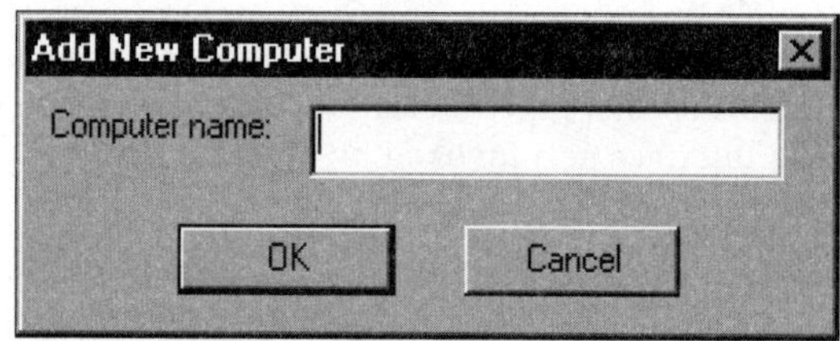

We generate a class, **CAddComputer**, to control this using the ATL object wizard, specifying a Dialog object rather than our usual Simple Object. If you've never done dialogs using ATL, don't panic – it's very straightforward. We haven't actually got many changes to make to what we're given by default, apart from changing the form layout. Here's the header file, **AddComputer.h**:

```
// AddComputer.h : Declaration of the CAddComputer

#ifndef __ADDCOMPUTER_H_
#define __ADDCOMPUTER_H_

#include "resource.h"       // main symbols

/////////////////////////////////////////////////////////////////////////////
// CAddComputer
class CAddComputer :
   public CDialogImpl<CAddComputer>
{
public:

   WCHAR m_wszComputer[32];

   CAddComputer();
   ~CAddComputer();

   enum { IDD = IDD_ADDCOMPUTER };

BEGIN_MSG_MAP(CAddComputer)
   MESSAGE_HANDLER(WM_INITDIALOG, OnInitDialog)
   COMMAND_ID_HANDLER(IDOK, OnOK)
   COMMAND_ID_HANDLER(IDCANCEL, OnCancel)
END_MSG_MAP()

   LRESULT OnInitDialog(UINT uMsg, WPARAM wParam, LPARAM lParam,
                        BOOL& bHandled);
   LRESULT OnOK(WORD wNotifyCode, WORD wID, HWND hWndCtl, BOOL&
                  bHandled);
   LRESULT OnCancel(WORD wNotifyCode, WORD wID, HWND hWndCtl,
                     BOOL& bHandled);
};

#endif //__ADDCOMPUTER_H_
```

That public member variable is our vehicle for getting the specified computer name back out of the dialog. Here's the implementation code:

```
// AddComputer.cpp : Implementation of CAddComputer
#include "stdafx.h"
#include "AddComputer.h"

/////////////////////////////////////////////////////////////////////////////
// CAddComputer

CAddComputer::CAddComputer()
{
}

CAddComputer::~CAddComputer()
{
}

LRESULT CAddComputer::OnInitDialog(UINT uMsg, WPARAM wParam, LPARAM lParam,
                                   BOOL& bHandled)
{
   return 1;  // Let the system set the focus
}

LRESULT CAddComputer::OnOK(WORD wNotifyCode, WORD wID, HWND hWndCtl,
                          BOOL& bHandled)
{
   *(WORD*) m_wszComputer = sizeof (m_wszComputer) - 1;

   WORD cbText = (WORD) SendDlgItemMessage (IDC_COMPUTER, EM_GETLINE,
                          0, (LPARAM) m_wszComputer);

   m_wszComputer[cbText] = 0;

   EndDialog(wID);
   return 0;
}

LRESULT CAddComputer::OnCancel(WORD wNotifyCode, WORD wID, HWND hWndCtl,
                              BOOL& bHandled)
{
   EndDialog(wID);
   return 0;
}
```

This is where ATL really loses out to MFC. We don't have nice things like **CEdit** classes, and we have to go back to straight C style Windows SDK programming to extract the string from the edit field. Nostalgic or what? Never mind, it's a very simple dialog.

Back in **CExtendContextMenu::DoNew()**, assuming that we've got a computer name, we then go through our little maneuver to get hold of the underlying **CItem** object (which represents the root item in this case):

```
// Get local item

IMyDataObject* pMyObject;
pDataObject->QueryInterface (IID_IMyDataObject,
                        (void**) &pMyObject);

long cookie;
pMyObject->get_Cookie (&cookie);
pMyObject->Release ();

LPITEM lpItem = reinterpret_cast<LPITEM> (cookie);
```

Now, we create an item to represent the new item as a sub-item to the root (we'll see the inner workings of this in a little while):

```
// Add new item to tree

LPITEM lpSubItem = lpItem->AddItem (add.m_wszComputer, NULL);
```

Next, we have to add it to the scope pane. This involves initializing a **SCOPEDATAITEM** structure...

```
// Now add it to scope pane

SCOPEDATAITEM sdi;

memset (&sdi, 0, sizeof (SCOPEDATAITEM));

sdi.mask = SDI_STR|SDI_PARAM|SDI_IMAGE|SDI_OPENIMAGE|SDI_PARENT;
```

The relative identifier is the identifier of the parent...

```
sdi.relativeID = lpItem->GetScopeItem ();
```

The display name will be set up in a callback (MMC doesn't allow us to do this directly)...

```
sdi.displayname = MMC_CALLBACK;
```

The new item pointer is set up as a parameter...

```
sdi.lParam = reinterpret_cast<LPARAM> (lpSubItem);
```

Now, something important almost slipped through there. We've set up the pointer to the current sub-item as the parameter in the scope data item structure. This will reappear as the cookie in a call to **QueryDataObject()** for this new item – see below for more details.

Finally, we decide which icons are to be used to represent the item in both open and closed state, and insert the item into the console name space:

```
      int level = lpSubItem->GetLevel ();

      if (level == 0)
      {
         sdi.nImage = 0;
         sdi.nOpenImage = 1;
      }

      else
      {
         sdi.nImage = 2;
         sdi.nOpenImage = 3;
      }

      m_pConsoleNameSpace->InsertItem (&sdi);
```

We save the identifier allocated so that we can use it for any subsequent children:

```
      lpSubItem->SetScopeItem (sdi.ID);
   }
```

MMC now has to get hold of **IDataObject** interfaces for each of the new items, so it calls the **QueryDataObject()** method of **IComponentData** that we saw earlier for *each* new item. This time, the cookie passed is the **lParam** member of the **SCOPEDATAITEM** structure, which we've set up to be a pointer to the underlying **CItem** object. If you feel that you're beginning to go round in circles at this point, don't worry. Take a break. Walk about for a bit, and then try again. It will become clear soon. Promise. Believe me, if you can get your head round this, you can tackle anything that Microsoft can throw at you...

Finally, I said that the display name would be set up by callback. The callback in question is an invocation of the **GetDisplayInfo()** method of **IComponentData**. This is what it looks like:

```
   STDMETHODIMP CComponentData::GetDisplayInfo (LPSCOPEDATAITEM pItem)
   {
      LPITEM lpItem = (LPITEM) pItem->lParam;

      pItem->displayname = lpItem->GetName ();
      return S_OK;
   }
```

So all we do is extract the name out of our underlying object and put it into the **SCOPEDATAITEM** structure. Don't ask me why we couldn't have done that without the callback... Once this is done, our new computer appears in the scope pane tree, just below the root:

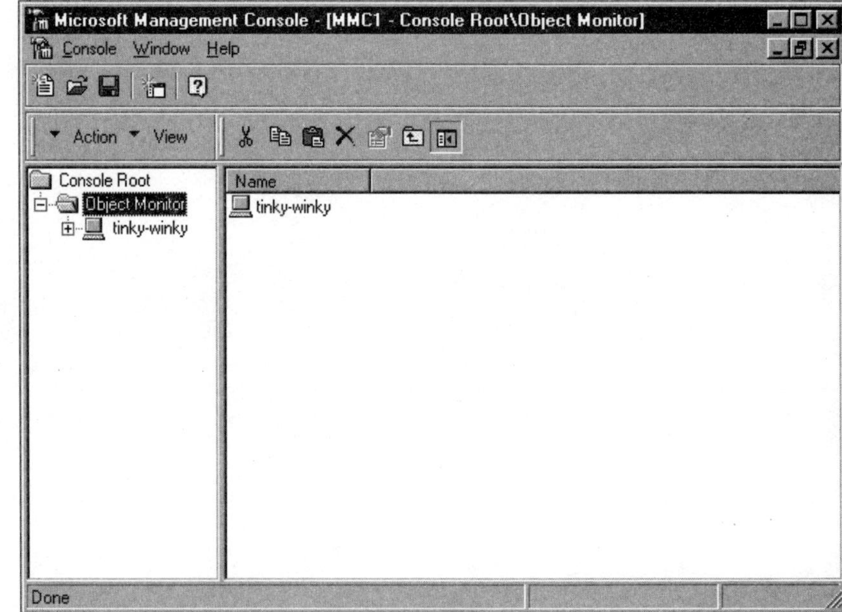

There's a nice little + sign next to it, too – but don't click on that just yet...

Populating the List of Objects

We skipped over something important in that last section. We blithely created a new **CItem** object without considering what that involved. Because the item in question represents a computer, creating it also involves populating it with a list of the monitored objects. I think it's time to look at our **CItem** class a little more closely.

First of all, let's take a quick look at the header files that we need:

```
// Item.cpp : Implementation of CItem
#include "stdafx.h"
#include "Item.h"
#include "SimpleMonitor.h"

#include <stdio.h>
```

Hey! **SimpleMonitor.h**! Where have you've been all this time? Don't say you're involved in this too? We'll see why we need this soon enough...

We've got two alternative constructors, a nice easy one for the root, and a more complex one for everything underneath it. Here's the first one:

```
CItem::CItem ()
{
   m_level = -1;
   m_nSub = 0;
   m_lpszName = new OLECHAR[5]
   lstrcpy(m_lpszName, L"Root");
   m_lpszClsid = 0;
   m_lpParent = 0;
   m_ping = 0;
}
```

This is used to create the root object in the snap-in. The other one is more interesting ...

```
CItem::CItem (ULONG level, LPOLESTR lpszName, LPOLESTR lpszClsid,
         LPITEM lpParent)
{
   // Set up local data from incoming arguments

   m_level = level;
   m_nSub = 0;
   m_lpParent = lpParent;
   m_ping = 0;

   int length = wcslen (lpszName);

   m_lpszName = new OLECHAR[length + 1];
   wcscpy (m_lpszName, lpszName);

   if (lpszClsid)
   {
      length = wcslen (lpszClsid);

      m_lpszClsid = new OLECHAR[length + 1];
      wcscpy (m_lpszClsid, lpszClsid);
   }

   else
      m_lpszClsid = 0;

   // If we're at level 0 (computers), get an IObjectList interface
   // to the monitor service

   if (m_level == 0)
   {
      //check if we want the local machine

      HRESULT hResult;

      MULTI_QI qis[1];
      memset (qis, 0, sizeof (MULTI_QI));

      qis[0].pIID = &IID_IObjectList;
```

```
WCHAR strMyName[MAX_COMPUTERNAME_LENGTH + 1];
DWORD dwSize = MAX_COMPUTERNAME_LENGTH + 1;
GetComputerName(strMyName, &dwSize);

if (lstrcmpi(strMyName, m_lpszName) == 0)
{
   hResult = CoCreateInstanceEx (CLSID_ObjectList, NULL,
        CLSCTX_ALL, NULL, 1, qis);
}
else
{
   COSERVERINFO serverInfo;
   memset (&serverInfo, 0, sizeof (COSERVERINFO));
   serverInfo.pwszName = m_lpszName;

   hResult = CoCreateInstanceEx (CLSID_ObjectList, NULL,
        CLSCTX_REMOTE_SERVER, &serverInfo, 1, qis);
}

if (FAILED (hResult))
   return;

CComPtr<IObjectList> pList =
         reinterpret_cast<IObjectList*> (qis[0].pItf);

// Enumerate the objects

long nObject;
pList->get_Count (&nObject);

IUnknown* pUnk;
pList->get__NewEnum (&pUnk);

CComPtr<IEnumVARIANT> pEnum;
pDispatch->QueryInterface (IID_IEnumVARIANT,
                 reinterpret_cast<void**> (&pEnum));

pEnum->Reset ();

for (int object = 0; object < nObject; object++)
{
   CComVariant vars;
   unsigned long count;
   pEnum->Next (1, &vars, &count);

   if (count == 0)
       break;

   // Get IMonObject interface for enumerated object

   IDispatch* pDispObj = vars.pdispVal;
```

```
            CComPtr<IMonObject> pObject;
            pDispObj->QueryInterface (IID_IMonObject,
               reinterpret_cast<void**> (&pObject));

            // Get name and class ID for object

            CComBSTR bstrName;
            pObject->get_Name (&bstrName);

            CComBSTR bstrClsid;
            pObject->get_CLSID (&bstrClsid);

            pObject->Release ();

            // Add item representing object to the tree

            AddItem (bstrName, bstrClsid);
         }

         pUnk->Release ();
      }
   }
```

This version of the constructor basically obtains an **IObjectList** interface from the monitor service on the computer in question, and uses it to enumerate all the monitored objects. A new **CItem** object is created for each one, and inserted into the tree below the computer's item using the **AddItem()** method.

Notice the use of smart pointers except for the **pUnk** pointer for the enumerator and the **pDispObj** pointer for the **MonObject**. In this latter case a smart pointer is not used because the interface is obtained from a **VARIANT** and the **CComVariant** ensures that the interface is correctly released. Also note that we check to see whether the requested machine is the same as the machine that the MMC is running on. This ensures that the **CLSCTX_REMOTE_SERVER** constant is only used when required; indeed, it's the instances of this constant in **item.cpp** that needs to be changed to **CLSCTX_SERVER** if you'd like to test the snap-in on your own machine before you spread it out across a network.

I should also emphasise that these items only exist in the local tree of **CItem** objects: they don't appear in the MMC scope pane. Yet.

You will notice that some memory is being allocated in the constructors. This is freed in the destructor:

```
CItem::~CItem()
{
   if (m_lpszName)
      delete [] m_lpszname;
   if (m_lpszClsid)
      delete [] m_lpszClsid
```

```
    for (int sub = 0; sub < m_nSub; sub++)
    {
        LPITEM lpItem = m_pSubs[sub];
        delete lpItem;
    }

    if (m_nSub)
    {
        delete [] m_pSubs;
    }
}
```

Here you can see that each **CItem** can be the parent of other items which are held in the **m_pSubs** array. This code deletes each item in the array and then the array itself. Whilst we're looking at **CItem**, let's look at some of the other local methods. Here's how we add a new item:

```
LPITEM CItem::AddItem (LPOLESTR lpszName, LPOLESTR lpszClsid)
{
    // Create item to hold new object details

    LPITEM pItem = new CItem (m_level + 1, lpszName, lpszClsid, this);

    // Extend array of sub-items from current item

    LPITEM* pSubs = new LPITEM[m_nSub + 1];

    if (m_nSub)
    {
        memcpy (pSubs, m_pSubs, m_nSub * sizeof (LPITEM));
        delete [] m_pSubs;
    }

    m_pSubs = pSubs;

    // Add new item into array of sub-items

    m_pSubs[m_nSub++] = pItem;

    return pItem;
}
```

These two methods get hold of the local member variables that were set up in the constructor:

```
LPOLESTR CItem::GetName ()
{
   LPOLESTR lpszName = new OLECHAR[wcslen (m_lpszName) + 1];
   wcscpy (lpszName, m_lpszName);

   return lpszName;
}

LPOLESTR CItem::GetClsid ()
{
   if (!m_lpszClsid)
      return NULL;

   LPOLESTR lpszClsid = new OLECHAR[wcslen (m_lpszClsid) + 1];
   wcscpy (lpszClsid, m_lpszClsid);

   return lpszClsid;
}
```

These two methods return the size of the tree and a pointer to one of the sub-items, respectively:

```
int CItem::GetCount ()
{
   return m_nSub;
}

LPITEM CItem::GetSubItem (int sub)
{
   if (sub >= m_nSub)
      return NULL;

   return m_pSubs[sub];
}
```

Finally, these three set the handle of the scope item relating to this node, retrieve it and get the current level in the tree, respectively.

```
void CItem::SetScopeItem (HSCOPEITEM hScopeItem)
{
   m_hScopeItem = hScopeItem;
}

HSCOPEITEM CItem::GetScopeItem ()
{
   return m_hScopeItem;
}

int CItem::GetLevel ()
{
   return m_level;
}
```

There are three more methods in **CItem**: **Ping()**, **GetPing()** and **ListErrors()**. These are getting dangerously close to the heart of what we're really up to here, so I'll put them on one side for now.

Expanding an Item

So what happens when you click on that little + next to the computer icon in the scope pane? Obviously, MMC needs to know what to show next, so it asks you. It does this by means of an invocation of the **Notify()** method in **IComponentData**. This is what our implementation of **Notify()** looks like. Notice that we're not particularly interested in anything apart from item expansions.

```
STDMETHODIMP CComponentData::Notify (LPDATAOBJECT lpDataObject,
                    MMC_NOTIFY_TYPE event, long arg, long param)
{
   // Only interested in item expansions

   if (event != MMCN_EXPAND)
      return S_OK;
```

This is similar to the stuff that we did when we added the new computer to the scope pane:

```
   // Set up scope item

   SCOPEDATAITEM sdi;

   memset (&sdi, 0, sizeof (SCOPEDATAITEM));

   sdi.mask = SDI_STR|SDI_PARAM|SDI_IMAGE|SDI_OPENIMAGE|SDI_PARENT;
   sdi.relativeID = static_cast<HSCOPEITEM> (param);
   sdi.displayname = MMC_CALLBACK;
```

Here's our usual code for getting hold of the underlying item:

```
   // Get local object

   IMyDataObject* pMyObject;
   lpDataObject->QueryInterface(IID_IMyDataObject, (void**) &pMyObject);

   long cookie;
   pMyObject->get_Cookie (&cookie);
   pMyObject->Release ();

   LPITEM lpItem = m_pRoot;

   if (cookie)
      lpItem = reinterpret_cast<LPITEM> (cookie);

     // Store incoming scope handle in local item

   lpItem->SetScopeItem (static_cast<HSCOPEITEM> (param));
```

Now let's just go through the list of sub-items (monitored objects in this case):

```
    int nSub = lpItem->GetCount ();

    // Go through list of sub-items

    for (int sub = 0; sub < nSub; sub++)
    {
       LPITEM lpSubItem = lpItem->GetSubItem (sub);
       sdi.lParam = reinterpret_cast<LPITEM> (lpSubItem);

       int level = lpSubItem->GetLevel ();
```

As before, when we added a new computer, we've set up the pointer to the current sub-item as the parameter in the scope data item structure. This will reappear as our cookie in a call to **`QueryDataObject()`** for this new item.

Next, we decide what icons to use, and then insert them into the console name space:

```
          // Decide on icon for scope pane display

       if (level == 0)
       {
          sdi.nImage = 0;
          sdi.nOpenImage = 1;
       }

       else
       {
          sdi.nImage = 2;
          sdi.nOpenImage = 3;
       }

          // Insert sub-item into namespace

       m_pConsoleNameSpace->InsertItem (&sdi);
    }

    return S_OK;
}
```

Once again, **`QueryDataObject()`** is invoked for each one to set up the **`IDataObject`** interface, and then **`GetDisplayInfo()`** is invoked to set up the display name.

User Actions

We covered the use of the menu to add a new computer to the list above; however, there are a couple of the other menu extensions that we haven't looked at yet. If the user selects a monitored object, and requests "Ping" from the "Task" menu, the **Command()** method of the **IExtendContextMenu** interface gets invoked, resulting in a call to **DoPing()**:

```
void CExtendContextMenu::DoPing (LPDATAOBJECT pDataObject)
{
   IMyDataObject* pMyObject;
   pDataObject->QueryInterface(IID_IMyDataObject,
                               (void**) &pMyObject);

   long cookie;
   pMyObject->get_Cookie (&cookie);
   pMyObject->Release ();

   LPITEM lpItem = reinterpret_cast<LPITEM> (cookie);

   lpItem->Ping ();
}
```

The **Ping()** method of **CItem** looks like this:

```
void CItem::Ping ()
{
   // Get class ID

   CLSID clsid;
   CLSIDFromString (m_lpszClsid, &clsid);

   // Instantiate, specifying IPing interface
   // first, check if we want the local machine

      HRESULT hResult;

   LPOLESTR lpszName = m_lpParent->GetName ();

   MULTI_QI qis[1];
   memset (qis, 0, sizeof (MULTI_QI));

   qis[0].pIID = &IID_IPing;

   WCHAR strMyName[MAX_COMPUTERNAME_LENGTH + 1];
   DWORD dwSize = MAX_COMPUTERNAME_LENGTH + 1;
   GetComputerName(strMyName, &dwSize);
   if (lstrcmpi(strMyName, lpszName) == 0)
```

```
    {
       hResult = CoCreateInstanceEx (clsid, NULL, CLSCTX_ALL, NULL,
          1, qis);
    }
    else
    {
       COSERVERINFO serverInfo;
       memset (&serverInfo, 0, sizeof (COSERVERINFO));
       serverInfo.pwszName = lpszName;

       hResult = CoCreateInstanceEx (clsid, NULL, C
          LSCTX_REMOTE_SERVER, &serverInfo, 1, qis);
    }

    delete [] lpszName;

    if (SUCCEEDED (hResult))
    {
         // Ping the object

       IPing* pPing = reinterpret_cast<IPing*> (qis[0].pItf);

       hResult = pPing->Ping ();

    pPing-> Release();
    }

    if (SUCCEEDED (hResult))
       m_ping = 1;
    else
       m_ping = -1;
}
```

In other words, it locates the object corresponding to the local item on the specified computer, and invokes **Ping()** on the **IPing** interface. The ping state of the local item is changed according to the result, and displayed in the result pane; the result pane is described below. There's also a method in **CPing** to get hold of the last known ping state:

```
LPOLESTR CItem::GetPing ()
{
    switch (m_ping)
    {
       case -1:
          return L"Failed";
       case 1:
          return L"Succeeded";
       default:
          return L"Unknown";
    }
}
```

We'll use this later on.

The other possible user action is to request an up to date error log for the selected monitored object. This results in a call to the **ListErrors()** method of **CItem**, which looks very similar to the code that is invoked to enumerate the monitored objects when a new computer is added:

```
void CItem::ListErrors ()
{
    // If we're not at level 1 (objects) bomb out

    if (m_level != 1)
        return;

    // Delete any sub-items (these represent previously fetched errors)

    for (int sub = 0; sub < m_nSub; sub++)
    {
        LPITEM lpItem = m_pSubs[sub];
        delete lpItem;
    }

    if (m_nSub)
    {
        delete[] m_pSubs;
        m_nSub = 0;
    }

    // Instantiate monitor service error object, specifying
    // IErrorList, on specified computer

    HRESULT hResult;
    LPOLESTR lpszName = m_lpParent->GetName ();

    MULTI_QI qis[1];
    memset (qis, 0, sizeof (MULTI_QI));

    qis[0].pIID = &IID_IErrorList;

    WCHAR strMyName[MAX_COMPUTERNAME_LENGTH + 1];
    DWORD dwSize = MAX_COMPUTERNAME_LENGTH + 1;
    GetComputerName(strMyName, &dwSize);

    if (lstrcmpi(strMyName, lpszName) == 0)
    {
        hResult = CoCreateInstanceEx (CLSID_ErrorList, NULL,
                CLSCTX_ALL, NULL, 1, qis);
    }
    else
    {
        COSERVERINFO serverInfo;
        memset (&serverInfo, 0, sizeof (COSERVERINFO));
        serverInfo.pwszName = lpszName;
        hResult = CoCreateInstanceEx (CLSID_ErrorList, NULL,
                CLSCTX_REMOTE_SERVER, &serverInfo, 1, qis);
    }
```

```
delete [] lpszName;

if (FAILED (hResult))
   return;

CComPtr<IErrorList> pList = reinterpret_cast<IErrorList*> (qis[0].pItf);

// Specify which object to enumerate errors for

CComBSTR bstrName = m_lpszName;
pList->put_Name (bstrName);

long nError;
hResult = pList->get_Count (&nError);

IUnknown* pUnk;
hResult = pList->get__NewEnum (&pUnk);

CComPtr<IEnumVARIANT> pEnum;
pUnk->QueryInterface (IID_IEnumVARIANT, (void**) &pEnum);

pUnk->Release();

pEnum->Reset ();

// Enumerate errors

for (int error = 0; error < nError; error++)
{
   CComVariant vars;
   unsigned long count;
   pEnum->Next (1, &vars, &count);

   if (count == 0)
      break;

   IDispatch* pDispErr = vars.pdispVal;

      // Query enumerated error object for IError interface

   CComPtr<IError> pError;
   pDispErr->QueryInterface (IID_IError, (void**) &pError);

      // Get descriptions

   CComBSTR bstrShort;
   pError->get_Short (&bstrShort);

   CComBSTR bstrLong;
   pError->get_Long (&bstrLong);
```

```
            // Add error details as new sub-item to tree

            AddItem (bstrShort, bstrLong);
        }
    }
```

The only other point worth noting is that, because the **`Notify()`** method will already have been called for this item, MMC has no knowledge of the sub-items. This is fine, because we don't want them to appear in the scope pane. However, we will want to see the error log in the result pane. Which brings us neatly on to the next subject for discussion...

Making Use of the Result Pane

The data in the result pane is manipulated by means of the **`IComponent`** interface. When you select an item in the scope pane, the corresponding result data gets displayed in the result pane. By default, the data to be shown will be the data for the next level down in the tree. For example, if you select one of the computers in the scope pane for our snap-in, full details of the monitored objects for that computer will be shown in the result pane. You can also add your own items to the result pane, if they aren't shown in the scope pane; for example, in our case, we don't show the errors logged in the scope pane, but we do add them in the result pane.

There is one **`IComponent`** interface for each item in the scope pane, and this gets created when the **`CreateComponent()`** method of **`IComponentData`** gets invoked:

```
STDMETHODIMP CComponentData::CreateComponent
                  (LPCOMPONENT* ppComponent)
{
   CComObject<CComponent>* pComponent;
   CComObject<CComponent>::CreateInstance(&pComponent);

   return pComponent->QueryInterface(IID_Icomponent,
      reinterpret_cast<void**>(ppComponent));
}
```

Nice and easy. OK, let's see what happens to **`IComponent`**. The first method to be invoked is **`Initialize()`**, which basically involves getting hold of a whole slew of interfaces from the console for later reference, and setting up the icon strip bitmap:

```
STDMETHODIMP CComponent::Initialize (LPCONSOLE lpConsole)
{
   lpConsole->QueryInterface (IID_IHeaderCtrl,
                  reinterpret_cast<void**> (&m_pHeaderCtrl));

   lpConsole->SetHeader (m_pHeaderCtrl);

   lpConsole->QueryInterface (IID_IResultData,
                  reinterpret_cast<void**> (&m_pResultData));
```

```
    lpConsole->QueryConsoleVerb (&m_pConsoleVerb);
    lpConsole->QueryResultImageList (&m_pImageResult);

    m_hBmp16x16 = LoadBitmap (ghInst, MAKEINTRESOURCE (IDB_16x16));
    m_hBmp32x32 = LoadBitmap (ghInst, MAKEINTRESOURCE (IDB_32x32));

    return S_OK;
}
```

Once again we are caching interface pointers, and we are loading GDI objects, so before we proceed we must make sure that these are released when the component goes away:

```
STDMETHODIMP CComponent::Destroy(long cookie)
{
    if (m_pHeaderCtrl)
        m_pHeaderCtrl->Release();
    if (m_pResultData)
        m_pResultData->Release();
    if (m_pConsoleVerb)
        m_pConsoleVerb->Release();
    if (m_pImageResult)
        m_pImageResult->Release();
    if (m_hBmp16x16)
        DeleteObject(m_hBmp16x16);
    if (m_hBmp32x32)
        DeleteObject(m_hBmp32x32);
    return S_OK;
}
```

The critical method in this interface is **`Notify()`**, which is invoked when an event occurs that affects the result pane. The selection of which events to handle depends on the required functionality. The key event is **`MMCN_SHOW`**. MMC triggers this when it needs to show the results for a given item.

```
STDMETHODIMP CComponent::Notify (LPDATAOBJECT lpDataObject,
              MMC_NOTIFY_TYPE event, long arg, long param)
{
    switch (event)
    {
        case MMCN_ACTIVATE:
        case MMCN_DBLCLICK:
        case MMCN_COLUMN_CLICK:
            break;

        case MMCN_ADD_IMAGES:
            DoAddImages (lpDataObject);
            break;

        case MMCN_SELECT:
            DoSelect (lpDataObject, arg);
            break;
```

```
        case MMCN_REFRESH:
        case MMCN_SHOW:
            DoShow (lpDataObject);
            break;
    }

    return S_OK;
}
```

Let's look at **DoShow()** more closely. We kick off with the usual stuff to extract the underlying item from the **IDataObject** interface:

```
void CComponent::DoShow (LPDATAOBJECT lpDataObject)
{
    IMyDataObject* pMyObject;
    lpDataObject->QueryInterface(IID_IMyDataObject,
                        reinterpret_cast<void**> (&pMyObject));

    long cookie;
    pMyObject->get_Cookie (&cookie);
    pMyObject->Release ();

    LPITEM lpItem = reinterpret_cast<LPITEM> (cookie);

    if (!lpItem)
        return;

    int level = lpItem->GetLevel ();
```

The action taken now depends on which level we are at. If we are at level -1 (i.e. the root item), we only need one column in the result pane, and we can let MMC decide which items to put into it:

```
    switch (level)
    {
        case -1:
            m_pHeaderCtrl->InsertColumn (0, L"Name", 0, 100);
            break;
```

If we are at level 0 (i.e. a computer item), we need three columns in the result pane, but we can still let MMC decide which items to put into it:

```
        case 0:
            m_pHeaderCtrl->InsertColumn (0, L"Name", 0, 100);
            m_pHeaderCtrl->InsertColumn (1, L"CLSID", 0, 250);
            m_pHeaderCtrl->InsertColumn (2, L"Ping state", 0, 100);
            break;
```

However, if we are at level 1 (i.e. a monitored object item), we need two columns in the result pane, and we also need to tell MMC what to put into it:

```
      case 1:
         m_pHeaderCtrl->InsertColumn (0, L"Short Description",
                                      0, 100);
         m_pHeaderCtrl->InsertColumn (1, L"Long Description",
                                      0, 300);

         m_pResultData->DeleteAllRsltItems ();
```

The code to insert the data into the results pane is similar to the code required to insert new items into the scope pane:

```
         RESULTDATAITEM rdi;
         memset (&rdi, 0, sizeof (RESULTDATAITEM));
         rdi.mask = RDI_STR | RDI_IMAGE | RDI_PARAM;
         rdi.nImage = 2;
         rdi.str = MMC_CALLBACK;

         int nSub = lpItem->GetCount ();

         for (int sub = 0; sub < nSub; sub++)
         {
            LPITEM lpSubItem = lpItem->GetSubItem (sub);
            rdi.lParam = reinterpret_cast<LPARAM> (lpSubItem);

            m_pResultData->InsertItem (&rdi);
         }
         break;
   }
}
```

What happens next? Well, MMC knows which items to display in the result pane, but it doesn't know what data to display for each one. So it invokes the **`GetDisplayInfo()`** method for each item.

```
STDMETHODIMP CComponent::GetDisplayInfo
            (RESULTDATAITEM* pResultDataItem)
{
   LPITEM lpItem = (LPITEM) pResultDataItem->lParam;

   if (!lpItem)
      return E_FAIL;

   if (pResultDataItem->str)
      delete [] pResultDataItem->str;

   int level = lpItem->GetLevel ();

   switch (level)
   {
```

Again, what we choose to display depends on which level we are at in the tree. At level 0 (i.e. a computer item), all we can show is the Name, in column 0:

```
        case 0:
           switch (pResultDataItem->nCol)
           {
              case 0:
                 pResultDataItem->str = lpItem->GetName ();
                 pResultDataItem->nImage = 0;
                 break;
           }
           break;
```

At level 1 (i.e. a monitored object item), we show the Name, Class ID and Ping state:

```
        case 1:
           switch (pResultDataItem->nCol)
           {
              case 0:
                 pResultDataItem->str = lpItem->GetName ();
                 pResultDataItem->nImage = 2;
                 break;

              case 1:
                 pResultDataItem->str = lpItem->GetClsid ();
                 break;

              case 2:
                 pResultDataItem->str = lpItem->GetPing ();
                 break;
           }
           break;
```

And at level 2 (i.e. a logged error item), we show the short and long descriptions (held in the **`Name`** and **`ClsID`** strings respectively):

```
        case 2:
           switch (pResultDataItem->nCol)
           {
              case 0:
                 pResultDataItem->str = lpItem->GetName ();
                 pResultDataItem->nImage = 2;
                 break;

              case 1:
                 pResultDataItem->str = lpItem->GetClsid ();
                 break;
           }
     }

     return S_OK;
  }
```

And that's about it for the results pane. I've taken a fairly simplistic approach to it for the purposes of this example. If you want, you can override most of its default behavior completely, and create some highly sophisticated displays – like, for example, the MTS snap-in.

Persistence

What if we don't want to set up our list of computers every time? What if we want the same ones to appear next time we open up the snap-in? MMC has the answer. If we implement **`IPersistStorage`** on our main snap-in object, it will *save* anything we want in a **`.msc`** file on exit, and re-load it next time.

As it happens, we only really need to implement two of the methods of **`IPersistStorage`**. Here's the **`Save`** method:

```
STDMETHODIMP CComponentData::Save (IStorage* pStorage,
                                   BOOL fSameAsLoad)
{
   // Construct enumerator for storage object

   CComPtr<IEnumSTATSTG> pEnum;
   pStorage->EnumElements (0, NULL, 0, &pEnum);

   // Go through  it, destroying everything in sight

   while (1)
   {
      STATSTG stat;
      ULONG found = 0;

      pEnum->Next (1, &stat, &found);

      if (found < 1)
         break;

      pStorage->DestroyElement (stat.pwcsName);
      CoTaskMemFree(stat.pwcsName);
   }

   // Get number of computers

   int nSub = m_pRoot->GetCount ();

   // Create a stream for each one

   for (int sub = 0; sub < nSub; sub++)
   {
      LPITEM lpSubItem = m_pRoot->GetSubItem (sub);
      LPOLESTR lpszName = lpSubItem->GetName ();
```

```
        CComPtr<IStream> pStream;
        HRESULT hResult = pStorage->CreateStream (lpszName,
                        STGM_READWRITE | STGM_SHARE_EXCLUSIVE,
                            0, 0, &pStream);
    }

    return S_OK;
}
```

Here, I've elected to store each computer name as a stream name. Crude, but effective. Here's what happens when the snap-in gets loaded next time:

```
STDMETHODIMP CComponentData::Load (IStorage* pStorage)
{
    // Construct enumerator for storage object

    CComPtr<IEnumSTATSTG> pEnum;
    pStorage->EnumElements (0, NULL, 0, &pEnum);

    // Go through streams, adding a computer for every one found

    while (1)
    {
        STATSTG stat;
        ULONG found = 0;

        pEnum->Next (1, &stat, &found);

        if (found < 1)
            break;

        m_pRoot->AddItem (stat.pwcsName, NULL);
        CoTaskMemFree(stat.pwcsName);
    }

    return S_OK;
}
```

Bear in mind, incidentally, that the operation of adding a new computer to the list will automatically establish a link with that computer's monitor service, and that should result in the list of known objects being populated.

The other **IPersistStorage** methods are not implemented and simply return **S_OK**.

Management, Monitoring and Control

That's about as far as I intend to go with the MMC for now. It's a tricky beast to master, with all those interactions between the different interfaces, but it's worth it. If nothing else, it's good COM practice ... Of course, there are many more things you can do with it – enough to fill several chapters of a book like this - but the example in this chapter should give you a good grounding.

As for the monitoring service that we developed, I'll go back to the point that I made at the outset. It's not intended to be an operational solution. It is, however, designed to make you think seriously about the problem of providing a monitoring system that's custom-built enough to be relevant to the needs of your support staff, but which presents itself in a standard recognisable form at the user interface.

The other question is: are there existing frameworks that could be used instead of building our own? Could we use the event log, perhaps? Well, yes, but remember that the event log is entirely passive. It's only part of the problem. With our own framework, we can actively investigate how the system is performing. We can time responses to a ping to the same object running on two different hosts, and perhaps switch future callers to the host that is currently responding faster – load balancing!

DCOM Troubleshooting

It can be a complicated business tracking down problems when things start to go wrong in a distributed system. Here's a set of guidelines to setting up your system with the aim of helping you find errors and put them right.

Follow these steps to help minimize DCOM problems:

1. Before you start, take some time to understand what you are doing. Make sure that you have a good grasp of COM fundamentals and the tools that you'll be using to create your distributed application. We recommend that you read *Professional DCOM Programming*, *Beginning ATL COM Programming*, and any other good COM books you can find.
2. Make sure an up-to-date version of DCOM is installed on both client and server machine:
   a. If either machine is Windows 95, install DCOM for Windows 95:
   `http://www.microsoft.com/com/dcom95/dcom95.htm`
   Or Internet Explorer 4:
   `http://www.microsoft.com/ie/download/`
   b. If either machine is Windows NT 4, install the latest NT service pack:
   `http://www.microsoft.com/windows/downloads/default.asp`

3. Make sure DCOM is enabled on both machines:

    a. Use `DCOMCnfg` to check the Enable Distributed COM on this computer check box on the Default Properties page

    b. Or check that the HKEY_LOCAL_MACHINE\Software\Microsoft\OLE\EnableDCOM registry entry is set to "Y"

4. If the server is on Windows 95, make sure that remote connections are enabled on the server machine. (This will need to be enabled on *both* machines if the 'server' calls back to the 'client').

    a. Use `DCOMCnfg` to check the Enable remote connection check box on the Default Security page.

    b. Or check that the HKEY_LOCAL_MACHINE\Software\Microsoft\OLE\EnableRemoteConnect registry entry is set to "Y"

5. Make sure that the machines are using a compatible network protocol.

    a. NT will dynamically load the right protocol, but DCOM for Windows 95 only works across TCP.

    b. There can be problems using RAS (make sure you have up-to-date service packs and hot fixes; check the DCOM mailing list archives and Microsoft's knowledge base for more details)

6. Ensure that your security settings will allow the client to *access* the server. Use `DCOMCnfg` to configure the access permissions for the server on the server machine:

    a. To allow everyone to access your server:

        - Select your application in the Applications list
        - Select the Properties... button
            - Select the Security page
                - Select Use custom access permissions
                - Select Edit...
                - Add access permissions for The World (Windows 95) or Everyone (Windows NT)

    b. Remember to configure security appropriately at both ends if the 'server' calls back to the 'client'.

7. On Windows NT, ensure that your security settings will allow the client to *launch* the server. Use **DCOMCnfg** to configure the launch permissions for the server on the server machine:

    a. To allow everyone to launch your server:

        - Select your application in the Applications list
        - Select the Properties... button
            - Select the Security page
                - Select Use custom launch permissions
                - Select Edit...
                - Add launch permissions for Everyone

8. On Windows NT, set the correct identity for your server. Use **DCOMCnfg** to configure the identity for the server on the server machine:

    a. If the server has a user interface, select Interactive User, otherwise select This User and choose a local or domain account.

    b. If the client uses callbacks then you can minimize the security settings by ensuring that the client and server run under the same account.

9. Make sure that the server is correctly installed on the server machine:

    a. Register the server and any necessary interface info (proxy-stub DLL or type library) on a local hard drive.

    b. If you're using ATL, you may need to register **ATL.dll**. Ensure that you register the correct version – the Visual C++ 5 CD features two versions of **ATL.dll**, the one in the **Redist\Ansi** directory will work on both Windows 95 and Windows NT. The other one is a Unicode DLL for Windows NT only.

10. Use the OLE/COM Object Viewer (**OLEView.exe**) on the server machine to check that the server can be instantiated locally.

11. Make sure that the client machine has any necessary interface info (proxy-stub DLL or type library) from the server registered on its local hard drive. If you're using ATL, you may need to register **ATL.dll**.

12. If your client is not DCOM-aware (e.g. a Visual Basic 5 or Java client), you will also need to adjust the client registry to have an AppID for the object class. Add the server into the RemoteServerName value of this key.

13. If the server is Windows 95, make sure that you prelaunch the server. Windows 95 security doesn't allow servers to be launched remotely. Also watch out for the server shutting down between test runs.

14. Use the OLE/COM Object Viewer (`OLEView.exe`) on the client machine to check that the server can be instantiated remotely from the client machine.

    a. If you have problems at this stage, verify the security settings one more time, and check the network connection using `ping` or other tools.

15. Use your client to test your server.

Still Having Trouble?

If you're still having trouble tracking down the problem after following these steps, here are a few more tips:

Reread those books.

Check the DCOM and ATL mailing list archives:

- `http://microsoft.ease.lsoft.com/archives/dcom.html`
- `http://microsoft.ease.lsoft.com/archives/atl.html`

Check the Microsoft site for updates:

- `http://www.microsoft.com/com/`

Check the Wrox Press sites for errata, information, and updates:

- `http://www.wrox.com/`
- `http://www.comdeveloper.com/`
- `http://www.worldofatl.com/`

If all else fails, we can offer support for any problems related to examples in this book, but we'll need you to help us to help you.

Send us some mail with the following information:

- Client OS
- Client OS service packs
- Client network protocols
- Server OS
- Server OS service packs
- Server network protocols
- Compilation tool
- Compilation tool service packs
- All relevant DCOM information
- All relevant security information
- A detailed description of the problem
- All steps taken to overcome the problem

CreateObjectEx()

```
Option Explicit
' This code is based on a sample from an unknown Microsoft programmer,
' posted by Charlie Kindel on the DCOM mailing list
' http://microsoft.ease.lsoft.com/
'                              scripts/wa.exe?A2=ind9612B&L=DCOM&P=R3412

' Modifications made by Alex Stockton:
'   CLSCTX_ constants no longer part of an Enum (for VBA compatibility)
'   MULTI_QI.pItf declared as IUnknown (rather than Object)
'   CreateObjectEx() uses new optional CLSCTX parameter
'   CreateObjectEx() queries and returns IUnknown interface

Public Const CLSCTX_INPROC_SERVER = 1
Public Const CLSCTX_INPROC_HANDLER = 2
Public Const CLSCTX_LOCAL_SERVER = 4
Public Const CLSCTX_REMOTE_SERVER = 16
Public Const CLSCTX_SERVER = CLSCTX_INPROC_SERVER + CLSCTX_LOCAL_SERVER _
                             + CLSCTX_REMOTE_SERVER
Public Const CLSCTX_ALL = CLSCTX_INPROC_SERVER + CLSCTX_INPROC_HANDLER _
                             + CLSCTX_LOCAL_SERVER + CLSCTX_REMOTE_SERVER

Public Const IID_IUnknown As String = _
                                 "{00000000-0000-0000-C000-000000000046}"
Public Const IID_IDispatch As String = _
                                 "{00020400-0000-0000-C000-000000000046}"
Public Const IID_IStream As String = _
                                 "{0000000C-0000-0000-C000-000000000046}"
```

```
Private Type MULTI_QI
   pIID As Long         'const IID*
   pItf As IUnknown     'IUnknown*
   hr As Long           'HRESULT
End Type

Private Type GUID
   Data1 As Long
   Data2 As Integer
   Data3 As Integer
   Data4(7) As Byte
End Type

Private Type COSERVERINFO
   dwReserved1 As Long   'DWORD
   pwszName As Long      'LPWSTR
   pAuthInfo As Long     'COAUTHINFO*
   dwReserved2 As Long   'DWORD
End Type

Private Declare Function CLSIDFromString Lib "OLE32" _
                         (ByVal lpszCLSID As Long, pclsid As GUID) As Long
Private Declare Function CLSIDFromProgID Lib "OLE32" _
                         (ByVal lpszProgID As Long, pclsid As GUID) As Long
Private Declare Function CoCreateInstanceEx Lib "OLE32" _
    (rclsid As GUID, ByVal pUnkOuter As Long, ByVal dwClsContext As Long, _
     pServerInfo As COSERVERINFO, ByVal cmq As Long, _
     rgmqResults As MULTI_QI) As Long


' Class is a ProgID or CLSID string:
'      "Excel.Application"
'      "{00000010-0000-0010-8000-00AA006D2EA4}"

' ServerName is the UNC, domain name, or IP address:
'      "\\server"
'      "server"
'      "server.com"
'      "www.server.com"
'      "135.5.33.19"

' Context is any of the CLSCTX_ constants defined above

Public Function CreateObjectEx(ByVal Class As String, _
                Optional ByVal ServerName As String, _
                Optional ByVal Context As Long = CLSCTX_SERVER) As IUnknown
   Dim rclsid As GUID
   Dim riid As GUID
   Dim hr As Long
   Dim ServerInfo As COSERVERINFO
   Dim mqi As MULTI_QI
```

```
    ' Convert IID_IUnknown string to binary IID
    hr = CLSIDFromString(StrPtr(IID_IUnknown), riid)
    If hr <> 0 Then Err.Raise hr
    mqi.pIID = VarPtr(riid)

    ' Convert provided CLSID or ProgID string into a binary CLSID
    If ((Left(Class, 1) = "{") And (Right(Class, 1) = "}") _
                                        And (Len(Class) = 38)) Then
       ' Create CLSID from string representation
       hr = CLSIDFromString(StrPtr(Class), rclsid)
       If hr <> 0 Then Err.Raise hr
    Else
       ' Create CLSID from ProgID
       hr = CLSIDFromProgID(StrPtr(Class), rclsid)
       If hr <> 0 Then Err.Raise hr
    End If

    ' Set up appropriate server info
    If ServerName <> "" Then
       ServerInfo.pwszName = StrPtr(ServerName)
    End If

  ' Create an instance of the object
  hr = CoCreateInstanceEx(rclsid, CLng(0), Context, ServerInfo, CLng(1), mqi)
  If hr <> 0 Then Err.Raise hr

    Set CreateObjectEx = mqi.pItf
End Function
```

References and Further Reading

Professional Visual C++ ActiveX/COM Control Programming
Sing Li and Panos Economopoulos (Wrox Press Ltd, 1997, ISBN 1-861000-37-5)

Professional DCOM Programming
Richard Grimes (Wrox Press Ltd, 1997, ISBN 1-861000-60-X)

Beginning ATL COM Programming
Alex Stockton, Richard Grimes, George Reilly and Julian Templeman (Wrox Press Ltd, 1998, ISBN 1-861000-11-1)

Essential COM
Don Box (Addison Wesley Longman, Inc, 1998, ISBN 0-201-63446-5)

Inside OLE, 2nd Edition
Kraig Brockschmidt (Microsoft Press, 1995, ISBN 1-55615-843-2)

Inside COM
Dale Rogerson (Microsoft Press, 1997, ISBN 1-57231-349-8)

SQL for Dummies, 2nd Edition
Allen G. Taylor (IDG Books Worldwide, Inc., 1997, ISBN 0-7645-0105-4)

The Road Ahead (Revised Edition)
Bill Gates (Penguin, 1996, ISBN 0-14-024351-8)

Being Digital
Nicholas Negroponte (Hodder and Stoughton, 1995, ISBN 0-340-64525-3)

Labyrinths: Selected Stories and Other Writings
Jorge Luis Borges (Penguin, 1989, ISBN 0-14-018029-X

The Physics of Star Trek
Lawrence M. Krauss (HarperCollins, 1995, 0-00-225485-9)

High Fidelity
Nick Hornby (Victor Gollancz, 1995, 0-575-05748-3)

How to Keep Your Volkswagen Alive, 1976 Edition
John Muir (John Muir Publications, 1976, 0-912528-33-8)

Truckers
Terry Pratchett (Doubleday, 1989, ISBN 0-385-26961-7)

The Phantom Tollbooth, Special 35th Anniversary Edition
Norton Juster (Random House, 1996, ISBN 0-394-81500-9)

Obviously, the major on-line resource for information on the technologies described in this book is `www.microsoft.com`. Much of this information is also available on the various CDs supplied to members of the Microsoft Developers' Network (MSDN).

Further information on Wrox Press books is available on `www.wrox.com`. Also check out Wrox's site for COM specialists, `www.COMDeveloper.com` and information on ATL from `www.WorldOfATL.com` Further information on Beanie Babies can be found at `www.ty.com`, and other unofficial sites too numerous to mention.

Index

SYMBOLS

A

D

E

F

G

H

I

J

K

L

M

N

O

P

Q

R

S

T

U

V

W

X

Beginning ATL COM Programming

Authors: Various

ISBN: 1861000111

Price: $39.95 C$55.95 £36.99

This book is for fairly experienced C++ developers who want to get to grips with COM programming using the Active Template Library. The Beginning in the title of this book refers to COM and it refers to ATL. It does not refer to Programming.

We don't expect you to know anything about COM. The book explains the essentials of COM, how to use it, and how to get the most out of it. If you do already know something about COM, that's a bonus. You'll still learn a lot about the way that ATL works, and you'll be one step ahead of the COM neophytes.

Neither do we expect you to know anything about ATL. ATL is the focus of the book. If you've never touched ATL, or if you've been using it for a short while, but still have many unanswered questions, this is the book for you.

Professional VB5.0 Business Objects

Author: Rockford Lhotka

ISBN: 186100043X

Price: $49.95 C$69.95 £45.99

In recent years, the concept of 'business objects' has taken hold in the developer community. Basically, these are the processes that deal with some input data and mediate the appropriate business response. Whether this be a stock-withdrawal from a warehouse supply system, an invoice-sender or whatever, writing the code in such a way that it can be used by an entire organization to maintain coherent information on the business is worthwhile.

Visual Basic 5 classes can be exposed as ActiveX objects. Such objects can use DCOM to communicate between machines, and can be both called and scripted by Active Server Pages and controlled by Microsoft Transaction Server. The book shows a variety of client-server designs, to illustrate how to design and deploy business objects.

- The only book dedicated to Business Objects with Visual Basic, the hottest topic for developers
- Covers component-based application development in Visual Basic 5
- Illustrates deployment of server-side Visual Basic 5 objects using DCOM
- Shows how to use Visual Basic 5, ASP and MTS to create an intranet application

Professional MFC with Visual C++ 5

Author: Mike Blaszczak

ISBN: 1861000146

Price: $59.95 C$83.95 £56.49

Written by one of Microsoft's leading MFC developers, this is the book for professionals who want to get under the covers of the library. This is the 3rd revision of the best selling title formerly known as 'Revolutionary Guide to MFC 4' and covers the new Visual C++ 5.0 development environment.

This book will give a detailed discussion of the majority of classes present in Microsoft's application framework library. While it will point out what parameters are required for the member functions of those classes, it will concentrate more on describing what utility the classes really provide. You will learn how to write a few utilities, some DLLs, an ActiveX control and even an OLE document server, as well as examining Microsoft's Open Database Connectivity (ODBC) and Data Access Objects (DAO) strategies. At the very end of the book, you'll take a look at what the Microsoft Foundation Classes provide to make programming for the Internet easier.

There's a CD ROM included which has the complete book in HTML format - now you can use any browser to read your book on the road.

Professional DCOM Programming

Author: Dr. Richard Grimes

ISBN: 186100060X

Price: $49.95 C$69.95 £46.99

This book is for Win32 programmers taking up the challenge of building applications using the distributed component object model. There is a strong emphasis on the practicalities of distributed object design and use, and the text is also a complete examination of COM programming. The code is described and developed using Visual C++ 5, MFC and ATL.